OPERATING SYSTEMS

AUTHOR

Dr. Sukomal Pal
Associate Professor
Department of Computer Science & Engineering
IIT (BHU), Varanasi, UP

REVIEWER

Dr. Sandeep Kumar
Associate Professor
Computer Science and Engineering Department,
IIT Roorkee, Uttarakhand

KHANNA BOOK PUBLISHING CO. (P) Ltd.
4C/4344, Ansari Road, Darya Ganj, New Delhi, India

All India Council for Technical Education
Nelson Mandela Marg, Vasant Kunj, New Delhi, India

Dear Readers,

To prevent the piracy, this book is secured with HIGH SECURITY HOLOGRAM on the front title cover. In case you don't find the hologram on the front cover title, please write us to at contact@khannabooks.com or whatsapp us at +91-99109 09320 and avail special gift voucher for yourself.

Specimen of Hologram on front Cover title:

Moreover, there is a SPECIAL DISCOUNT COUPON for you with EVERY HOLOGRAM.

How to avail this SPECIAL DISCOUNT:

Step 1: Scratch the hologram

Step 2: Under the scratch area, your "coupon code" is available

Step 3: Logon to www.khannabooks.com

Step 4: Use your "coupon code" in the shopping cart and get your copy at a special discount

Step 5: Enjoy your reading!

ISBN: 978-93-5538-547-5

Book Code: UG427EN

Operating Systems

by Dr. Sukomal Pal

First Edition: 2026

Originally Published by:

All India Council for Technical Education, Ministry of Education, GOI

Exclusively Published & Distributed by:

Khanna Book Publishing Co. (P) Ltd.
4C/4344, Ansari Road, Daryaganj,
New Delhi (INDIA)

Visit us at: **www.khannabooks.com**
Write us at: **contact@khannabooks.com**

To view complete list of books,
Please scan the QR Code:

KPH

Printed in Bharat.

प्रो. टी. जी. सीताराम
अध्यक्ष
Prof. T. G. Sitharam
Chairman

सत्यमेव जयते

आज़ादी का अमृत महोत्सव

अखिल भारतीय तकनीकी शिक्षा परिषद्
(भारत सरकार का एक सांविधिक निकाय)
(शिक्षा मंत्रालय, भारत सरकार)
नेल्सन मंडेला मार्ग, वसंत कुंज, नई दिल्ली–110070
दूरभाष : 011–26131498
ई–मेल : chairman@aicte-india.org

ALL INDIA COUNCIL FOR TECHNICAL EDUCATION
(A STATUTORY BODY OF THE GOVT. OF INDIA)
(Ministry of Education, Govt. of India)
Nelson Mandela Marg, Vasant Kunj, New Delhi-110070
Phone : 011-26131498
E-mail : chairman@aicte-india.org

FOREWORD

Engineers are the backbone of any modern society. They are the ones responsible for the marvels as well as the improved quality of life across the world. Engineers have driven humanity towards greater heights in a more evolved and unprecedented manner.

The All India Council for Technical Education (AICTE), have spared no efforts towards the strengthening of the technical education in the country. AICTE is always committed towards promoting quality Technical Education to make India a modern developed nation emphasizing on the overall welfare of mankind.

An array of initiatives has been taken by AICTE in last decade which have been accelerated now by the National Education Policy (NEP) 2020. The implementation of NEP under the visionary leadership of Hon'ble Prime Minister of India envisages the provision for education in regional languages to all, thereby ensuring that every graduate becomes competent enough and is in a position to contribute towards the national growth and development through innovation & entrepreneurship.

One of the spheres where AICTE had been relentlessly working since past couple of years is providing high quality original technical contents at Under Graduate & Diploma level prepared and translated by eminent educators in various Indian languages to its aspirants. For students pursuing 2nd year of their Engineering education, AICTE has identified 87 books, which shall be translated into 12 Indian languages - Hindi, Tamil, Gujarati, Odia, Bengali, Kannada, Urdu, Punjabi, Telugu, Marathi, Assamese & Malayalam. In addition to the English medium, books in different Indian Languages are going to support the students to understand the concepts in their respective mother tongue.

On behalf of AICTE, I express sincere gratitude to all distinguished authors, reviewers and translators from the renowned institutions of high repute for their admirable contribution in a record span of time.

AICTE is confident that these outcomes based original contents shall help aspirants to master the subject with comprehension and greater ease.

(Prof. T. G. Sitharam)

ACKNOWLEDGEMENT

The author is grateful to the authorities of AICTE, particularly Prof. T. G. Sitharam, Chairman; Dr. Abhay Jere, Vice-Chairman; Prof. Rajive Kumar, Member-Secretary; Dr. Ramesh Unnikrishnan, Advisor-II and Dr. Sunil Luthra, Director, Training and Learning Bureau for their planning to publish the books on Operating Systems. We sincerely acknowledge the valuable contributions of the reviewer of the book Dr. Sandeep Kumar, Associate Professor, IIT Roorkee for making it students' friendly.

I believe that everything happens as per the will of the Supreme Power. It came through my parents (my father Late Damodar Pal who showed how aiming for perfection can be done with goodness and grace and my mother Smt. Renu Pal whose zeal for providing us higher and better education enabled me pursuing an academic life) to dream of authoring a textbook. My PhD supervisor Prof. Mandar Mitra introduced me to the realm of operating systems. He not only taught me how to teach the subject but also how to live and play with its different incarnations. At the onset of drafting the manuscript, he provided me with insightful materials and much-needed guidance. During the drafting, I was also assisted by many colleagues and students, mainly through their thoughtful suggestions and constructive feedback. I also owe to the contribution of my student Shivam Solanki, who provided me with a set of questions collected from different sources and, of Supriya Chanda who did last minute proof-reading and corrections. I am thankful to my loving and ever-encouraging family for their constant support and understanding.

This book is an outcome of various suggestions of AICTE members, experts and authors who shared their opinion and thought to further develop the engineering education in our country. Acknowledgements are due to the contributors and different workers in this field whose published books, review articles, papers, photographs, footnotes, references and other valuable information enriched us at the time of writing the book.

Dr. Sukomal Pal

PREFACE

The book titled "Operating Systems" is an outcome of my teaching of operating systems courses. The motivation of writing this book is to expose operating system to the engineering students, the fundamentals of operating systems as well as enable them to get an insight of the subject. Keeping in mind the purpose of wide coverage as well as to provide essential supplementary information, we have included the topics recommended by AICTE, in a very systematic and orderly manner throughout the book. Efforts have been made to explain the fundamental concepts of the subject in the simplest possible way.

During the process of preparation of the manuscript, several standard textbooks are consulted and accordingly questions are developed with answer keys and hints. Emphasis has also been laid on definitions and explaining concepts with easy real-life examples so that students can readily relate to. Each chapter ends with a summary and pointers to resources for further learning.

The book starts with an introduction to the concept of operating systems, placing it appropriately under the computer black box, as a set of programs in the core of system software. It covers the evolution of computer as well as that of operating system side by side. In the second unit, some fundamental concepts like program, process and threads are developed, with their activities and interactions. Third unit deals with co-ordination among different cooperating processes in a multiprogramming environment. Process synchronization is discussed in reasonable detail with sample pseudo-codes. One severe fall-out of concurrent execution of several co-operating processes is deadlock when neither of the processes / threads can proceed. The definition of deadlock, when it can form, how it can be avoided and remedies, if it is formed are discussed in Unit 4. Memory is the second most important component of any computer. Program code and data are stored in different memory elements and brought to main memory and registers for processing. How operating systems manage these code and data in the main memory and cache are discussed in Unit 5. The final chapter deals with management of peripheral and devices by an operating system.

Even though several books on operating systems are available in the market, this book provides all the necessary introductory materials in a very concise manner. However, 'Know More' sections are also provided for the inquisitive students in each chapter. Questions are designed following Blooms' taxonomy incorporating the latest relevant ones from different competitive examinations.

I sincerely hope that the book will inspire the students to learn and discuss the ideas behind operating systems and will surely contribute to the development of a solid foundation of the subject. We would be thankful to all constructive comments and suggestions which will contribute to the improvement of the future editions of the book. It gives me immense pleasure to place this book in the hands of the teachers and students.

Dr. Sukomal Pal

OUTCOME BASED EDUCATION

For the implementation of an outcome-based education the first requirement is to develop an outcome-based curriculum and incorporate an outcome-based assessment in the education system. By going through outcome-based assessments evaluators will be able to evaluate whether the students have achieved the outlined standard, specific and measurable outcomes. With the proper incorporation of outcome-based education there will be a definite commitment to achieve a minimum standard for all learners without giving up at any level. At the end of the programme running with the aid of outcome- based education, a student will be able to arrive at the following outcomes:

PO1. Engineering knowledge: Apply the knowledge of mathematics, science, engineering fundamentals, and an engineering specialization to the solution of complex engineering problems.

PO2. Problem analysis: Identify, formulate, review research literature, and analyze complex engineering problems reaching substantiated conclusions using first principles of mathematics, natural sciences, and engineering sciences.

PO3. Design / development of solutions: Design solutions for complex engineering problems and design system components or processes that meet the specified needs with appropriate consideration for the public health and safety, and the cultural, societal, and environmental considerations.

PO4. Conduct investigations of complex problems: Use research-based knowledge and research methods including design of experiments, analysis and interpretation of data, and synthesis of the information to provide valid conclusions.

PO5. Modern tool usage: Create, select, and apply appropriate techniques, resources, and modern engineering and IT tools including prediction and modeling to complex engineering activities with an understanding of the limitations.

PO6. The engineer and society: Apply reasoning informed by the contextual knowledge to assess societal, health, safety, legal and cultural issues and the consequent responsibilities relevant to the professional engineering practice.

PO7. Environment and sustainability: Understand the impact of the professional engineering solutions in societal and environmental contexts, and demonstrate the knowledge of, and need for sustainable development.

PO8. Ethics: Apply ethical principles and commit to professional ethics and responsibilities and norms of the engineering practice.

PO9. Individual and team work: Function effectively as an individual, and as a member or leader in diverse teams, and in multidisciplinary settings.

PO10. Communication: Communicate effectively on complex engineering activities with the engineering community and with society at large, such as, being able to comprehend and write effective reports and design documentation, make effective presentations, and give and receive clear instructions.

PO11. Project management and finance: Demonstrate knowledge and understanding of the engineering and management principles and apply these to one's own work, as a member and leader in a team, to manage projects and in multidisciplinary environments.

PO12. Life-long learning: Recognize the need for, and have the preparation and ability to engage in independent and life-long learning in the broadest context of technological change.

COURSE OUTCOMES

After completion of the course the students will be able to:

CO-1. Create processes and threads.

CO-2. Develop algorithms for process scheduling for a given specification of CPU.

CO-3. Utilization, Throughput, Turnaround Time, Waiting Time, Response Time.

CO-4. For a given specification of memory organization develop the techniques for optimally allocating memory to processes by increasing memory utilization and for improving the access time.

CO-5. Design and implement file management system.

CO-6. For a given I/O devices and OS (specify) develop the I/O management functions in OS as part of a uniform device abstraction by performing operations for synchronization between CPU and I/O controllers.

Table for CO and PO attainment

Course Outcomes	Expected Mapping with Programme Outcomes (1- Weak Correlation; 2- Medium correlation; 3- Strong Correlation)											
	PO-1	PO-2	PO-3	PO-4	PO-5	PO-6	PO-7	PO-8	PO-9	PO-10	PO-11	PO-12
CO-1	3	3	2	2	1	-	-	-	-	-	-	-
CO-2	3	3	3	2	1	-	-	-	-	-	-	-
CO-3	3	3	3	3	2	-	-	-	-	-	-	-
CO-4	3	3	3	3	2	-	-	-	-	-	-	-
CO-5	3	3	2	2	1	1	-	-	-	-	-	-
CO-6	3	3	2	2	1	1	-	-	-	-	-	-

GUIDELINES FOR TEACHERS

To implement Outcome Based Education (OBE) knowledge level and skill set of the students should be enhanced. Teachers should take a major responsibility for the proper implementation of OBE. Some of the responsibilities (not limited to) for the teachers in OBE system may be as follows:

- Within reasonable constraint, they should manoeuvre time to the best advantage of all students.
- They should assess the students only upon certain defined criterion without considering any other potential ineligibility to discriminate them.
- They should try to grow the learning abilities of the students to a certain level before they leave the institute.
- They should try to ensure that all the students are equipped with the quality knowledge as well as competence after they finish their education.
- They should always encourage the students to develop their ultimate performance capabilities.
- They should facilitate and encourage group work and team work to consolidate newer approach.
- They should follow Blooms taxonomy in every part of the assessment.

Bloom's Taxonomy

Level	Teacher should Check	Student should be able to	Possible Mode of Assessment
Create	Students ability to create	Design or Create	Mini project
Evaluate	Students ability to justify	Argue or Defend	Assignment
Analyse	Students ability to distinguish	Differentiate or Distinguish	Project/Lab Methodology
Apply	Students ability to use information	Operate or Demonstrate	Technical Presentation/ Demonstration
Understand	Students ability to explain the ideas	Explain or Classify	Presentation/Seminar
Remember	Students ability to recall (or remember)	Define or Recall	Quiz

GUIDELINES FOR STUDENTS

Students should take equal responsibility for implementing the OBE. Some of the responsibilities (not limited to) for the students in OBE system are as follows:

- Students should be well aware of each UO before the start of a unit in each and every course.
- Students should be well aware of each CO before the start of the course.
- Students should be well aware of each PO before the start of the programme.
- Students should think critically and reasonably with proper reflection and action.
- Learning of the students should be connected and integrated with practical and real life consequences.
- Students should be well aware of their competency at every level of OBE.

ABBREVIATIONS AND SYMBOLS

General Terms			
Abbreviations	**Full form**	**Abbreviations**	**Full form**
CAS	Compare & Swap	Mutex	Mutual Exclusion
CLI	Command Line Interface	NRU	Not Recently Used
CS	Critical Section	OPT	Optimal
CSP	Critical Section Problem	OS	Operating Systmem
DLL	Dynamic Link Libraries	PCB	Process Control Block
DMA	Direct Memory Access	PT	Page Table
FCFS	First Come First Serve	RAG	Resource Allocation Graph
FIFO	First In First Out	RAID	Redundant Array of Inexpensive Disk
HAL	Hardware Abstraction Layer	RM	Resident Manager
I/O	Input / Output	RTOS	Real Time Operating System
IPC	Interprocess Communication	SC	Second Chance
JVM	Java Virtual Machine	TSL	Test & Set Lock
KLT	Kernel Level Thread	ULT	User Level Thread
LRU	Least Recently Used	VM	Vrtual Machine
LWP	Light Weight Process	VMM	Virtual Machine Manager

CONTENTS

UNIT 2: PROCESSES, THREADS and their SCHEDULING

UNIT 3: INTERPROCESS COMMUNICATION and PROCESS SYNCHRONIZATION

UNIT 5: MEMORY MANAGEMENT

1 Introduction

UNIT SPECIFICS

Through this unit we have discussed the following aspects:

- *Concept of Operating Systems*
- *Generations of Operating systems*
- *Types of Operating Systems, OS Services, System Calls*
- *Structure of an OS - Layered, Monolithic, Microkernel Operating Systems*
- *Concept of Virtual Machine*
- *Case study on UNIX and WINDOWS Operating System.*

This chapter introduces operating systems and their uses in computers. It also provides an intuitive understanding of the entire book in a nutshell. Emphasis is placed on lucidly discussing the topic with simple real-life examples that a novice reader can readily relate to and remember the underlying concept easily. The examples should not be taken as precise and exact, but approximate ones to serve the purpose in general.

Besides giving several multiple-choice questions as well as questions of short and long answer types marked in two categories following lower and higher order of Bloom's taxonomy, assignments through several numerical problems, a list of references and suggested readings are given in the unit so that one can go through them for practice. It is important to note that for getting more information on various topics of interest, appropriate URLs and QR code have been provided in different sections which can be accessed or scanned for relevant supportive knowledge.

We also have a "Know More" section. This section has been carefully designed so that the supplementary information provided in this part becomes beneficial for the users of the book. This section mainly highlights the initial activity, examples of some interesting facts, analogy, history of the development of the subject focusing the salient observations and finding, timelines starting from the development of the concerned topics up to the recent time, applications of the subject matter for our day-to-day real life or/and industrial applications on variety of aspects, case study related to the topic, and finally to serve the inquisitiveness and curiosity of the readers related to topics.

RATIONALE

This introductory unit on operating systems helps students to get a primary idea about the system software that works at the core of a computer system and as an important layer between the bare hardware and the users. It starts with the rudimentary division of a computing system into hardware and software and then where and why an operating system fits in this binary division. This basic understanding is very important to start the study of operating systems properly. It then discusses different activities of an operating system and its evolution over the years. All these are discussed with simple real-life examples for important concepts and necessary details to develop the subject. Keeping in mind the need of intended readers, efforts are made to keep the content minimum and language simple.

Operating Systems is an important subject of Computer Science. As a user of any computing device from a large-size mainframe or a server of a datacentre to a personal computer or a smartphone, even a smart domestic appliance like washing machine or dishwasher, we interact with operating system interfaces. Hence, basic understanding of operating systems is more than necessary for everyone in this world of today driven by knowledge. For an academician or a practitioner of computer science, it is an absolute necessity as it enriches the understanding of both system software and application programs. This enables one to comprehend the functions and behaviours of different computing devices, what they can do and what they cannot, and thus use the computers in a better way in everyday life. At the same time, it equips one to design a software, write programs and implement different algorithms in an efficient and effective manner.

PRE-REQUISITES

Basics of Computer Organization and Architecture

Fundamentals of Data Structures

Introductory knowledge of Computer Programming

UNIT OUTCOMES

List of outcomes of this unit is as follows.

U1-O1: Define an operating system.

U1-O2: Describe the operations of an OS in a computer system.

U1-O3: Understand the evolution of computer system along with OS.

U1-O4: Realize the services of an operating system.

U1-O5: Analyse and compare given any two operating systems.

U1-O6: Design a sketch of an ideal operating system.

Course Outcomes

After completion of the course the students will be able to:

1. Create processes and threads.
2. Develop algorithms for process scheduling for a given specification of CPU.
3. Utilization, Throughput, Turnaround Time, Waiting Time, Response Time.
4. For a given specification of memory organization develop the techniques for optimally allocating memory to processes by increasing memory utilization and for improving the access time.
5. Design and implement file management system.
6. For a given I/O devices and OS (specify) develop the I/O management functions in OS as part of a uniform device abstraction by performing operations for synchronization between CPU and I/O controllers.

Unit-1 Outcomes	EXPECTED MAPPING WITH COURSE OUTCOMES (1- Weak Correlation; 2- Medium correlation; 3- Strong Correlation)					
	CO-1	CO-2	CO-3	CO-4	CO-5	CO-6
U1-O1	2	2	1	1	1	1
U1-O2	2	1	1	1	1	1
U1-O3	1	1	1	1	1	1
U1-O4	2	1	1	1	1	1
U1-O5	1	1	1	1	1	1
U1-O6	1	1	1	1	1	1

1.1 COMPUTER FUNDAMENTALS

A computer is a powerful information processing machine. It has two broad categories of components: *hardware* and *software*.

Hardware is the tangible (that we can touch and feel) components like processor (a physical chip that houses one or more central processing units or CPUs), memory (RAM, ROM, HDD, flash drives), peripheral devices (Input devices like keyboard, mouse, joystick; output devices like monitor, printers) and network devices like network interface cards. Some of the hardware units are *essential* like CPU and memory while others can be *optional* like peripheral devices monitors, printers, scanners and secondary and tertiary memories. Hardware is supposed to manipulate, transmit and store information.

Software, on the other hand, is intangible but stored electronically. It refers to programs that are executed on a computer. It is broadly classified as: *system software* (that help the users operate the hardwares in a pre-decided manner or provide users a limited set of services), and *application software* (a set of user-designed programs that can perform any computing task as per user's design).

An operating system (OS) is a software. It is the **core of system software** that conceptually sits on top of the hardware and below the application software. It runs all the time, if a present-day computer runs and interacts with the hardware and all application software (*application programs* as well as *utilities*) for the convenience of the users.

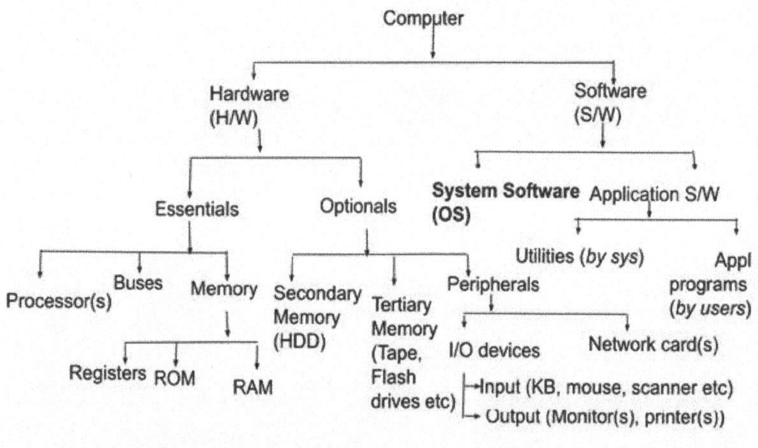

Fig. 1.1: Different components of a computer system

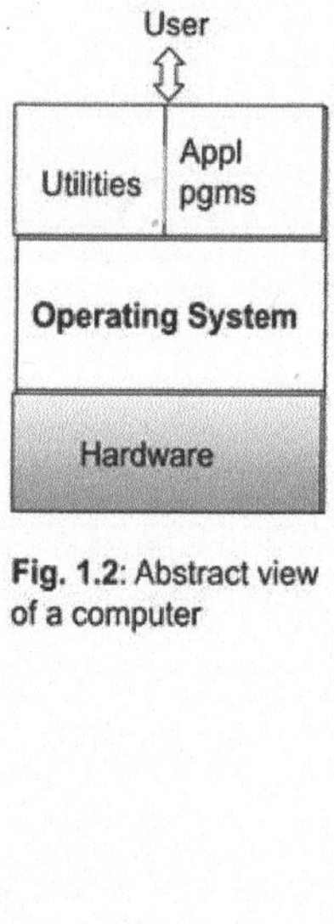

Fig. 1.2: Abstract view of a computer

1.1.1 What an Operating System does?

A computer takes some input (software and raw data) and produces output as designed by the programmer. The programs that are executed by the computer hardware to perform a desired task are written in a low-*level* **machine language.** This language is often *difficult to understand*, and very *difficult to use, error-prone* and *time-consuming.* Ordinary programmers (most of the developers) are comfortable with high-level languages (C, C++, Java, Python etc.), which cannot directly talk to the computer hardware. Operating systems come at this point to bridge the gap between the users (programmers or end-users) and the hardware. An OS provides an "easy-to-use" platform to the users over the "difficult-to-use" bare-bone hardware.

A simple analogy can be made with the railway operation here. A train can certainly run on the tracks without a station. However, it will be difficult to get in and out of the train for the passengers (the users). Railways not only provide platforms for easy boarding and deboarding but several facilities for passengers' convenience. Railways provide drivers with guards and signalling staff with a signalling for smooth running of the train. Ticket counters at the station enable us to buy tickets for journeys and other services in the station premises. Think of different services like waiting rooms, washrooms, food stalls and so on.

Fig 1.3: An analogy with Railways

Keep this example of a railway system in mind to understand different activities of an operating system. Rail tracks, some signals or train rakes can be considered analogous to the hardware components of a computer. Railway reservation system, on the other hand, is a software in every sense.

The entire railway system is built to serve two basic purposes: 1. to cater passengers (users) and 2. to manage railways resources (trains, other physical resources and manpower). Loosely put, an operating system is like the railways system. Its functions can thus also be viewed from two perspectives: 1) User View and 2) System View as briefly described below.

User View

In most cases, a personal computer (PC) or a laptop is used by a *single user* (**Fig 1.4**) at a given point of time. The user monopolizes the resources (hardware resources like processors, memories, I/O devices etc or software resources like programs, files, databases etc). The primary job of the operating system is to ensure **ease of use** of the resources.

However, in a multi-user environment (**Fig. 1.5**), several users work on a single system (mainframe, minicomputer, workstation or a server) connected through their own terminals. The users share different computing resources (h/w and s/w) and exchange information. Here, **resource utilization** in an *equitable* and *fair* manner is very important. The job of an OS is not only to offer **ease of use** to the users, but also to ensure that every user gets a *fair share* of the resources (both h/w and s/w) and maximise the overall performance (e.g., maximum resource utilization, lowest overall CPU time etc) of the system from all the users' point of view.

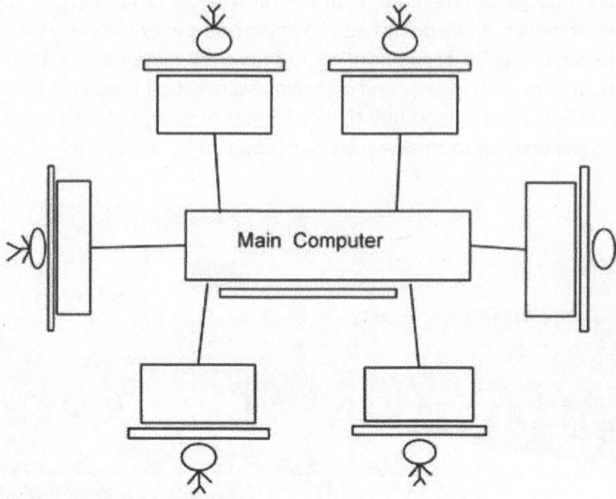

Fig 1.4: Single-User OS

Fig 1.5 Multi-User OS

Smartphones and tablets of today's world are single-user computers, but they connect to a server and cloud through cellular or wireless networks. The OS provides a touchscreen (or keypad) to interact with the user as well as with a remote server and/or a cloud to provide service to the user.

However, there are few embedded systems where the operating system does not or very rarely interact with the user (home appliances like refrigerators, washing machines, dishwashers or car indicators).

System View

As an OS can directly interact with the hardware of the system and the user programs cannot, OS must ensure the **resource allocation** to all users. These resources can be hardware resources like CPU time, memory blocks, I/O and network devices as well as software resources like programs, file systems etc. From a computer's point of view, these resources need to be controlled, managed and allocated by an operating system. Hence, an OS is also seen as a **control program** or **resource allocator** for a computer.

1.2 GENERATIONS OF OPERATING SYSTEMS

The earliest computers did not have any operating systems. Gradually, the need of developing system software was felt to facilitate the users and several efforts were made in an uncoordinated way. Hence, it is difficult to put up a coherent chronology of the evolution of computers and operating systems. An attempt is made to put the evolution divided in the following generations and major phases (highlighted text) (according to [Han00][1]). A quick graphical summary is shown in **Fig 1.6**.

1.2.1 First Generation (1940s - 50s)

The first electronic computer came in 1940 to replace the mechanical computer. It did not have any OS and was used to do simple calculations using plug-boards. For more than a decade, the computing systems developed did

[1] THE EVOLUTION OF OPERATING SYSTEMS∗ PER BRINCH HANSEN (2000) (available at http://brinch-hansen.net/papers/2001b.pdf) [as on 16.6.2022]

not support any OS and the users had to manually feed the program and the data. This period is also called the **Open Shop** phase. Each user was allotted a fixed amount of time to use the computer. Time for setting up was much higher than actual time of computation. The exercise was extremely laborious and error prone. IBM 701 machine is an example of an Open Shop machine.

1.2.2 Second Generation (1955-1965)

Huge wastage of users' time was drastically reduced by appointing skilled professionals (operators) in the computer room. The users were asked to prepare their 'job' (punched cards of programs and data) and submit to the operators who run the jobs on users' behalf. Similar jobs (based on requirement of similar set of resources) were put in a batch and jobs scheduled for execution sequentially one after another batch-wise. This phase is also known as **Closed Shop** (as users were not allowed in the computer room) or **batch processing.** Even though much improved over the Open shop era, it was still plagued by slow speed of I/O devices. The SHARE operating system for the IBM 709 was an early batch processing system.

1.2.3 Third Generation (1965-1980)

Sequential execution in batch processing forced the computer processor to stall or remain idle during I/O operation leading to poor utilization of CPU time. Advancement in large core memories, secondary storage with random access, data channels, and hardware interrupts enabled more powerful operating systems. Multiple programs were simultaneously loaded in the main memory and interrupts enabled a processor to switch execution of one program to another. When one program went for an I/O operation (taking input or displaying / printing output), the CPU was idle and so is used by another program. From a user's point of view, as if several programs were concurrently executed with simultaneous input/output operations. This generation is thus known as **multiprogramming.** Since input devices, the processor and the output devices could run simultaneously, this was also called ***spooling*** (acronym for *simultaneous peripheral operation on-line*). CPU utilization was improved, but user programs were still executed in the background without offering the users to observe, correct or respond to the results of execution interactively. Atlas Supervisor, Burroughs B5000 Master Control Program, Exec II systems are examples of multiprogramming operating systems.

The need for interactive computing was met in **time-sharing** phase. The computer was connected to several terminals where each terminal can offer interaction with a user. While a user interacts with the terminal (I/O operation), the processor could execute other users' programs as processor speed is much faster than that of a user. It provided an illusion as if each user was having a dedicated processor. CTSS (acronym for *Compatible Time-Sharing System*), designed at MIT, USA and MULTICS (MULTiplexed Information and Computing Service) designed at AT&T Bell Labs were two early examples of time-sharing systems. Later, UNIX was developed in 1971 following the principles of MULTICS. Concepts of file system, file protection, passwords also came as part of time-sharing systems.

Concurrent Programming was the next logical step. Computers gradually evolved into such a complex system that the problems due to multiprogramming and time-sharing features (*deadlocks,* to be discussed later) could not be solved in an *ad hoc* fashion. Conceptual basis was developed to design complex systems in a principled manner that can offer simultaneous execution of several tasks without problems. Synchronization primitives like semaphore, monitor etc (discussed later) were introduced. THE (acronym for *Technische Hogeschool Eindhoven* or Technical School of Eindhoven, the Netherlands) operating system by Edger Djikstra (1968), RC 4000 operating system by P Brinch Hansen (1970) included concurrent programming.

1.2.4 Fourth Generation (1980-Now)

Advancement in microprocessors and semiconductor memories and their cheap availability in the 70s enabled computing within the reach of individuals. Gradually **Personal Computing** became a reality with focus shifting to single-user environment (user convenience preferred over resource utilization). GUI (*graphical user interface*), interaction through mouse clicks were included in the operating systems. MS-DOS, Windows 95, Macintosh are examples of single-user operating systems.

The above phases of OS development discussed so far considered self-contained, stand-alone systems. With the advancement of networking and communication technologies, the need of sharing computations among several computer systems was felt. Specific responsibilities were assigned to different computers connected to do a certain task in a cooperative manner. Servers and resource sharing became common with remote procedure calls (RPC), and distributed programming as dominant concepts leading to development of **Distributed Systems.** WFS File Server, Amoeba, Unix with additional layers of distributed computing are examples of distributed systems.

Real Time systems[2] are those that respond to events within predictable and specific time constraints. They are used in several time-critical systems like air traffic control systems, process control systems, autonomous driving systems, robotics etc. Often sensors send the data to the computer and output is produced within a specific time so that the appropriate next action initiates, otherwise the system fails (think of robot actions). Precise timeliness, time synchronization among different agents and priority-based actions are important attributes of the RT operating systems (RTOS). It is characterized as a small, fast, responsive, and deterministic OS. VxWorks is a RTOS. An **Embedded System** is a small operating system that lies within a larger machine - e.g., a microcontroller within a robotic arm. Often a RTOS is used as an embedded system when timeliness and reliability are critical. Symbian (used in basic cellular phones) is an embedded operating system.

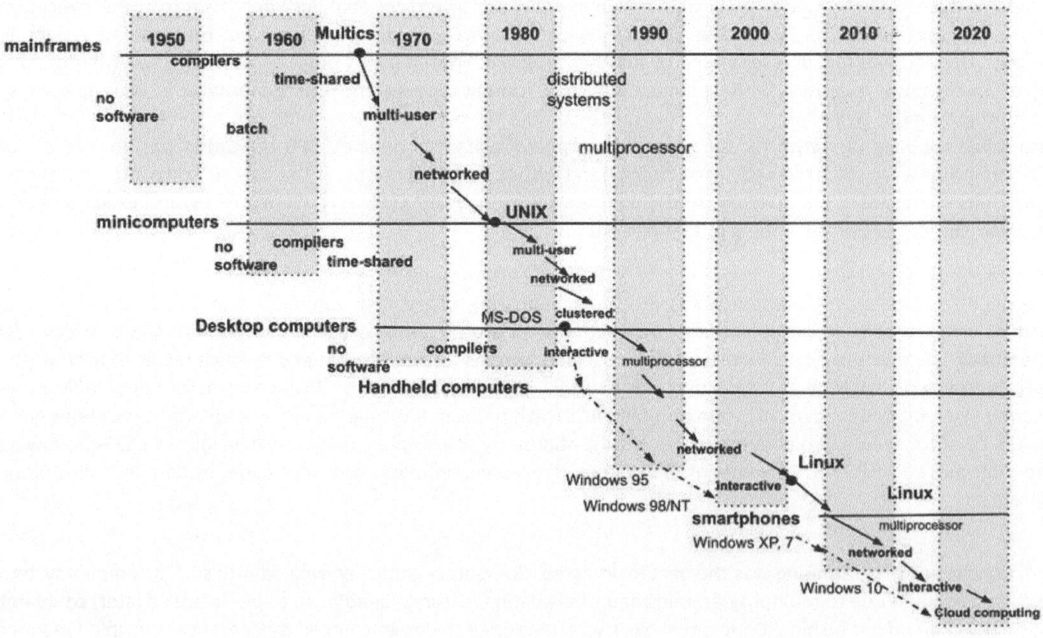

Fig 1.6: Evolution of OS (focusing on UNIX and Windows)

[2] https://www.windriver.com/solutions/learning/rtos [as on 17-Jun-2022]

1.3 TYPES OF OPERATING SYSTEMS

Several operating systems have been developed over the years as we saw above. Not one operating system can serve all types of requirements.

Depending on the features, operating systems can be divided into several categories.

Based on the *mode of data entry* and *response time* (the time between request for a service from a system and the first response from it), some types are briefly mentioned below.

1.3.1 Batch Systems

As already mentioned earlier, these systems date back to the 1950s. Even today, the periodic tasks of the same types as payroll, billings, group membership mails are clubbed together, put in a queue for automatic execution and, if necessary, the results are looked at later. The tasks need to be such that they do not require user intervention while being executed. Today, these tasks even can be submitted from an interactive session. Operating systems like IBM's MVS (*Multiple Virtual Storage*[3]) initially was a batch processing one with JCL (*job control language*) interface.

1.3.2 Interactive Systems

These systems were designed to provide faster response time so that users can debug their programs. Operating systems required to support the quick interaction was time-sharing software. One of the early such systems was IBM MVS with CICS (*Customer Information Control System*) and TSO (*time sharing option*) interfaces. Most of the prevalent OSs like different versions of Windows, UNIX and Linux are interactive ones.

1.3.3 Hybrid Systems

Some systems are a combination of both batch as well as interactive ones. Individual users can interactively execute their programs while the system accepts and runs batch programs when interactive load is low. Operating systems of many large computers are hybrid ones.

1.3.4 Real-time Systems

Real-time Systems are already introduced above. They are of two basic types based on its response time: hard real-time and soft-real time systems. A hard real-time OS has high consistency in completing a type of task (in the order of a few milliseconds), whereas a soft real time operating system allows relaxation (few hundred milliseconds with more variability or more 'jitter').

Based on the *number of users, processors, and programs and their connections*, operating systems can be classified into several categories as given below.

1.3.5 Single Processor Systems

The systems having only one *general purpose processor* with a single core (core is the component that executes instructions and store/fetch data in/from registers from the local storage) are known as single processor (or uniprocessor) systems. These systems, however, can have several *special-purpose processors* for managing specific I/O devices like keyboard controllers, disk controllers, graphic controllers etc. These device-specific processors execute a limited number of instructions and are not used to run user programs. An operating system can send

[3] https://en.wikipedia.org/wiki/MVS [as on 20-Jun-2022]

instructions to these special processors and monitor their status but cannot directly control the operation of the devices. While controllers work, the general-purpose CPU remains free from I/O devices management and OS uses it to execute another program. Operating systems working on a uniprocessor system are simple in design. However, very few present-day computer systems are single processor systems.

1.3.6 Multi-processor Systems

Most modern-day computer systems, from mobile devices (smartphones, tablets, laptops) to servers have multiple general-purpose processors. One processor can house one or more CPUs in the processor chip while each CPU can have one or more cores. The processors share system buses and the system clock. Each processor can have its own main memory or share the same along with peripheral devices. Multiprocessor systems are thus also called *tightly coupled systems* (contrast to distributed systems which are loosely *coupled*). The system can independently run several streams of execution simultaneously depending on the number of cores. Multiprocessor systems are of two basic types. *Symmetric multiprocessor systems* (SMP) run the same copy of the operating system on each processor, with each processor taking independent decisions and cooperating with each other to ensure smooth operation of the entire system. *Asymmetric multiprocessor system,* each processor is assigned a specific role and a master processor allocates the job to each processor and coordinates all the subordinate processors. The operating system is thus designed to have separate modules for master and subordinate processors. Increasing the number of processors and/or that of cores within a single processor increases the overall *throughput* (number of tasks completed in unit time) of the system. However, the relation between number of processor (or core) vs throughput is not linear as law of diminishing return sets in due to contention for shared resources and time needed for coordination among the processors. Operating systems need to incorporate complex and sophisticated mechanisms for task scheduling, load balancing and synchronization among processors (and/or cores) (discussed later in *Process Synchronization*).

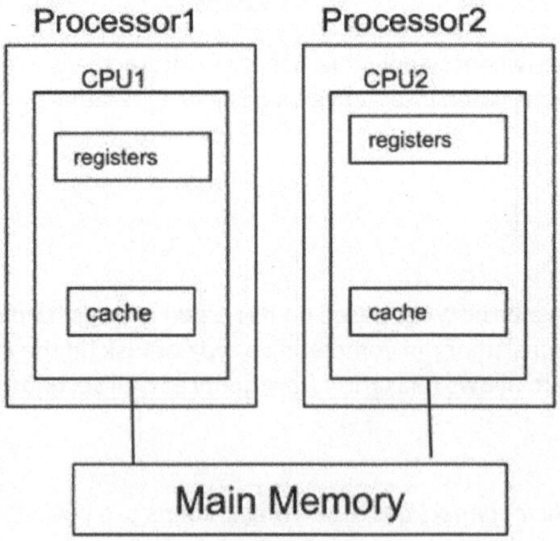

Fig 1.7 SMP System

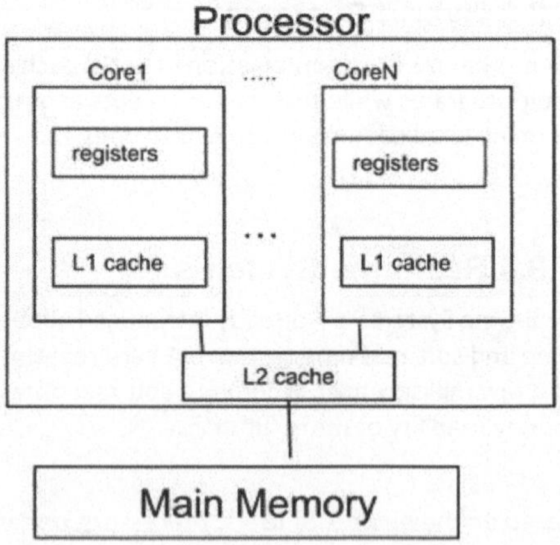

Fig 1.8 Multicore System

1.3.7 Multi-user Systems

As the name suggests, a multi-user system has many users. The operating system here must provide support to multiple users at the same time. The users can run their programs simultaneously (through multiple processors/cores) or can share a single processor for a slice of time in such a manner that each user feels as if she uses a system dedicated to her (time-multiplexing) (**Fig 1.9** - **Fig. 1.11**). The OS allocates the resources in a fair and orderly manner to all the users, without bothering the users. Security is a major issue here. OS must ensure that each user works within her own authorized area (for her program and data) and does not transgress beyond her authority. OS also needs to track usages of resources by each user and to pre-empt the resource(s) and/or user when a user unduly monopolizes a set of resources and others wait indefinitely for them. Workstations and servers are multiuser systems.

1.3.8 Multiprogram Systems

When many application programs are allowed to run concurrently in a system the system is called a multiprogram system. The main memory needs to accommodate all the application programs (either from a single user or multiple users) simultaneously. These applications have some private code and data but can also share some program modules like library files and stubs. Memory management is therefore important. OS needs to allocate private memory space for each application as well as (See **Fig 1.9**).

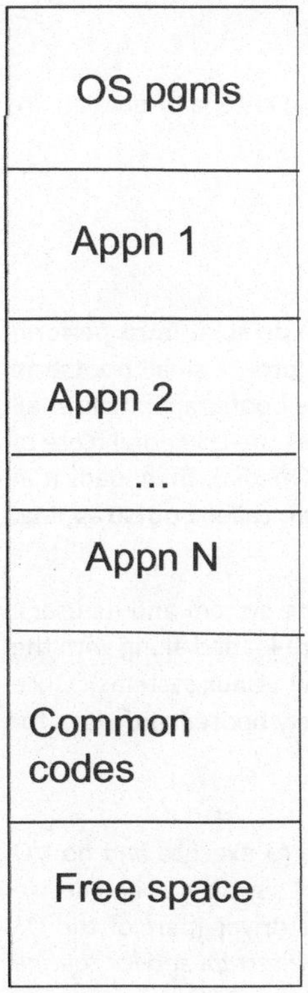

Fig 1.9 Main memory in multiprogram system

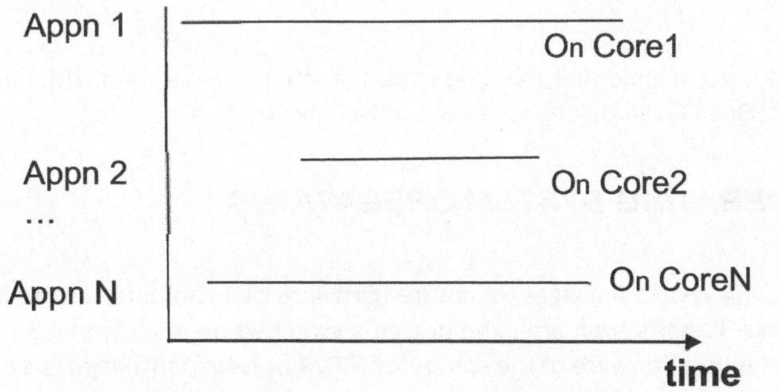

Fig 1.10 Multiprogramming in a multi-core system (true *parallelism*)

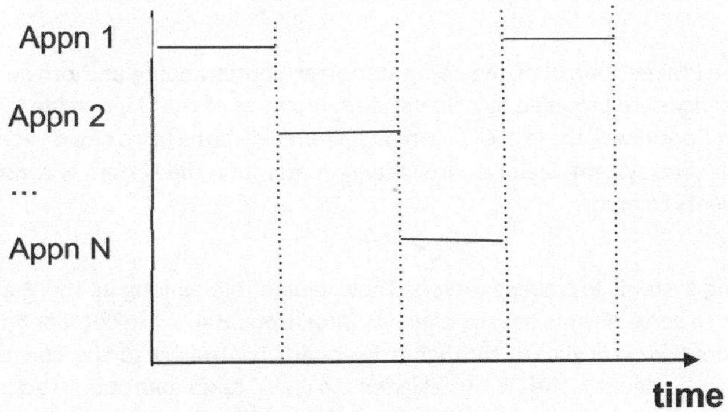

Fig 1.11 Multiprogramming in 1-core system (*concurrency* with time-sharing or time-interleaving)

Point to note that most of our computers are both multiuser and multiprogram systems. Most of today's single-user systems like mobile devices are also multiprogram ones.

1.3.9 Distributed Systems

As already introduced, distributed systems are extensions of multiprocessor systems where several independent computers are connected through a network. Users of a computer can use resources of another computer in the network. Operating systems here help users to communicate with non-local computers through various mechanisms like message passing, remote procedure calls (RPC) and so on and the user *feels* the networked system as a uniprocessor one. One of the key motivations for distributed systems is to withstand faults and failures of a local system through fault-tolerant mechanisms. Present day **clustered systems** are examples of distributed systems.

1.3.10 Embedded Systems

As we already discussed earlier, an embedded operating system is a small, special purpose OS embedded within a large machine to do a specific task. Often RTOSs are embedded within our car components, washing machines, and robots for executing certain tasks. These OSs are small (a RTOS takes only a few MB space) and contain either no or extremely limited user interfaces.

We must keep in mind that this kind of classifications can overlap with one another, as the criteria of division are different. One OS can belong to several of the above types.

1.4 OPERATING SYSTEM OPERATIONS

An operating system manages the entire hardware of a computer and serves its users. To do so, it must perform many tasks. It starts soon after the power is switched on in a computer. To boot a computer, a small **bootstrap** code kept in the firmware of the computer (ROM or its variant) needs to be executed. The bootstrap initializes all necessary hardware (CPU registers, memory contents and I/O device controllers). It locates the OS *kernel* (core of the operating system) in the memory (usually HDD or some external media disks or flash media), then loads it in the main memory (RAM) and initiates kernel execution leaving the control to it. This process is called **bootstrapping.**

The kernel takes control of the computer after bootstrapping and provides services to the system and its users. Some services are provided by other system modules of the OS, outside the kernel, that are loaded along with the kernel at boot time - these are known as **system daemons (`systemd`** is one such daemon in Linux systems). Once the kernel and system daemons are loaded in memory, the system is considered completely booted and waits for some events to occur.

Operating systems are **event driven.** They remain idle as long as there are no programs to execute and no I/O requests to serve. Events are signalled via **interrupts.** Hardware components raise interrupt signals through device controllers (like a keyboard through a keyboard controller) to the corresponding device driver (part of the OS managing the device). The OS kernel listens to it and takes appropriate action executing an *interrupt service routine* (ISR). These interrupts are called **hardware interrupts.** There can be **software interrupts** also, known as **traps** or **exceptions** which occur when some illegal operations are attempted by programs (like division by zero). Appropriate ISRs are invoked and executed for software interrupts as well. All these interrupts are assigned a priority level. If more than one interrupts occur simultaneously, high priority interrupts are served before the low-priority ones. Often user programs can explicitly request OS services to access some system resources (e.g., memory allocation, scanning input, printing output, system files etc) through a special operation known as **system calls** (discussed in the next section).

The interrupts, service routines and system calls are some of the mechanisms through which an OS either receives notifications from or controls and manages different resources of a computer system. This overall management can be classified into a few broad categories as briefly discussed below.

1.4.1 Resource Management

Operating systems work as the **resource manager** of a computer. These resources are processes, memory, filesystem and I/O devices. We briefly introduce here how these resources are managed by operating systems in general.

1.4.1.1 Process Management

A software program is a set of instructions that are executed in the CPU to accomplish a specific task. Programs are *passive* entities (like stationary rail rakes in a car-shed) unless they are in execution. A program in execution is the *active entity* (as if a running train) and called a **process**. A process is more than a program (*like a person is more than just an anatomical body or a running train with a lot of passengers*) and needs a lot of hardware and software resources during its execution. In a multiprogram OS, several processes run simultaneously either in parallel on different CPU cores or in a single core in a time-multiplexed (each process gets a slice of CPU time) manner. An operating system does the following tasks related to the process management:

creation and deletion of processes

scheduling of processes (or threads aka sub-processes) for CPU time

suspending and resuming processes

communication and coordination among several cooperating processes

resolving contention among competing processes

We shall discuss these issues in detail in **Module 2-4**.

1.4.1.2 Memory Management

Even though there are different types of memory elements (**Fig 1.12**), the main memory is central to computation. Processor and I/O devices quickly share data kept in main memory. Also, processors see main memory as the largest memory element that it can directly access and store data. It is a large array of bytes, each byte having a fixed memory address. CPU fetches instructions from main memory addresses (during instruction-fetch cycle), accesses (read & write) data from there during the data-fetch cycle (in Von Neumann architecture).

The main memory (henceforth referred as only memory) stores all the processes (OS kernel, other system modules and from users' programs) that are running in a system (**Fig 1.9**).

While the OS kernel resides in the memory if the computer is running, other processes come and go. If we can accommodate many processes, the **degree of multiprogramming** increases, but a processor core can serve only one process at a time. Higher number of processes will cause a higher number of **context switches** (attaching a CPU core from one process to another). How many processes can be kept, for how long, when a process needs to be pre-empted (removed) - are some of the important management issues.

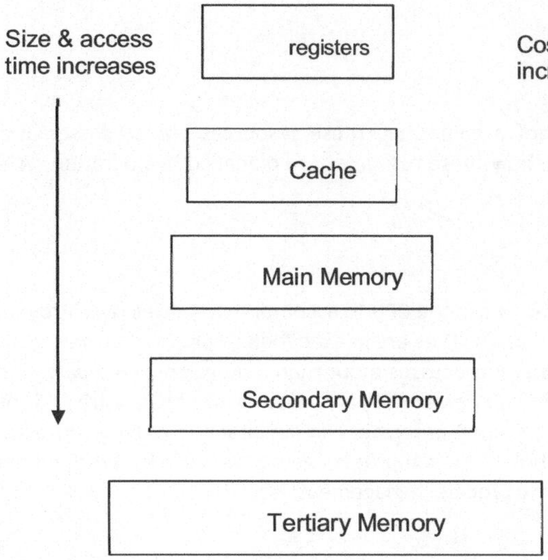

Fig 1.12: Memory Hierarchy

As part of memory management, OS does the following:

1. keeping track of memory addresses being accessed and by whom (process-id)
2. allocating and deallocating memory space to different processes
3. deciding which processes (or their parts) and their data needs to be brought into and removed from memory.

1.4.1.3 File-system Management

Program code and data are stored temporarily in registers, cache and main memory during the program execution. But, in the long term, they are stored in secondary (HDD) and tertiary storage (CD, floppy, DVD, pen drive, magnetic tape etc). These media stores data *persistently* (can retain information even when the computer is shut down). The information (code + data) is stored in the logical unit of files. A file is a sequence of records. Each file is a device-independent concept (e.g., a `.txt` file is `.txt`, no matter what physical device stores it or an `.exe` is always an `.exe` irrespective of storage media). But each physical storage medium has different physical characteristics with diverse ways of storing and retrieving data. Operating systems provide abstraction of files and map the logical files onto physical media.

File management subsystem, a part of an OS, also helps organize the files into directories (or folders) that users think are a logical collection of related files.

Specifically, an operating system does the following jobs as part of file system management:

1. formatting the media into file system type (e.g., DOS, Windows, Unix file system etc.)
2. mapping files onto physical media
3. creation, modification, and deletion of files
4. creation, modification, organization, deletion of directories (and sub-directories)
5. copying (backing up) files and directories from one media to another.

File system management will be discussed in **Module 6**.

1.4.1.4 I/O Management

A computer can have several different I/O devices (keyboard, mouse, touchpad, styler pen, monitor, scanner, printer, external disk etc). These devices enter, store and/or retrieve data. All application programs use I/O devices during their execution. These devices are made of different physical materials, have different physical characteristics, and thus require different handling techniques. Performance of a computer is dependent on proper management and control of the I/O devices and application programmers need to be kept free of their low-level nitty-gritties which can be diverse and complex. Operating systems provide a general device driver for related categories of I/O devices and specific ones when necessary. The drivers interact with the device-controllers and manage the devices. Operating systems provide users simpler interfaces to interact with the devices. In most of the operating systems, an I/O subsystem does the job, by specifically providing:

1. a memory management module to buffer, cache, and spool data transfer
2. a general device driver interface
3. specific device driver interfaces.

I/O Management will be discussed in detail in **Module 6**.

1.4.2 Security and Protection

Many users can concurrently use a computer in a multiuser, multiprogram environment. One user program can inadvertently or intentionally (with malicious intention) access a resource and/or execute a code that it is not supposed to. Any computer should have some policy and mechanism to restrict access to important resources. **Security** and **Protection** are often loosely referred to as similar concepts. However, semantically, security talks about the policies to safeguard a system from external attacks, while protection refers to the implementation of mechanisms to primarily deal with internal attacks.

A computer system implements various kinds of protection schemes: some are at the *hardware level* and some at the *software* (or *operating system*) *level*.

1.4.2.1 Processing mode

At the hardware level, every processor supports at least two operation modes: **kernel** (or **supervisor, system** or **privileged**) **mode** and **user mode**. A **mode-bit** is used to denote (say, kernel-mode 0 and user-mode 1) in which mode the processor is executing the instructions. In the kernel mode, a processor can execute all instructions like accessing all hardware and code from any user programs. But in used mode, the processor can execute instructions only from the designated memory regions (*user area*) and cannot access the hardware. If the user program needs to access hardware or execute a code beyond its designated area (beyond the boundaries in **Fig 1.9**), it needs to raise a service request to the operating system through a **system call (or syscall)**. Syscalls change the processor mode from user to kernel. The syscalls are services of the operating system. They are first checked by the OS and if approved, necessary codes are executed on behalf of the user program by kernel. However, if the user program tries to forcefully do the same without syscall, there are hardware protection mechanisms to raise interrupts. Also, if illegal operations happen, there are software traps or exceptions. In either case, immediately the mode is changed from user to kernel and proper ISR is invoked by the OS kernel. Hence, protection is ensured at hardware level and supported by the operating system.

Some processors support more than two operating modes (e.g., Intel has 4 protection rings or modes, ARMv8 has 7 modes).

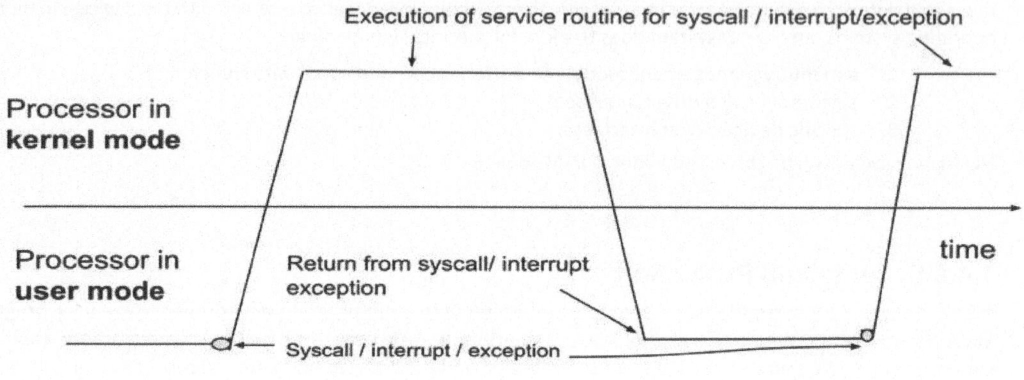

Fig 1.13: Dual mode operation (h/w + s/w protection mechanism)

1.4.2.2 Address Space

Every process is allocated memory that may not be physically contiguous and not entirely loaded in the RAM while the program is being run. However, the process sees conceptually (or *virtually*) the space as contiguous. It is referred to as *virtual address space* and such memory is called *virtual memory.* Most operating systems support virtual memory. Dedicated hardware (memory management unit or MMU) translates the virtual address space to physical addresses so that the processor can access them. A fixed portion of virtual address space of each process maps the kernel code and data - this portion is called **kernel space or system space** that can only be accessed in kernel mode. Operating system kernel maintains some global data structures and some per-process objects. Two important per-process objects are *user area* and *kernel stack.* User processes are not allowed to modify the objects and can only be modified in kernel mode. These data structures may be implemented as part of process address space but considered belonging to kernel space and operated on in kernel mode. User processes cannot access kernel space, if they need to execute some portion from kernel, they should use system calls.

1.4.2.3 Execution context

Kernel functions may run for the need of the kernel itself or due to request of the user programs. When they are run by the kernel for its own reasons (system wide maintenance & managerial purpose initiated mostly by interrupts), it is called *system context*. During this time, it usually does not need to access user address space, user area or kernel stack of the current process. However, when kernel functions are run by kernel on behalf of the requesting process, it is called to be run in *process context.* Kernel may access and modify *process address space, user area* and *kernel stack* of the current process.

It is important to note that the term *kernel* comes in 3 different contexts:

i. kernel can mean the core of operating system software (code + data)

ii. hardware operating mode (kernel mode) and

iii. virtual memory space (kernel space).

We must understand the meaning from the context.

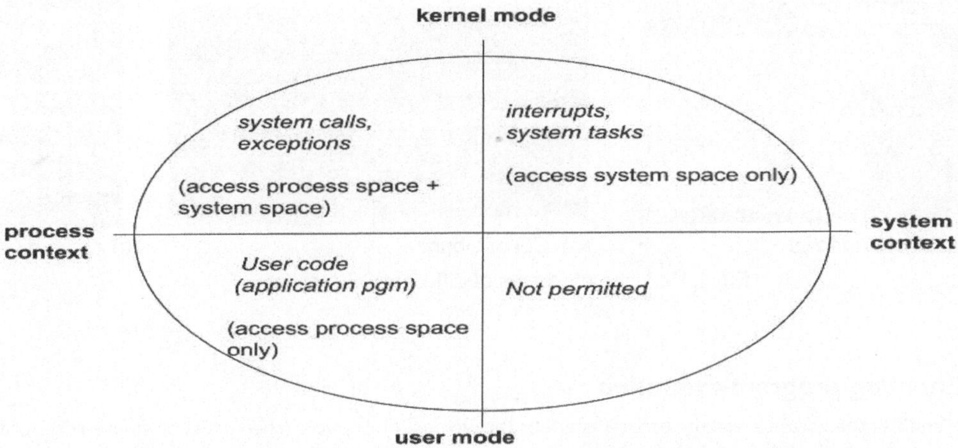

Fig 1.14: Relation among processor mode, execution context, address space

Also, we need to understand the distinctions between user and kernel mode, process, and system (or kernel) space and process and system context (**Fig 1.14**). User codes run in user mode and process context and can access only process address space. System calls and exceptions are handled in process context but in kernel mode and can access both process and kernel space. Interrupts are handled in system context, kernel mode and access only system space.

Even though a system has adequate protection, it can fail and/or be vulnerable to inappropriate access to its resources. User's authentication information may be stolen, her code and data can be copied and deleted. Such vulnerabilities can spread across the system and come through viruses and worms and materialise as identity theft, denial-of-service and/or theft of service attacks. Prevention of some of these attacks are the job of operating systems and some OSs offer some security measures for the same. All modern OSs maintain a list of users and offer user-ids (UID). During login, UIDs are checked and only on successful authentication, users are allowed to use the operating system. All processes (and sub-processes) are associated with the UIDs and monitored for use of resources. In some operating systems, users are grouped based on their privileges to access files and other resources (e.g., group-id or GIDs in UNIX/Linux systems). Only privileged groups can access some of the resources.

1.5 OPERATING SYSTEM SERVICES

Operating systems provide different services to the users and application programs. Recall that users view an operating system as a service provider (**Sec 1.1.1**). The services offer ease-of-using the computer. These services vary from one OS to another. Here, we list some of the general and common services: first, from the users' perspective and then from the system's perspective.

1.5.1 Providing user interfaces

All OSs offer user interfaces (UIs). Modern operating systems provide graphical user interfaces (GUIs). Desktop computers provide different work windows within the GUI that can be operated with mouse or touch, smartphones, tablets and high-end laptops provide touchscreen interfaces that can be operated with finger touches. PC-based OSs also offer command-line interfaces (CLIs) that take input only through text.

(a) GUI of Windows (b) CLI of Ubuntu (c) Android GUI

Fig 1.15: User interfaces of different OS systems

1.5.2 Enabling program execution

Every OS enables the users to execute programs either through user interfaces (shell in CLI or mouse-clicks or tap in GUI) or through other programs (one program can invoke another). An OS also ensures that the program completes execution with expected outcome or OS indicates the error(s) for abnormal termination.

1.5.3 Enabling I/O handling

No user programs can directly handle I/O devices, but they often need to do so (like reading from a file, an input device or a network device and/or writing onto one or more of them), during their execution. Operating systems facilitate this through different system calls.

1.5.4 Enabling filesystem organization

Users can access and modify the contents of a file through a program or through UIs. OSs provide mechanisms for creating, opening, modifying, and deleting files as well as organizing them in a hierarchy of directories and subdirectories. An OS also enables users to create, modify and delete folders or directories and sub-folders (sub-directories) using programs or through UIs.

1.5.5 Enabling interprocess communication

Processes interact with one another within a single machine or between two or more remote machines connected through a network. Operating systems provide communication mechanisms like shared memory (within the same physical system) or message passing (remote processes) over communication channels.

1.5.6 Detecting errors and enabling correction

Errors can occur during program execution - they are trapped by hardware like CPU (e.g., division by zero), or memory (e.g., illegal memory access) or I/O devices (e.g., no pages in printer). OS monitors the hardware, checks for the exceptions and notifies the concerned programs (ISRs) so that the program can take appropriate action. Sometimes, if need arises, the OS terminates the rogue process(es) to ensure smooth operation of other processes and the entire system.

These services are to provide an easy-to-use environment to the *users*. However, the computer system also requires some services for its smooth operation and improvement of overall performance. Some of these services are briefly mentioned below that are common to most operating systems.

1.5.7 Allocation of resources

In a single user, single process environment, all the resources are monopolized by one process at a time. But, in a multiprogram environment, several processes may demand a resource (say CPU) at the same time. Operating systems need to implement a scheduling algorithm (CPU scheduling for the example) so that every candidate processes can access the resource in a fair manner. This is true for all the resources of a computer like CPU, memory, and other peripheral devices. The contention and thus complexity increases when we go from multi-user, multiprogramming systems to distributed or clustered systems. An operating system has to play the role of a fair allocator of all the resources to all the candidates and of an arbitrator to resolve disputes and pre-empt unfair occupation of resources.

1.5.8 Monitoring

Use of all resources by all processes and their users therefore need to be closely monitored in terms of CPU usage, main memory usage, usages of cache, and different I/O buffers in real time. Operating systems keep track of the same and help the super user (system administrator) to take punitive action, if required.

1.5.9 Protection and security

As already mentioned earlier, for smooth running of a computer, we need both protection and security. Protection mechanisms of OS ensure that one process cannot trespass into another's memory region or that of kernel processes or cannot access hardware resources on its own. Every process is owned by a user and each user has a certain set of privileges that are strictly checked and ensured by the OS to adhere to. Security features like user's authentication credentials are also checked by the OS during local login and remote access so that unauthorized access is not allowed to mess up the operation of a system.

1.6 SYSTEM CALLS (as well as exceptions and interrupts)

User programs make system calls when they need to execute privileged instructions. These are like function calls offered by operating systems to user programs mainly for accessing the hardware. As given in **Fig 1.13** and **1.14**, system calls are executed in *kernel mode* but initiated by the user process. Hence, they run in *process context* and access both *process space* and *kernel space*.

Actually, a system goes into the kernel mode under three events: *interrupts* (from an I/O device to the processor, e.g., when reading from an input device or writing on an output device is complete), *exceptions* (generated due to an error in a running process) or a *system call* (explicit request from a running process). For an operating system, they are treated in a similar fashion.

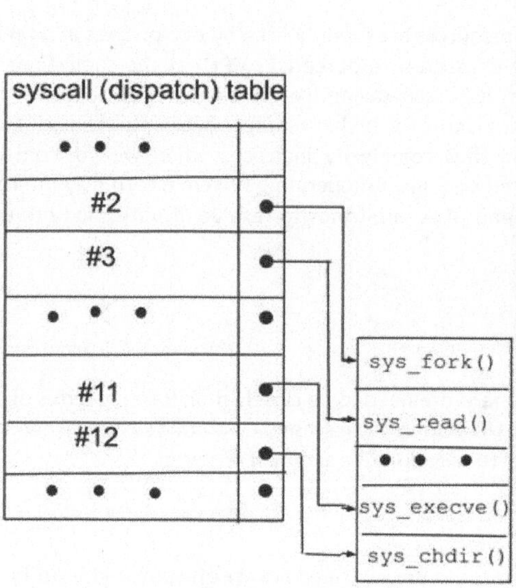

Fig 1.16: System call table in Linux

Service type	Windows	Unix

Process Control	CreateProcess()
	ExitProcess()
	WaitForSingleObject()
	...
		`fork()`
		`exit()`
		`wait()`
		...

File Management	CreateFile()
	ReadFile()
	WriteFile()
	CloseHandle()
	...
		`open()`
		`read()`
		`write()`
		`close()`
		...

Device Management	SetConsoleMode()
	ReadConsole()
	WriteConsole()
	...
		`ioctl()`
		`read()`
		`write()`
		...

Information Maintenance	GetCurrentProcessID()
	SetTimer()
	Sleep()
	...
		`getpid()`
		`alarm()`
		`sleep()`
		...

Communications	CreatePipe()
	CreateFileMapping()
	MapViewOfFile()
	...
		`pipe()`
		`shm_open()`
		`mmap()`
		...

Protection	SetFileSecurity()
	SetSecurityDescriptorGroup()
	...
		`chmod()`
		`chown()`
		...

Fig 1.17: Some example syscalls

In each case, an interrupt signal (`int <n>`, where `n` is an integer pointing to interrupt type) is generated and the kernel receives the control. It immediately suspends the normal execution of the processor and saves some important information related to the running state (program counter value, process status word or PSW) of the suspended process so that the processor can resume execution from the point of suspension at a suitable later time. It then consults a system call table (in Linux, it is called a *dispatch table*) (**Fig 1.16**). Corresponding to interrupt number (`n`), an appropriate *interrupt handler (or interrupt service routine* or ISR) is invoked. ISR is executed in kernel mode and system space (ISRs remain in system space only).

However, it is important to understand the differences among system calls, exceptions and interrupts. Interrupts can come from any I/O device that may be active due to any process, not necessarily the currently running one. Hence, it is an asynchronous event and therefore, depending on its priority level, the hardware interrupts can be serviced immediately or later.

Exceptions are caused by illegal instructions that happen in the process space, and user mode and are synchronous events. They need to be handled by the kernel in the kernel mode but in process context. It may access the user area of the kernel as well as system space. System calls are very much like exceptions with the difference that they are lawful requests from the running process.

Once the ISR (typically called `syscall()`) completes its execution, kernel checks and sets the return value or error status in appropriate registers, restores the saved state information of the suspended process from its user area of the kernel space and returns to user mode and returns the control to the suspended process. Note that mode change is a privileged instruction and can be done in kernel mode, kernel space and kernel context only.

1.6.1 Application Programming Interfaces (APIs)

Syscalls can be considered as buying tickets for the services of an operating system. Like we can buy tickets for different services of a railway station, we can request different system calls (**Fig 1.17** and **Fig 1.18**). An application program may need several syscalls to complete its intended task.

Fig 1.18: Syscalls are like railway counters

For example, a simple program for copying some content (say, only first-names) from an input file (having first-names and surnames) to an output file involve several I/O operations or syscalls like:

i. opening the input file (1)

ii. opening the output file (2)

within a loop till there is content in (1)

iii. reading the input file (1)

iv. writing on the output file (2)

v. closing the file (1)

vi. closing file (2).

Each of these operations is to be done through different syscalls (**Fig 1.17**) that the user program is supposed to request to the underlying operating system running on a system. Exact nomenclatures of syscalls (*function-names*) are different from one operating system to another (Windows and Unix syscalls are different, even within the same family it can vary from one version to another). For an application programmer, it is difficult to remember all these syscall function-names. Also, the program written under one OS (say Windows) cannot run on another operating system (say Unix) if the user program uses direct syscall functions. Operating systems therefore provide a *system call interface* that interacts with different compilers, shells and programming language libraries (Often system call interface lies within a runtime environment or RTE that comes bundled with the OS). Application programming languages (like C, C++, Java) directly talk to system call interfaces on behalf of the programs to make necessary syscalls and offer *application programming interfaces* (APIs) to the programmers. These APIs are functions available in the standard libraries of the programming languages (e.g., `libc` for standard C library) that correspond to different syscalls. (APIs can be loosely compared to different ticket booking mechanisms for railway services like using mobile apps, browsers, or agents).

As shown in **Fig 1.19**, user programs use APIs provided by library functions for making system calls. The compiler transfers it to the kernel's system call interface that changes the processor mode (user to kernel) (Step 1). The interface raises an interrupt signal with the necessary number (remember `int n`) (Step 2). In the system call table, it is resolved which system call is to be invoked (Step 3). Once the appropriate ISR completes execution, control goes back to the system call interface (Step 4). Return value is checked for error messages. If no error is found, program state and other status variables are restored, with change in operating mode (from kernel mode to user mode) and control is returned to the user program so that execution can resume from the point where it was interrupted (Step 5).

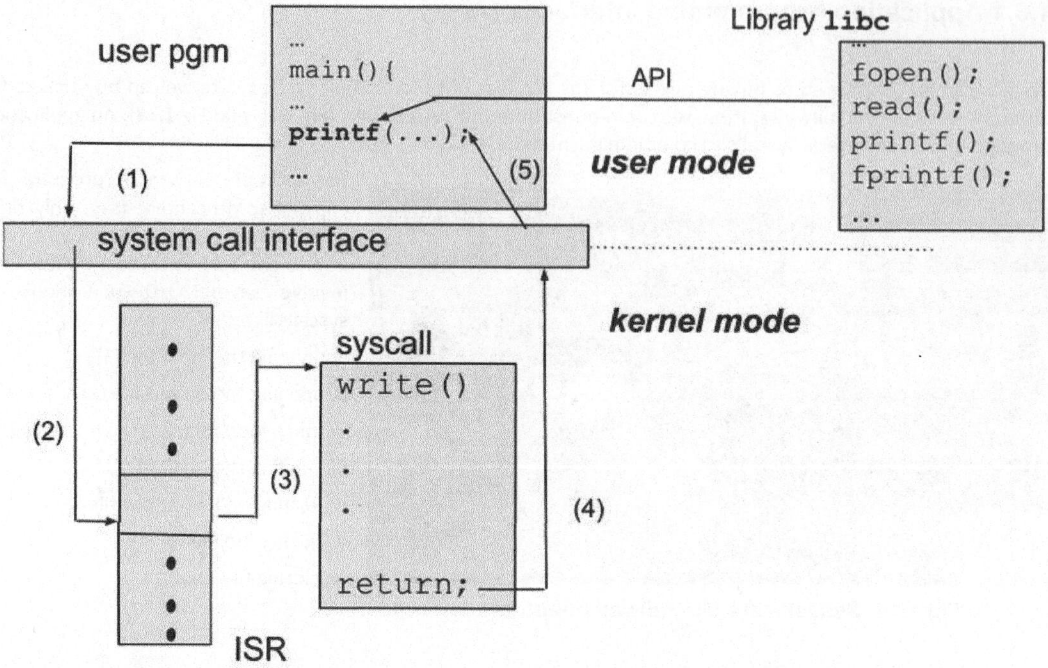

Fig 1.19: Interaction between system call and API

1.7 OPERATING SYSTEM STRUCTURE

From a user's perspective, three key requirements from an OS are:

i. *multiplexing* of the resources: several processes can run and use resources concurrently, hence time-sharing of them

ii. *isolation* of resources and processes: contention for the resources should be fairly arbitrated and a process should not interfere into address space of other processes and

iii. *interaction* among processes: processes should communicate among themselves for load-sharing.

Also from the designer's viewpoint, the operating system must have following two properties:

i. portability: the same OS can easily run on different underlying hardware architecture

ii. extensibility: newer features can be easily added and incorporated into the existing OS.

These requirements often compete and meeting all of them together is difficult. Designing an operating system is a complicated task and has some trade-offs. Requirements of multiplexing, isolation and interaction are met with kernel mode of operation. But the question comes *how much of the OS operation will be in kernel mode?*

This question drives different structural organization of the OS family and offers a few types of OS as briefly discussed below.

1.7.1 Monolithic Kernel

As the name suggests, the entire operating system runs as a single program and all the services that an OS offers to the applications are done in kernel mode.

It has a few obvious advantages like

i. *simplicity*: it is very simple in design.
ii. *centralization*: a single code controls all the resources.
iii. *close coupling*: all functionalities are in a single kernel space bypassing hassle of communications.
iv. *performance:* it is fast and easy to maintain.

However, it has also serious drawbacks like

i. *size:* Being big in size, it eats up good amount of memory (fails in *portability*)
ii. adding a new functionality incurs the cost of compiling the entire code every time (fails in *extensibility*)
iii. for any bug in a particular service, the entire kernel may fail and abort all the running processes (poor *reliability*).

Original Unix was a monolithic OS. Due to its simplicity, speed and efficiency, it still has partial presence in some of the latest versions of Unix, Linux and Windows systems.

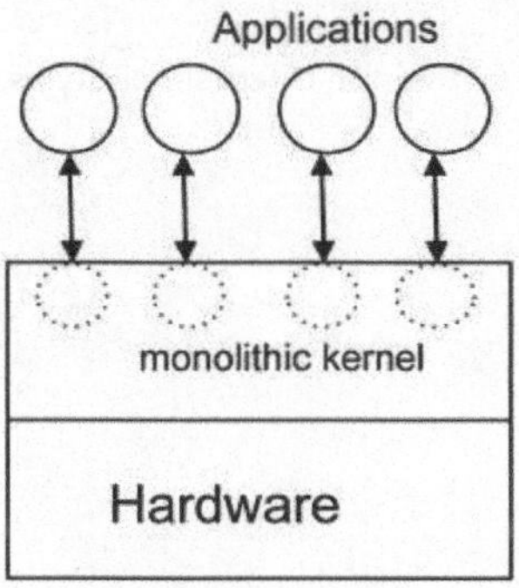

Fig 1.20: Monolithic kernel

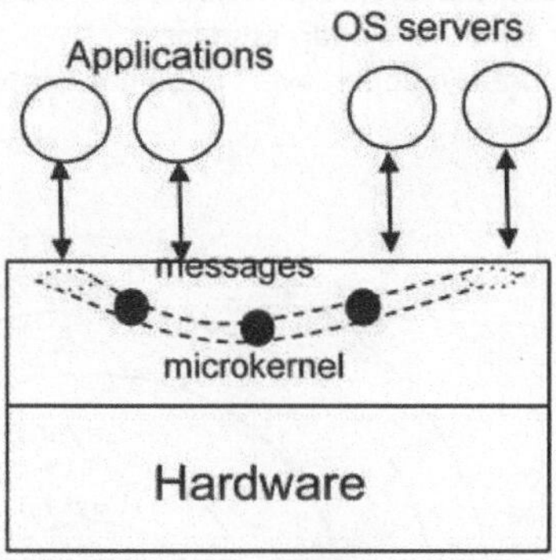

Fig 1.21: Microkernel

1.7.2 Microkernel

An opposite design strategy can be to keep the amount of kernel mode code to a bare minimum and leave most of the OS services offered in user mode. This type of OS organization is called *microkernel.* OS kernels provide minimal process and memory management with interprocess communication facility. Bulk of the OS services including device drivers, filesystem, system call handling are run as processes (like user processes) and are called *servers.* Processes (both user and system level ones alike) interact with OS servers using message passing via OS kernel.

The scheme has several advantages like:

i. *good portability*: since the kernel is small, it is easily portable and manageable.
ii. *greater reliability:* problems in OS servers do not cause kernel to fail.
iii. *easy extensibility*: adding newer functionalities or modifying the existing ones is simple due to robust implementation of the isolation.

On the other hand, it has a few disadvantages as well like:

i. *increased communication*: heavy amount of message passing through kernel for different OS services.

ii. *increased use of space:* every message is copied in two different process address spaces (of requester and server) as well as in kernel space.
iii. *poor performance*: increase in the overall workload of the kernel and thereby drop in overall performance.

Originally Mach (developed at CMU in the 1980s) brought the concept of microkernel. Darwin, the core of Apple's MacOS and iOS uses a microkernel. Several embedded systems, like QNX, use microkernel architecture.

1.7.3 Layered Approach

An alternative to both monolithic and microkernel approaches is having a layered approach. The entire functionalities of an OS are divided into well-defined layers, where the innermost layer (layer 1) deals with the bare-bone hardware (layer 0) and the uppermost layer (layer N) offers services to the applications. In-between, each layer interacts exactly with an upper and a lower layer and facilitates communication across the layers. Each layer has a specific and limited functionality and can directly use the services only of the immediate lower layer and similarly can directly serve only the immediate upper layer.

The scheme has benefits like:

i. *portability*: each layer can be independently designed, maintained when the layers are well-defined.
ii. *isolation*: the layers can interact only through a pre-defined set of interfaces and cannot interfere with each other's address space.
iii. *transparency*: upper layers need not know the details of lower layers - this also offers simplicity as well.

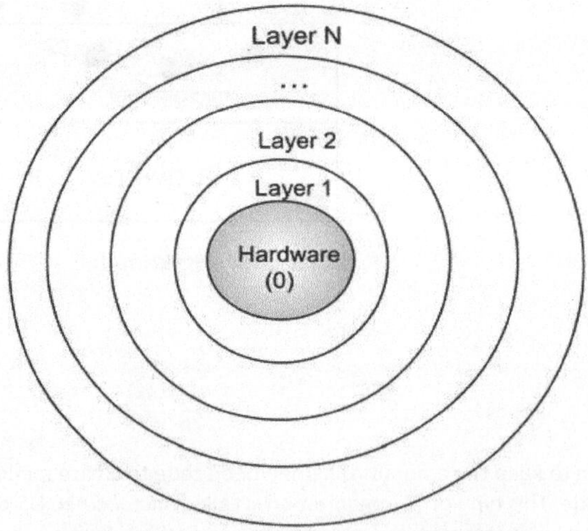

Fig 1.22: Layered Architecture of OS

However, at the same time, it has some demerits:

i. *no consensus*: The layers are easy to work with, if already well-designed. But there is no consensus on what well-designing means - which functionalities should go at what layers.
ii. *difficult stratification:* Not all functionalities can be elegantly broken down into the same number of layers.

iii. *increased communication*: there is substantial increase in communication cost as each OS service involves communication through several layers leading poor *performance.*

THE multiprogramming system (in the 1960s) implemented pure layered architecture. However, THE system had hardware-dependent layered architecture that fails the portability requirement. Few modern OSs use a limited number of layers with more functionalities added in each layer.

1.7.4 Modular Approach

A recent trend is the use of modular architecture. The kernel is divided into a set of core components and can link to several additional modules that can be dynamically loaded as and when required after bootup. These modules are called *loadable kernel modules* (LKMs).

The approach is a mixture of microkernel and layered architecture. Very few services constitute the core components and other services are dynamically attached (or "inserted" in) to the kernel. The LKMs can be removed from the kernel during runtime as well.

Linux systems use this modular approach.

1.7.5 Hybrid Approach

Very few modern OSs strictly implement one of the above approaches, rather there are combinations of two or more approaches. For example, Linux is monolithic broadly following the Unix philosophy. However, it has modular architectures with LKMs. Windows is also largely monolithic but contains some properties of microkernels with provision of separate subsystems that run as user processes.

1.8 VIRTUAL MACHINES

Virtual machines are non-real or illusory computing environments created over a single real, physical computer system. Often, we simultaneously need different operating systems but are limited by hardware constraints (e.g., having a single CPU, single memory and a single set of I/O devices) (**Fig 1.23**). Different operating systems run simultaneously on a single set of hardware (a real physical computing system) where each such OS 'feels' as if it is exclusively owning the system hardware. Each such OS can be considered as a virtual machine (VM) (**Fig 1.25**). Note that this setup is different from a computer with multiple boot options. In a multi-boot system, the hard disk is partitioned and only a single OS is booted at a time and works solo till it is shutdown. Not two or more OSs can be booted at the same time. But virtualization enables simultaneous booting and working of multiple OSs on a single real machine (on different virtual machines). A loose analogy can be multiple roles played by an actor in different movies (multi-boot), to double / triple / multiple roles of an actor in a single movie (VMs).

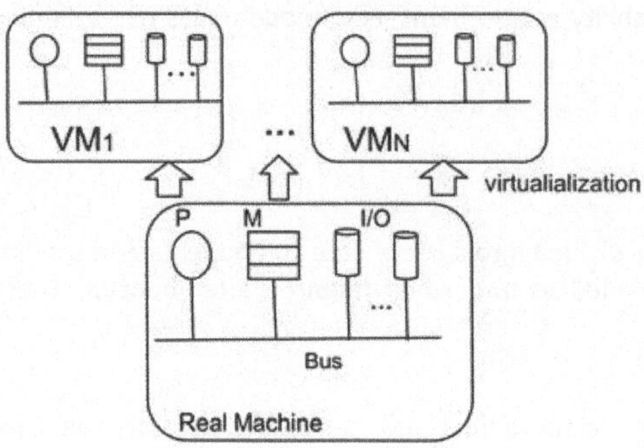

Fig 1.23: Single h/w m/c virtualized to multiple virtual m/cs (*system-level virtualization*)

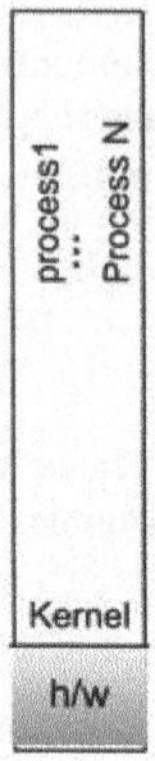

Fig 1.24: Single OS on a single m/c

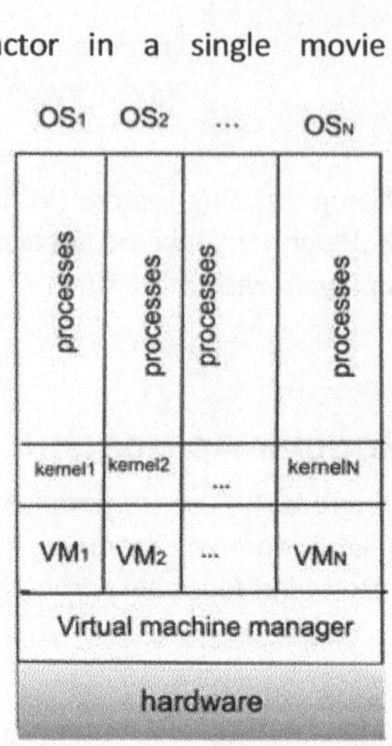

Fig 1.25: Virtual Machines on a single m/c

Virtual machine implementation consists of a few components (**Fig 1.25**). The base has the hardware components, known as the **host.** The host is managed by a **virtual machine manager (VMM)** that virtualizes the computing environment (as if it creates replicas of the underlying hardware) to several virtual machines (**Fig 1.23** and **Fig 1.25**). Each virtual machine offers a *'feel'* of an independent hardware machine and can run an OS on it. Each OS can run processes and use virtual resources independently, oblivious of the fact that there are other OSs running simultaneously on the same real machine. The OSs running on VMs are called **guest** OSs and the application processes on them are **guest** applications.

1.8.1 Types of VMMs

VMMs are also called **hypervisors** and can be of several types as described below.

Type-0 Hypervisor: Underlying hardware supports virtualization through creation and management of VMs via firmware. Mainframe and large size servers like IBM LPARs, Oracle LDOMs contain Type-0 VMMs.

Type-1 Hypervisor: VMMs here are more like operating systems that interact with both host hardware and virtual machines as intermediaries. VMs almost work like processes running on the host OS or Type-1 hypervisors. VMWare ESX, Citrix XenServer are examples of Type-1 hypervisors.

Type-2 Hypervisor: These hypervisors are applications that run on some host OS and allow some other OS to run inside the application. Obviously, these hypervisors offer very limited features and compromised performance. VMWare Workstation and Fusion, Oracle VirtualBox are examples of Type-2 hypervisors.

Virtual machines are very popular for cross-platform software development and testing due to the following reasons.

i. *Cost-effectiveness*: One does not need different hardware to test a newly developed OS as a VMM can simulate the same. Similarly, a new application can be developed and tested for multiple OS platforms using VMs.

ii. *Isolation:* VMs provide isolation between the host OS and guest OSs as well as between any two guest OSs. A bug or virus or worm within a particular OS cannot play havoc on other OSs.

iii. *Consolidation*: In data centers two or more lightly loaded systems can be combined in a virtual machine to run on a single real system. This way load can be consolidated and balanced with better resource utilization.

iv. *live migration*: Some VMMs include the feature that allows some guests to move from one host system to another without any interruption. This live migration enables better resource management also.

1.8.2 Other types of virtualization

Sometimes virtualization comes with different flavours. For example, ***paravirtualization*** does not offer *pure virtualization* where all the hardware is simulated as per the need of a guest OS. Rather, the guest OS can customize itself to the basic set of virtual hardware. This scheme reduces the volume of virtualization software.

Virtualization can also happen at application level. For example, ***Java Virtual Machine (JVM)*** is actually virtualization of the programming environment. JVM provides an execution environment that is independent of operating systems. Java programs are compiled into **bytecodes** that are executed in a JVM irrespective of the OS that is running the JVM.

Virtualization, discussed so far, takes care of different OSs running on the same instruction set architecture (same processor). However, when programs compiled in one instruction-set architecture (guest) need to be run on another instruction set (host), the entire guest instruction-set needs to be converted. ***Emulator*** software, sitting on the host system, translates each of the guest instructions into a host instruction and enables execution of the guest executables. This **emulation** is also virtualization of instruction-set - which is complicated and challenging, but very popular, particularly in gaming softwares.

Present day **cloud computing** is enabled by massive virtualization of hardware resources over the Internet. The processing and storage are offered as a service to the users but are actually done in remote data centers.

1.9 OS CASE STUDIES

There are quite a few operating systems in the market. However, most of the general-purpose OSs belong to either of the two popular families: UNIX and WINDOWS. We shall briefly provide an overview of the two families here.

1.9.1 UNIX

UNIX, first developed in 1971 (See Sec **1.2.3**), is one of the most successful operating systems. It has been widely used and is still available in variants and offshoots with different open-source and commercial versions, both in academia, research and the business world. UNIX is a multi-user, multiprogramming OS. It has simplicity and elegance in its design from the system's point of view. It also provides simplicity, clarity, and ease-of-use from the user's point of view.

1.9.1.1 System Design

Fig 1.26 provides an overview of high-level design of UNIX architecture. The UNIX kernel directly interacts with the hardware and isolates it from the other programs by providing a set of services. Traditionally UNIX has a command line interface (CLI) where programs like sh(ell) (there can be different types of shells like `csh`, `tcsh`, `bash` etc) are used. Shell offers a number of commands (few are shown in the middle layer of **Fig 1.26**), each one is an executable program. These programs and editors (`vi` and `ed`) interact with the kernel invoking system calls. Even the user program (`a.out`) can be in this layer. A standard C compiler (`cc`) is found in the outermost layer which invokes a pre-compiler (`cpp`), 2-pass compiler (`comp`), assembler (`as`), and linker-loader (`ld`) from the lower-layer. Other applications remain in the outermost layer that can use different lower-layer programs to invoke syscalls. This architecture is generic, different variants have different numbers of layers and UNIX, being open source since inception, allows extension on the hierarchy of layers.

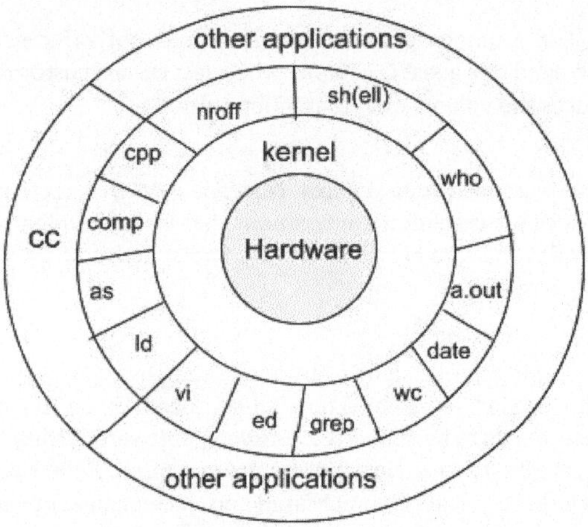

Fig 1.26: UNIX architecture

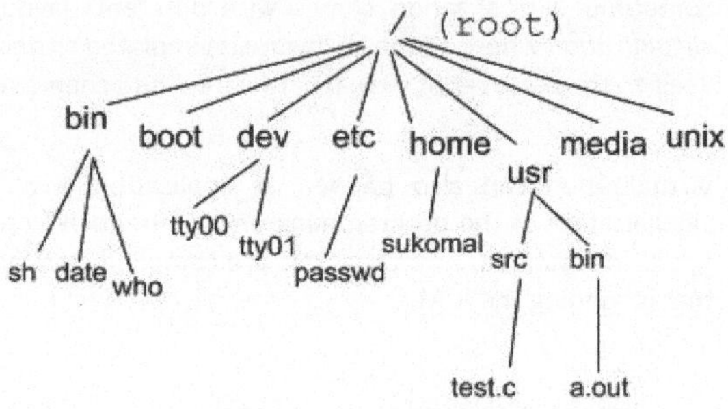

Fig 1.27: UNIX File system organization

1.9.1.2 User Perspective

At the high level, UNIX provides a set of simple and consistent features.

Filesystem: UNIX has a hierarchical filesystem (**Fig 1.27**) where '/' is the root and all directories and files are arranged in a tree structure. Leaf-nodes are files and non-leaf nodes are directories and subdirectories. But UNIX treats all files and folders alike as an unformatted stream of bytes. Every file is considered unique by the system and identified by the path from the root to leaf (e.g., `/usr/src/test.c`). Even the devices are also treated as files, as `tty01` and `tty02` represent 2 devices.

Processing environment: A program is any executable binary file (e.g., `a.out`), but during execution, UNIX sees it as a process (a running instance of a program). Several processes can run concurrently. A process can create another process (using `fork()` system call), execute a program within the process (using `exec()` syscall), and communicate with one another using IPC mechanisms (e.g., signals and pipes).

System primitives: Shell is a powerful tool that comes with UNIX offering a few building block primitives. These primitives help users write small modular programs that can be combined to create complex programs. One such primitive is *redirection of I/O*. Processes easily access *standard input, standard output* and *standard error* of the CLI as 3 files and can independently redirect any of the files to another location. Another useful primitive is *pipe* where output of one process can be treated as input to another process.

1.9.1.3 OS Services

UNIX provides the following standard services. Privileged services are provided in kernel mode.

Process management: The kernel does process creation, termination, suspension and communication. It ensures fair process scheduling using time-sharing.

Memory management: UNIX kernel allocates memory to all executing processes ensuring isolation between the kernel space and user space and among the address spaces of several user processes. It also takes care of virtual memory when main memory is low.

File management: For persistent storage, UNIX formats the disk space, allocates to different files and directories and allows users to organize and manage it. It also provides well-structured security at folder and file levels.

I/O Management: UNIX allows processes to access I/O devices like terminals, disk drives, network devices in a controlled manner.

Interrupt and exception handling: UNIX allows peripheral devices and the system clock to asynchronously interrupt CPU and support exception handling synchronously. Interrupts have defined priority levels. When a high priority interrupt is serviced, all interrupts below its priority level are blocked.

Even though earlier versions of UNIX had only CLI, present-day UNIX also has GUIs. Linux and open-source versions have made UNIX freely distributed and well accepted across the globe.

1.9.2 WINDOWS

Windows, developed by Microsoft (MS) Corporation, is a family of operating systems that are perhaps the most used OSs across the world. It started with Windows 1.0 in 1985 that came following MS-DOS (1981), a collaborative effort of MS and IBM for IBM personal computers. Windows 10 and Windows Server 2016 with annual updates are the latest in the family and briefly discussed.

1.9.2.1 System Design

Windows is a monolithic operating system with layered structure and some features of a microkernel. Majority of OS and device driver code run in kernel mode with the processes running in user mode (**Fig 1.28**). There are several layers with some major components.

In the user mode, processes and dynamic link-libraries (DLLs) are executed.

1. Processes: Windows considers processes of 4 categories.

i. **user processes:** These are Windows applications developed by users.
ii. **service processes:** These are Windows services independent of user logins like Task Scheduler and Print Spooler services including MS SQL Server or Exchange Server services.
iii. **system processes:** These are some fixed processes not considered Windows services like logon process, Session Manager process.
iv. **environment subsystem processes:** These are part of support for other OS environments like OS/2 and POSIX systems by Windows. However, they are now discontinued.

2. Sub-system DLLs: DLLs are stand-alone executable routines that are linked by applications (different processes) and they translate functions to the lower level native system calls.

3. NTDLL.dll: These have the Windows lower-level system calls that are executed in the kernel mode.

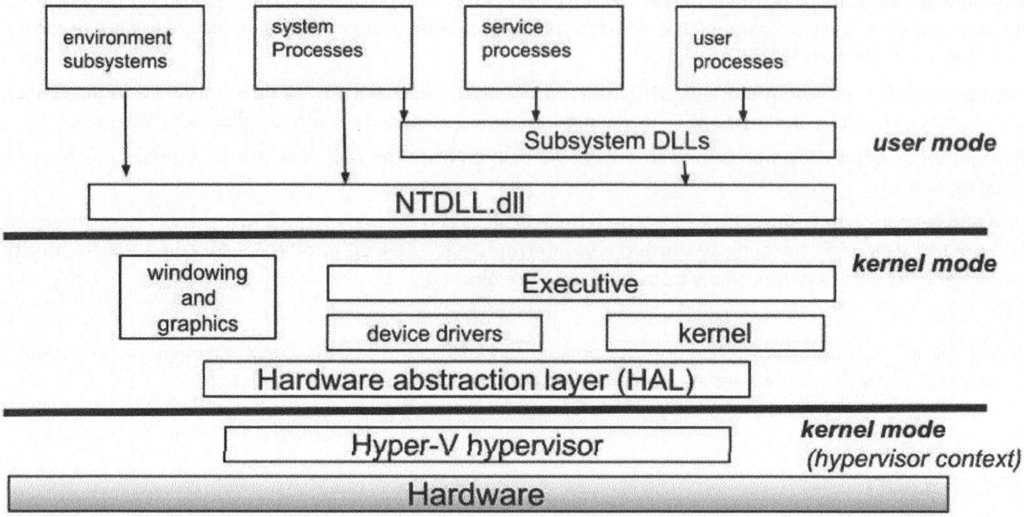

Fig 1.28: Overview of Windows architecture

In the kernel mode, several components work.

4. Executive: It contains the basic OS services like memory management, process and thread management, security, I/O, networking and IPC.

5. Kernel: It consists of low-level OS functions, such as thread scheduling, interrupt and exception handling, and multiprocessor synchronization and provides a set of routines for Executive.

6. Device drivers: Hardware device driver codes translate user I/O function calls into specific hardware device I/O requests, and non-hardware device drivers, such as file system and network drivers.

7. Windowing and graphics system: Windows brought rich GUIs for the users. This section deals with GUI functions (known as USER and GDI functions), interface controls and drawing.

8. HAL: Hypervisor interacts with a hardware abstraction layer (HAL) that isolates the kernel, device drivers and other Windows executives from hardware-specific details.

9. Hypervisor: At the base, the hypervisor (Hyper-V) runs with privileges higher than a traditional kernel. It virtualizes and isolates all the hardware resources of a host system and provides them virtualization-based-security (VBS). The hypervisor has its own internal layers and services to manage the hardwares ad to offer virtual machines.

1.9.2.2 User Perspective

Filesystem: Windows supports Windows native filesystem, called NTFS along with some other formats like CDFS, UDF, FAT12, FAT16, FAT32, exFAT etc. Files are organized into directories, where each directory is a B+ tree.

Processing environment: Windows manages processes through threads where each process has one or more threads. Kernel creates the first thread during process creation and other threads are created on need basis. Kernel threads execute kernel code, but application threads can execute both application and kernel codes. An application can also own some kernel threads, mainly to access device drivers.

Interprocess communication: Processes communicate using two schemes:

1. directly with each other using shared memory and memory-mapped files in the user space

2. indirectly using local procedure call (LPC) or RPC where message passing technique is used via kernel space.

1.9.2.3 OS Services

Process management: Windows kernel does process creation, termination, suspension and communication. Kernel uses a scheduler (called *thread dispatcher*) for CPU time management with pre-emption (forceful eviction of threads from CPU). Windows use objects to manage processes and threads (named as EPROCESS and ETHREAD objects respectively). Windows also supports fibers (sub-thread) and jobs (a group of processes).

Memory management: Windows divides main memory into 2 halves and allocates almost equally to user processes (lower memory region is called user half) and kernel processes (upper memory region is called kernel spaces). Virtual memory with paging is used.

File management: For persistent storage, Windows formats the disk space, allocates to different files and directories and allows users to organize and manage it. Files are managed in terms of *volumes* where a master file table (MFT) takes care of each volume. Files are protected through security mechanisms.

I/O Management: Windows I/O manager along with device drivers does the I/O management. Windows I/O subsystem covers device drivers, filesystem drivers, network drivers, a cache and message buffers.

Interrupt and exception handling: Generic name for interrupts, exceptions and system calls is *trap* in Windows. Traps have 32 interrupt request levels or IRQLs (0-31). Hardware interrupts have high IRQLs (3-31), followed by software interrupts (IRQL 2 and 1). A processor always runs with a single IRQL. Normal user thread executes in IRQL 0.

Windows has greatly evolved over the years from a PC-based OS to a complex Windows-as-a-service (WaaS) in a cloud computing environment implementing virtualization. Microsoft has a good deal of its documentation with other resources at https://docs.microsoft.com/en-us/. The most authentic source to learn about the latest version of Windows is [YIR17].

UNIT SUMMARY

- *An operating system is a software, the core of system software that runs all the time from booting to shutdown of a computing device. It acts as the intermediary between the bare hardware of the system and its users.*
- *It provides a lot of services to the users so that they need not bother about the specialties of the underlying hardware as that can vary across the systems. An OS allocates the hardware whenever user programs need them, controls and manages them. An OS also manages execution of user programs. through process management.*
- *OSs have evolved a lot since the 1950s as computer systems did with time. From the open shop era when there was no OS to today's cloud computing, OS has seen batch processing, multiprogramming, time-sharing, concurrent programming, personal computing, distributed computing and embedded systems.*
- *Based on needs, OS has various types like: batch system, multiprogramming system, interactive system, multi-user systems, distributed systems, embedded and realtime systems.*
- *Again, based on organization and architecture, there are variations like monolithic, microkernel, hybrid and loadable kernel modules.*
- *These classifications are not non-overlapping. Most of the available operating systems actually belong to several categories simultaneously.*
- *However, most of the OSs do process management, memory management, file management, I/O device management and provide security and protection to hardware & software entities and the users.*
- *OS ensures protection in collaboration with the hardware through different isolation schemes like operating modes (kernel and user), address spaces (kernel space and process space) and execution context (system and process).*
- *The isolation schemes are assisted by another set of hardware-software mechanisms: interrupts, exceptions and system calls.*
- *The chapter concludes with case studies of two popular OS families: UNIX and Windows.*

EXERCISES

Multiple Choice Questions

Q1. Which of the following standard C library functions will always invoke a system call when executed from a single-threaded process in a UNIX/Linux operating system?

A. exit **B.** malloc **C.** sleep **D.** strlen GATE (2021)]

Q2. Which combination of the following features will suffice to characterize an OS as a multiprogrammed OS?
(a). More than one program may be loaded into main memory at the same time for execution.
(b). If a program waits for certain events such as I/O, another program is immediately scheduled for execution.
(c) If the execution of a program terminates, another program is immediately scheduled for execution.

A. a **B.** a and b **C.** a and c **D.** a, b and c [GATE (2002)]

Q3. Fork is
A. the creation of a new job
B. the dispatching of a task
C. increasing the priority of a task
D. the creation of a new process

Q4. Which of the statements are true?

S1: At the end of system call OS generates an interrupt which switches CPU back to USER MODE

S2: Whenever user calls system call OS generate an interrupt which switches CPU from KERNEL MODE to USER MODE

S3: In kernel mode instructions to manipulate hardware can be executed by CPU

A. S1 and S3

B. S1 and S2

C. S2 and S3

D. only S1

Q5. close system call returns _____
(A) 0
(B) 1
(C) -1
(D) 0 and -1

Q6 In UNIX Which of the following command is used to set task priority

A. init

B. nice

C. kill

D. ps [UGC NET CS (2012)]

Answers of Multiple Choice Questions

1. A and C 2. B 3. D 4. A 5. D 6. B

Short Answer Type Questions

Q1. What does the CPU do when there are no programs to run?

Q2. What characteristics are common to trap, interrupts, supervisor calls and subroutine calls?

Q3. Why must a computer start in kernel mode when power is first turned on?

Q4. What is kernel?

Q5. Define a process. What is it used for?

Q6. What is spooling? Why is it used?

Long Answer Type Questions

Q1. What are the key differences between a trap and an interrupt?

Q2. What are the main differences between operating systems for a mainframe computer and a personal computer?

Q3. What is bootstrapping ? What is its purpose ? Briefly describe how it is performed?

Q4. What are the two different kinds of multiprocessor operating systems? Discuss their differences.

Q5. What are the differences between (processor) preemption and interruption? When and in what way can they be similar?

Numerical Problems

Q1. How many of the following instructions should be privileged _____

1) set mode to kernel mode 2) reboot 3)read the program status word 4) disable interrupts 5) write the instruction register

Q2. How many bits are required to control Windows IRQLs?

PRACTICAL

1. Install any Linux operating system in your computer. There are many free OS available at `https://distrowatch.com/` and Internet tutorials on installing Linux.
2. Check on the Internet, how Ubuntu can be activated and used from Windows and explore the Ubuntu CLI.
3. Learn details of different syscalls in the UNIX and Windows. [Hint: For Unix commands, try `man <cmd> or info <cmd>`]

KNOW MORE

- Evolution of Computer systems as well as that of operating systems can be studied from [Mil11], [SGG18], [Hal15], [Han00].
- Types of operating systems can be learned more from [Dha09].
- Operation of Interrupts is detailed in [Sta12].
- Virtualization was covered from [Hal09] and [SGG18].
- [Bac05] and [Vah12] give a broad overview as well as details of UNIX.
- Windows is discussed in reasonably great detail in [Hal15] and [SGG18].
- However, to work with Windows in exploratory details, one must refer [YIR17].

REFERENCES AND SUGGESTED READINGS

[Bac05] Maurice J Bach: The Design of the UNIX Operating System, Prentice Hall of India, 2005.

[CKM16] Russ Cox, Frans Kaashoek, Robert Morris: xv6, a simple, Unix-like teaching operating system, available at https://www.cse.iitd.ac.in/~sbansal/os/book-rev9.pdf

[Dha09] Dhananjay M. Dhamdhere: Operating Systems, A Concept-Based Approach, McGraw Hill, 2009.

[HA09] Sibsankar Haldar and Alex A Aravind: Operating Systems, Pearson Education, 2009.

[Hal15] Sibsankar Haldar: Operating Systems, Self-Edition 1.1, 2015.

[Han00] Per Brinch Hansen: The Evolution of Operating Systems, (2000) (available at http://brinch-hansen.net/papers/2001b.pdf) ((as on 8-Jul-2022).

[Mil11] Milan Milenkovic: Operating Systems - Concepts and Design, 2nd edition, Tata McGraw Hill, 2011

[SGG18] Abraham Silberschatz, Peter B Galvin, Greg Gagne: Operating Systems Concepts,10th Edition, Wiley, 2018.

[Sta12] William Stallings: Operating Systems Internals and Design Principles, 7th Edition, Prentice Hall, 2012.

[Vah12] Uresh Vahalia: UNIX Internals, The New Frontiers, Pearson, 2012.

[YIR17] Pavel Yosifovich, Alex Ionescu, Mark E. Russinovich, and David A. Solomon: Windows Internals, Seventh Edition (Part 1 and 2), Microsoft, 2017. https://docs.microsoft.com/en-us/sysinternals/resources/windows-internals (as on 8-Jul-2022).

Dynamic QR Code for Further Reading

2 Processes, Threads and their Scheduling

UNIT SPECIFICS

Through this unit we have discussed the following aspects:

- *Processes: Definition, Process Relationship, Different states of a Process, Process State transitions, Process Control Block (PCB), Context switching*
- *Thread: Definition, Various states, Benefits of threads, Types of threads, Concept of multithreads*
- *Process Scheduling: Foundation and Scheduling objectives, Types of Schedulers*
- *Scheduling criteria: CPU utilization, Throughput, Turnaround Time, Waiting Time, Response Time*
- *Scheduling algorithms: Pre-emptive and Non preemptive, FCFS, SJF, RR;*
- *Multiprocessor scheduling*
- *Real Time scheduling: RM and EDF.*

This chapter introduces the basic units of program execution: processes and threads. A process is a running instance of a set of instructions, called a program. Execution of a program is facilitated and managed by the OS on the computing hardware. Operating system sees it in terms of a process, allocates resources to the process and its sub-units, called threads, and allows the CPUs to execute the instructions for a process and threads. We develop necessary concepts centred around program execution with a focus on CPU scheduling.

Like the previous unit, many multiple-choice questions as well as questions of short and long answer types following Bloom's taxonomy, assignments through several numerical problems, a list of references and suggested readings are provided. It is important to note that for getting more information on various topics of interest, appropriate URLs and QR code have been provided in different sections which can be accessed or scanned for relevant supportive knowledge. "Know More" section is also designed for supplementary information to cater to the inquisitiveness and curiosity of the students.

RATIONALE

This unit on process management starts with the discussion on functioning of an operating system in detail. The unit helps students understand the fundamental concepts of program execution under the control of an OS. A program is a set of instructions stored in the persistent memory. They need to be brought to the main memory and then executed on the processor using different hardware units to produce a desired output. In a multi-user, multi-program environment, several programs from several users run. But every program essentially needs a processor to execute and other resources (both software and hardware) to complete its intended task. How these resources are allocated, when they are allocated, deallocated and reclaimed - are central questions to understand the overall functioning of an OS. We define the fundamental concepts of program execution - processes and threads here. We also define other necessary concepts related to process management. How different resources are allocated to processes, how their usages are tracked and monitored, which data structures help them in this tracking are discussed here. Out of several hardware resources, the processor or CPU is the most important one. How a CPU is allocated to a process, for how much time, when it is taken off from the process - are discussed as part of CPU Scheduling. All these are discussed with respect to uniprocessor, multiprocessor and real time operating systems.

This unit builds the fundamental concepts to understand the functioning of an OS. The concepts will be used in all the forthcoming units of the book.

PRE-REQUISITES

- *Basics of Computer Organization and Architecture*
- *Fundamentals of Data Structures*
- *Fundamentals of Algorithms*
- *Introductory knowledge of Computer Programming*
- *Introduction to Operating Systems (**Unit I** of the book)*

UNIT OUTCOMES

List of outcomes of this unit is as follows:

U2-O1: *Define a process, a thread, PCB, context switch, performance metrics.*

U2-O2: *Describe the life cycle of a process through different states, PCB, different scheduling algorithms.*

U2-O3: *Understand the state transitions of a process and context switching.*

U2-O4: *Realize the need of threads and their differences with processes.*

U2-O5: *Analyse and compare different CPU scheduling algorithms.*

U2-O6: *Design CPU scheduling algorithms to optimize performance.*

Course Outcomes

After completion of the course the students will be able to:

1. Create processes and threads.
2. Develop algorithms for process scheduling for a given specification of CPU.
3. Utilization, Throughput, Turnaround Time, Waiting Time, Response Time.
4. For a given specification of memory organization develop the techniques for optimally allocating memory to processes by increasing memory utilization and for improving the access time.
5. Design and implement file management system.
6. For a given I/O devices and OS (specify) develop the I/O management functions in OS as part of a uniform device abstraction by performing operations for synchronization between CPU and I/O controllers.

Unit-2 Outcomes	EXPECTED MAPPING WITH COURSE OUTCOMES (1- Weak Correlation; 2- Medium correlation; 3- Strong Correlation)					
	CO-1	CO-2	CO-3	CO-4	CO-5	CO-6
U2-O1	3	3	3	2	1	1
U2-O2	3	3	3	2	1	1
U2-O3	3	3	3	2	1	1
U2-O4	3	3	3	2	1	1
U2-O5	3	3	3	2	1	1
U2-O6	3	3	3	2	1	1

2.1 PROGRAMS and PROCESSES

A computer essentially contains two components: hardware and software (See **Fig 1.1** in *Unit 1*). Software is composed of one or more programs written in programming languages. *A program is a set of instructions* that need to be executed on the processor or CPU of the computer. When the program is not run, it is a *passive* entity. It remains only as a file, stored in some persistent memory (secondary memory like hard drive or a tertiary memory like flash drive, CD, DVD, tapes etc). From the point of view of an OS, a program is any *executable* file (`a.out` in UNIX or `.exe` in Windows). Note the difference with *source codes* (`.c` or `.java` files which are written in high-level languages and therefore not executable and not programs). A source code, after being compiled, produces an executable that is referred to as a program.

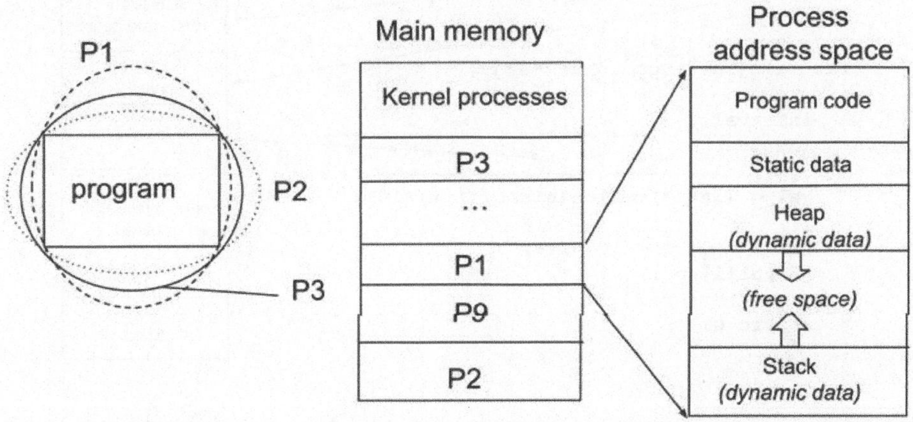

Fig 2.1: A program having 3 processes, running with others processes simultaneously

When a program is executed, it becomes a process. *A process is a program in execution.* It is an active entity and dynamically changes. An OS considers processes as units of program execution or simply, computation. When we talk of multiprogramming, we mean that multiple processes run simultaneously. A process is much more than a program. For an OS, a process subsumes a program which is a sequence of instructions (code), but also contains data and a lot of other entities. A single program can have multiple instances as multiple processes running at the same time on a given machine. For example, a word processor (a program) can open several documents, each one can be considered as a separate process (each document as data is different) and the OS tracks each process individually. As a loose analogy, a person can be considered as a program, but she can be a mother, a daughter-in-law, wife at the same time in a family and play different roles simultaneously. Different roles can be considered as processes that can come from a single program (a single person).

Some of the processes can belong to application programs or user programs (called *user processes*), and some OS programs (called *kernel processes*).

Each process holds some attributes assigned by the OS as follows.

Process-id: a process identifier (often referred to as `pid`)

User-id: the process is owned by a specific user (owner's user identifier or user-id, referred as `uid`)

Process Group-id: Every process is supposed to belong to a group, based on the task. The group has a process group identifier (or `pgid`)

Address space: main memory space (known as *process address space*) where it stores

i. program (code or text)
ii. static data
iii. dynamic data in the form of
    a. heap and

b. stack.

Kernel processes reside in kernel space (of main memory), execute OS kernel code in kernel mode, while user processes remain in user space and run user code in user mode and can make system calls (Recall Sec **1.4.2.3**).

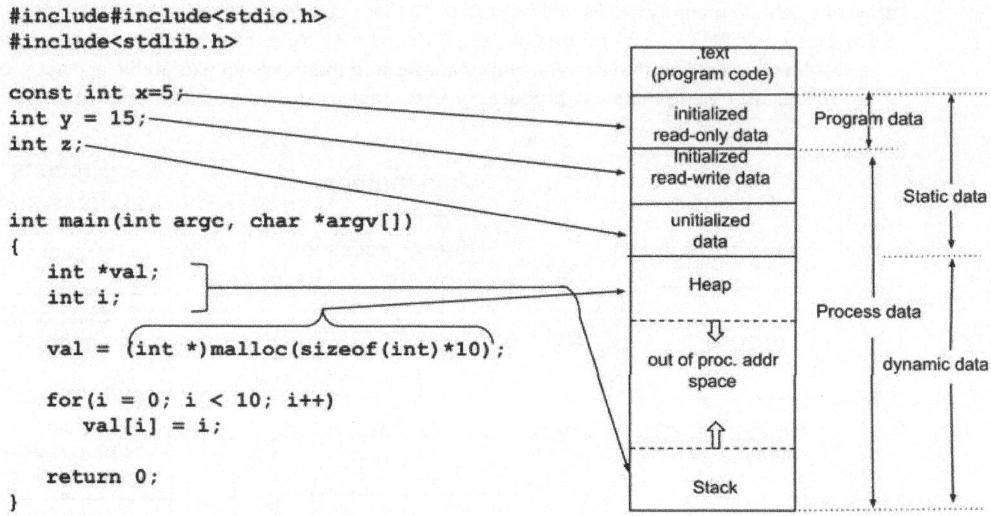

Fig 2.2: Different parts of process address space

2.1.1 Process Address Space

When a program is executed, it is allocated space in the main memory. The space is called process address space. The space may be physically contiguous or non-contiguous depending upon the memory allocation technique used by the OS (will be covered in **Memory Management**, Unit 5). However, logically (or *virtually*) the space is considered contiguous, and a hardware mechanism does necessary address translation from virtual (logical) to physical address space. The process address space essentially contains the following sections (**Fig 2.1** and **Fig 2.2**).

A. Text Section: It stores the program code (in executable form, not the source code). All the instructions are stored here.

B. Data Section: This section stores the data that are used by the process. Some data comes attached to the program code that cannot be dynamically changed (globally declared and initialized as read-only data) - we call this as program data. However, most of the data belong to the two major classes as follows.

i. Static data: This data is statically bound to program code and can be allocated space during compilation. This can be initialized as read-only data (program data) or initialized read-write data or uninitialized data (**Fig 2.2**).

ii. Dynamic data: This data is not allocated during compilation, rather can only be allocated during program execution or in the run-time. It can grow or shrink during execution depending on the requirement of the process. It has two important sub-sections.

a. Heap: During program execution the process dynamically allocates memory (as done by `malloc()` in **Fig. 2.2**) based on requirement and deallocates when the need is over. Often actual data size of such need is not known during code development or programming and is left to run-time. Such data is allocated from the heap space. The space is allocated from the free space of the main memory by the OS after getting a syscall from the process. Thus, the heap can grow in size, requesting free space from the OS. This causes an increase in the process address space also. It again shrinks in size when the space is freed by the process via a syscall and reclaimed by the OS.

b. Stack: This space is used by the arguments, local variables, return values of a function or a method within a source program. For each function call, stack stores the above variables and data structures for it. When several functions are called in succession, space for each called but not yet terminated functions are maintained here. The stack space thus grows with function calls and is removed as the function terminates.

For the given example C-source code (**Fig 2.2**), when compiled using GNU C compiler (`gcc`) and a program is created as `a.out`. Some portions of different sections discussed, and its process address space is mentioned below (using shell command `size -A a.out`).

```
a.out  :
section          size    addr
...
.text             437    4192
...
.rodata             8    8192
...
.data              20   16384
...
Total            2265
```

2.2 PROCESS RELATIONSHIP

Processes are related among themselves as we find human relationships in a family. All processes in an OS are created by some other process, except the first process (`init` or `systemd` process which is created during bootstrapping). `init` process is rather considered as the original creator (or parent) of all processes. All user processes are children of `init` or `systemd`, either directly or indirectly as its sub-children (See **Fig. 2.3**).

Each process has a number of links. It has a link to its parent process, its own children and sibling processes. When a process does not have a parent or a child or a sibling that particular link points to a NULL value (recall definition of a structure with pointers in C). Children of a process are the ones created by the process in question (`init(9)` is a child of `init(1)` in **Fig 2.3**). Sibling processes are all those processes having the same parent (`init(9)` and `init(116)` are siblings). In the left-hand side of **Fig 2.3**, sibling links are not shown for the sake of simplicity (only children links are provided). However, the right side shows them where processes p2, p3 and p4 are children of p1 and thus are siblings to each other.

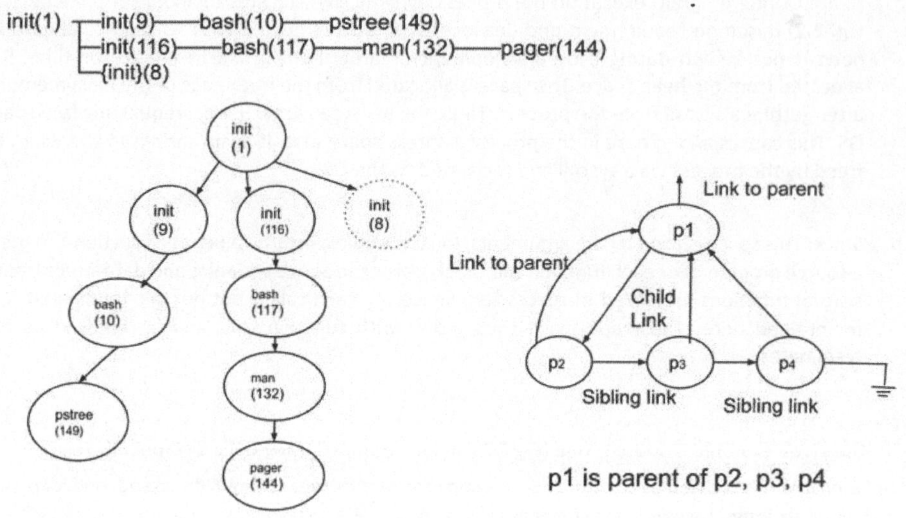

Fig 2.3: Process tree with *pids* (Linux command: `pstree -p`)

2.2.1 Child processes

A process can create another process using a system call (recall **Fig 1.17**). In the example below (**Fig 2.4**), a child process is created through `fork()` syscall. (Try yourself in any UNIX based system). A `fork ()` creates a new process (child) as a duplicate of the calling process (parent). On success, it returns two different integer values to two different processes: the parent gets the child's process-id, while the child gets a value zero (0). On failure, no child process is created and the calling process gets a negative return value (usually -1). This is an interesting example where the same code is being shared by two processes but their process address spaces are different. Local variables (e.g., `pr_id` here), and different other software contexts are also replicated. Both the processes start execution immediately after the `fork()` call, but from two different process contexts. `getpid()` and `getppid()` return process id and parent's process-id to the calling process respectively. These three functions (`fork()`, `getpid()` and `getppid()`) are declared in the C header file `<unistd.h>`. The child process created can be used to load another program file in its process address space by invoking `exec()` and its several variations. There is no guaranteed order whether the child will execute first or the parent. However, the parent can make a system call `wait()` to ensure that the parent waits till the child completes its execution. Otherwise, the parent may complete its execution and exit first and the child process then becomes an **orphan** process. When a process terminates, but its parent has not yet invoked `wait()` call, the process is said to be in **zombie** state. Every process becomes a zombie process before its process id and entry in the process table are taken away. Try on your own to learn more about `fork`([4]), `wait()` and `exec()`[5] and their interaction.

---

[4] https://www.csl.mtu.edu/cs4411.ck/www/NOTES/process/fork/create.html (as on 21-Jul-2022)

[5] https://ece.uwaterloo.ca/~dwharder/icsrts/Tutorials/fork_exec/ (as on 21-Jul-2022)

```
#include<stdio.h>
#include<unistd.h>

int main(){
int pr_id;
if ((pr_id = fork()) == 0)
     printf("\nfrom child with pid=%d, ppid=%d and fork-return
value=%d\n", getpid(), getppid(), pr_id);

else if (pr_id >0)
     printf("\nfrom parent with pid=%d, ppid=%d and fork-return
value=%d\n", getpid(), getppid(),pr_id);

else
     printf("\nerror in in fork pid=%d, ppid=%d and fork-return
value=%d\n", getpid(),getppid(), pr_id);
}
```

The results obtained

```
from parent with pid=264, ppid=10 and fork-return value=265
from child with pid=265, ppid=264 and fork-return value=0
```

Fig 2.4: Example of process creation and parent-child relation

2.3 PROCESS STATES and their TRANSITIONS

The state of any object defines and/or represents its circumstance, situation or form. Any dynamic object changes its state from one to another. A process is very much a dynamic object that goes through various states as described below (see **Fig 2.5**).

New: This is the first state of a process. When a process is created or a program is invoked the OS creates a new execution context (recall Sec **1.4.2.3**), allocates a process address space in the main memory and other necessary per-process resources in the kernel mode.

Ready: Once the per-process resources are created, the process becomes ready for execution. It needs a processor (actually, a core of a processor, to be specific) to be allocated.

Running: As soon as a processor is allocated, the process starts executing the instructions from the program text. Here, the program can run in user mode, However, for privileged instructions, it can go to kernel mode also.

Waiting: When the process needs an I/O to be done or explicitly waits (via a system call like `wait()`), the process is taken off the processor and is considered to be waiting. When the I/O is complete or the explicit wait is over, the process becomes ready and joins the ready queue. It can run only when it is allocated to the processor.

Terminated: When the process completes normally (even abnormally also), process address space is reclaimed by the OS. All process-related resources are also de-allocated. This state is called a terminated state. A process cannot be made to run from this state. As mentioned above, the state when the process completes execution, but its resources are not yet deallocated, is known as a zombie state.

Nomenclatures of these states vary from one OS to another. However, other than the running state, all other states happen in kernel mode only. From kernel to user mode or vice versa can happen in the running state of a process.

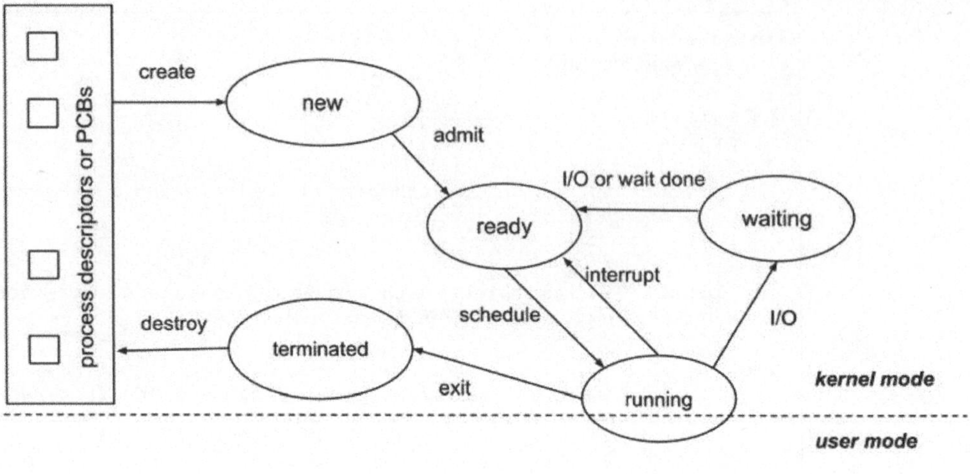

Fig 2.5: Process states and their transitions (life-cycle of a process)

2.4 PROCESS CONTEXT

After a process is created, it changes its states from one to another as it proceeds in its life cycle (very much like infancy, childhood, adolescence, youth, middle-age, old-age of a person). Along with the states, there are several other parameters of a live process that the OS kernel has to keep track of. For example, which instruction a process is currently running and thus where the CPU will find the next instruction from (remember program counter or PC), how many special purpose registers (SPRs) like stack pointer (SP), program status word (PSW), condition codes (CC) it is using and what are their values, how many general purpose registers (GPRs) the current process holds, what are their values, what are values of base register and limit register with respect to the process, how many I/O devices it is currently allotted, etc. This information is particularly important when a process moves from running to waiting or running to ready state, because we have to resume the process exactly from the same condition where it was suspended (before the state transition). As if we need to take a snapshot of the running condition of the process with values of all the controlling variables and accounting parameters and preserve the snapshot. All such control information related to a process collectively defines an execution context of the process and is called the *process context* (recall the definition of execution context in **Sec 1.4.2.3**). In a multiprogramming environment where resources are shared among several processes, maintaining and keeping track of process contexts is absolutely critical for correct and smooth running of the system.

2.5 PROCESS CONTROL BLOCK (PCB)

The OS kernel maintains a special data-structure called process control block (PCB) or process descriptor in its kernel space for each live process. This is a per-process data structure that stores the context of a process. A user process may not need it for its running, but the kernel maintains it for managing and monitoring the process and providing protection to other processes.

The PCB has a number of attributes, some of which are the following (**Fig 2.6**).

- **Process id:** Every process has a unique identifier.
- **User id:** The owner of the process.
- **Process state:** Process state is kept track of that can be new, ready, running, waiting, terminated etc.

- **Scheduling information:** For CPU allocation to a process, process priority, pointers to scheduling queues, and other scheduling parameters need to be maintained.
- **Memory-management information:** Information like value of the base and limit registers and the page tables, or segment tables.
- **Accounting information:** Information like amount of CPU time used, wait time, time limits etc.
- **Software context:** This can be a list of *open files, open sockets* (ip-address + port-address, used for communicating with remote processes) and *memory regions*.
- **Hardware context:** There are a number of hardware information that need to be kept track of like
  - *Program counter* - stores the address of the next instruction to be executed
  - *Stack pointer* - points to the top of the procedure that is being executed
  - *Other CPU registers* - values held by accumulators, PSW, CC and other GPRs
  - *I/O devices* - list of I/O devices held by the process
- **Pointers to different data structures:** There are other data structures that are needed by the kernel for managing a process - pointers to all of such data structures are kept in the PCB which are dynamically added and deleted.

2.5.1 Process Table

In a multiprogramming OS, multiple processes concurrently run. The kernel thus has to maintain more than one PCB. Often the PCBs are stored as a list in a table. This is a kernel data structure called a Process Table (**Fig 2.6**).

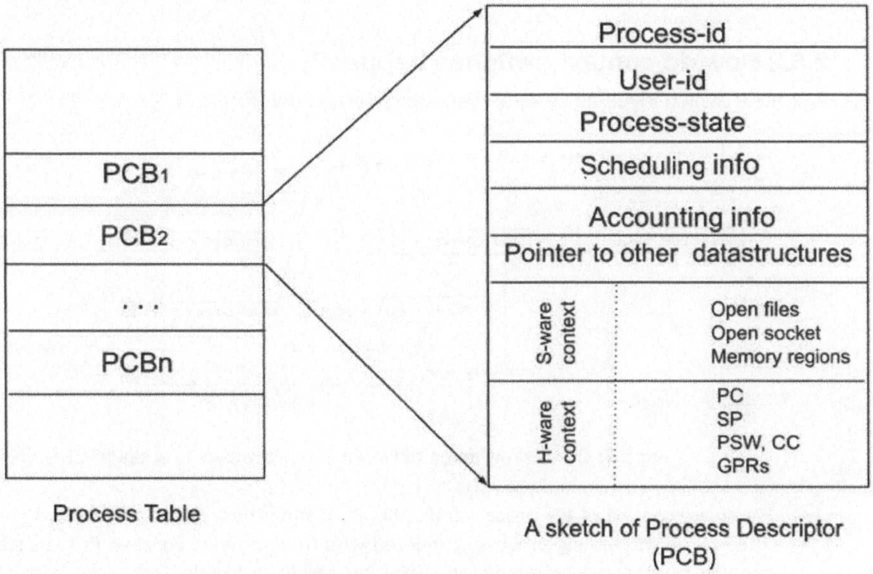

Fig. 2.6: Process Table and PCB

2.6 CONTEXT SWITCH

When the CPU is changed from one process to another, the context of the first process is saved and that of the second process is loaded into appropriate registers and other data structures. We call this *context switching* or *process switching*. Mind that process switching happens from one process to another in relation to a CPU allotment and is managed by the OS. But, mode switching (user mode to kernel mode or vice versa) is essentially a processor mode activity - that happens within the context of a running process. Context switch is a kernel activity and seen only in a multiprogramming environment. It is done to improve the performance of the OS (to increase throughput, reduce average execution time for a set of processes etc).

2.6.1 Who causes the context switch and when?

Recall from the last chapter that running of an user process is disturbed only under three events: interrupts, system call and trap.

1. **Interrupts:** An interrupt is an asynchronous activity. That can come from
    i. *the timer* when time slice allocated for the running process is over and another process scheduled to run next needs to get the CPU.
    ii. *I/O devices* when some tasks assigned by some process to an I/O device is complete and the processor is notified. The process is to be scheduled for the CPU (either immediately or later) as decided by the OS. If the notification comes from a device and the interrupt was not blocked, there will be a process switch (currently running process will be halted and a kernel process will start) to handle the interrupt.
2. **System calls:** It happens when the running process itself requires to execute a privileged instruction. Most system calls are for accessing hardware, like memory units or I/O devices. However, note that interrupts are caused by I/O devices to the processor, but system calls go from a running process to devices through the OS kernel. Context of the running process is saved, and a suitable kernel process is executed to meet the requirement.

3. Trap / exception: When a running process encounters some errors, attempts illegal operation or to access restricted resources, traps are flagged and handled in kernel mode by kernel processes.

2.6.2 How do context switches happen?

A context switch involves several steps as given below (**Fig 2.7**).

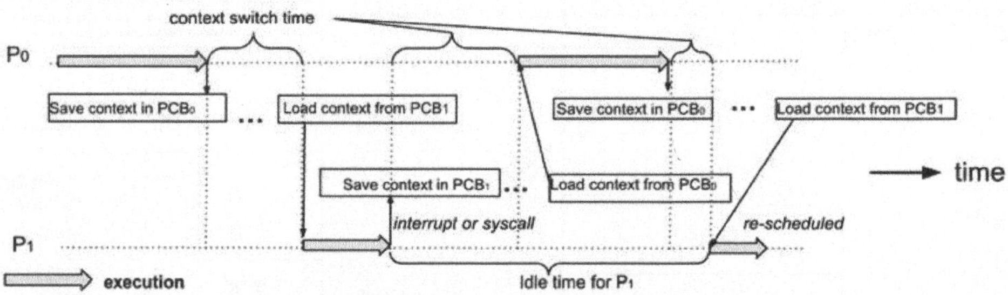

Fig 2.7: Context switches between two processes in a single CPU core

- Hardware context of the processor (PC, SP, PSW and other registers) are saved.
- The PCB of the running process is updated with the hardware context. Process state is changed from running to other appropriate states (waiting, ready or terminated) along with other relevant fields including accounting information.
- The PCB is put to the appropriate queue (ready queue, blocked on some event queue, I/O queue etc).
- Another PCB is selected based on the priority and position of the process in the scheduler queue.
- The selected PCB is updated with process state (from earlier state to running state).
- Memory management data-structures are updated (e.g., base register, limit register of the processor)
- All the hardware context of the processor is restored from the selected PCB.

A context switch thus takes some amount of time to complete these tasks. In comparison, processor mode switching (user to kernel or vice-versa) is less time-consuming.

2.7 THREADS

Processes have been discussed so far as units of program execution and resource allocation & utilization. Traditional OSs allocate computing resources at process level and monitor execution of each process as if it has a single flow of execution. The flow is suspended when it goes for some system call or I/O operation.

However, in many tasks, there are many independent subtasks that can be done in parallel. For example, in real life, you can solve some numerical problems as well as listen to music simultaneously. Any busy lawyer handles several cases simultaneously - since a single case does not get dates of hearing continuously, but after days of interval. After one hearing, while a case waits for the next hearing, the lawyer can handle other cases.

In the world of computing, the task of matrix multiplication can be divided into several independent subtasks. If A_{mxn} and B_{nxp} are two matrices that are multiplied to generate another matrix C_{mxp},

such that $C[i,j] = \sum_{k=1}^{n} A[i,k] * B[k,j]$ *for* $i = 1, \ldots, m$ and $j = 1, \ldots, p$.

Here, each of *(mxp)* entries of matrix *C* can be computed independently and finally compiled together to generate matrix *C*.

Recent advances in processor architecture provide multiple CPU units within a single processor and even multiple cores within a single CPU. Hence, if a task can be intelligently divided into several independent subtasks, they can be allocated to different cores of a CPU and the entire task can be efficiently accomplished in a short period of time.

These facts have been instrumental in bringing the concept of threads.

2.7.1 Definition

A thread is a single flow of execution and considered a basic unit of CPU utilization. A process can have one or more threads. A traditional process is considered to have a single thread of control, but most modern OSs support processes to have more than one thread.

Each thread can run independently. If there are multiple CPUs or multicores within a CPU, threads of a single process can execute in parallel simultaneously. Each thread has a thread ID, and holds a program counter (PC), a register set, and a stack on its own. However, code section, data section, and other operating-system resources, such as open files and signals are shared by all threads within a process (**Fig 2.8**).

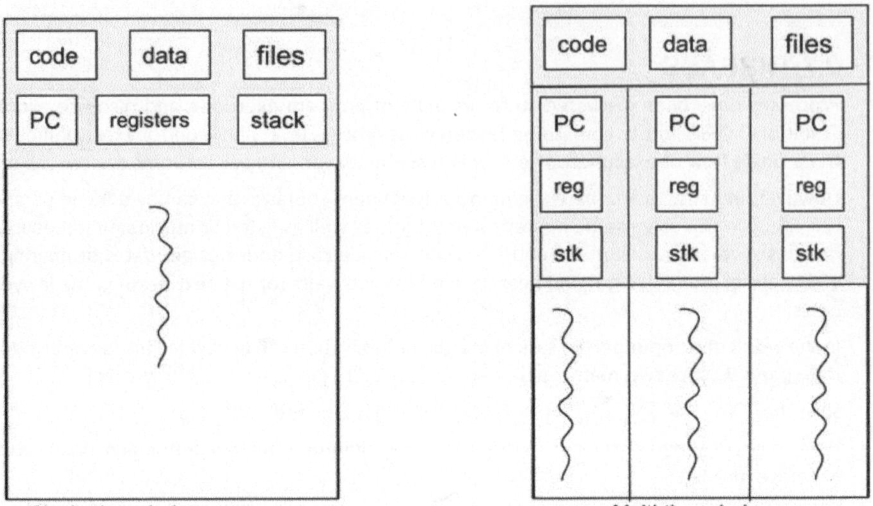

Fig. 2.8: Relation between a process and threads

There are several applications of threads as follows.

1. A thread in a word processor can listen to keystrokes while another thread can do the spell checking.
2. A server can simultaneously attend several clients by creating threads for each individual client. Here, all are similar threads executing the same code but with different parameter values.

2.7.2 Thread States

Like processes, threads also have states that change during their life cycle, however within the context of a process. Once a thread is created, it can go to the following principal *states* as follows:

- **Ready:** the thread is prepared to go for execution, but not yet scheduled a CPU core
- **Running:** after a CPU core is allocated, the thread executes instructions from code
- **Blocked:** If the thread waits for some event to complete.

Related to states, there are the following four *operations* on threads that change the states.

- *Spawn:* When a process is created, a thread is also created at the same time. Such thread creates or spawns other threads as and when necessary. A new thread is given an instruction pointer to start from (PC value), register context and stack space (kernel and user stack) and put on the ready queue of a CPU core.
- *Block: A thread often needs to wait for some event to complete. The thread then blocks (saves execution context including PC, SP values and other register values in the thread descriptor) so that another ready thread (either from the same process or another process) can execute.*
- *Unblock:* When the event for which the thread was waiting completes, the thread is put on Ready state.
- *Finish:* When a thread completes, its registers and stack space are deallocated.

Threads are managed using *thread descriptors* and *thread switching* is done with appropriate updates in the thread descriptors.

2.7.3 Pros and Cons of Threads

Threads are beneficial for many reasons. Some of them are listed below.

- **Improved performance:** Multithreading enables division of a task into several independent subtasks, each of which can be performed by a thread. This reduces the blocking time of processes increasing overall CPU utilization and user responsiveness. This is particularly useful in interactive applications where the user does not have to wait for completion of one action before invoking another, especially when such action is time-consuming.
- **Resource sharing:** Threads belonging to a process share the memory and the resources by default. This increases the overall resource utilization by a set of processes of a system.
- **Low cost:** Allocating memory and resources to processes are costly in terms of both space and time. Thread creation takes almost 10 times less time than a process creation. A thread switch is also less expensive than a process switch in terms of space and time.
- **Scalability:** Several threads of a process can run in parallel on different CPU cores, whereas a single-threaded process can run on only one processor, no matter how many cores are available. Threading thus unleashes the advantage of exploiting the full potential of modern multi-core multi-processor architecture.

However, there are a few disadvantages as well.

- **Increased stack space:** Since each thread needs a stack that comes from the stack space of the corresponding process, usually restriction is set on per-thread stack size. Thread stack size cannot always grow on demand - often a bottleneck for application development.
- **Increased complexity:** Multi-threaded applications exhibit non-deterministic behaviour as ordering of threads is difficult to implement. Designing and developing concurrent multi-threaded applications, debugging and correcting them are very complex and demanding exercises.

Overall, advantages often outweigh disadvantages and use of multi-threading is on the rise across applications.

2.7.4 Types of Threads

There are two categories of threads: user level threads (ULTs) and kernel level threads (KLTs). KLTs are also called Lightweight processes (LWPs).

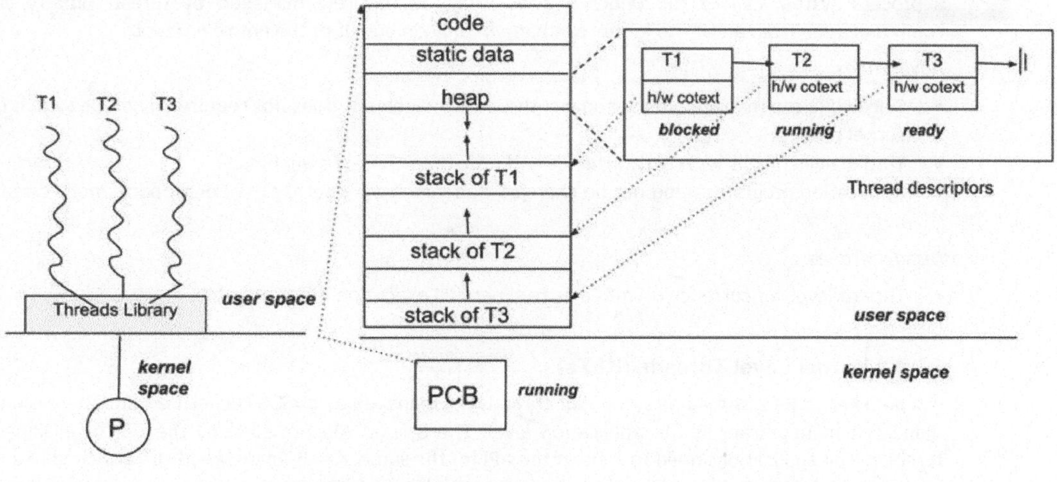

Fig 2.9: User Level Threads

2.7.4.1 User Level Threads (ULTs)

User level threads exist in the user space. The kernel may not be aware of the ULTs. When the OS does not inherently support multi-threading, ULTs are managed by the threads library in the user space only and the OS kernel remains completely unaware of ULTs. This arrangement is called pure user level threading (or pure ULT) (**Fig 2.9**).

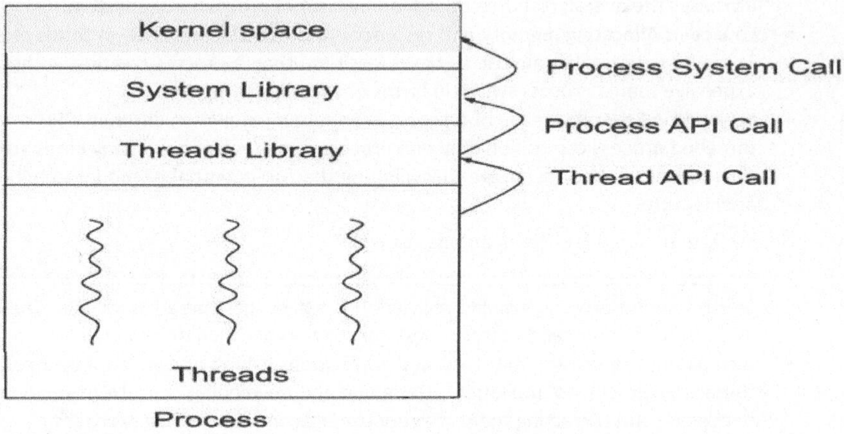

Fig 2.10: ULT interaction with kernel

Threads are created, managed and destroyed in the user space by the threads library. User heap space maintains the thread descriptors and user stack space is divided into thread stack spaces. In a pure ULT system, the kernel allocates only a single CPU core to the process and thread concurrency is achieved at the user level via threads library. Only a single ULT can run at a time while other threads need to wait in blocking or ready state. True parallel execution is therefore not possible in a pure ULT system. To interact with the kernel, an ULT first makes a thread API call provided by threads library (**Fig 2.10**). But the OS can see only processes. So it is modified to a process API call as provided by the system library which again converts it to a process system call of the underlying OS. ULTs are entirely managed by threads library and any communication from an ULT to kernel can happen only on behalf of the entire process.

Advantages:

- Since ULTs are managed in user space, thread management does not require any mode switch (user to kernel mode).
- Thread switching is less costly in space and time than context switching.
- Application programs need not be changed depending on whether the OS supports multi-threading or not.

Disadvantages:

- Thread-level concurrency is limited as true parallel execution is not possible.

2.7.4.2 Kernel Level Threads (KLTs)

In a pure kernel level threading system, all threads are managed by the OS kernel itself and there is no thread management necessary at the application level. There is an API provided by the OS for availing thread facilities. The applications need to contact the API for the same. An ULT can directly be attached to a KLT and can run independently. Thread descriptors are managed in the kernel space either as part of the PCB or linked to the PCB. Multiple threads of a process can simultaneously run as individual threads are separately scheduled to different CPU cores. True execution parallelism is achievable in a pure KLT system, if there are multiple CPU cores available (**Fig 2.11**).

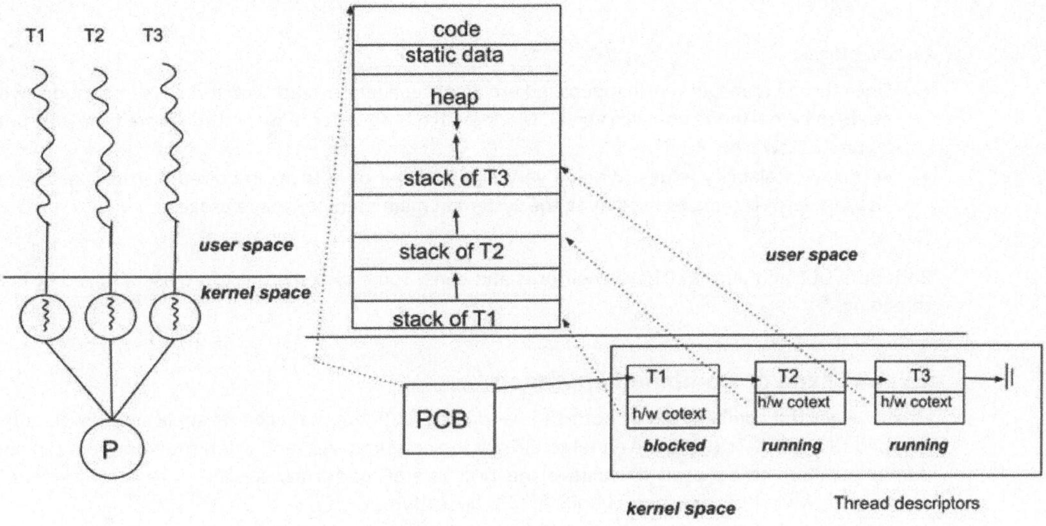

Fig 2.11: Kernel Level Threads

User threads can directly interact with the kernel space with necessary mode switch (user to kernel mode). An ULT through a KLT can make a system call independent of other threads from the same process (**Fig 2.12**). There can be thus two or more system calls from a single process at the same time.

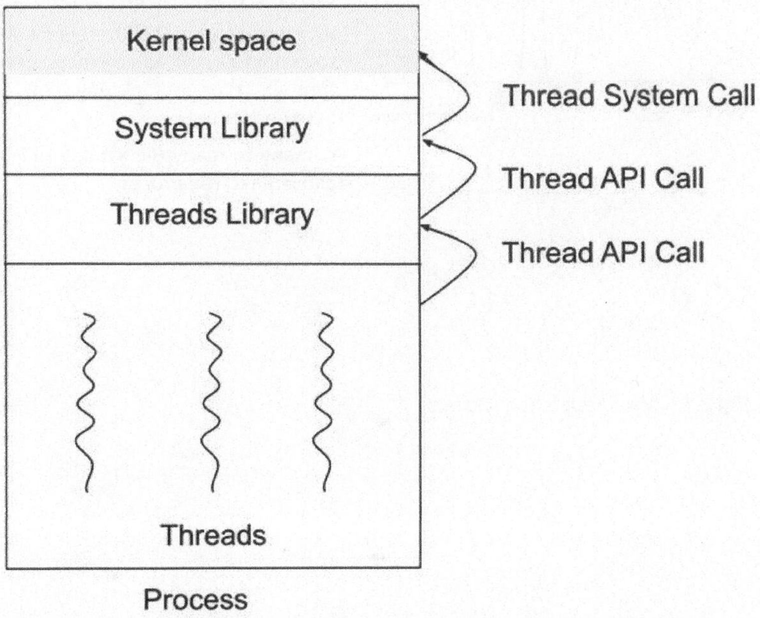

Fig 2.12: User application interaction with kernel in KLT

Advantages:

- KLTs help to achieve true parallelism and provide substantial speed up in execution.

Disadvantages:

- Since thread management happens in kernel space, every thread switch results in a mode switch (user mode to kernel mode and vice versa). Mode switch is an order of magnitude more time-consuming than a pure ULT switch.
- KLTs have scalability issues. When a very high number of KLTs are required, kernel space requirement also increases leading to burdening the system in main memory space usage.

Both pure ULT and pure KLT have their pros and cons. Some systems therefore use a mixed or hybrid kind threading.

2.7.4.3 Mixed or Combined approach

Here, we get the combination of both ULTs and KLTs. ULTs are managed at application level, and they are mapped to a few KLTs (ULTs are equal to KLTs or less in number). Application programmers can control the number of KLTs to be used to achieve the best overall performance. ULTs are seen as units of work assignment, while KLTs are seen as units of CPU allocation.

Solaris uses this mixed system. There ULTs do not directly get attached to KLTs but through an intermediary called lightweight processes (LWPs). A process is allocated at least one LWP. ULTs can be hooked to a LWP and each LWP can attach one available KLT.

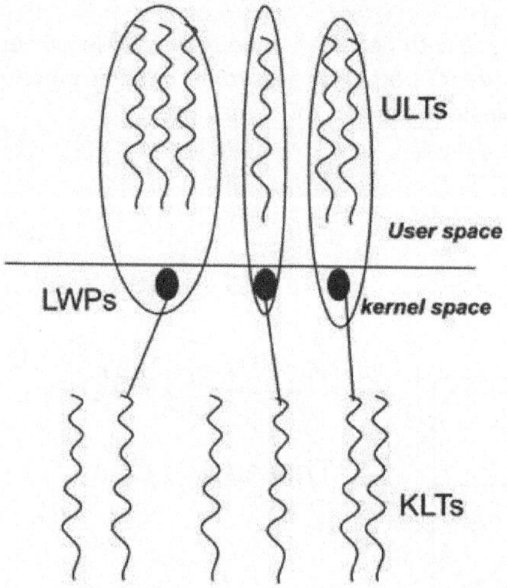

Fig 2.13: Mixed approach (Solaris)

A process can own one or more LWPs. There are different types of mapping possible between ULTs and LWPs as given below.

a. one-to-one (1:1): one ULT can be hooked to only one LWP. It is restrictive and thus not very efficient.

b. many-to-one (M:1): several ULTs can be hooked together to a LWP and can access the kernel concurrently through time-multiplexing. An ULT cannot switch between LWPs.

c. many-to-many (M:N): any ULT can hook to any LWP allocated to the process.

2.7.5 Concept of Multithreading

As evident from the previous discussion, user level threading can yield better performance when the OS also supports multi-threading. Most modern OSs like Windows, UNIX and MacOS support kernel level threading. But how are ULTs attached to KLTs? There are three popular variants, known as multithreading models.

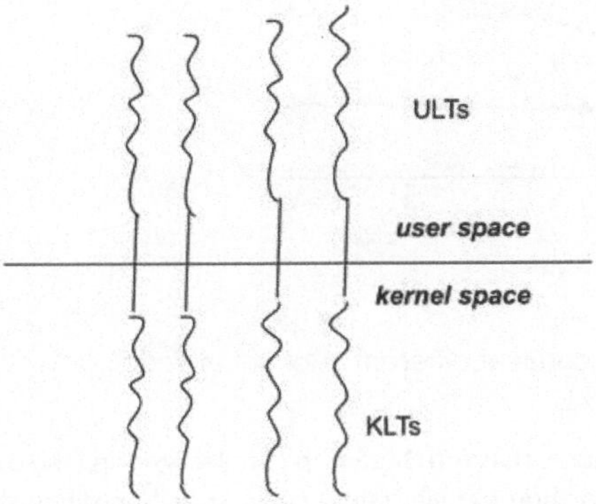

Fig 2.14: One-to-one model

One-to-one model: For every ULT, there is exactly one KLT assigned. Compared to the many-to-one model, better concurrency is achieved. However, creation of every ULT causes that of a KLT increasing the burden on kernel space. Linux and Windows use the model (**Fig 2.14**).

Many-to-one model: More than one ULT map to one KLT. Thread management is done at user level by threads library. If a thread makes a blocking system call, all other threads from the same process need to wait. Hence concurrency cannot be fully exploited. Green threads - a thread library in the older Solaris system implemented this model. However, recent OSs do not use this because of the issue mentioned (**Fig 2.15**).

Many-to-many model: Here, many ULTs map to a smaller or equal number of KLTs. How many KLTs will be assigned to a process varies depending on the application or the architecture. A multi-core processor can allocate a higher number of KLTs (**Fig 2.16**).

Although theoretically a higher number of cores can run multiple threads in parallel leading to increase in performance, the speed-up is not linear. This follows **Amdahl's Law** that justifies the diminishing return.

$$speed\text{-}up = \frac{\text{time to execute using a single thread}}{\text{time to execute using multiple threads}} = \frac{1}{s + (1-s)/N}$$

where *s* is the fraction of serial code that cannot be parallelized, and *N* is the number of threads.

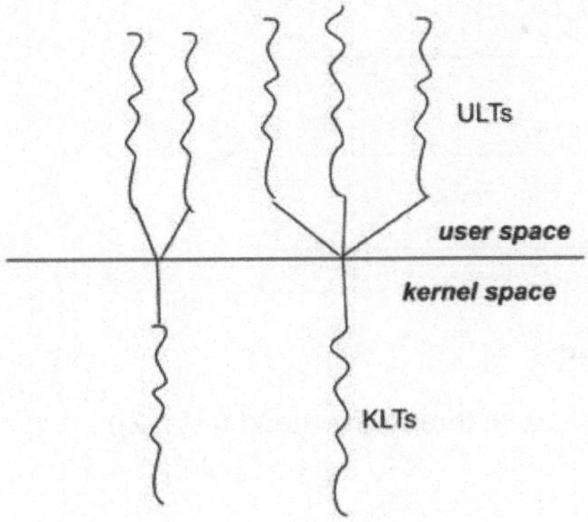

Fig 2.15: Many-to-one model

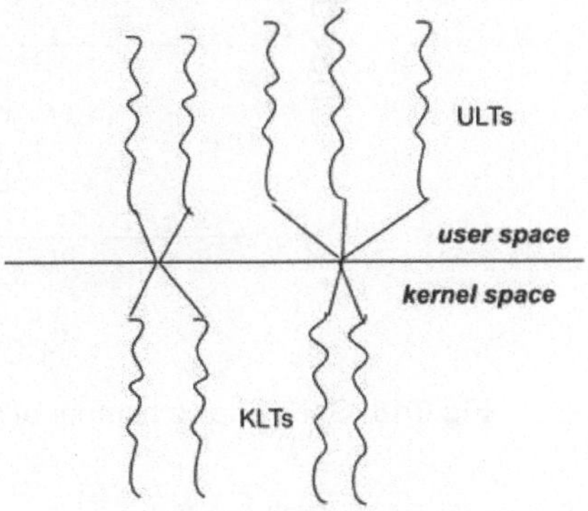

Fig 2.16: Many-to-many model

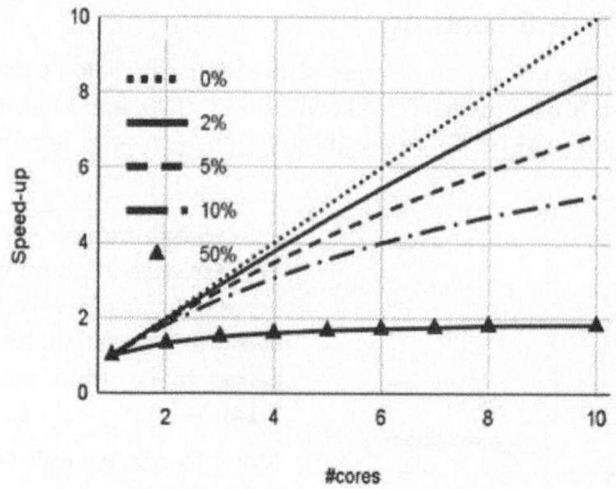

Fig 2.17: Speed-up vs number of cores at different % of serial code

Fig 2.17 shows the variation in speed up vs number of cores that run threads in parallel, ignoring the overhead of creating threads. With a higher fraction of serial (or non-parallelizable) code, speed-up diminishes. For example, with 50% of serial code, maximum speed-up can be 2, attainable only when a huge number of CPU cores are employed. When the overhead of creating threads and thread-switches is considered, speed-up is even worse. In fact, speed-up falls after reaching a highest point due to increase in cost of thread management (**Fig 2.18**).

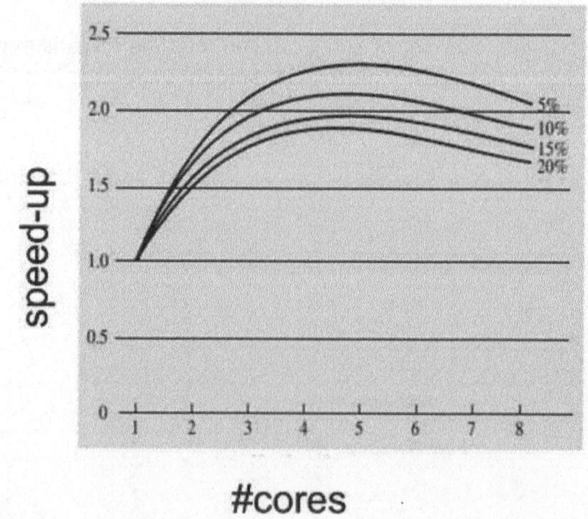

Fig 2.18: Speed-up vs number of cores with thread overhead ([Sta12])

2.7.5.1 Example of Multithreading

Following C code (**Fig 2.19**) is an example of using POSIX threads available as `pthread` library.

`pthread_create()` is a function that creates a thread. The function takes 4 arguments and returns an integer (0 when successful, an error number otherwise) . The function creates a thread with a thread-id (the first argument of type `long int`) and invokes a function (the third argument) to execute with the thread. The fourth argument of `pthread_create()` is the sole parameter to the thread-function. The second argument is for specifying the thread attributes which take the default values if mentioned as NULL.

`pthread_join()` is used to make the calling thread (the `main()` function here) to wait till the thread in the argument completes. If this function is not called, the main program (main thread) can terminate before the thread-function is complete. This is possible because all threads are independently scheduled for CPU time. They can even run in parallel on different CPU cores. In that case, the main thread terminates, before the thread-task completes - a situation that defeats the main purpose of multi-threading.

You can comment-out one or more `pthread_join()` and see the effect.

Also, if you run the program several times you can observe that the threads can execute in any order, not necessarily in the order of their creation. You can see the header file `<pthread.h>` or do `man pthread_create` or `man pthread_join` in any UNIX-based system to learn more about the functions.

```
#include <stdio.h>
#include <stdlib.h>
#include <pthread.h>

void *print_function( void *ptr ){
    char *message;
    message = (char *) ptr;
    printf("%s \n", message);
}

main()
{
    pthread_t thread1, thread2, thread3;
    char *message1 = "From Thread 1";
    char *message2 = "From Thread 2";
    char *message3 = "From Thread 3";

    int  ret1, ret2, ret3;

   /* Create independent threads each of which will execute function */

    ret1 = pthread_create( &thread1, NULL, print_function, (void*) message1);
    ret2 = pthread_create( &thread2, NULL, print_function, (void*) message2);
    ret3 = pthread_create( &thread3, NULL, print_function, (void*) message3);

    pthread_join( thread1, NULL);    /* Wait till threads are complete */
    pthread_join( thread2, NULL);   /*otherwise process can terminate */
    pthread_join( thread3, NULL);   /* before threads are complete */

    printf("Thread 1 returns: %d\n",ret1);
    printf("Thread 2 returns: %d\n",ret2);
    printf("Thread 3 returns: %d\n",ret3);

    exit(0);
}
```

Compile it with `gcc -pthread <file_name.c>` and run as `./a.out`.

Fig 2.19: An example of multithreading using POSIX threads library

2.8 PROCESS SCHEDULING

CPU is the most important resource of any computing system as it is the only resource that executes instructions. Every process needs a CPU core non-sharably to execute its code (like every train needs a track). During its life-time, a process uses CPU for execution and other resources (persistent memory and I/O devices) for other activities like read, write, display, print and so on. When the process uses other resources and does not require CPU, the CPU remains idle (recall from **Fig 2.7**). In a single process system, this is not a problem as the process can monopolize the CPU. But in a multiprogramming system where several processes are waiting to access a CPU core, keeping the CPU idle is a waste of time. To maximize the performance of a system, the CPU utilization should be maximum. In other words, whenever a CPU is free, we should allow other processes to use it. But at a single point in time, only one process can use the CPU. In a single-core CPU, all the processes that require CPU should be allocated some CPU time one after another. Even in multi-core CPU or multiprocessor systems, the number of processes are much higher than the number of cores. Hence, not all processes get the CPU core as and when required. So *which process* should get a CPU core, *when* and *for how long* - are very important questions. Remember from Unit 1 (**Sec 1.1**) that resource allocation is an important responsibility of any OS and CPU is the most important resource. *Process scheduling or CPU scheduling is the task of an OS dealing with the allocation of a CPU or a CPU core to a set of processes.*

CPU Scheduling is a kernel activity that involves context switch and change of states in the processes (from ready to running and running to ready or running to wait/blocked states). CPU scheduling is managed by an OS program - known as CPU scheduler. The scheduler runs in quick intervals, checks the queue of ready processes and allocates a CPU core to one process when the core is free.

2.8.1 Scheduling objectives

Many processes concurrently run in a computer and require a number of resources. Simultaneous demands for a resource by many processes lead to contention and thus requires a policy of allocation of the resource. For all the computing resources in a multiprogram environment, the OS has the responsibility of implementing allocation policies. OS allocates CPU time to all needy processes in an orderly manner implementing some rules or algorithms. These rules are called CPU scheduling algorithms.

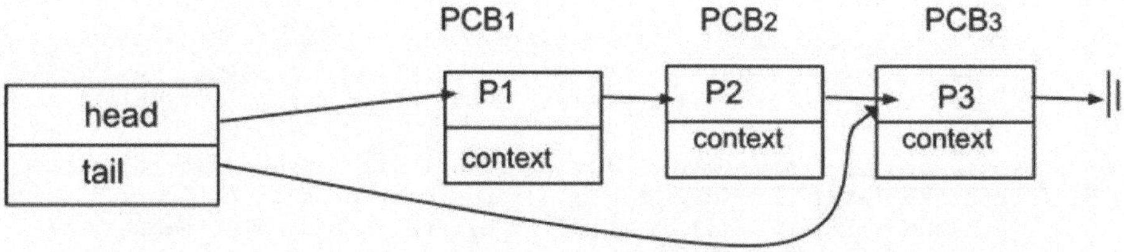

Fig 2.20: A queue of processes waiting for accessing a resource

These algorithms ensure:

- orderly allocation of CPU to all needy processes maintaining a queue of such processes (**Fig 2.20**).
- increased overall performance of the system in terms of *throughput* (unit of tasks completed in unit time), *degree of multiprogramming* (how many programs are active and reside in main memory).

2.8.2 Types of Schedulers

CPU schedulers work in two levels of abstraction (**Fig 2.21**) as given below.

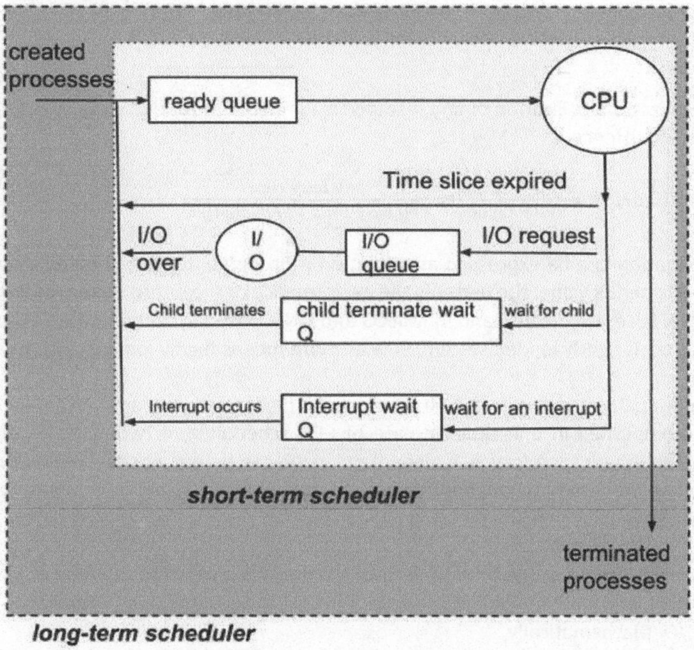

Fig 2.21: Schedulers and different queues

Long-term scheduler: At the coarse level, the scheduler decides how many processes and exactly which processes will be brought in the ready queue of a CPU. The decision may be based on how many processes can be accommodated in the main memory and/or other OS design-related restrictions. This scheduler thus determines the degree of multiprogramming. Often this scheduler takes a process away (*swap out*) from the main memory and puts it in the hard drive and again brings it in (*swap in*) when space is available. Hence, a long-term scheduler is also called a *swapper*. In some books, swapper is also considered as a *medium-term scheduler*.

Short-term scheduler: Once processes are brought into the CPU ready queue, which process out of them will be assigned the CPU next, what will be the selection criteria for CPU allocation, when it will be assigned and for how long - these fine level decisions are taken by a short-time scheduler. This is also called **dispatcher.**

The job of CPU scheduler or dispatcher is to

a) ensure context switch from one process to another,
b) switch to user mode (from kernel mode),
c) pointing to the appropriate location in the user program to start / resume the process.

2.8.3 Scheduling Criteria

The aim of a CPU scheduler is to achieve "goodness" with respect to some measurable criteria. Different systems have different criteria, some are user-oriented and some system-oriented. Goodness according to each criterion is measured in terms of a performance metric. Some performance metrics are defined below.

- **CPU Utilization:** Utilization of any resource is defined as a ratio of its busy time and total time including its idle time. Hence,

  $$CPU\ Utilization = \frac{\text{CPU busy time}}{\text{CPU total time}} = \frac{CPU\ busy\ time}{CPU\ busy\ time + CPU\ idle\ time}$$

  The utilization can be expressed as a fraction or in percentage. It should lie between 0 to 1 (or 0% to 100%). Higher its value, the better is the performance of the entire system as it means the CPU has lower idle time. (Use `top` command in MacOS and UNIX based systems to see CPU utilization. Its value 40% or less means lightly loaded system, 90% or more means highly loaded system.)

- **Throughput:** Throughput is used to measure the performance of any system in terms of units of work or task accomplished in unit time. In case of CPU scheduling, it is defined as the number of processes completed in unit time (say in 1 second). Its value can be any positive real number per unit time. For a set of long processes, throughput can be a fractional value (say, 0.05 per sec), whereas for very short processes, we can have integers (say, 10 per sec).

- **Turnaround Time:** It is the total time since a process is created to the time of its completion. Hence, it is the sum of wait time in the ready queue, CPU execution time, wait time in the I/O queue and time for doing I/O. Mathematically,

  $$Turnaround\ (TA)\ time = total\ wait\ time\ in\ ready\ Q + total\ execution\ time\ in\ CPU + total\ wait\ time\ in\ I/O\ Q + time\ for\ doing\ I/O.$$

For any process, instruction execution in CPU and I/O activities are not contiguous. Both these activities rather happen in spells - few CPU bound instructions are followed by an I/O bound action and then again CPU bound instructions and so on.

These spells are also called *bursts.* A CPU burst (a continuous sequence of CPU-bound instructions) is followed by an I/O burst and vice versa. Any process can be considered as a sequence of several CPU bursts and I/O bursts having start and end mandatorily with CPU bursts.

- **Burst time** is defined as the time spent for executing the activity in the burst excluding the wait time in the queue. Hence, TA time can also be defined as the sum of all *CPU bursts* and *I/O bursts* and *wait-times* in different queues.

  $$TA\ time = \sum CPU\ bursts + \sum I/O\ bursts + \sum\ waiting\ times$$

TA time is any positive real number usually expressed in microseconds, milli-seconds or seconds.

- **Waiting Time:** A process has to wait for any resources if there is a high demand for the resource. Every resource is generally associated with a queue (**Fig 2.20**), where processes wait to access the resource. Waiting time is the time spent in the queue for the resource starting from joining the queue to using the resource. In CPU scheduling, waiting time means waiting in the CPU ready queue, unless otherwise mentioned.

- **Response Time:** In interactive processes, users are more interested in getting the responses from the system. Users may tolerate delay in completion of the entire task if it may take time and continue in the background. In those cases, turnaround time is not that important, but what matters is the time spent in getting the first response from the system. Hence, response time is defined as the time between submission of a request and getting the first response from the system (not completion of production of the response).

For a good scheduling algorithm, we expect high CPU utilization, high throughput, low TA time, low wait time and low response time. However, not all such criteria can be met in a single algorithm. There are different algorithms to prioritize different criteria. We shall learn a few algorithms here.

2.8.4 Scheduling Algorithms

CPU allocation or scheduling is to be done when there is at least one process in the ready queue and a CPU core is idle. For a single-process system, this is a trivial case and does not need any policy or algorithms. However, in a multiprogram environment (no matter whether a single core CPU or a multi-core one or multiple CPUs, number of processes are often way higher than the number of available cores), several processes contest to get a CPU core for executing instructions. We need a scheduling policy to determine which process will get the chance first and next, when and for how long. Scheduling algorithms implement one or more of such policies.

CPU scheduling is needed under the following circumstances (revisit **Fig 2.21**).

1. A newly created process joins the ready queue, and the process needs to be immediately executed.
2. the time slice allocated to a process is over and another process needs to get the CPU.
3. a process needs an I/O before it can proceed any further.
4. a process waits for its children to complete first before it proceeds further.
5. a process waits for some interrupt (other than timer) and the interrupt occurs.
6. a process completes its execution.

A little thought over the above cases will say that some of the cases (Circumstances 1, 2, 5) need eviction of the CPU from a currently executing process, unless it voluntarily releases it. In other cases (Circumstances 3, 4, 6), the CPU can be voluntarily released by the executing process. It is up to the designer of the OS to decide whether the OS will apply force to evict CPU from the running process or not. If scheduling algorithms allow forceful eviction (or *preemption*) of the CPU, they are called **preemptive algorithms.** When no preemption is allowed and the processes can only voluntarily release CPU, corresponding scheduling algorithms are called **non-preemptive algorithms.** Obviously, non-preemptive algorithms have the potential problem of monopolizing the CPU, particularly by long processes when other processes suffer from *indefinite block* or *starvation*. The starvation can lead to a catastrophe if the executing process goes into an infinite loop due to some programming errors. Preemptive algorithms do not suffer from this problem. But they cause frequent context switches and incur associated overhead. Also, a context switch can lead to a serious issue when the preemption occurs in the middle of a modification of a shared data. If the process modifying the shared data could not complete it before the context switch, and another process uses the data immediately after - the second process gets incorrect data. This problem, called *data inconsistency problem,* adds complexity and is discussed in *process synchronization*. Nevertheless, most modern OSs (Windows, Linux, UNIX, MacOS) use preemptive algorithms nowadays.

Let us focus on a few popular scheduling algorithms below.

2.8.4.1 First-Come-First-Served (FCFS) Algorithm

This is the simplest non-preemptive CPU scheduling algorithm. Every process is scheduled based on its arrival time (time of joining the ready queue of the CPU) and continues to run until it is complete or voluntarily leaves CPU for some I/O operation. When the CPU is free, the process that has the earliest arrival time is scheduled next. FCFS can be implemented using a FIFO ready queue. Even though it is simple, it is not a very efficient algorithm as far as performance is concerned. The long processes can hold the CPU for long causing starvation to late comers (See **Example 1**).

2.8.4.2 Shortest-Job-First (SJF) Algorithm

This algorithm looks at the CPU burst times of all the waiting processes in the ready queue and allocates the CPU to the one with the shortest CPU burst time. The shortest job will complete its execution quickly and reduce the wait time for the next candidate. In this strategy, all the processes will have the least possible wait time and hence least turnaround time as well. Let us look at the following example to understand the finer points of the algorithm. First, the non-preemptive version of SJF (**Example 2**).

Example 1: *Consider the following set of processes, with the arrival times and the CPU-burst times given in milliseconds. Find the average waiting time and average turnaround time in the FCFS algorithm.*

Process	Arrival Time (ms)	Burst Time (ms)
P1	0	5
P2	1	3
P3	2	3
P4	4	1

Soln. Following is the arrival time CPU burst times of different processes.

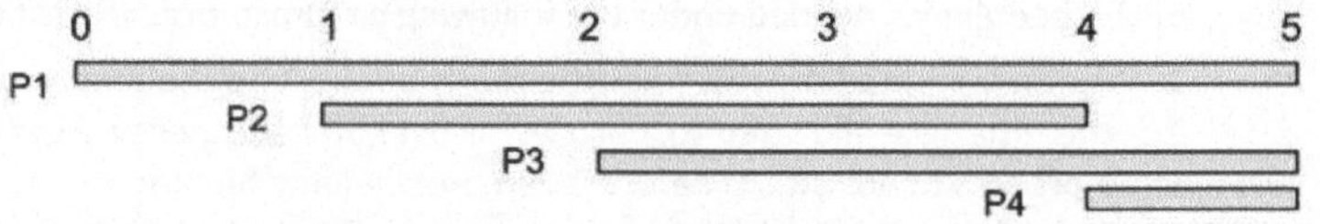

According to FCFS, P1 will execute undisturbed, followed by P2, then P3 and P4.

Hence CPU will be held by them as per following timing diagram (called *Gantt chart*).

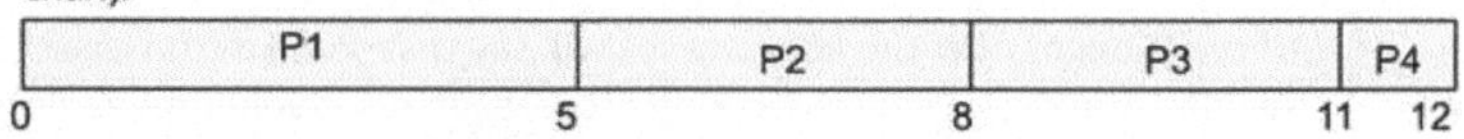

A process waits from arrival till it gets the CPU. Hence wait times are as follows:
for P1 = 0 ms
P2 = (5-1) = 4ms
P3 = (8-2) = 6ms
P4 = (11-4) = 7ms

Avg wait-time = (0+4+6+7)/4 = **4.25ms**

Turnaround time for each process is its time of completion minus its time of arrival.

Hence, TA times are as follows:
for P1 = (5-0) = 5ms
P2 = (8-1) = 7ms
P3 = (11-2) = 9ms
P4 = (12-4) = 8ms

Avg TA-time = (5+7+9+8)/4 = **7.25ms**

Example 2: *The following set of processes arrive at the same time, however in the following order with the given CPU-burst times in milliseconds. Find the average waiting time and average turnaround time in the SJF algorithm.*

Process	Arrival Time (ms)	Burst Time (ms)
P1	0	5
P2	0	3
P3	0	3
P4	0	1

Soln. Following is the arrival time CPU burst times of different processes.

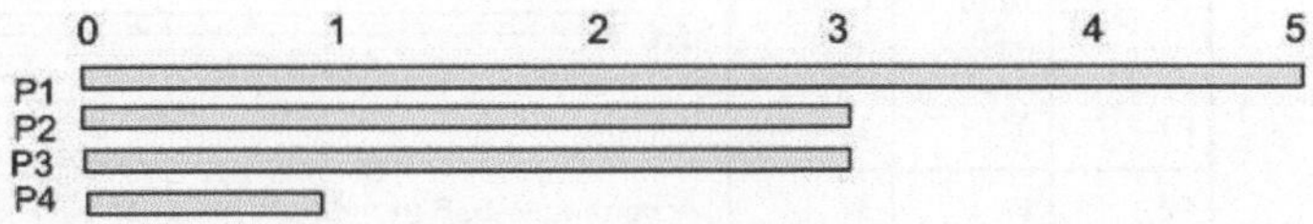

According to SJF, P4 will execute first, followed by P2, then P3 (since P2 & P3 have same CPU bursts, arrival order is given preference) and P1 at last.

Hence corresponding *Gantt chart* looks like the following.

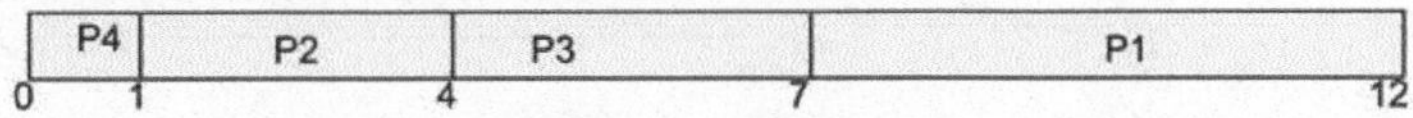

A process waits from arrival till it gets the CPU. Hence wait times are as follows:
for P1 = (7-0) = 7 ms
P2 = (1-0) = 1ms
P3 = (4-0) = 4ms
P4 = 0ms

Avg wait-time = (7+1+4+0)/4 = 3.0 ms

Turnaround time for each process is its time of completion since its time of arrival.

Hence, TA times are as follows:
for P1 = (12-0) = 12ms
P2 = (4-0) = 4ms
P3 = (7-0) = 7ms
P4 = (1-0) = 1ms

Avg TA-time = (12+4+7+1)/4 = 6.0 ms

If we compare **Example 1** and **Example 2,** the processes have the same CPU burst times but different arrival times. Processes arrive at different time points in **Ex 1** but at the same time in **Ex 2**. We considered the same arrival time in **Ex 2,** to illustrate the non-preemptive SJF algorithm.

It seemingly shows performance gain in both average time and average TA time in Ex 2. However, the comparison is not fair as the processes have different arrival times in the two problems. Hence, we revisit the problem of **Example 1** in **Example 3** with a non-preemptive SJF algorithm again.

Example 3: *Consider the same problem as in* **Example 1.** *Find the average waiting time and average turnaround time in the SJF algorithm (non-preemptive).*

Soln. Following is the arrival time & CPU burst times of different processes.

Process	Arrival Time (ms)	Burst Time (ms)
P1	0	5
P2	1	3
P3	2	3
P4	4	1

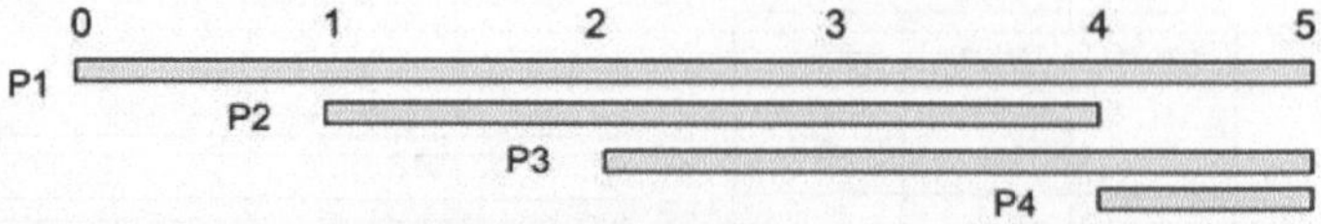

According to SJF (non-preemptive), P1 will execute first undisturbed, since other processes did not arrive then. But before P1 finishes, P2, P3, P4 arrived. Hence, P4 will execute next, followed by P2 and then P3 (though P2 & P3 are of same length, P2 is given preference for arriving early). Hence *Gantt chart* will look like the following.

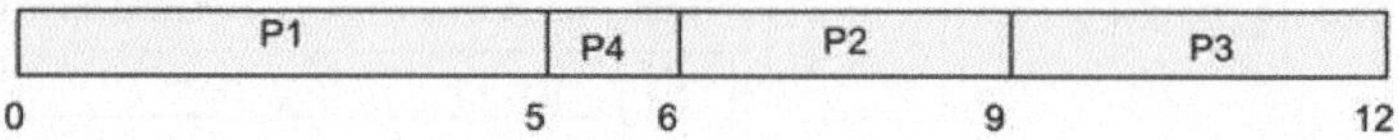

A process waits from arrival till it gets the CPU.
Hence wait times are as follows:
for P1 = 0 ms
P2 = (6-1) = 5ms
P3 = (9-2) = 7ms
P4 = (5-4) = 1ms

Avg wait-time = (0+5+7+1)/4 = **3.25ms**

Turnaround time for each process is its time of completion since its time of arrival.

Hence, TA times are as follows:
for P1 = (5-0) = 5ms
P2 = (9-1) = 8ms
P3 = (12-2) = 10ms
P4 = (6-4) = 2ms

Avg TA-time = (5+8+10+2)/4 = **6.25ms**

Example 4: *Consider the same problem as in* **Example 1.** *Find the average waiting time and average turnaround time in the SJF algorithm (preemptive).*

Soln. Following is the arrival time & CPU burst times of different processes.

Process	Arrival Time (ms)	Burst Time (ms)
P1	0	5
P2	1	3
P3	2	3
P4	4	1

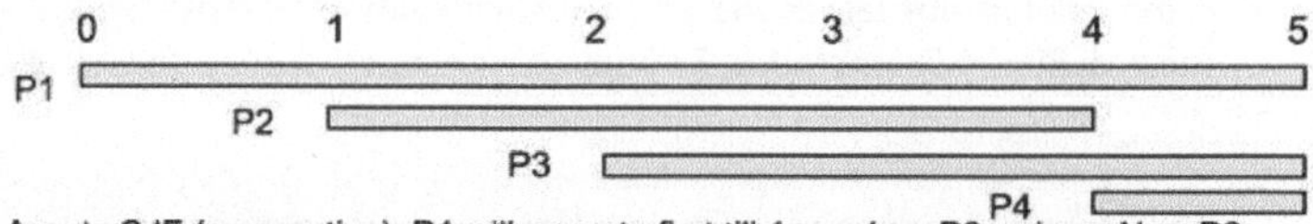

Acc. to SJF (preemptive), P1 will execute first till 1ms when P2 arrives. Now P2 needs 3ms of CPU whereas P1 needs 4ms. Hence P2 will execute till 2ms when P3 arrives. Here P2 has the smallest CPU burst (3-1 = 2ms) whereas P1 has = (5-1) = 4ms, and P3 has 3ms. At time = 4ms, P2 completes and P4 arrives with CPU burst 1ms (the smallest). Hence P4 will execute next. P3 will start after P4 as its CPU burst time (3ms) is smaller than than that of P1 (4ms). Hence *Gantt chart* will look like the following.

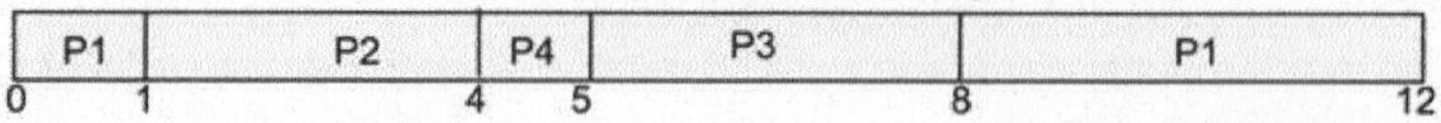

A process after arrival waits whenever it is not using CPU.
Hence wait times are as follows:
for P1 = (8-1) =7ms
P2 = (1-1) =0 ms
P3 = (5-2) = 3ms
P4 = (4-4) = 0ms

Avg wait-time = (7+0+3+0)/4 = **2.5ms**

Turnaround time for each process is its time of completion since its time of arrival.

Hence, TA times are as follows:
for P1 = (12-0) = 12ms
P2 = (4-1) = 3ms
P3 = (8-2) = 6ms
P4 = (5-4) = 1ms

Avg TA-time = (12+3+6+1)/4 = **5.5ms**

Example 3 shows improvements over the FCFS. But can we do any better? What if we can suspend P1 as soon as P2 arrives with 3ms of execution when P1 has 4ms of execution left? Can there be any gain if we preempt P1 and run P2? In other words, what will be the gain in a preemptive SJF? In preemptive SJF, we check CPU burst time of every process whenever a new process joins the ready queue. We schedule a new process preempting the current one only if the new process has the smallest CPU burst time. This is therefore also called the **Shortest Remaining Time Next (SRTN) or Shortest-Remaining-Time-First (SRTF) algorithm**. Let us revisit Example 1 with SRTN or preemptive SJF below.

Compare **Example 3** and **Example 4** carefully. We have done better both in terms of average waiting time and average TA time in preemptive SJF or SRTN.

SJF, though elegant, is difficult to implement as we do not know the CPU bursts of the processes before they execute. Sometimes, the next CPU burst of a process is estimated from its past CPU bursts as an exponential average like

$\tau_{n+1} = \alpha t_n + (1 - \alpha)\tau_n$, where τ_{n+1} is the estimate for next CPU burst and t_n is the observed CPU burst. α is the weightage ($0 \leq \alpha \leq 1$) given to real burst time and (1- α) to the estimated burst time (at the *n*-th time) in the new estimate. The estimated burst times can be used for implementing SJF algorithms.

2.8.4.3 Round-Robin (RR) Algorithm

Round-robin is a preemptive algorithm with FCFS at the core. Every process is preempted from the CPU core after a fixed time-interval and put at the back of the ready queue. The time-interval is called *time-slice* or *time-quantum* of the RR algorithm. The wait-time of a process depends on the number of processes in the ready queue and the length of a time-quantum. Let us take an example (**Example 5**). We also see the same problem with higher quantum value in **Example 6**.

With small time-slice, processes with smaller CPU bursts definitely gain as they can quickly get the CPU. If their CPU burst times are smaller or equal to the time slice, they can complete the execution in 1 time slice. Hence, they gain in terms of individual wait time and TA time (See the values of P4). However, there is a substantial increase in the number of context switches.

Example 5: *The following set of processes arrive at the same time, however in the following order with the given CPU-burst times in milliseconds. Find the average waiting time and average turnaround time in the RR algorithm with time-slice of 1ms.*

Process	Arrival Time (ms)	Burst Time (ms)
P1	0	5
P2	0	3
P3	0	3
P4	0	1

Soln. Following is the arrival time CPU burst times of different processes.

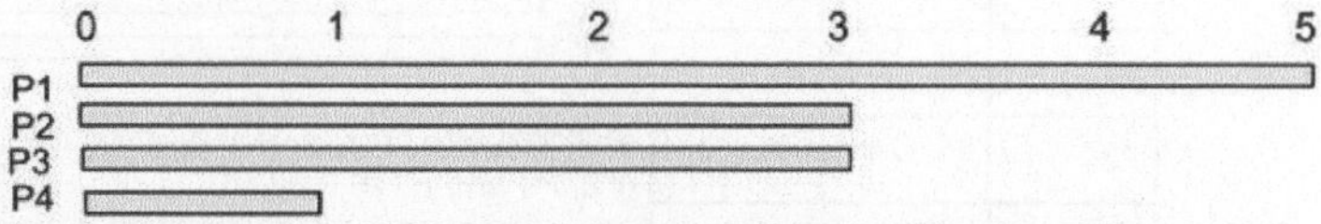

According to RR, P1 will execute first for 1ms, followed by P2, P3 and P4 each for 1ms in the order. Then again the next cycle will start with P1 and so on. Since P4 will complete in the 1st cycle itself, it will not feature in the 2nd cycle.

Hence corresponding *Gantt chart* looks like the following.

P1	P2	P3	P4	P1	P2	P3	P1	P2	P3	P1	P1

0 1 2 3 4 5 6 7 8 9 10 11 12

A process waits from arrival till it gets the CPU. Here, wait happens multiple times for a process.

Hence wait times are as follows:
for P1 = (3+2+2) = 7 ms
P2 = (1+3+2) = 6ms
P3 = (2+3+2) = 7ms
P4 = 3ms

Avg wait-time = (7+6+7+3)/4 = **5.75 ms**

Turnaround time for each process is its time of completion since its time of arrival.

Hence, TA times are as follows:
for P1 = (12-0) = 12ms
P2 = (9-0) = 9ms
P3 = (10-0) = 10ms
P4 = (4-0) = 4ms

Avg TA-time = (12+9+10+4)/4 = **8.75 ms**

Let us see the same problem with higher quantum value in **Example 6**.

Example 6: *The following set of processes arrive at the same time, however in the following order with the given CPU-burst times in milliseconds. Find the average waiting time and average turnaround time in the RR algorithm with time-slice of 4ms.*

Process	Arrival Time (ms)	Burst Time (ms)
P1	0	5
P2	0	3
P3	0	3
P4	0	1

Soln. Following is the arrival time CPU burst times of different processes.

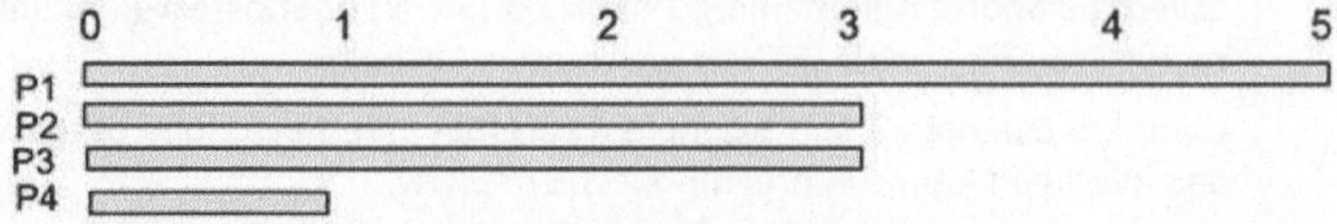

According to RR, P1 will execute first for 4ms, followed by P2, P3 and P4 each for maximum 4ms in the order. Then again, the next cycle will start with P1 and so on. Since P2, P3, and P4 have burst times less than the time quantum (4ms), they will complete in the 1st cycle itself except P1 that will feature in the 2nd cycle. Hence corresponding *Gantt chart* looks like the following.

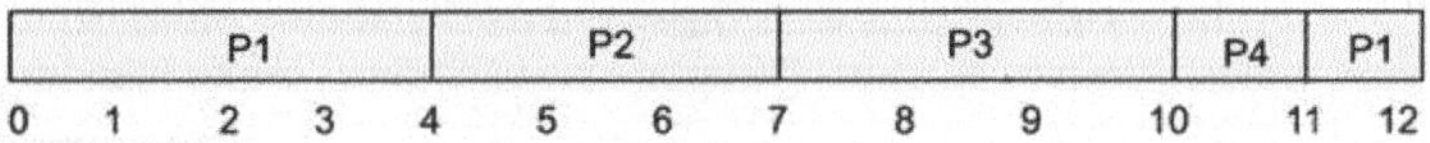

Wait time is the total time spent in ready queue of the CPU. Here, wait happens multiple times.

Hence wait times are as follows:
for P1 = (11-4) = 7 ms
P2 = (4-0) = 4ms
P3 = (7-0) = 7ms
P4 = (10-0)=10ms

Avg wait-time = (7+4+7+10)/4 = **7.0 ms**

Turnaround time for each process is its time of completion *since its time of arrival.*

Hence, TA times are as follows:
for P1 = (12-0) = 12ms
P2 = (7-0) = 7ms
P3 = (10-0) = 10ms
P4 = (11-0) = 4ms

Avg TA-time = (12+7+10+4)/4 = **8.25 ms**

Example 7: *The following set of processes arrive at the same time, however in the following order with the given CPU-burst times in milliseconds. Find the average waiting time and average turnaround time in according to the priority based scheduling.*

Process	Burst Time (ms)	Priority
P1	5	4
P2	3	2
P3	3	1
P4	1	3

Soln. Following is the arrival time CPU burst times of different processes.

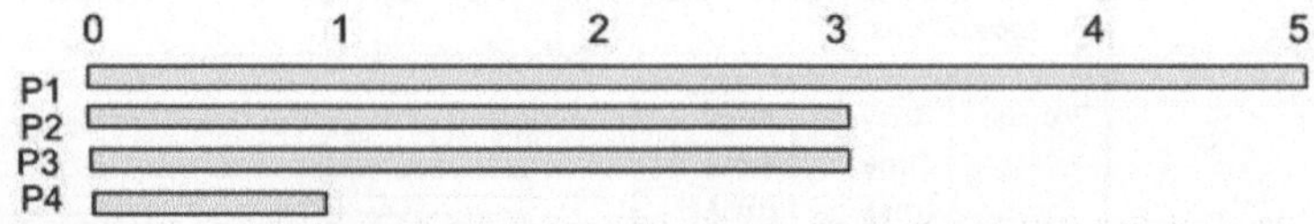

According to priority-based scheduling, P3 will execute first undisturbed, followed by P2, P4 and P1 at the last.

Hence corresponding *Gantt chart* looks like the following.

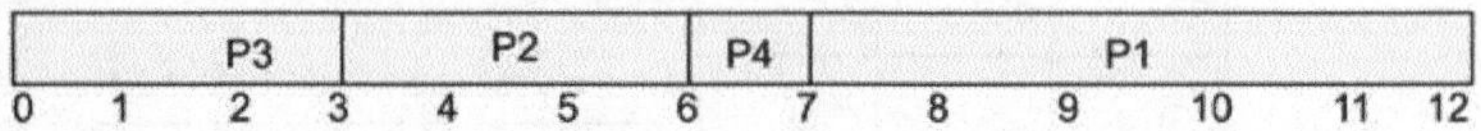

A process waits from arrival till it gets the CPU.

Hence wait times are as follows:
for P1 = (7-0) = 7 ms
P2 = (3-0) = 4ms
P3 = 0ms
P4 = (6-0)= 6ms

Avg wait-time = (7+4+0+6)/4 = **4.25 ms**

Turnaround time for each process is its time of completion since its time of arrival.

Hence, TA times are as follows:
for P1 = (12-0) = 12ms
P2 = (6-0) = 6ms
P3 = (3-0) = 3ms
P4 = (7-0) = 7ms

Avg TA-time = (12+6+3+7)/4 = **7.0 ms**

With higher quantum, processes with smaller CPU bursts suffer, especially if they join the ready queue late (see **P4** in **Example 6**). If we use a very high time quantum (say 5ms or higher in **Example 6**), it becomes FCFS. However, the number of context switches decreases (4 in **Example 6** compared to 11 in **Example 5**).

We did not consider the overhead time of context switch here, but that is not always negligible. Therefore, time quantum must be way greater than time of context switch time. Quantum is generally kept 10 to 100 milliseconds in modern OSs, while a context switch takes in the order of a few microseconds.

The RR algorithm can be implemented using a circular queue and a timer interrupt that interrupts to invoke the dispatcher after the time quantum expires and causes a context switch. The dispatcher picks the process from the front of the queue.

2.8.4.4 Priority-based Scheduling Algorithm

Generally, all processes are associated with a priority level. A scheduler allocates CPU to the process with the highest priority among all the processes in the ready queue. If two or more processes have the same priority level, they are then scheduled according to the FCFS principle.

SJF can be considered as a special case of the priority algorithm whereas if priority of a process is decided by the reciprocal of its CPU burst time (longest process is assigned the lowest priority). Let us see in **Example 7**.

Here, we considered a non-preemptive version of the priority algorithm. It suffers from the problem of indefinite blocking and causing starvation to other waiting processes. Hence, **preemptive priority-based algorithms** (whenever a higher priority process arrives, the current process is preempted and the high-priority one is scheduled immediately) or **RR based priority algorithms** are more popular. The RR-based algorithm is also implemented using **multi-level priority queues** where each queue is supposed to store processes of the same priority level. Every process executes for a time quantum and then preempted and put at the end of the ready queue of the same priority level. Often **multi-level priority queues with feedback** are used where *short processes* (for example, interactive processes) are put in queues with *higher priority* and *low time quantum* and long processes (batch jobs) are put in queues with low priority and high time quantum. Processes can move from high-priority queue to low-priority one after execution of a time slice and from low to high-priority after spending a threshold of waiting time in a queue.

2.8.5 Thread Scheduling

CPU scheduling is discussed so far in terms of processes. However, in most modern OSs, threads are considered units of work and can be independently scheduled. Thread scheduling is supported in two ways.

2.8.5.1 One-level thread scheduling

Threads are directly assigned to a CPU core. Scheduling criteria and principles can be applied the same way to the threads as we have discussed in traditional process scheduling.

2.8.5.2 Two-level thread scheduling

CPUs are allotted to processes. Each process manages the thread scheduling at the application level through thread libraries (for user-level threads) or at OS level (for kernel level threads). User level thread-scheduling is cheap in terms of time and space logistics and is done only when a process is allotted a CPU. These 2-level scheduling can be implemented using one scheduler (only kernel-level scheduler) or 2 schedulers (one within application level, another at the kernel level).

Solaris 2 supports both ULT and KLT through a middle-layer abstraction LWP (See **Sec 2.7.3.3**). Here LWPs connect ULTs to KLTs where each KLT is attached to a CPU.

Some OSs also support assigning relative priorities among sibling threads and thus priority scheduling.

Thread scheduling is beyond the scope of the book. Interested readers can find relevant material in general in [SGG18] and [Sta12].

2.8.6 Multiprocessor Scheduling

The algorithms discussed above are mostly with respect to a single CPU core. Most modern computing systems come with a multi-core CPU or a set of multicore CPUs. Multiple CPU cores allow parallel execution of several processes and/or several threads simultaneously. This makes CPU scheduling more complex. Multiprocessor would earlier mean a system with multiple units of physical single-core CPUs. But in present times, a multiprocessor system may also refer to any of the following system architectures:

1. Homogeneous multiprocessing
   a. *Multiprocessor scheduling*: a multi-core CPU or a set of multicore CPUs
   b. *Multicore processor scheduling*: multi-threaded cores
   c. *Non-Uniform Memory Architecture (NUMA)* systems
2. Heterogeneous multiprocessing.

2.8.6.1 Homogeneous multiprocessing

All the processors and processor cores here are identical in terms of their configuration and capabilities.

a. Multiprocessor scheduling:

First let us consider multiple processor units. Several processors can work in either of the two ways:

- *Asymmetric multiprocessing*: A processor acts as the master server while others as the slaves. The master takes all the scheduling decisions, I/O processing and other system activities. The slaves execute only user code. This is simple from the viewpoint of process scheduling and management, but not a very good solution in terms of performance. All the processors look for the master, which is heavily loaded. Also, the entire set-up is prone to a single-point failure as the server breakdown can cause total system breakdown (**Fig 2.22a**).

- *Symmetric multiprocessing (SMP):* Each processor can schedule on its own. They can either have a single global ready queue shared by all the processors or each processor can have their own local and private ready queue (**Fig. 2.22b**). The queues are shown optional, either a single global one or the local queues.

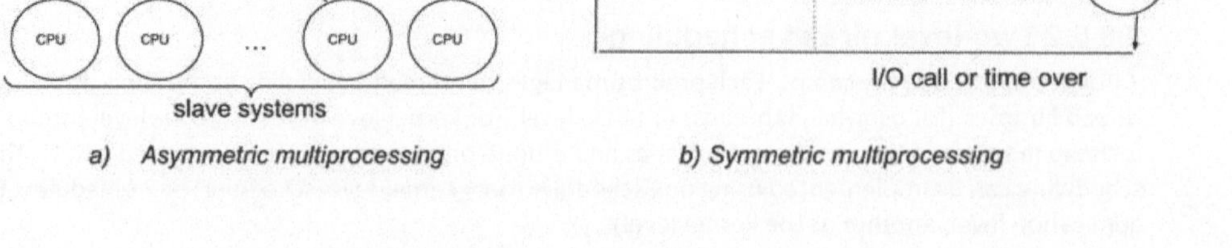

Fig 2.22: Homogeneous multiprocessor scheduling

Two important issues need to be discussed in relation to SMP systems:

a. Load balancing: As SMP systems can have independent scheduling per core, some of the cores might be overloaded while others are lightly loaded. Load balancing is particularly necessary when cores have their private ready queues. This is achieved by **push migration** (a special process that runs periodically to check the loads of each processor and pushes some threads from a highly loaded processor to a lightly loaded one) or **pull migration** (an idle processor pulls threads from the queue of a loaded processor). Some SMP systems use both push and pull migrations.

b. Processor Affinity: When a process / thread runs on a processor, some of its code and data remain in its cache attached to the processor. When the process (or thread) migrates to a different processor, the corresponding cache does not have the code and data and it needs to store them again. Had the process / thread been scheduled with the old processor again, old copies of the code and data could be re-used, and time could be saved. OS often attempts to schedule a given thread to a single processor, even though the allotment is not always guaranteed (the situation is called *soft affinity*) or allows processes to make system calls for scheduling to a given processor (*hard affinity*).

ii. Multicore processor scheduling:

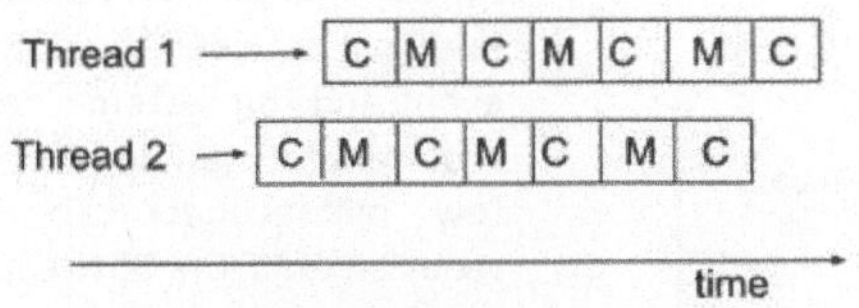

Fig 2.23: Multi-threaded core

Several computing cores are put in a single processor chip nowadays. Each core can work independently and appears to the OS as an individual logical CPU. Nowadays, such cores implement multithreading. For a cache miss, a thread has to often wait for fetching data from memory (called **memory stall**) due to mismatch in speed of processing in the core and that of memory hardware. To utilize that idle time in the core, chip-level hardware threads are supported. When one hardware thread does computation (C), another thread handles memory stall (M) in an interleaving fashion (**Fig 2.23**).

Intel processors use the term **hyperthreading** to refer to these hardware threads. Present i7 processors have 2 hyper-threads per core while Oracle Sparc M7 supports eight threads per core.

iii. Non-Uniform Memory Access (NUMA) Architecture:

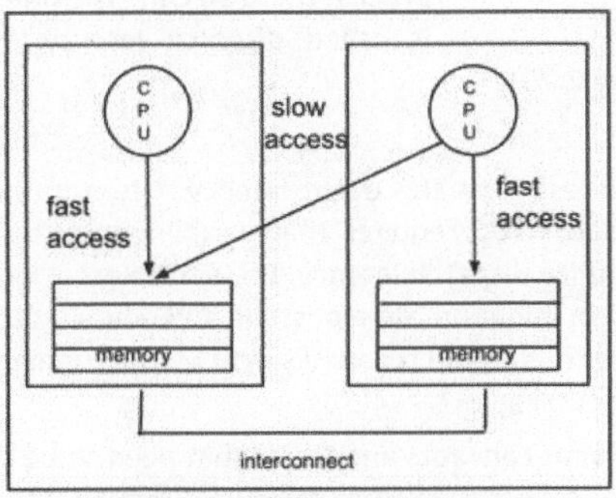

Fig 2.24: NUMA architecture

Here multiple processor chips are interconnected, with each chip associated with a CPU and its own memory unit.

Time required by a processor to access its own memory is less than that for a non-local memory. If OS scheduling and the memory management algorithms consider NUMA architecture, the threads can be allocated the CPU that is closest to the memory where the thread is loaded.

Load balancing and processor affinity often contradict each other, and the scheduler needs to balance the two. Most modern OSs including Windows, Linux, MacOS, iOS and Android implement SMP.

2.8.6.2 Heterogeneous multiprocessing

Some of the present day mobile devices use multicore processors of different processing attributes (clock speed, power requirement etc.). Such systems are called heterogeneous multiprocessing (HMP). This is mainly used to save battery power for long hours. For example, in ARM processors, a processor with high computational capability and high power requirement (called **big**) is used for interactive processes and gaming threads for a short period of time, while low power-requiring and slower processors (called **littles**) are used for background processes that run for longer duration. The *littles* save energy while the bigs deliver performance. Windows 10 supports HMP scheduling.

2.8.7 Real-Time Scheduling

Real Time systems need to respond to events within predictable and specific time constraints (recall **Sec 1.2.4**). *Hard real-time systems* have hard deadlines that must be met without fail, else the purpose of the system fails. They are used in mission-critical systems like defence systems of weapon-delivery or nuclear reactor control, space navigation and guidance and industrial machine control. *Soft real-time systems* are little tolerant to missing deadlines, but the delay must be predictable and bounded. Digital audio, multimedia systems, virtual reality systems, domestic consumer appliances are some examples of soft real-time systems.

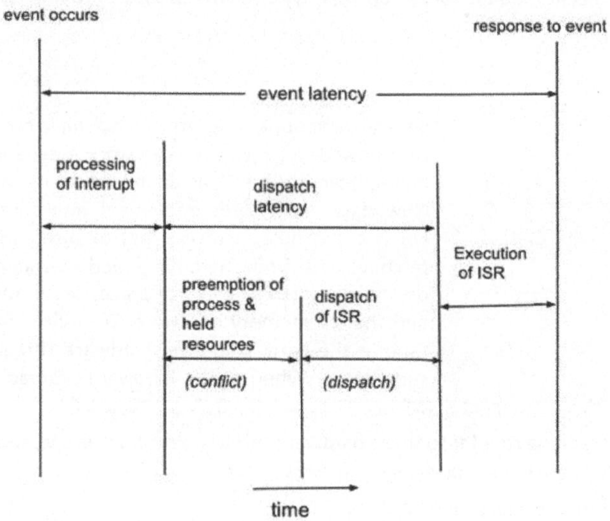

Fig 2.25: RTOS Scheduling: important latencies

The OS used in these systems, or Real Time operating systems (RTOSs) are characterised by precise timeliness, time synchronization among different agents and priority-based actions. A RTOS scheduler has to respond to real-time events that have strict *latency* (the time gap between the occurrence of an event and the system's response to it) requirements (a few microseconds to a few milliseconds). To meet these requirements, the OS has to listen to the respective interrupt, determine interrupt type, determine appropriate ISR (interrupt service routine) and invoke the ISR - all these make *interrupt latency*. Also, we need to consider the time required to suspend any running process, save its context, and do the context switch to dispatch a new process (here an ISR) - the time required is called *dispatch latency*. Here, the interrupt latency also subsumes the dispatch latency (**Fig 2.25**).

For a hard RTOS scheduler, interrupt latency must be less than the event latency. Often interrupts are disabled when some kernel data structures are accessed. RTOS requires that disabling interrupts can be allowed only for a very short time period. Also, to minimize dispatch latency, the RTOS kernel needs to be preemptive. Whenever a high priority processor arrives, in minimum time possible, CPU should be allocated to it preempting any running process of low-priority and freeing the resources held by the running process. Hence, RTOS should have priority-based preemptive scheduling.

With respect to RTOS scheduling, there are some important concepts and terms that need to be discussed. RTOSs are mostly used within embedded systems which collect data from sensors at regular intervals. The tasks that are performed at regular intervals are called **periodic** and the time between initiation of two successive such tasks is called a **period** (*p*) (**Fig 2.26**).

In preemptive scheduling, a running task may not be complete at one go (like in a non-preemptive scheduling), however the time required for completing the task (*t*) must be smaller than the deadline (*d*). Generally, $0 \leq t \leq d \leq p$. The rate of a periodic task is the frequency of appearing the task (*1/p*) in unit time and is often expressed in Hertz (Hz).

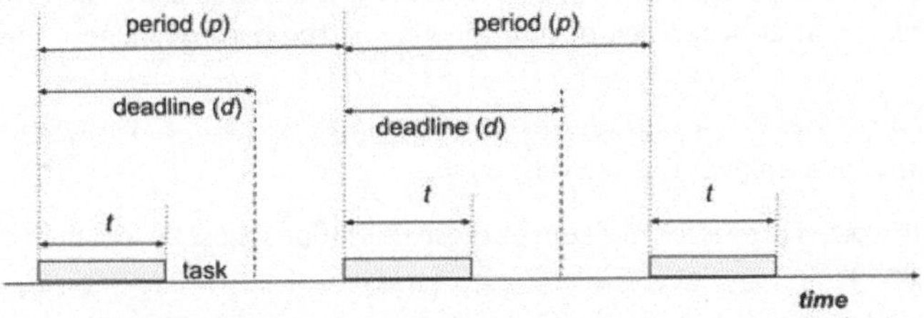

Fig 2.26: Periodic tasks with deadlines in a RTOS

Deadline (*d*) is a time-constraint by which a task should either start or end. Typically, completion or end deadlines are more popular.

There are some tasks which occur from time to time, but not in regular intervals. They are called **aperiodic**. For example, closing of a valve in a duct when fluid level reaches a certain threshold is an aperiodic task.

With this background we can discuss two scheduling algorithms that are popularly used in RTOSs.

2.8.7.1 Rate Monotonic (RM) Scheduling Algorithm

It is a static priority-based preemptive scheduling algorithm for periodic tasks. Every process is assumed to have a specific period (*p*) or rate (*1/p*). The processes are statically assigned priorities based on the period or rate: the higher the rate, the higher is the priority. A process with the shortest period or the highest rate is given the highest priority and the process with the longest period gets the lowest priority. The highest priority process is allocated to the CPU first, as soon as possible, preempting any other low-priority processes. Let us take an example (**Ex 8**).

Example 8: *A set of periodic processes arrive at the same time with the following execution times and periods. Deadlines for each process can be considered as before the start of next period. Show their possible scheduling according to the RM algorithm.*

tasks	Exec Time (c) (ms)	Period (p)
T1	25	150
T2	15	50
T3	20	100

Soln. Here, T2 has the shortest period, followed by T3 and then T1. Hence, the scheduling order will be T2 → T3 → T1.

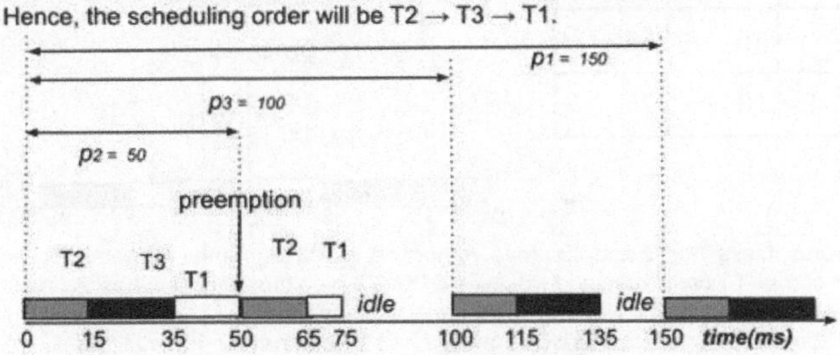

At *t=0ms*, tasks T1, T2 and T3 arrive. According to RM algorithm, T2 gets CPU and run entirely.
At *t= 15ms*, T2 completes and releases CPU. T3 gets the CPU as it has the next highest priority, and can complete as it needs 20ms of execution, well within the first period of 50ms.
At *t=35ms*, T3 completes, leaves the CPU and T1 can run for 15ms till 50ms.

At t=50ms, T2 arrives for the second time with the highest priority. T1 is therefore preempted and T2 starts.
At *t =65ms*, T2 completes and leaves the CPU. T1 is the only remaining task that can run the remaining part of T1 (10ms) and completes at 75 ms. The CPU remains idle for next 25ms.

At *t=100ms*, both T2 and T3 arrive. T2 run first for 15 ms, followed by T3 for 20 ms.
At *t=135ms*, T3 leaves CPU and there is no task remaining. The CPU remains idle for 15 ms.

At *t=150ms*, all of T1, T2 and T3 arrive again. Here, the scenario beginning at *t=0* starts repeating.

One important concept related to hard RT scheduling is *schedulability* - i.e., whether a given set of periodic processes can be at all scheduled or not, meeting all the hard deadlines. This is checked in terms of CPU utilization.

If the set of processes $T_1, T_2, \ldots, T_n$ have execution times $c_1, c_2 \ldots, c_n$ with periods $p_1, p_2 \ldots, p_n$ respectively, then utilization of each task T_i is given by $u_i = \frac{c_i}{p_i}$.

For the entire set of processes, the sum of these utilizations must be less than or equal to maximum possible utilization, i.e. 1.

In other words, $\frac{c_1}{p_1} + \frac{c_2}{p_2} + \cdots + \frac{c_n}{p_n} \leq 1$

However, it is shown that, there is a tighter upper-bound $\frac{c_1}{p_1} + \frac{c_2}{p_2} + \cdots + \frac{c_n}{p_n} \leq n\left(2^{\frac{1}{n}} - 1\right)$.

When $n \rightarrow \infty$, the upper bound $\rightarrow \ln 2 \rightarrow 0.693$.

For, n=3, this bound is $3\left(2^{\frac{1}{3}} - 1\right) = 0.779$. In **Example 8**, the sum of utilizations is $(\frac{25}{150} + \frac{15}{50} + \frac{20}{100}) = 0.67$, which is less than the upper-bound. Hence the set of tasks are schedulable, and we could find one according to the RM algorithm.

This schedulability criterion is a sufficient, but not necessary condition. If the criterion is satisfied, there is a guarantee of RM schedulability. But even if the criterion is not fulfilled, we can sometimes (not always) find a RM schedule, meeting all the hard deadlines. **Example 9** illustrates the point.

Example 9: *A set of periodic processes arrive at the same time with the following execution times and periods. Deadlines for each process can be considered as before the start of the next period. Show their possible scheduling according to the any algorithms.*

tasks	Exec Time (c) (ms)	Period (p)
T1	25	100
T2	15	50
T3	20	75

Soln. Let us first check the schedulability. According to schedulability criterion, for 3 processes, this bound is 3(2^(⅓)-1)= 0.779. Here, the sum of utilizations is (25/100+15/50 + 20/75) =0.817 which is greater than the bound (0.779). Hence, we are not guaranteed to find a schedule with all hard deadlines met according to the RM algorithm. However, let us see below.

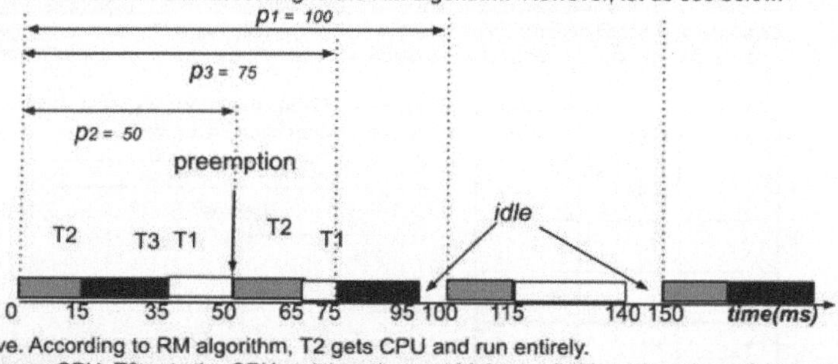

At *t=0ms*, tasks T1, T2 and T3 arrive. According to RM algorithm, T2 gets CPU and run entirely.
At *t= 15ms*, T2 completes and releases CPU. T3 gets the CPU as it has the next highest priority, and can complete as it needs 20ms of execution, well within the first period of 50ms.
At *t=35ms*, T3 completes, leaves the CPU and T1 can run for 15ms till 50ms.

At t=50ms, T2 arrives for the second time with the highest priority. T1 is therefore preempted and T2 starts.
At *t =65ms*, T2 completes and leaves the CPU. T1 is the only remaining task that can run the remaining part of T1 (10ms) and completes at 75 ms.

At *t=75ms*, T3 arrives. T3 runs for 20 ms till 95 ms. No other process is there and CPU remains idle for 5ms.
At *t=100ms*, T1 and T2 arrive. Acc to RM, T2 runs entirely (till 115ms) followed by T1 running completely till 140ms. The CPU can remain idle for 10 ms.

At *t=150ms*, T2 and T3 arrive again. Both can comfortably complete as sum of their execution times (15+20) is less than 50, before any new period starts (T1, T2 come at t = 200ms).
Hence, we can even find a schedule according to RM algorithm, even if schedulability criterion is not satisfied.

2.8.7.2 Earliest Deadline First (EDF) Scheduling Algorithm

EDF algorithm is a preemptive priority scheduling algorithm used in RTOSs that can be applied for aperiodic tasks including the periodic ones. Priorities are decided dynamically: earlier the deadline, higher is the priority. At any point in time, the highest priority task is scheduled for the CPU that has the earliest deadline. Let us take an example (**Ex 10**).

Example 10: *The following set of aperiodic processes arrive at the mentioned time with the given execution times and deadlines. Show their possible scheduling according to the EDF algorithm.*

Tasks	Arrival time (ms)	Exec Time (c) (ms)	End-deadline (ms)
T1	0	25	40
T2	5	10	20
T3	10	20	50

Soln. Here, T1 appears first when there are no other processes. Hence, it can start and execute till 5ms when T2 arrives.

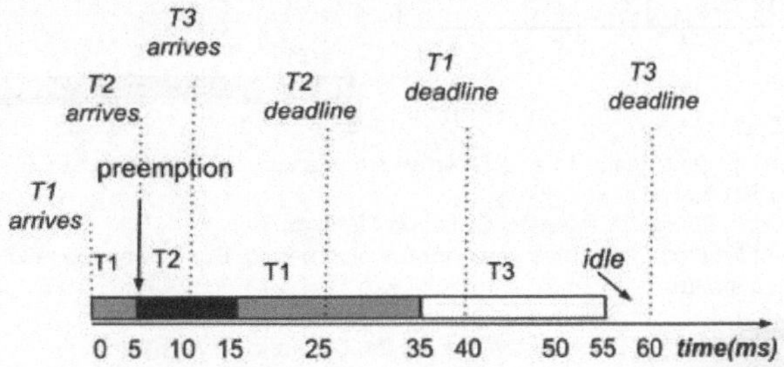

At *t=5ms*, task T2 arrives with deadline at (5+20)=25ms, earlier than that of T1 [at 40ms], hence T1 is preempted *and T2 starts running.*

At *t= 10ms,* T3 arrives with deadline at (10+50) = 60 ms, later than that of T2. Hence T2 continues till its end, i.e. till 15ms.

At *t= 15ms,* T2 leaves CPU. Now T1 has deadline earlier than that of T3, hence T1 gets CPU and completes rest of its execution (20ms) till (15+20)=35ms.

At *t=35ms,* T1 completes, leaves the CPU and T3 can run for 20ms till 55ms.

At *t=55ms,* T3 completes its execution comfortably as it had the latest deadline at 60 ms.

Hence, all three tasks complete well within their end-deadlines according to the EDF algorithm.

In **Example 10**, little thought will reveal that instead of EDF, if we follow a non-preemptive FCFS algorithm, T1 would continue for 25ms. When T1 releases the CPU, we miss the end-deadline of T2 which is (5+20) = 25ms itself.

EDF can also be applied for periodic tasks (Please see **Example 11**). The example can also be tried with the RM algorithm. The RM schedulability criteria will show that there is no guarantee of finding a solution. And, in fact, applying RM to **Example 11** will lead to a situation where we cannot meet all the deadlines. The students are strongly encouraged to try on their own and get convinced.

Example 11: *The following pair of periodic processes arrive at the same time with the given execution times and periods. Deadlines for each process can be considered as before the start of next period. Show their possible scheduling according to the EDF algorithm.*

Soln.

tasks	Exec Time (c) (ms)	Period (p)
T1	25	50
T2	35	75

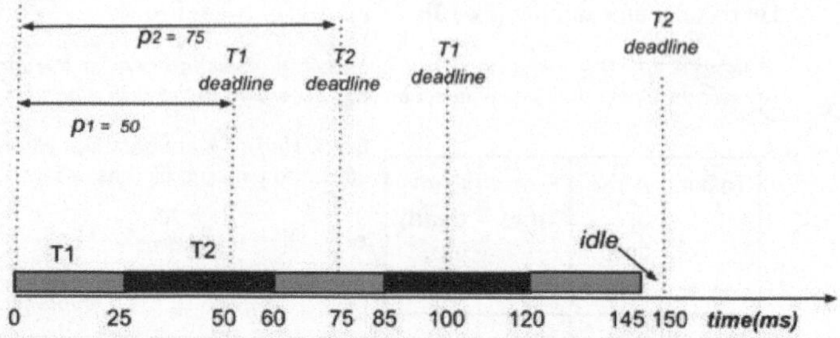

At *t = 0ms*, tasks T1 and T2 arrive simultaneously. According to EDF algorithm, T1 with earlier deadline (at 50ms) gets the CPU first and run entirely.
At *t= 25ms*, T1 releases CPU and T2 starts.
At *t=50ms*, T1 comes again for the next period. But T1 has the next deadline at 100ms, while T2 at 75ms. Hence T2 continues.

At *t=60ms*, T2 completes, leaves the CPU and T1 can start.

At *t=75ms*, deadline for T2 strikes, but T2 already completed at 60ms. T2 comes for the second cycle, but T1 has earlier deadline at 100ms and so continues.
At *t = 85ms*, T1 completes and leaves the CPU. T2 for the second cycle starts.

At *t=100ms*, T1 comes again for the third cycle with its deadline at 150ms, while T2 also has at 150ms. Hence T2 continues applying FCFS.
At *t=120ms*, T2 completes it burst of 35ms and leaves CPU. T1 starts and continues for 25ms of its burst.
At *t=145ms*, T1 completes 25ms of burst and leaves CPU. CPU remains idle for 5ms.

At *t=150ms*, both T1 and T2 arrive again. Here, the scenario beginning at *t=0* starts repeating.

In both the scheduling algorithms related to RTOSs, it was assumed that tasks or processes are independent. However, they may have interdependence among them. Then precedence constraints will necessitate topological sort of the processes to find an execution order. Deadline-based scheduling policy may involve other constraints also. Some of them will be discussed in the later units.

UNIT SUMMARY

This chapter introduced the basic units of program execution: processes and threads.

- *A process is a running instance of a program which is a set of instructions. Execution of a program is facilitated and managed by an OS on the computing hardware. An OS sees it in terms of a process and allocates resources to the processes.*
- *A process may have more than one independent flow of execution, each of them can be executed concurrently. Each such execution flow is called a thread. Processes are units of resource allocation by an OS while threads are units of work.*
- *There are different terms related to a process: process states, process control block, context switching and similarly that of threads like thread states, thread types and multi-threading.*
- *Every process has a life cycle where it is first created and is assigned resources. After it becomes ready to run, it is allocated CPU to begin execution. When it needs I/O, it goes to wait state and then rescheduled for CPU. After one or more CPU and I/O bursts, It finally terminates.*
- *Processes are connected to each other in a parent, child and siblings relationship.*
- *Threads are of two types: ULTs and KLTs. ULTs are managed in user applications through threads library. KLTs are managed by the OS.*
- *There are different CPU scheduling algorithms for single processor systems. Some are preemptive where the scheduler applies force to evacuate a currently running process from CPU. Non-preemptive ones rest on voluntary releases of the CPU cores by the processes.*
- *FCFS algorithm schedules processes according to the time of arrival. SJF gives preferences to the shortest remaining job at any moment. The RR algorithm offers a fixed time slice to all processes in the queue. Priority scheduling prefers important processes over the not-so-important ones.*
- *Different scheduling algorithms have different purposes to serve. Their performance can be measured using different metrics like CPU utilization, throughput, average wait time, average turnaround time, response time etc.*
- *Multiprocessor systems are nowadays quite commonplace even for PCs. Load balancing, processor affinity are two important issues in homogeneous multiprocessor scheduling.*
- *Heterogeneous multiprocessing is seen in mobile computing devices nowadays to save battery power.*
- *Scheduling in real time systems is deadline driven. Hard real time systems require that deadlines to be met for all tasks. Soft real time systems need predictable and time bound responses. The RM algorithm is used for periodic RTOS tasks, but EDF can be used for both periodic and aperiodic tasks.*

EXERCISES

Multiple Choice Questions

Q1. In UNIX Which of the following command is used to set task priority

A init

B nice

C kill

D ps [UGC NET CS (2012)]

Q2. Consider the following code fragment:

```
if (fork() == 0){
a = a + 5;
printf("%d, %p\n", a, &a);
}
else{
a = a - 5;
printf ("%d, %p\n", a, &a);
}
```

Let (u,v) be the values printed by the parent process and (x,y) be the values printed by the child process. Which one of the following is **TRUE**?

A. u=x+10 and v=y

B. u+10=x and v=y

C. u=x+10 and v!=y

D. u+10=x and v!=y [GATE (2005)]

Q3. What is the output of the following program?

```
main(){
    int a = 10;
    if(fork()) == 0))
        a++;
    printf("%d\n",a);
}
```

A. 10 and 11

B. 10

C. 11

D. 11 and 11 [ISRO (2017)]

Q4. Which of the following does not interrupt a running process?

A device

B. Timer

C. Scheduler process

D. Power failure [GATE (2001)]

Q5. Which combination of the following features will suffice to characterize an OS as a multi-programmed OS?

a. More than one program may be loaded into main memory at the same time for execution

b. If a program waits for certain events such as I/O, another program is immediately scheduled for execution

c. If the execution of a program terminates, another program is immediately scheduled for execution.

A. (a) **B**. (a) and b. **C**. (a) and (c) **D**. (a), (b) and (c) [GATE (2002)]

Q6. Consider the following statements with respect to user-level threads and kernel-supported threads

I. context switch is faster with kernel-supported threads

II. for user-level threads, a system call can block the entire process

III. Kernel supported threads can be scheduled independently

IV. User level threads are transparent to the kernel

Which of the above statements are true?

A. (II), (III) and (IV) only

B. (II) and (III) only

C. (I) and (III) only

D. (I) and (II) only [GATE(2004)]

Q7. Which one of the following is **FALSE**?

A. User level threads are not scheduled by the kernel.

B. When a user level thread is blocked, all other threads of its process are blocked.

C. Context switching between user level threads is faster than context switching between kernel level threads.

D. Kernel level threads cannot share the code segment. [GATE (2014)]

Q8. Threads of a process share

A. global variables but not heap

B. heap but not global variables

C. neither global variables nor heap

D. both heap and global variables [GATE(2017)]

Q9. Which scheduling policy is most suitable for a time-shared operating system?

A. Shortest Job First **B**. Round Robin

C. First Come First Serve **D**. Elevator [GATE(1995])

Q10. Four jobs to be executed on a single processor system arrive at time **0** in the order **A, B, C, D**. Their CPU burst time requirements are **4, 1, 8, 1**-time units respectively. The completion time of **A** under round robin scheduling with a time slice of one-time unit is.

A. 10 **B.** 4 **C.** 8 **D.** 9 [GATE (1996), ISRO(2008)]

Q11. The process state transition diagram of an operating system is as given below. Which of the following must be false about the above operating system ?

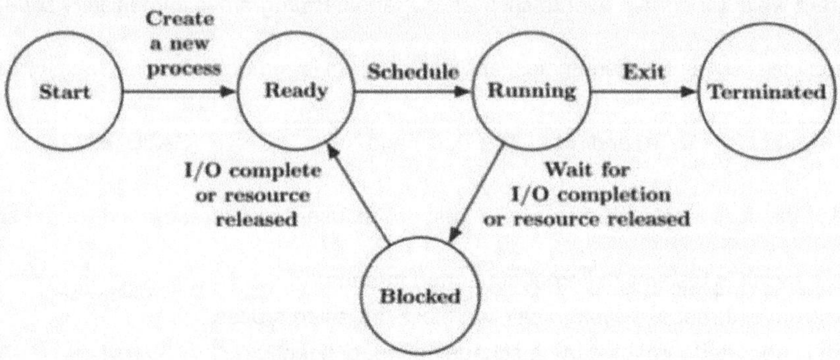

A. It is a multiprogrammed operating system

B. It uses preemptive scheduling

C. It uses non-preemptive scheduling

D. It is a multi-user operating system [GATE(2006)]

Q12. Consider an arbitrary set of CPU-bound processes with unequal CPU burst lengths submitted at the same time to a computer system. Which one of the following process scheduling algorithms would minimize the average waiting time in the ready queue?

A. Shortest remaining time first

B. Round-robin with the time quantum less than the shortest CPU burst

C. Uniform random

D. Highest priority first with priority proportional to CPU burst length [GATE(2016)]

Answers of Multiple Choice Questions

1. B 2. B 3. A 4. C 5. B 6. A 7. D 8. D 9. B 10. D 11. B 12. A

Short Answer Type Questions

Q1. On a system call with N CPUs what is the minimum number of processes that can be in the ready, run and blocked state?

Q2. What is the principal advantage of multiprogramming?

Q3. What is the principal disadvantage of too much multiprogramming?

Q4. What are the differences between process switch and thread switch? When do they occur?

Q5. What are process execution modes? Explain their purpose.

Q6. What is the difference between turnaround time and response time?

Q7. What is the purpose of a ready queue?

Q8. Explain two level thread scheduling.

Q9. On a system using round robin scheduling what would be the effect of including one process twice in the list of processes?

Q10. In the following process state transition diagram for a uniprocessor system, assume that there are always some processes in the ready state:

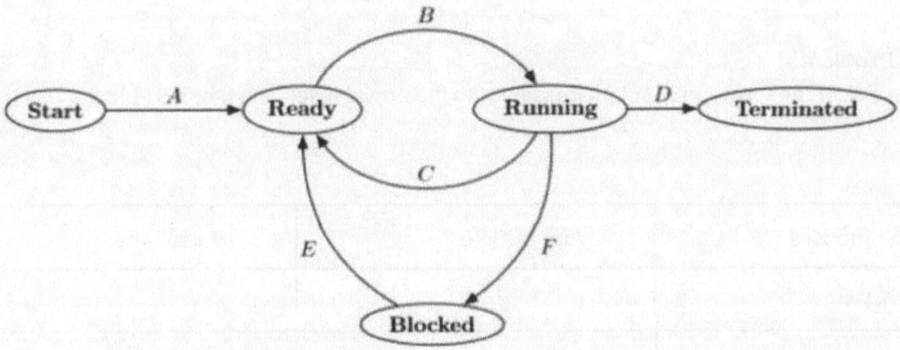

Now consider the following statements:

I. If a process makes a transition D, it would result in another process making A transition immediately.

II. A process P2 in a blocked state can make transition E while another process P1 is in a running state.

III. The OS uses preemptive scheduling.

IV. The OS uses non-preemptive scheduling.

How many of the above statements are TRUE? Justify.

Long Answer Type Questions

Q1. The operating system protects one process from another one. Why does it not protect one thread from its sibling thread?

Q2. What are user-threads and kernel-threads? Write the similarities and differences between them.

Q3. Why does the UNIX system use the zombie state? Is this an execution state of a thread or a process?

Q4. Define system throughput and CPU utilization. Are these two related to one another?

Q5. Explain FCFS scheduling and discuss its advantages and disadvantages.

Q6. What is priority-based scheduling? Explain the difference between preemptive priority scheduling and non preemptive priority scheduling.

Q7. Is a non-preemptive scheduling algorithm a good choice for an interactive system? Justify your answer.

Q8. Draw the process state transition diagram of an OS in which (i) each process is in one of the five states: created, ready, running, blocked (i.e., sleep or wait), or terminated, and (ii) only non-preemptive scheduling is used by the OS. Label the transitions appropriately.

Q9. How is uniprocessor scheduling different from multiprocessor scheduling? Explain.

Q10. What are the issues of real time scheduling? Discuss its specialities in comparison to uniprocessor systems.

Numerical Problems

Q1. Consider the following set of processes, with the arrival times and the CPU-burst times given in milliseconds.

Process	Arrival Time	Burst Time
P1	0	5
P2	1	3
P3	2	3
P4	4	1

What is the average turnaround time for these processes with the preemptive shortest remaining processing time first (SRPT) algorithm? [GATE(2004)]

Q2. Consider three CPU-intensive processes, which require 10, 20 and 30 time units and arrive at times 0 , 2 and 6,respectively. How many context switches are needed if the operating system implements a shortest remaining time first scheduling algorithm? Do not count the context switches at time zero and at the end. [GATE(2006) ISRO (2009)]

Q3. Consider three processes, all arriving at time zero, with total execution time of 10, 20 and 30 units, respectively. Each process spends the first 20% of execution time doing I/O, the next 70% of time doing computation, and the last 10% of time doing I/O again. The operating system uses a shortest remaining compute time first scheduling algorithm and schedules a new process either when the running process gets blocked on I/O or when the running process finishes its compute burst. Assume that all I/O operations can be overlapped as much as possible. For what percentage of time does the CPU remain idle? (upto 2 decimal place)

Q4. Consider the following four processes with arrival times (in milliseconds) and their

length of CPU bursts (in milliseconds) as shown below:

Process	p1	p2	p3	p4
CPU arrival time	0	1	3	4
CPU burst time	3	1	3	Z

These processes are run on a single processor using the preemptive Shortest Remaining Time First scheduling algorithm. If the average waiting time of the processes is 1 millisecond, then the value of **Z** is _____? [GATE(2019)]

Q5. Consider a uniprocessor system executing three tasks T1 ,T2 and T3 each of which is composed of an infinite sequence of jobs (or instances) which arrive periodically at intervals of 3, 7 and 20 milliseconds, respectively. The priority of each task is the inverse of its period, and the available tasks are scheduled in order of priority, which is the highest priority task scheduled first. Each instance of T1, T2 and T3 requires an execution time of 1, 2 and 4 milliseconds, respectively. Given that all tasks initially arrive at the beginning of the 1st millisecond and task preemptions are allowed, the first instance of T3 completes its execution at the end *of_______________________milliseconds.* *[GATE (2015)]*

Q6. Consider the set of processes with arrival time (in milliseconds), CPU burst time (in milliseconds), and priority (0 is the highest priority) shown below. None of the processes have I/O burst time.

process	Arrival time	Burst time	Priority
p1	0	11	2
p2	5	28	0
p3	12	2	3
p4	2	10	1
p5	9	16	4

The average waiting time (in milliseconds) of all the processes using preemptive priority scheduling algorithm is ____.

PRACTICAL

1. Study different process management-related POSIX calls like: i. *fork()* ii. *exec()* iii. *wait()* iv. sleep v. *kill()* vi. *exit()* vii. *getpid()* viii. *getppid()* and use them in your program.

2. Use multithreading to find the sum of integers 1 to 20 using
   i. 2 threads
   ii. 4 threads.
   iii. 10 threads

   See execution time in each case. Compare them with execution time using a single thread (without multithreading). What could be the reasons for the differences?

3. For a set of processes with arrival times and CPU burst times provided, implement FCFS, SJF, RR algorithm. Use different POSIX calls to simulate the same and find out average waiting time, TA time.

KNOW MORE

Process creation and management in UNIX & Linux are elaborately discussed and demonstrated in [RR03] and [SR05] for hands-on experiences. Similarly for Windows [YIR17] contains the manual.

UNIX processes and their scheduling are detailed in [Bac05] and [Vah12] and about UNIX threads in [Vah12], while for Windows threads [YIR17] stands as the authentic source.

For general discussion on processes, threads and their scheduling [SGG18], [Sta12] and [Hal15] are good books. [Mil11] and [Sta12] contain good accounts of scheduling.

Discussion on multiprocessing environments is covered in [SGG18] and [Sta12].

For real time systems, [Nar14] provides a brief but nice overview. Real time scheduling was elaborately covered in [SGG18], [Sta12] and [Nar14].

REFERENCES AND SUGGESTED READINGS

[Bac05] Maurice J Bach: The Design of the UNIX Operating System, Prentice Hall of India, 2005.

[HA09] Sibsankar Haldar and Alex A Aravind: Operating Systems, Pearson Education, 2009.

[Hal15] Sibsankar Haldar: Operating Systems, Self Edition 1.1, 2015.

[Mil11] Milan Milenkovic: Operating Systems - Concepts and Design, 2nd edition, Tata McGraw Hill, 2011

[Nar14] Naresh Chauhan: Principles of Operating Systems, Oxford University Press, 2014.

[RR03] Kay A. Robbins, Steven Robbins: Unix™ Systems Programming: Communication, Concurrency, and Threads, PrenticeHall, 2003.

[SR05] Richard W Stevens, Stephen A Rago: Advanced Programming in the UNIX Environment (2nd Edition), Addison-Wesley Professional, 2005.

[SGG18] Abraham Silberschatz, Peter B Galvin, Greg Gagne: Operating Systems Concepts,10th Edition, Wiley, 2018.

[Sta12] William Stallings: Operating Systems Internals and Design Principles, 7th Edition, Prentice Hall, 2012.

[Vah12] Uresh Vahalia: UNIX Internals, The New Frontiers, Pearson, 2012.

[YIR17] Pavel Yosifovich, Alex Ionescu, Mark E. Russinovich, and David A. Solomon: Windows Internals, Seventh Edition (Part 1 and 2), Microsoft, 2017. https://docs.microsoft.com/en-us/sysinternals/resources/windows-internals (as on 8-Jul-2022).

Dynamic QR Code for Further Reading

3 Interprocess Communication and Process Synchronization

UNIT SPECIFICS

Through this unit we have discussed the following aspects:

- *Inter-process Communication: Critical Section, Race Conditions, Mutual Exclusion, Hardware Solution, Strict Alternation, Peterson's Solution, The Producer Consumer Problem, Semaphores, Event Counters, Monitors, Message Passing,*
- *Classical IPC Problems: Readers & Writers Problem, Dining Philosopher Problem etc.*

This chapter discusses interaction among processes and threads. Often a number of processes together accomplish a job where individual processes contribute through sharing information and resources. Information is shared through different interprocess communication (IPC) schemes following two models. The shared memory model works in the user space, but the message passing model is implemented in kernel space. In a multiprogramming environment, concurrent execution of these cooperating processes often leads to simultaneous access-attempts to these shared data and data structures. However, simultaneous access cannot be allowed, but needs to be ordered in a mutually exclusive way to avoid different undesirable situations like race conditions and data inconsistencies. All relevant concepts related to process coordination and synchronization are defined, developed and explained with reasonable detail. The problems and their solutions at different levels of abstraction are discussed.

Like the previous unit, several multiple-choice questions as well as questions of short and long answer types following Bloom's taxonomy, assignments through several numerical problems, a list of references and suggested readings are provided. It is important to note that for getting more information on various topics of interest, appropriate URLs and QR code have been provided in different sections which can be accessed or scanned for relevant supportive knowledge. "Know More" section is also designed for supplementary information to cater to the inquisitiveness and curiosity of the students.

RATIONALE

This unit on interprocess communication and process synchronization starts with the discussion on different IPC models and techniques in reasonable detail. The unit helps students learn the fundamental concepts of communication techniques and some examples of their implementations. Interprocess communication increases utilization of available resources in a computer and its overall efficiency through increase in modularity and reduction in redundancy of codes. But concurrent execution on the IPC data structures creates serious issues like race conditions leading to data inconsistency and thus program malfunctioning. The sections of code within the cooperating processes where shared data structures are accessed are called critical sections. Access to these critical sections needs to be done in mutual exclusion to each other. The problems arising out of simultaneous attempts to access these critical sections are called critical section problems. Necessary definitions with relevant examples are provided and other necessary concepts are developed. Basic primitives required towards solution to critical section problems and offered at hardware level are described. A few more powerful primitives developed using the basic tools at algorithmic level as well as operating system, and high-level programming language levels are then discussed. Finally, a few classic and standard IPC problems are explained and how their solutions can be designed using different synchronization and then are described in detail. This unit builds the fundamental concepts to understand the concurrent (and parallel) programming environment of an OS. The concepts developed here are central and critical to the utilization of computing resources and their management by OS and will be used in other forthcoming units of the book.

This unit builds the fundamental concepts to understand the concurrent (and parallel) programming environment of an OS. The concepts developed here are central and critical to the utilization of computing resources and their management by OS and will be used in other forthcoming units of the book.

PRE-REQUISITES

- *Basics of Computer Organization and Architecture*
- *Fundamentals of Data Structures*
- *Fundamentals of Algorithms*
- *Introductory knowledge of Computer Programming*
- *Introduction to Operating Systems (***Unit I** and **Unit II** *of the book)*

UNIT OUTCOMES

List of outcomes of this unit is as follows:

U3-O1: Define process communication models, race condition, critical section, different solution primitives and tools like mutex, semaphores, monitors.

U3-O2: Describe methods of process communication like shared memory model, message passing model and their implementation, different critical section problems and their solutions using various synchronization tools and primitives.

U3-O3: Understand the need for process cooperation and the problems arising out of sharing data and resources among cooperating resources.

U3-O4: Realize the importance of process coordination and synchronized execution of critical sections.

U3-O5: Analyze and compare different process synchronization techniques at different levels of hardware and software.

U3-O6: Design solutions to different classical IPC problems as well as some novel (non-classical) problems.

Course Outcomes

After completion of the course the students will be able to:

1. Create processes and threads.
2. Develop algorithms for process scheduling for a given specification of CPU.
3. Utilization, Throughput, Turnaround Time, Waiting Time, Response Time.
4. For a given specification of memory organization develop the techniques for optimally allocating memory to processes by increasing memory utilization and for improving the access time.
5. Design and implement file management system.
6. For a given I/O devices and OS (specify) develop the I/O management functions in OS as part of a uniform device abstraction by performing operations for synchronization between CPU and I/O controllers.

Unit-3 Outcomes	EXPECTED MAPPING WITH COURSE OUTCOMES (1- Weak Correlation; 2- Medium correlation; 3- Strong Correlation)					
	CO-1	CO-2	CO-3	CO-4	CO-5	CO-6
U3-01	3	3	3	2	1	2
U3-02	3	3	3	2	1	2
U3-03	3	3	3	2	1	2
U3-04	3	3	3	2	1	2
U3-05	3	3	3	2	1	2
U3-06	3	3	3	2	1	2

3.1 INTERPROCESS COMMUNICATION

Processes can execute within a multiprocess OS in two ways. Either they share some information among them or do not do it at all. When they share information (code and/or data) among them during execution, they are called **cooperating processes,** otherwise **independent processes**. Cooperating processes collaborate to accomplish a task through various *interprocess communication (IPC)* techniques. These techniques belong to either of the two popular IPC models: *shared memory (SM)* and *message passing.*

3.1.1 Shared Memory Model

Processes are allowed to use a memory region in the user space for communication. The OS provides system calls to create, manage and destroy the shared memory space. Any process can create a shared memory. Any other process, if it requires use of the shared memory, attaches to the space. The region is then considered part of its process address space and can access it as its own memory. Any process attached to the shared memory can write on and read from the space (**Fig 3.1a**).

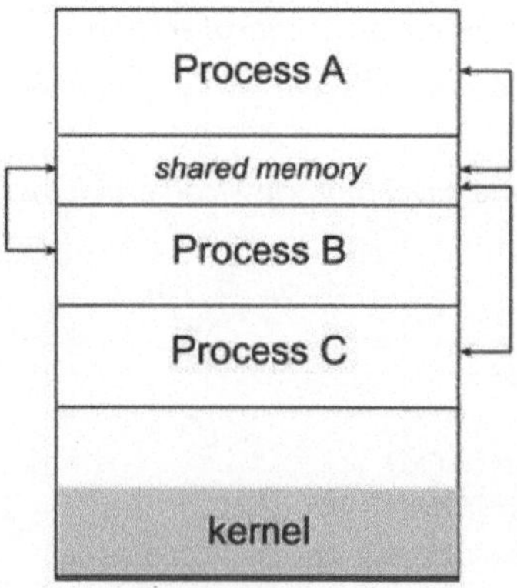

(a)

```
/*****WRITER-PROCESS (shm-writer.c) **/

#include <stdio.h>
#include <sys/ipc.h>
#include <sys/shm.h>

int main(){
// ftok to generate unique key
key_t key = ftok("shmfile",65);
// shmget returns an identifier in shmid
int shmid =
shmget(key,1024,0666|IPC_CREAT);

// shmat to attach to shared memory
char *str = (char*) shmat(shmid,(void*)0,0);
// read input from console
scanf("%s", str);

printf("Data written in memory: %s\n",str);

//detach from shared memory
shmdt(str);

return 0;
}
```

(b)

```
/**READER (shm-reader.c)**/

#include <stdio.h>
#include<string.h>
#include <sys/ipc.h>
#include <sys/shm.h>

int main(){
// ftok to generate unique key
key_t key = ftok("shmfile",65);

// shmget returns an identifier in shmid
int shmid =
shmget(key,1024,0666|IPC_CREAT);

// shmat to attach to shared memory
char *str = (char*)
shmat(shmid,(void*)0,0);

printf("Data read from shared memory:
%s\n",str);

//detach from shared memory
shmdt(str);

// destroy the shared memory
shmctl(shmid,IPC_RMID,NULL);

return 0;
}
```

(c)

Fig 3.1: (a) Shared Memory Model (b) - (c) IPC implementation of a SM model

A process can detach itself from the shared memory when its use is over, but the SM remains in the main memory until it is explicitly destroyed by some process (not necessarily the creator). If several processes want to access the space simultaneously, the OS kernel does not have any control on it. Concurrent access to the shared memory is thus to be managed at the user level only.

Fig 3.1b and **Fig 3.1c** show a simple example of SM implementation in a Unix-based system. The writer process (**Fig 3.1b**) reads an input string from the console and writes it on the shared memory. The reader process (**Fig 3.1c**) can attach to it and then read from the shared memory, if it is not destroyed. The reader can also write on it. Any other process can attach to the shared memory and use it freely. Students are strongly encouraged to run the code and play with them by modifying the programs. (They can learn more about the necessary syscalls by doing (man <shm-service-name>) in UNIX based systems.

3.1.2 Message Passing Model

When the information to be shared among a set of cooperating processes is seen as a message that is sent by a process and is received by one or more processes, the paradigm is called message passing model. Message passing happens through the kernel space involving the OS kernel (**Fig 3.2**). There are several IPC mechanisms that implement message passing. Few of them are briefly discussed below.

3.1.2.1 Signal System

Signal system was originally implemented in UNIX systems and is the simplest IPC mechanism of message passing model. Every process has a signal descriptor in its kernel space to get notified on different signals (occurrence of interrupts and/or traps). Generally, a single bit is used for each of the signals and a particular bit is designated for it within the signal descriptor (**Fig 3.3**).

Either the kernel process (for interrupts and traps) or any other cooperating process through a syscall sets a particular signal bit ON to notify the recipient process about the corresponding signal. POSIX has about 20 signal types like SIGTERM, SIGSEGV, SIGINT etc, but a signal descriptor can accommodate more. The recipient process invokes a signal handler appropriate to the signal received in response and then the signal bit is reset by the kernel. The template of the signal handlers is provided by default by the kernel. However, it can be customized by the process and executed in the process address space. A process can block a signal by notifying its signal type in another signal descriptor meant for blocking. Blocked signals (e.g., signal type 1, 28, 29, 31 are blocked in **Fig 3.3**) are not received by the recipient unless it unblocks the signals.

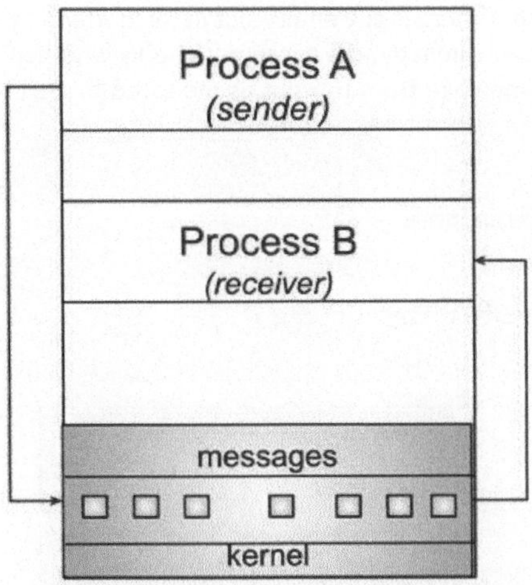

Fig 3.2: Message passing Model

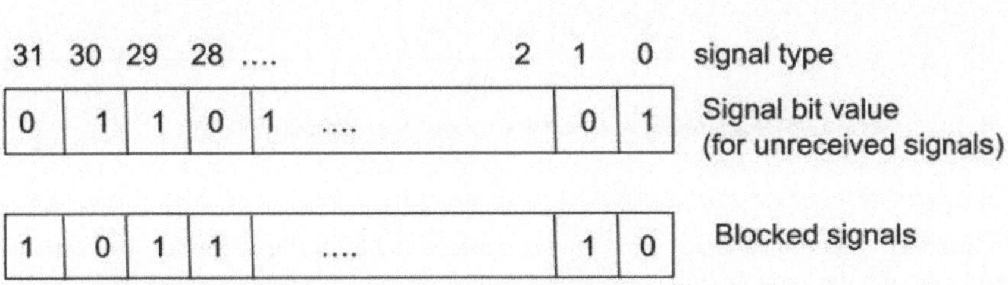

Fig 3.3: Signal descriptor and blocking of signals

3.1.2.2 Message Queuing (MQ)

Message queues are the best examples of implementing a message passing model as shown in **Fig 3.2**. Messages are considered shareable information units, finite in size, that are created by one or more sender processes, sent to a designated region in kernel space (called a *message buffer*) and consumed by other processes. A message buffer acts like a queue and works in strictly FIFO (first-in-first-out) fashion. An OS manages message queues but does not see the message contents. The OS only provides mechanisms in terms of IPC primitives for

i. creating message queues (e.g., `msgget()` function is used in UNIX[6])
ii. opening an existing queue (`msgget()` function with suitable flags)
iii. sending a message to an open queue (`msgsnd()` function)
iv. receiving an available message from an open queue (`msgrcv()` function)
v. destroying the queue (`msgctl()` function).

A message queue is often implemented with a circular queue following a *producer-consumer model*: a producer(s) produce(s) messages, put(s) them in the buffer and the consumer(s) collect(s) them from the buffer (**Fig 3.4a**). MQ is an *asynchronous* IPC technique - the producers keep on producing the items and put them in the buffer until the buffer is full. Similarly, the consumers keep on collecting the items until the buffer is empty.

Let us consider a simple implementation using a bounded buffer of size N (**Fig 3.4a**) with a single producer (**Fig 3.4b**) and a single consumer (**Fig 3.4c**). The circular buffer has N slots, each slot can hold one message only. The producer checks whether there is any empty slot in the buffer and puts the message in the slot, pointed to by `in` (a shared variable). Similarly, the consumer checks whether there is at least one message in the queue and consumes the message from the slot as indicated by `out` (another shared variable).

Initialisation:

```
#define BUFFER_SIZE N
typedef struct {
...
} msg;
msg buffer[BUFFER_SIZE];
int in = 0;
int out = 0;
Int count =0;
```

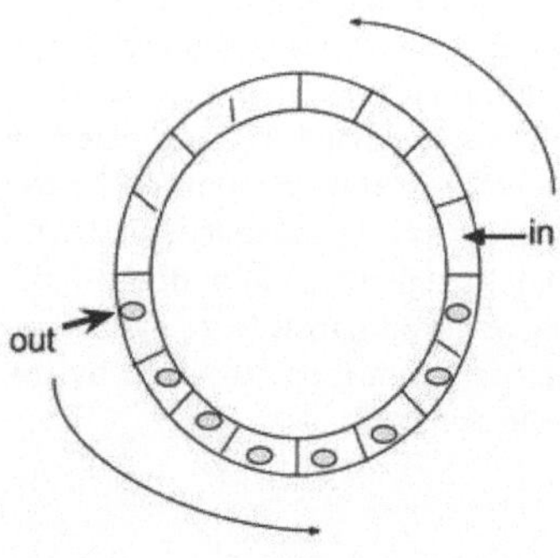

(a)

```
/****PRODUCER *****/
produce() {

 msg next_produced;

 while (true) {

   while ((count == BUFFER_SIZE)
     ; /* do nothing */

   buffer[in] = next_produced;
   in = (in + 1) % BUFFER_SIZE;
   count++;
  }
}
```

(b)

```
/****CONSUMER *****/

consume(){

 msg next_consumed;

 while (true) {
  while (count == 0)
     ; /* do nothing */

  next_consumed = buffer[out];
  out = (out + 1) % BUFFER_SIZE;
  count - -;
  }
}
```

(c)

Fig 3.4: Message Queue implementation using a bounded circular buffer

Data structure `buffer` and the variable `count` are accessed by both the processes. The variable `in` is only used by the producer, and the variable `out` by only the consumer, variable count is updated by both.

---

[6] https://users.cs.cf.ac.uk/dave/C/node25.html

3.1.2.3 Pipes

Pipes are an asynchronous and uni-directional message passing mechanism between two *related* processes. These pipes are created in kernel space and generally un-named. Usually, parent and child processes communicate through unnamed pipes (**Fig 3.5**).

In UNIX, a pipe is treated almost like a file. However, each process has two file descriptors for a pipe: one for read and another for write. Writer uses the write-descriptor and closes the read-descriptor, while the reader process uses the read-descriptor, closing the write-descriptor (**Fig 3.5b**). In shell programming, pipes are used to send output of one command to be used as input of another command. For example, two popular commands **'ls | more'** use here a pipe denoted by '|'. Output of **ls** is sent as input of **more**. In the UNIX shell, a series of commands can be cascaded using pipes this way.

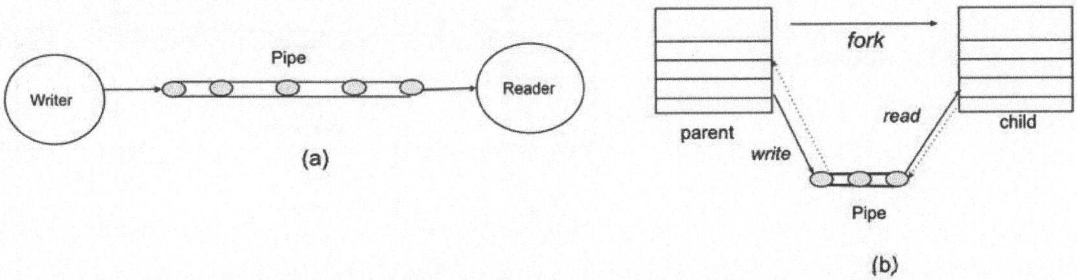

Fig 3.5: (a) Pipe scheme (b) UNIX implementation of pipe

3.1.2.4 Named pipes

Construction-wise, named pipes are the same as unnamed pipes except that they have names. In UNIX, they are called FIFO and created using **mkfifo** syscall. FIFOs can be used by any processes (related or unrelated) like a file for reading and writing. But, unlike files, unread data does not persist after system reboot.

3.1.2.5 Sockets

Sockets are endpoints of a bi-directional communication channel through which two processes communicate. The processes can be related or unrelated, local or remote. A socket represents a port on a host machine through which a process sends or receives data. Sockets implement *indirect IPC*, i.e., any process (including the sender) that connects to the other end of the channel, i.e., another socket, can receive or send data (**Fig 3.6a**).

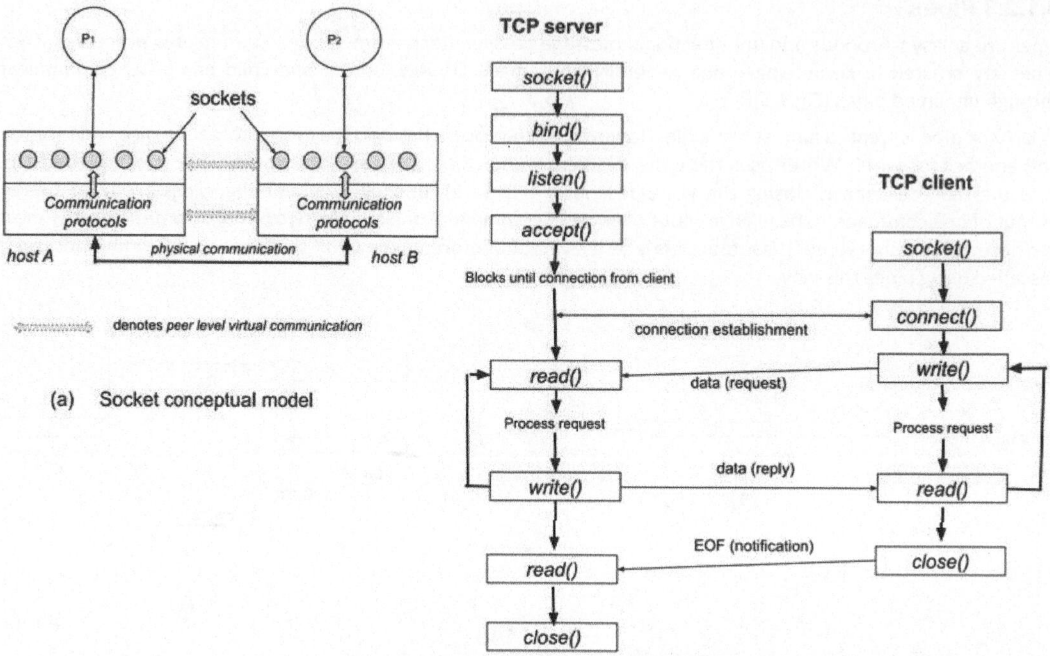

(a) Socket conceptual model

(b) Block diagram for TCP client-server socket implementation

Fig 3.6: Sockets

Sockets are mostly used in client-server configurations between two remote processes. Each socket is supposed to have a host address where the host id depends on the domain (domain can be UNIX or Internet). In the Internet domain, a host address consists of a 32-bit ip-addr and 32-bit port number. In the UNIX domain, it is a unique name like a filename.

An operating system provides the following system calls to implement a socket.

i. *socket()*: to create a socket. It returns a socket descriptor.
ii. *bind()*: the server binds the created socket to a local port.
iii. *listen()*: the socket is ready to communicate, waits for some request from other processes.
iv. *connect()*: the other process (client) connects to the remote socket (server-side) as given by the host address.
v. *accept()*: the server accepts the request of remote host, creates another socket at the server for communication
vi. *close()*: closes the socket.

Once connection is established, the socket is accessed like a file within the host programs and data is read from or written to the socket.

Sockets can be implemented using different communication protocols like UDP, TCP, or IP. **Fig 3.6b** shows a block diagram of the sequence of data flow in a client server implementation of sockets following TCP.

Fig 3.7 shows the actual implementation in a single UNIX system. Both the programs need to be executed simultaneously to see the communication. Sockets are here implemented at the user level with the APIs provided by the OS. The control lies with the OS kernel as the necessary message buffers are created in the kernel space. When several processes simultaneously attempt to access the same socket, how it will be managed is a kernel prerogative.

```
/******SERVER********/
#include<sys/types.h>
#include<sys/socket.h>
#include<string.h>
#include<sys/un.h>
#include<stdlib.h>
#include<stdio.h>
#define ADDRESS "testsocket" /*socket-addr */

int main(){
char c, *server_str = "msg from server\n";
int fromlen;
FILE *fp;
int sd, cd, len;
struct sockaddr_un servaddr, fsaun;

sd = socket(AF_UNIX, SOCK_STREAM,0);      /*create socket */
servaddr.sun_family = AF_UNIX;
strcpy(servaddr.sun_path, ADDRESS);

unlink(ADDRESS);      /* remove earlier file with same name*/
len = sizeof(servaddr.sun_family) + strlen(servaddr.sun_path);
bind(sd, (struct sockaddr *)&servaddr, len);      /*bind socket */
listen(sd, 5);      /*listen to client */
cd = accept (sd, &fsaun, &fromlen);      /*accept client request*/
fp = fdopen(cd, "r");      /*open a fd to read from client */
send(cd, server_str, strlen(server_str), 0);      /*send msg to client*/
while (( c = fgetc(fp)) != EOF) {
putchar(c);      /*print msg from client*/
if (c == '\n')
break;
}
close(sd); /*close server-side socket */
exit(0);
}
```

```
/**************CLIENT ********/

#include <sys/types.h>
#include <sys/socket.h>
#include <sys/un.h>
#include <stdlib.h>
#include <stdio.h>
#define ADDRESS "testsocket" /* socket-addr to connect */
char *strs = "A message from client\n"; /*to be sent to server*/

int main(){
char c;
FILE *fp;
int s, len;
struct sockaddr_un saun;

s = socket(AF_UNIX, SOCK_STREAM, 0); /*create socket */
saun.sun_family = AF_UNIX;
strcpy(saun.sun_path, ADDRESS);
len = sizeof(saun.sun_family) + strlen(saun.sun_path);

if (connect(s, &saun, len) < 0)  /*connect to socket */
printf ("error: connect\n");

fp = fdopen(s, "r"); /* opening a fd to read from socket */

while ((c = fgetc(fp)) != EOF){ /*reading from socket */
putchar(c);      /*writing on console */
if(c=='\n')
break;
}
send(s, strs, strlen(strs), 0); /*sending msg to server */
close(s);
exit(0);
}
```

Fig 3.7: Client-Server implementation in the UNIX domain

Sockets are an important part of networking and socket programming is considered an integral part of network programming. You can learn more on sockets and their implementations from the given links[7].

3.2 SYNCHRONIZATION

In both the IPC models across the implementation schemes discussed, there are several shared data structures: a shared memory region, or a shared message buffer and shared variables. All the cooperating processes either share data through them or modify them. It may happen that more than one process attempts to simultaneously access the same data-structure (or shared variables) at the same time. Simultaneous read of a given shared data by several processes may lead to a contention in a single processor system as to who gets the first chance to read. Even though this is a scheduling issue, it is not a serious problem. All processes are supposed to read the same value of the variable or face the same state of the shared data structure.

But when simultaneous read and write attempts are made or simultaneous writes are attempted on a shared data item by more than one process - their execution order has serious implications.

If the writer writes before the reader, while the read should happen before any write - the reader gets the modified data. It may lead to an undesirable effect. Similarly, if reading of a data item should happen after a write, but it happens in the opposite order - it is also a potentially serious issue.

---

[7]https://www.ibm.com/docs/en/ztpf/1.1.0.15?topic=considerations-unix-domain-sockets
https://users.cs.cf.ac.uk/dave/C/node28.html#SECTION00280000000000000000

These issues may arise because of two reasons:

1. difference in processing speeds among the cooperating processes
2. lack of coordination or synchronization among the cooperating processes.

In a uniprocessor system, processor speed is the same for all the processes. However, the frequency of repetitive reads or writes of a shared data in a loop depends on the inherent logic of the program - a factor intrinsic to the process and is beyond the control of the operating system.

But coordination or synchronization among the cooperating processes is necessary to ensure that simultaneous reads & writes are properly serialized to mitigate undesirable program behaviour. It is one of the most important issues in concurrent programming (refer **Sec 1.2.3** and **Sec 1.3.8**) that needs to be taken care of either by the application developers or the operating system.

The synchronization issue not only arises among cooperating *user processes* involved in IPC but also among several *kernel processes* accessing kernel data structures, among several *threads* of a process sharing global data and in a multiprocessor system, and among several *processors* sharing a global CPU queue.

However, we shall focus here on process synchronization considering both user and kernel processes.

In a non-preemptive uniprocessor system, a process is allowed to execute as long as it wants until it voluntarily leaves the processor. Only one process gets the chance to use CPU and complete the read or write operations at a given time unhindered. Hence, this kind of erroneous sequence is not supposed to occur unless there is a mistake within the process committed by the programmer.

In a non-preemptive multiprocessor system, however, speeds of the processors also need to be taken into account. Scheduling cooperating processes on different processors with different computing speeds can create serious synchronization issues.

The problem can aggravate in a preemptive scheduling system because a process can be preempted while it is in the middle of a write operation. The write may not be complete before the preemption and another cooperating process may read the same data unaware of the preemption. If the read is supposed to happen after the write, but the write is not complete, and the reader is not aware of it - this leads to the problem of *data inconsistency.* The reader will get wrong data which can lead to further undesirable effects.

Let us first analyse the case very carefully with an example and then discuss the possible remedies.

3.3 RACE CONDITIONS

Concurrent multiprogramming involving cooperating processes is a challenge for operating systems. To illustrate the point, consider the shared variable `count` in **Sec 3.1.2.2.** The variable is updated in both producer (`counter++`) and consumer (`counter--`) processes. Both the processes run concurrently (in interleaved fashion in a single processor system or in parallel in a multiprocessor system). It may happen that both the processes attempt to update `count` simultaneously. Then it is a case of simultaneous writes.

Even though a write is a single operation in a high-level language, it involves several low-level instructions as depicted below (**Fig 3.8**). Consider any possible value of `count` (say, `3`) before the simultaneous writes, and the execution order of instructions during the simultaneous writes in a parallel or in an interleaved processing (CPU preemption happens after data-read in the producer and then after data-write in the consumer). At the end, the value of `count` will be 4 in the producer and 2 in the consumer. Had there been proper synchronization, the appropriate value of `count` should be 3 at the end in both the producer and the consumer, as there is one production and one consumption.

But depending on whether Step 4 or Step 6 is executed last, the final value of `count` that will prevail in the system can be either 2 or 4 respectively. Both are undesired or inconsistent. This is a case of *data inconsistency* that resulted because of uncoordinated updates of a shared data by two concurrent processes. When two or more concurrent processes simultaneously update, the final value is unpredictable, depending on who updates last (like who wins the race). Hence, this is called a *race condition*.

Race conditions are an undesirable situation and must be avoided in concurrent execution.

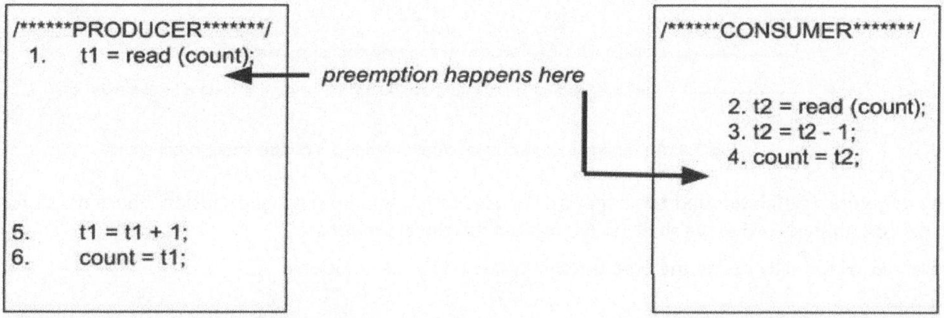

Fig 3.8: Example of a race condition

3.4 CRITICAL SECTIONS

A close look into the above example will reveal that even though the update within the *consumer* happened in one go in a coherent manner (no break in the sequence 2,3,4), it was not the case within the *producer.* Had the Step 1, 5, 6 been taken together continuously (without break), either before the Steps 2, 3, 4 or after Steps 2, 3, 4 - the data would have been consistent (count value would be 3 in either case at the end). In other words, the update needs to be indivisible or *atomic, i.e.,* if it has started, it must be complete, or it should be rolled back and should start afresh. The problem occurred as preemption was allowed within an update of a shared variable. Operating systems must ensure that shared variables are updated in an atomic manner - preemption should not happen while shared data is being modified. The section of code where a shared data is accessed is thus very critical - the section is called a *critical section (CS).* For example, where a database file is updated is a critical section. In the above example (**Fig 3.8**), both `count++` and `count--` statements are critical sections in their respective processes. When a shared variable is accessed in a process, the first instruction with which the access begins marks the start of a CS and the instruction where manipulation is complete marks the end of a CS. For a given shared variable, there can be several CS for it within a process. Also, for the same shared variable, there can be different CS in different processes. The length of a CS can vary depending on the type of data structure and its manipulation type. A process can have several critical sections related to a single or multiple shared objects.

3.5 MUTUAL EXCLUSION

Each access (read or write) to a critical section is to be ensured in a protected manner. Only one process should be allowed at a time to access a critical section shared by many processes. If some shared data is updated, then it should be done in an atomic way (either update should be complete or not done at all). While the update is in progress, no other processes should interfere but wait till it is complete. In other words, access to critical sections is to be done *mutually exclusively.*

Fig 3.9 shows an example of 3 cooperating processes A, B, C sharing a CS and all of them start concurrent execution at time t_0. Both process A and process C then attempt to get into a critical section at time t_1 . But only one of them can be allowed. A goes to execute in CS, when C must wait. C can start CS execution only when A leaves (at time t_2). But B can continue with normal (non-critical section) execution. At time t_3, process B wants to execute its CS, but it must wait since C is in CS. Process B can start once C leaves the CS at time t_4. The figure illustrates the difference between concurrent execution and execution of a CS. While normal execution can be concurrent or parallel, CS execution should only be done obeying mutual exclusion. When one process is in CS, other processes intending to go into the same CS must wait (either they block or loop around) to get into the CS - no effective execution takes place during that time for those processes (between time t_5 and t_6 for both A and C).

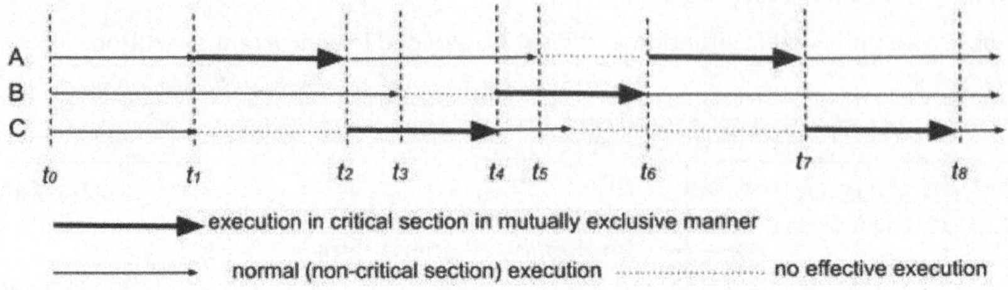

Fig 3.9: An example of mutual exclusion among 3 cooperating processes

There are several techniques and tools that an OS uses to implement mutual exclusion. There needs to be a few more desired properties that we shall discuss related to critical sections.

However, let us formally define the problem first followed by the solutions.

3.6 CRITICAL SECTION PROBLEM (CSP)

```
while (1) {

    entry section

    critical section

    exit section

    remainder section
}
```

Fig 3.10: critical section structure

Let us consider a system of *n* processes $P_0, P_1, \dots, P_{n-1}$ sharing at least a shared data item among them. Each of the processes has a critical section where the process accesses or modifies data that is shared with at least another process. As already discussed, no two processes should be allowed to access the CS at the same time. Any process that wants to access a CS must make a request to enter the CS. If there is no other process executing the CS, the requesting process will be allowed to enter the CS, otherwise it needs to wait. The section of code where the request is made, and the process is granted permission or needs to wait is called an *entry section.* Every CS will be preceded by an entry section. Similarly, when the execution of a CS is done by a process, some bookkeeping jobs need to be done, so that other processes waiting for permission to enter the CS, can enter in their CS. This portion of code where book-keeping work is done just after a CS is called an *exit section.* Every CS will be followed by an exit section. Other portions of the code in each of the processes are called the *remainder section* (**Fig 3.10**).

Any good solution to the critical section problem must have three following properties:

Mutual Exclusion: One and only one process is allowed to execute in a critical section corresponding to a shared data object at any time. In other words, access to the CS is done mutually exclusively. This is also known as the *safety* property.

Progress: If no process is executing in a CS, but some other process(es) want(s) to enter the CS, then the processes which are *not in the remainder section* (that means processes in either *entry* or *exit* or *critical sections*) will decide which process can enter in the CS next. Also, this decision must be taken within a bounded time. This is also known as *finite arbitration* or *liveness* property.

Bounded wait: Once a process has made a request to enter a critical section, there must be a limit or bound on how many times other processes can be allowed to enter the CS before the requesting process is granted access to enter the CS. This is also called the property of *starvation freedom.*

Property 1 is self-explanatory.

Property 2 ensures that every process gets a chance to enter a CS if it wants to. The decision as to which process will go into the CS next is taken by processes which are either in the entry section, critical section or exit section.

The processes which are in the remainder section have either already completed execution of the CS some time back and/or are not interested now in CS - hence these processes are excluded. The rest of the processes are immediate stakeholders and thus take part in the decision. The bound on the time ensures that the decision is actually taken and not indefinitely postponed for some reasons or other.

Property 3 ensures that the wait for going into a CS for every process is well defined. A process cannot go into a CS indiscriminately denying access to other processes.

All the three properties are necessarily satisfied in a solution to a CSP. Note that Property 2 does not necessarily ensure Property 3. For example, out of n processes in the system, a proper subset of n processes (say $P_0, P_1, \ldots, P_{i-1}$) can have a collusion to deprive another proper subset of processes (P_i, $P_{i+1}, P_{i+2}, \ldots, P_{n-1}$) entering into a CS ($0 < i < n$).

These three properties are essential ones of a good solution to a CSP. There are a few other desirable properties as well.

One of them is the property of *fairness* - i.e., there should not be any undue priority to any process for entering into the critical section when other processes are waiting. Fairness can be implemented in different ways like: *FCFS fairness* (no overtaking of a waiting process by another to enter a CS) or *LRU fairness* (the process that received the service least recently will get services next) etc.

3.7 SYNCHRONIZATION SOLUTIONS

Solutions to CSPs can be implemented in different ways and at different layers of abstractions. Some of the synchronization tools are available at the basic hardware level, extended hardware level or at different software levels. Some examples of solution tools or primitives are shown in **Fig 3.11**. While some are supportive tools, some are ready-made solutions based on some basic or extended tools. We shall discuss their implementation details below and analyse how many of the necessary and desirable criteria are satisfied by them.

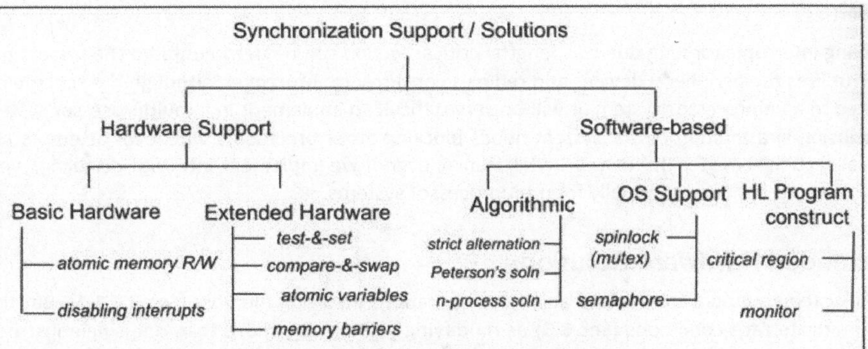

Fig 3.11: Different types of synchronization tools

3.7.1 Basic Hardware Solutions

Some synchronization services are obtained from the basic hardware like the memory units, processors and/or interrupts.

3.7.1.1 Atomic memory operations

Memory cells store the data which are read and written through machine instructions executed by the processor. Simultaneous access to different memory locations does not cause any synchronization issue, but on the same memory location may do. In a uniprocessor system, only one instruction can be executed by the processor at a single point in time. After invoking a memory read or memory write operation, the CPU stalls or blocks the process. It does not proceed until the memory operation is over. Hence, no other instructions from the same process can invoke the same memory access in a non-preemptive kernel. In a preemptive system, the CPU can go to other threads or other processes that can attempt to read or write from the same memory location. However, even in a preemptive kernel, only one memory operation is generally allowed at a time. When one memory read / write is going on, other attempts to the same memory location are blocked by the hardware. Another memory operation by the same or another process is allowed only after the current one is completed. Simultaneous attempts to memory access are, however, serialized in an arbitrary manner - whoever executes the memory operation instruction first, gets to access the memory. The memory operation is atomic - i.e., if it is started, the memory access hardware ensures that it is done in a mutually exclusive manner.

This atomic memory access feature is only basic, as it provides only mutual exclusion. It does not have any mechanism to ensure progress (Property 2) and bounded wait (Property 3). Also, often a critical section includes memory access to compound data structures involving several memory cells. Ensuring synchronization among simultaneous accesses to several memory cells is not trivial with only atomic memory access.

3.7.1.2 Disabling interrupts

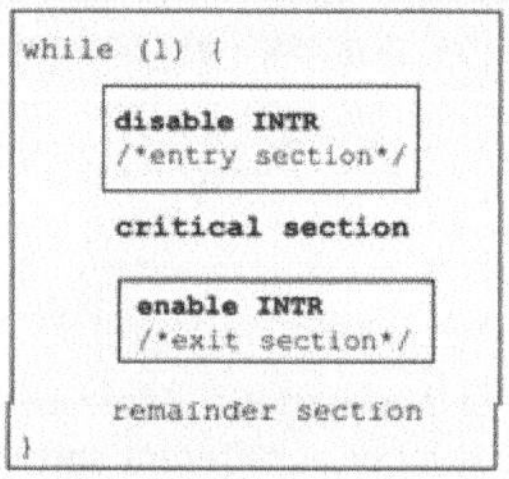

Fig 3.12: Disabling interrupts within process

One solution to stopping simultaneous attempts for accessing the same critical section can be dis-allowing preemption, i.e., not allowing any interrupts to occur during CS execution. However, disabling interrupts can only be done in kernel mode. Hence, user processes cannot implement it in user mode. Kernel processes can implement it by disabling interrupts from devices, timer or other processes (traps) in the entry section before going into the critical section. Again, after execution in CS is over, the process enables the interrupt so that interrupts from timer, other devices and processes can happen. Also, another kernel process can disable interrupt and enter the CS.

This scheme ensures *mutual exclusion*, but not *progress* and *bounded wait*. More than just disabling and enabling interrupts needs to be done in entry and exit sections respectively to achieve other properties.

Also, disabling interrupts for long due to a lengthy critical section can be detrimental to the system performance, as it under-utilizes the peripheral devices and reduces concurrency. Moreover, although the scheme can be easily implemented in a uniprocessor system, it will be very difficult to implement in a multiprocessor system. Ensuring mutual exclusion in a multiprocessor system needs blocking other processors whenever attempts to access the same critical section is made. This is non-trivial. Hence, even if we implement interrupt disabling, we need other synchronization mechanisms, especially for multiprocessor systems.

3.7.2 Extended Hardware Solutions

All modern systems support atomic load and store operations involving memory (**Sec 3.7.1.1**). But these are not enough to mitigate race conditions (**Sec 3.3**) as modifying value needs more than one single instruction. But, if increment / decrement of a variable can be made atomic, the race conditions arising in a shared variable (like `count` in **Sec 3.1.2.2**) could be solved. Based on the atomic load / store, several instructions are proposed that support two memory operations like read and write or read and test in one instruction cycle, hence two simultaneous operations are atomic. The operations cannot be divided, or preemption cannot happen in-between their execution. We shall discuss below a few such hardware instructions that can help implement atomic increment / decrement.

3.7.2.1 test-&-set lock (TSL)

```
boolean testAndset(boolean *val){
 boolean temp = *val;
 *val = true;
 return temp;
}
```

`testAndset()` is an instruction that tests and returns the value of its argument (type boolean) and sets its value if it was originally false.

If two or more processes attempt to execute `testAndset()` simultaneously, the instructions will be run atomically, but in an arbitrary manner. Whoever gets the first chance, will be able to set `val`. Others can check that it is already set.

3.7.2.2 compare-&-swap (CAS)

```
int compareAndswap(int *target, int exp, int newval){
 int temp = *target;

 if (*target == exp)  *val = newval;

 return temp;
}
```

`compareAndswap()` is another hardware instruction that compares values of two arguments (target variable with an expected one) and if they are equal, sets to a new value (third argument) and returns the original value of the target variable. CAS deals with integers.

Both these primitives can be used to implement mutual exclusion (**Fig 3.13**). All the processes that want to get into the critical section have the similar code and run concurrently. `lock` is a shared variable among the cooperating processes. `lock` is used to get exclusive access to the critical section and initialised to value false or zero (0).

```
/****** use of test-&-set ****/

while (1) {
     while (testAndset(&lock))
     ; /*entry section*/

     critical section

     lock = false; /*exit section */

     remainder section
}
```

(a)

```
/****** use of compare-&-swap ****/

while (1) {
     while (compareAndswap(&lock, 0, 1) != 0)
     ; /*entry section*/

     critical section

     lock = 0; /*exit section */

     remainder section
}
```

(b)

Fig 3.13: Implementation of mutual exclusion using extended hardware support (special instructions)

Variable `lock` in case of `testAndset` (**Fig 3.13a**) is checked in the entry section of every process. But whoever gets the first chance to set it (the *first* process finds false as the return value of `testAndset()`), can enter into the critical section. Other processes find the value of `testAndset()` as true and loops around in the entry section. When the first process completes the critical section, it resets the lock (making *lock = false*) in the exit section. Other processes then again can fight for entering the critical section. Only one process can set the lock and thus enter the critical section at a time. Hence mutual exclusion is ensured.

The implementation using `compareAndswap()` (**Fig 3.13b**) is exactly the same except the entry section where we replace `testAndset`. The `lock` initially has value 0. Hence the first process that executes `compareAndswap()`, finds return value 0, sets `lock = 1`, and enters CS. Other processes find 1 as the return value of `compareAndswap()` and loop in the entry section. After CS execution is done, in the exit section, lock is reset to 0 to allow other waiting processes to acquire the lock and enter their CS. Mutual exclusion is thus ensured.

Both the implementation also ensures that which process can go into the CS next is decided by processes in the entry and exit section only. Hence, progress is also ensured by both. But there is no guarantee on which process among several contenders will get the chance to go into the CS. There is a possibility that a group of processes are deprived if they cannot acquire the lock. Hence bounded wait is not met by the above implementation.

We shall see later implementations that meet all necessary properties, but that involves other shared data-structures and their orderly management.

3.7.2.3 Atomic variables

Synchronizing instruction like CAS is not typically used directly for mutual exclusion. Rather, CAS is more used in implementing atomic increment or decrement of a variable (Remember that an increment / decrement of a shared variable like `count` can cause a race condition in **Sec 3.1.2.2**). A function for atomic decrement for an integer `var` can be called within a program as:

```
decrement (&var);
```

```
void decrement(atomic_int *v)
{
    int tmp;

    do {
    tmp = *v;
    } while (tmp != compareAndswap(v, tmp, tmp-1));
}
```

The function can be implemented in the following way. The value var is decremented only once by only one process that tried to execute the CAS first.

The increment can also be done in the same manner. This implementation can ensure atomic updates: no two processes can update at the same time.

CAVEAT*: *This may not always mitigate the race condition. For example, in the bounded buffer implementation of multiple producers-consumers problem, if a producer produces one message and puts it in the empty buffer, two or more consumers can come out of the while loop (busy wait loop) in the entry section if busy wait checks are not done in mutual exclusion (**Fig 3.4c**) before doing any modification in the buffer. But only one process can consume, others will not. Nevertheless, the system will be in an inconsistent state or race condition.*

3.7.2.4 Memory barriers

Modern processors and/or compilers can reorder the instructions when they seem to be independent to each other. For example, consider the following case involving two threads (**Fig 3.14**) that share the following data initialized globally as:

```
boolean flag = false;
int x = 0;
```

```
/******Thread 1 ****/
while (!flag)
;
display x;
```

(a)

```
/******Thread 2 ****/
X = 10;
flag = true;
```

(b)

Fig 3.14: Data sharing by two threads and instruction reordering

Here, Thread 1 is supposed to print 10 as it should be in a busy wait state due to the while loop initially and can proceed only after Thread 2 executes. This is the expected behaviour.

But if the processor / compiler does *instruction reordering* in Thread 2, `flag` may be set to `true` before x = 10. If the thread-switch happens immediately after the flag is set, Thread 1 can show 0, not expected behavior.

If instruction reordering happens in Thread 1, not in Thread 2: i.e., `x` is printed before `flag`, `x` can display 0, again another undesired behavior.

In a shared memory multiprocessor environment, this kind of instruction reordering involving memory load / store can lead to inconsistency. To mitigate, a hardware instruction is used that propagates any memory updates within a processor to all other threads running on other processors. These instructions are called *memory barriers* or *memory fences.* When a memory barrier is executed, the system ensures that all load and store instructions are completed and visible to other processors before any subsequent load or store can happen. The memory barriers are thus used to synchronize events across processors. To revisit our example above, *memory barriers* can ensure that the `flag` is checked before printing `x` in Thread 1. Also, `x` is guaranteed to get updated before the `flag` is set in Thread 2 (**Fig 3.15**).

```
/******Thread 1 ****/
while (!flag)
 memory_barrier();
display x;
```

```
/******Thread 2 ****/
x = 10;
memory_barrier();
flag = true;
```

(a) (b)

Fig 3.15: Use of memory barrier to stop instruction reordering

These hardware supports for synchronization do not directly provide solutions to CSP. But they are used to design solutions. Nevertheless, their use is limited to kernel processes, as user level processes cannot directly access these hardware tools and instructions.

3.7.3 Algorithmic Solutions

Algorithmic solutions to CSP fall within the broad category of software solutions. However, they are built on the hardware support and use some of the hardware synchronization primitives. We start with a 2-process scenario and then generalize to a n -process case $(n > 2)$.

3.7.3.1 Strict Alternation

A simple or naive solution to 2-process CSP is to alternately allow the processes to enter CSP in a mutually exclusive manner. The solution uses a single shared boolean control variable `turn`, and two local boolean variables `self` and `other`. The general solution is given in terms of i-th process P_i where i = 0 or 1. (**Fig 3.16a**).

```
shared volatile boolean turn = 0;
const boolean self = i;
constant boolean other = 1 - i;

while (1) {

 while (turn != self)
  ; /*entry section */

 <critical section>

turn = other; /*exit section */

}
```

```
turn = 0;
self = 0;
other = 1;

while (1) {

 while (turn != self)
 ;/*entry section*/

 <critical section>

  turn = other;
 /*exit section */
}
```

```
turn = 0;
self = 1;
other = 0;

while (1) {

 while (turn != self)
  ;/*entry section*/

 <critical section>

  turn = other;
 /*exit section */
}
```

(a) Process P_i (b) Process P_0 (c) Process P_1

Fig 3.16: Strict Alternation for 2-process CSP

The two processes are assumed to have similar structure and are running similar code concurrently. The variable `turn` denotes whose turn it is to go into the critical section and is initialized to 0 (there is no harm if it is initialized to 1). Variable `self` denotes the own process number and the `other` the counterpart. In the entry section, both the processes check whether the `turn` is set for it or not (**Fig 3.16b** or **Fig 3.16c**). If not, it is in the busy wait loop, otherwise it can execute the critical section. In the exit section, the process that executed the critical section, changes the value in `turn` so that the other process can enter CS next. Since turn can be either 0 or 1 at a given moment, only one process can enter and execute CS. Hence mutual execution is satisfied. Progress is also ensured as the exit section changes the turn to the other process. Bounded wait is also met as for any process wait time is maximum 1 process as processes alternately execute CS if both want to execute CS.

Even though all 3 necessary conditions are satisfied, it assumes that both processes would like to enter CS all the time. That is not a realistic situation. Consider a case when one of processes (say P0) does not want to enter CS, but turn is set to 0. Now the other process (here, P1) cannot enter CS, even though it wants to get into the CS. This will cause indefinite wait for the process wanting to get into the CS. Hence, progress will not be ensured in case one of the processes does not want to get into the CS. Also, after executing a CS, a process cannot go into the CS next time, if the other process does not execute the CS in between.

Variable `turn` is declared as a volatile type to notify that turn should not be reordered by compilers - as reordering the instructions involving update to `turn` can cause indefinite wait also (see **Sec 3.7.2.4**).

3.7.3.2 The Peterson Solution

To take into consideration the intent of the process to enter CS, two flag variables are introduced in Peterson's solution to 2-process CSP. Remaining parts of the solution are almost like earlier naive solution to 2-process CSP (**Fig 3.17**).

```
shared volatile boolean turn = 0;
Shared volatile boolean flag[2] = 0;

while (1) {
   flag[i] = 1;
   turn = 1 - i;

   while (flag[1-i] && turn == 1-i)
     ; /*entry section */

  <critical section>

  flag[i] = 0; /*exit section */
}
```

(a) Process P_i

```
turn = 0;
flag[0]=0; flag[1]=0;

while (1) {
 flag[0] = 1;
 turn = 1;
 while (flag[1] &&
turn == 1)
 ;/*entry section*/

<critical section>

  flag[0] = 0;
 /*exit section */
}
```

(b) Process P_0

```
turn = 0;
Flag[0] = 0; flag[1]=0;

while (1) {
 flag[1] = 1;
 turn = 0;
 while (flag[0] && turn
== 0)
 ;/*entry section*/

  <critical section>

  flag[1] = 0;
 /*exit section */
}
```

(c) Process P_1

Fig 3.17: Peterson's solution to 2-process CSP

Both the flag variables and `turn` are boolean shared variables, and not intended to be reordered by compilers (declared volatile). They are all initialized to 0 (the algorithm will behave the same with other initialisations also). In the entry section, the process sets its intent flag, but turn is set for the other process, as if for courtesy (compare **Fig 3.17b** and **Fig 3.17c**). For concurrent executions, nobody knows which process will set the turn variable last that will prevail. If the other process intends to enter CS (as available in `flag[1-i]`), the process loops in a busy wait and lets the other process go into CS. Since `turn` can be either 0 or 1 at a moment, only one process can enter CS. Hence, mutual exclusion is met. Also, if the other process does not intend to go into the CS, irrespective of the value of `turn`, the process can enter CS. Hence, progress is also ensured. In the exit section, a process resets its intent flag so that the other process, if intending, can enter CS. Hence bounded wait is also satisfied.

3.7.3.3 *n* - process Solution ($n > 2$)

The above solutions do not work for n-process CSP ($n > 2$) as they are built based on alternation principle. For n- processes, we need the following shared variable:

```
shared boolean volatile flag[n] = false;
shared boolean volatile lock = 0;
```

The scheme is shown in **Fig 3.18**. The first one is for any process P_i ($0 \leq i \leq n-1$). The second and third are for specifically two example processes P0 and Pn-1 respectively. The flag variable is defined for each of the *n* processes that notifies the intent of any process to get into the CS. It can be modified inside any process. The shared variable `lock` needs to be set (=1) to get into the CS.

In the entry section, every process sets its flag variable and then tests the lock within the hardware primitive *`test-&-set`* (one can use CAS also). If the lock was not acquired (lock = 0), a process gains it (lock = 1) invoking `test-`

&-set().The TSL returns 0 and gets into CS by breaking the busy-wait while loop. Since TSL is an atomic operation, only the first process can set the lock uninterrupted, out of several simultaneous contenders. Other processes will get return value 1 and will loop around in the busy-wait state. Hence *mutual exclusion is ensured.*

while (1) {
flag[i] = true;
 	
while (flag[i] &&
testAndset (&lock));
/*busy-wait*/
flag[i] = false;
 	
<critical section>
 	
j = (i + 1) % n;
while ((j != i) && !flag[j])
j = (j + 1) % n;
 	
if (j == i)
lock = 0;
else
flag[j] = false;
 	
/ remainder section */*
}
	while (1) {
	flag[0] = true;
	
	while (flag[0] &&
	testAndset(&lock)); /*busy-wait*/
	flag[0] = false;
	
	<critical section>
	
	j = (0 + 1) % n;
	while ((j != 0) && !flag[j])
	j = (j + 1) % n;
	
	if (j == 0)
	lock = 0;
	else
	flag[j] = false;
	
	/ remainder section */*
	}
		while (1) {
		flag[n-1] = true;
		
		while (flag[n-1] &&
		testAndset(&lock)); /*busy-wait*/
		flag[n-1] = false;
		
		<critical section>
		
		j = (n) % n;
		while ((j != n-1) && !flag[j])
		j = (j + 1) % n;
		
		if (j == n-1)
		lock = 0;
		else
		flag[j] = false;
		
		/ remainder section */*
		}

P_i	P_0 ...	P_{n-1}

Fig 3.18: ***n*-process algorithmic solution to CSP**

The process getting into the CS voluntarily resets its intent flag in the entry section. This ensures that the process executing CS now will not try to have another turn immediately.

In the exit section, the algorithm finds the next intending process to go into the CS in a principled manner. The next process is the intending process (flag[j) is set) with higher process-id in the circular sequence {0, 1, 2, ..., n-1}. If one is found, its intent flag is reset as that process is certainly looping in busy-wait condition in the entry section of process Pj. Such process Pj can thus come out of the while loop and enter the CS. The lock seems to be transferred to the process Pj. If we cannot find one among the remaining processes (j==i), the lock is reset (=0) so that any process that intends to go into the CS in future, can acquire the lock.

If the flag[j] is already reset in the exit section, again resetting it within the entry section of process Pj is redundant. But we do not know how the process comes into the CS. Also, this redundant action does not harm but helps *achieve progress.*

The implementation ensures checking the turn in a circular fashion all the processes with id 0, 1, 2, ..., n-1. Hence, no process waits more than (n-1) times, after it notifies its intent to go into CS and before it actually gets the chance. Hence, the *bounded wait is also met.*

Like earlier, the updates on the shared variables flag[j] and lock are very important, and they are to be done in the given order in all the processes. *Instruction reordering* can create race conditions and affect synchronization. Hence, we declared them as volatile.

3.7.4 Operating System Support

Hardware primitives are neither available to the programmers for synchronizing user processes, nor are they easy to use even for kernel processes. Operating systems use the hardware tools to implement some easy-to-use synchronizing tools for the application developers. We shall discuss two such types below.

3.7.4.1 Mutex locks

Mutex is the acronym of **mut**ual **ex**clusion. A mutex lock is a simple synchronization tool designed to ensure mutual exclusion of two or more processes sharing a critical section. It can be thought of as a simple data structure containing a boolean variable, say `avail`. The variable `avail` is initialised as `true`. A mutex lock allows two simple operations: `acquire()` and `release()`. The `mut_lock` is acquired (only if `avail` is `true`) by a process before going into a CS, and released (`avail` is set to `true`) when the execution in the CS is done (**Fig 3.19**). Operation `acquire()` resets the variable `avail` (=false) so that other processes that want to execute CS loops around in the busy wait condition. However, if a process that holds the lock releases it, another process can acquire and go into the CS.

```
typedef struct {
boolean avail;
} mut_lock;
```

(a) Definition of a mutex lock

```
acquire(){
   while (!avail);
    /* busy wait */

avail = false;
}
```

(b) Acquiring a mutex lock

```
release(){
avail = true;
}
```

(c) Releasing a mutex lock

Fig 3.19: Definition of a simple mutex lock and its implementational prototype

The two operations `acquire()` and `release()` are considered atomic. They can be implemented using hardware primitives like TSL or CAS.

This type of mutex locks has a busy-wait loop where a process intending to go into CS loops around. These are also, therefore, called **spinlocks.**

NOTE: *Even though we encountered busy-wait loops before, spinlocks are different from them. In spinlocks we check only the lock variable* `avail`*, whereas in other busy-waiting loops we can have a predicate involving one or more variables. Thus, spinlocks are simpler to check, and computationally lighter.*

But still spinlocks are not good from the performance point of view. The process interested to go into a CS, spins to get a lock and wastes CPU cycles. For a single-core system, it cannot be also implemented, as that will require context switches within atomic operations.

Nonetheless, spinlocks are beneficial when critical sections are very small needing mutual exclusion for only short duration. A thread can `spin' on acquiring a lock in a processing core when another thread can execute the critical section on another core of a multi-core processor. This obviates the need of blocking a process for mutual exclusion and causing a context switch which is costly in terms of time and other logistics.

3.7.4.2 Semaphores

Semaphores are improvements and generalizations over mutex locks. A semaphore S can be considered as an integer variable that is, after initialisation, accessed and updated only by two atomic operations `wait()` and `signal()` **(Fig 3.20).** The semaphore integer variable (`val`) keeps track of simultaneous access to a critical section that can be allowed. It is initialized with an integer indicating maximum of such simultaneous accesses (often simultaneous reads to a CS data item is allowed, but simultaneous read & write are to be done mutually exclusively). `wait()` allows the use of a semaphore and decrements `val`. When no more simultaneous access is allowed (`val` <=0), a process spins in busy-wait. `signal()` increments semaphore value to allow other waiting processes to use the semaphore. `wait()` is also known as **down()** or **P()** (short of Dutch term *proberen* meaning 'to test') and `signal()` as **up()** or **V()** (short for Dutch term *verhogen* meaning to increment) in the literature.

```
typedef struct {
int val;
} semaphore;

semaphore S;
```

(a) Definition of a semaphore

```
wait(S){
  while (S.val <=0);
      /* busy wait */

  S.val-- ;
}
```

(b) waiting with busy probing

```
signal(S){
S.val++;
}
```

(c) semaphore release

Fig 3.20: Simple definition of semaphore and its basic operations

Semaphore types

There are two types of semaphore.

A **counting semaphore** allows multiple but limited number of processes to simultaneously access a shared resource (including reading). When non-negative, the semaphore value represents how many more processes can still be *allowed to simultaneously access a shared resource.* When negative, *semaphore shows the number of processes* waiting to access the shared resource.

A restricted type is the **binary semaphore** that is like a mutex lock. Its `val` thus can be 0 or 1. However, mutex lock (or spinlock) is different from binary semaphore in that mutex requires the same process to unlock it that locked it. On the other hand, binary semaphores are operated by any process that has access to it (not necessarily the same process).

Implementation of a semaphore

As mentioned earlier, busy-wait is a wastage of CPU time. Instead of spinning, a process can rather block and have a context switch to let other processes execute when its competitor(s) are executing in CS. The semaphores, therefore, get rid of busy wait loops by maintaining a list of such blocked processes. Necessary changes in the implementation are shown in **Fig 3.21**.

```
typedef struct {
int val;
struct process *list;
} semaphore;

semaphore *S;
```

(a) Definition of a semaphore

```
sem_wait(S){
  S→val--;
  if (S→val < 0) {
    add this process to S→list;
    sleep();}
}
```

(b) wait without busy loop

```
sem_signal(S) {
   S→val++;
if (S→val <= 0) {
remove process P from S→list;
wakeup(P);}
}
```

(c) signal

Fig 3.21: A semaphore and its implementational prototype

A semaphore is always initialized with a non-negative integer. Then its value is inspected and updated only by two functions. In the wait function `sem_wait()`, semaphore value is decremented first and then the calling process is blocked, if the semaphore value becomes negative. The blocked processes wake up only through a call of signal function (`sem_signal()`) invoked by some other process. In the signal function, semaphore value is incremented first and if it becomes non-positive (≤ 0), a blocked process is woken up and allowed to continue. The list of processes is implemented using a pointer to the linked list of PCBs of blocked processes.

The two functions `sem_wait()` and `sem_signal()` must be executed atomically. In other words, these functions can also be considered critical sections for a semaphore. Hence, they must be implemented using disabling interrupts (Sec **3.7.1.2**) or CAS or mutex locks. Implementation of the semaphores needs judicious consideration of processor architecture (single-core or SMP multi-core or heterogeneous) and basic hardware synchronization primitives.

Use of semaphores

Semaphores are offered by OS to ease the job of synchronization for application programmers. Primary use is in mutual exclusion of a critical section (CS) among a set of cooperating processes. A binary semaphore `s` is initialized with value 1. The process that wants to execute a CS, calls `sem_wait(s)` in the entry section. If no other process is in CS, it can go into the CS. In the exit section, it calls `sem_signal(s)` to let others go (**Fig 3.22a**). The code looks simpler and tidy from the application programmers' end.

A binary semaphore can also be used for ensuring serialization of events, tasks or statements. Suppose we want to ensure that statement S_1 of process P_1 need to execute before the statement S_2 of the process P_2 where both processes are running concurrently (recall the problem of using a *memory barrier* as it needs kernel access in **Sec 3.7.2.4**). We can do the following implementation using a semaphore `sync`, initialized to 0 (**Fig 3.22b**). Since `sync` has initial value 0, P_2 will block due to `sem_wait()` and cannot execute S_2 in P_2. Once S1 in P_1 is executed and then `sem_signal()` increments the semaphore `sync`, S_2 in P_2 can execute.

```
sem_wait(s); /*entry section */

<critical section>

sem_signal(s); /*exit section */
```

(a) Semaphore for mutual exclusion

`/* process P1 */`	`/* process P2 */`
`S1;` `sem_signal(sync);`	`sem_wait(sync);` `S2;`

(b) Semaphore for serializing sentences

Fig 3.22: Illustrative uses of semaphores

Counting semaphores are often used for managing simultaneous access of a resource by more than one process. A counting semaphore can keep track of the accesses to resources that have multiple instances like scanners, printers, shared buffers, files etc. and can stop further attempts when the maximum limit is reached.

We shall soon see more use of semaphores in solving some of the classical critical section problems.

3.7.5 Programming Language Constructs

The synchronizing tools discussed so far are elementary in nature. The hardware tools are the most basic and are used to develop little more sophisticated ones. But, even then, tools like mutex lock, spinlock or semaphores do not provide ready-made solutions to CSPs. They need to be intelligently used along with their associated functions. Little sloppiness in their use can cause problems like the following silly mistakes in **Fig 3.23.**

```
sem_wait(s); /*entry section */

<critical section>

sem_wait(s); /*exit section */
```

(a) Wrong use of semaphore for mutual exclusion

`/* process P1 */`	`/* process P2 */`
`S1;` `sem_wait(sync);`	`sem_signal(sync);` `S2;`

(b) Wrong use of semaphore for serializing sentences

Fig 3.23: Examples of wrong uses of semaphores

In **Fig 3.23a,** instead of `sem_signal()`, if `sem_wait()` is again invoked by mistake, other processes waiting in the blocked state or looping around in the busy-waiting state can not come out and execute the CS - this will cause *starvation* to them. Or as in **Fig 3.23b,** if `sem_wait()` and `sem_signal()` are interchanged by mistake, the intended ordering of sentences S_1 and S_2 will not be ensured. There can be several such errors like omission of invoking a `sem_wait()` or `sem_signal()` or invoking with wrong semaphore name etc. Note that this kind of silly mistakes, or unintentional errors on the part of developers are very commonplace, and not detectable during compilation. We shall get *undesired results in an irregular fashion* (synchronization issues only come up occasionally depending on dynamic conditions of several processes). Hence, they are not easily reproducible and are very difficult to detect and debug.

Different programming languages provide a few synchronization primitives built on the elementary tools. These high-level primitives relieve the developers from the hassle of painstakingly invoking the correct procedures with correct parameters every time.

Below we mention two broad such categories.

3.7.5.1 Critical Regions

A critical region is a region consisting of one or more critical sections. General construct of a critical region is like:

"region cr do S;"

cr is the critical region variable, S is a critical section. cr ensures that S is executed in mutual exclusion. If several processes want to execute a critical region with the same critical region variable, only one will execute at a time mutually exclusively. However, critical sections belonging to different critical regions can run concurrently. Compiler of the language takes care of the mutual exclusion. This kind of critical region is called unconditional.

Unconditional critical regions are not always sufficient to meet the requirement of an application. For example, if a process within a critical region wants to check the value of a shared variable and based on the value it can proceed or block. This needs a special provision that the **Conditional Critical Region** provides. General construct of this primitive is as follows.

"region cr do S_1; ... **await (E)** .... S_n;"

The entire set of statements "S_1; ... **await (E)** .... S_n;" is a critical section within the critical region and cr is the condition variable here. **await** is a new synchronization primitive that will check the boolean expression **E** and either proceed or block within the critical section based on the evaluated value of the expression **E**. If the process blocks within a critical section, it sleeps on an event queue of cr and allows the critical region to be used by another process. When the event happens due to execution in another process, and the first process gains access, the blocked process can resume the critical section.

In case of an unconditional critical region, the expression E needs to be checked and then block is implemented using a busy-wait loop - a scheme that wastes CPU cycles. **await()** in a conditional critical region helps implement this without the busy-wait loop.

3.7.5.2 Monitors

Monitors are more powerful and sophisticated tools than critical regions provided by programming languages. They can be considered as abstract data types (ADT) that encapsulate both data and methods, resembling objects in C++ or Java. A user can define her own monitor based on her need using the prototype as given in **Fig 3.24a.** Each monitor has the provision of defining a set of shared variables that can represent the states of the monitor, a set of condition variables whose values determine the progress of the monitor, and a set of functions that can be executed in a mutually exclusive manner. A process enters a monitor by invoking a function or method within it. Within an invoked function, the parameters, shared variables and condition variables defined can be accessed. A condition variable here is like that in a conditional critical region. The variable determines whether to proceed in execution of the monitor-function that it is executing or to block, based on the value of the variable. Since only one of the monitor functions is active at a given time, and no other functions from the same monitor can be active that time, several processes can wait or block to enter a given monitor. Again, within a monitor-function, a process can check a condition variable and block itself. This condition variable is a shared variable on which several processes can block. Hence, there can be two sets of blocked processes. One set of blocked processes have not entered the monitor (called *inactive* processes) and another set of processes that are within the monitor (and hence, *active*) but blocked on condition variables. Inactive processes can enter a monitor when no other processes are active in the monitor. They are not directly dependent on any control variable.

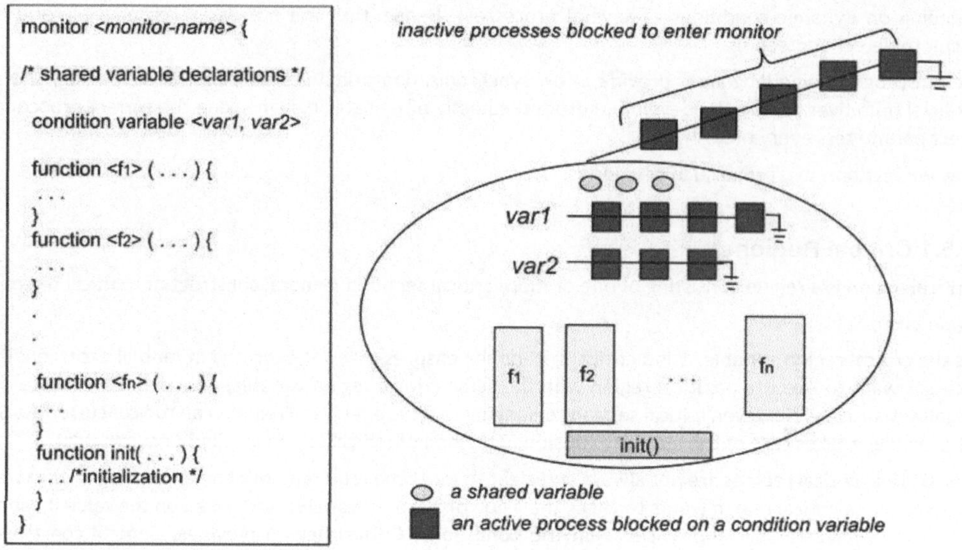

a) structure of a monitor

b) conceptual diagram of a monitor

Fig 3.24: A monitor and condition variables and blocked processes

Each condition variable x within a monitor is associated with two functions: *x.wait()* and *x.signal()*. Very much like a semaphore, *x.wait()* blocks an active process running within a monitor. *x.signal()* wakes up a blocked active process, if any. If there are no blocked processes, *x.signal()* does not have any effect (unlike normal semaphore). However, once a *x.signal()* is invoked by a process (say A) and there is a process (say B) waiting on *x.wait()*, a pertinent question is: which process can start execution inside the monitor immediately?

There are two possible answers as strategies given below.

1. *Signal and wait:* Process A signals and then waits until B completes execution in the monitor.

2. *Signal and continue:* Process A signals and continues while process B waits until A completes execution in the monitor.

Any one of the strategies is followed in an implementation. However, both have their advantages and disadvantages and are used in different implementations. Java, C# support monitors.

Implementation of a monitor using semaphores

Monitors can be implemented using semaphores. Two sets of semaphores are needed. One set is to ensure mutual exclusion among processes using a monitor. One among them is a binary semaphore (say `mutex`, initialized to 1). When a process enters the monitor, it invokes `wait(mutex)` and when it leaves the monitor, it invokes `signal(mutex)`.

However, there are two categories of processes waiting in two different types of queues. While one is outside the monitor waiting in a queue to enter the monitor, the other is a set of active processes inside the monitor that are waiting on different condition variables. Now depending on the scheme (*signal-and-wait* or *signal-and-continue)* we need to also make the mutual exclusion among two processes signalling and then signalled ones.

If we consider the *signal-and-wait* scheme, then we need another binary semaphore (say *next,* initialized to 0) to make the signalling process wait and resume the next process (signalled). We also need to keep track of the count

```
wait(mutex);
  ...
<monitor-function>;
  ...
if (next_count >0)
    signal(next);
else
   signal  (mutex);
```

Fig 3.25: An implementation of monitor using semaphores

of such processes that have signalled and are waiting. Let us consider such a variable as `next_count`. Hence, a call to the monitor will look like **Fig 3.25**. The process will enter after making a wait call on `mutex`. After execution of the monitor function, it will signal `next` if there are other waiting processes inside the monitor. If not, then `mutex` will be signalled to allow other processes waiting outside the monitor.

Now, for each condition variable (say x), we need to implement x.wait() and x.signal(). For each such x, a binary semaphore sem_x (initialized to 0) can be used with an counter variable x_count. An illustrative x.wait() and x.signal() is shown in **Fig 3.26**.

For wait due to x, x_count increases. If there are other processes inside the monitor waiting (`next_count >0`) they are woken up. Otherwise, processes waiting outside the monitor are allowed to enter the monitor. The calling process then goes to wait for the condition variable x.

For signal from x, we need to see how many processes are waiting on x. If there is at least one, then we need to wake up the process. Also, the calling process will exercise signal-and-wait. hence `next_count` is incremented first and then the processing on x is woken up. The calling process itself goes to wait.

```
/*** x.wait() ***/

x_count++;

if (next_count > 0)
   signal (next);
else
   signal(mutex);

wait(sem_x);
x_count--;
```

```
/*** x.signal() ***/

if (x_count > 0){
        next_count++ ;

        signal (sem_x);

        wait (next);
        next_count-- ;
}
```

Fig 3.26: Illustrative implementation of condition variable actions of a monitor

3.7.6 Solutions without enforcing mutual exclusion

In some applications, it is difficult to ensure mutual exclusion, especially in distributed systems involving several processors and communication networks with uncontrolled delays. [RK79][8] proposed two synchronization primitives that can be used to design solutions to CSP without enforcing mutual exclusion. Instead of protecting the manipulation of shared variables that control ordering of events through mutual exclusion, the scheme directly orders the events through two primitives as briefly described below.

3.7.6.1 EventCounts

Eventcounts are abstract objects that take integer values to keep track of occurrences of events. Each *eventcount* corresponds to events of a particular event-type. There are three operations defined on an *eventcount* E,

i. $advance(E)$: increments the value of E by 1. It indicates occurrence of an event of a particular event type.
ii. $await(E, v)$: blocks the calling process until E reaches the value v.
iii. $read(E)$: reads the current value E.

Eventcounts are initialized to 0 and then operated by these primitive operations inside the cooperating processes. However, these operations may happen concurrently in an uncontrolled manner and need not be done mutually exclusively.

[8] http://www.cs.uml.edu/~bill/cs515/Eventcounts_Sequencers_Reed_Kanodia_79.pdf (as on 23-Sep-2022)

3.7.6.2 Sequencers

Sequencers, like eventcounts, are abstract objects but are needed to ensure ordering of a set of events of a particular type. Often, we need to know which of the several processes should execute an event first (e.g., simultaneous write attempts), as that can decide other follow-up events. A *sequencer* S ensures sequencing a set of events by issuing tokens (a token is a sequence number that we come across for getting services in banks, bakery, reservation counters etc.). The operation defined on the abstract object *S* is `ticket (S)` that always generates non-negative integers (*S* is initialised to 0). Two calls to `ticket(S)` will give two different numbers that indicate serial numbers of their operations.

While eventcounts can be used independently for handling concurrent processes, sequencers are always used along with eventcounts, especially to ensure mutual exclusion.

Solutions to several standard critical section problems (CSPs) can be designed using eventcounts and the combination of eventcounts and sequencers. Even synchronizing tools like semaphores can be designed using the two primitives as illustrated in **Fig. 3.27.** A semaphore S should have an eventcount S.E and a sequencer S.T. The initial value of the eventcount before calling the *sem_wait()* is represented by S.I.

```
sem_wait(S){
  int t = ticket (S.T);
  await (S.E, t - S.I);
}
```

```
sem_signal(S){
  advance(S.E);
}
```

Fig 3.27: Implementation of semaphore using an eventcount and a sequencer

3.8 CLASSICAL IPC PROBLEMS

With necessary background on the interprocess communication, synchronization, critical section problems and their solution attempts using different synchronizing tools, we discuss a few classical IPC problems where there are a few CSPs. Let us describe the problems and their solutions.

3.8.1 The Producer-Consumer Problem

This is a classic problem found in many systems across the domains where a component produces some items or objects and stores them in a place one after another from where they are picked up (or consumed) in the same order by another component of the system downstream **(Fig 3.28)**. The buffer is accessed in FIFO (first-in-first-out) manner. The producer-consumer problem can have different forms and flavours as given below.

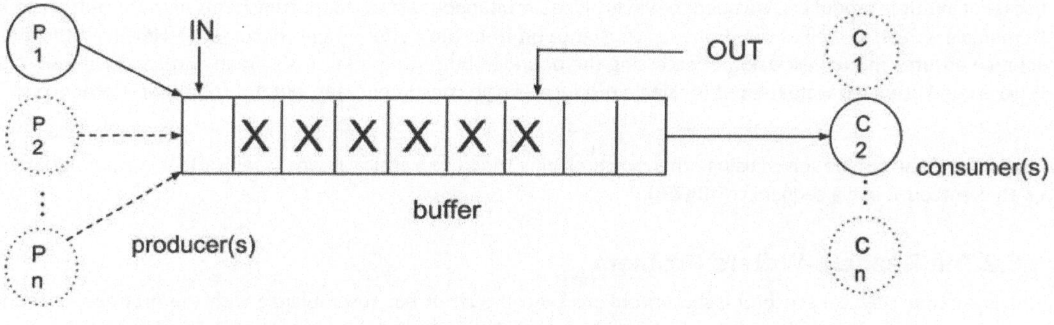

Fig 3.28: Producer-Consumer Model

Based on the IPC mechanism, it can follow

- *Synchronous communication*: the producer produces only when the consumer is ready to consume.
- *Asynchronous communication:* the producer(s) produces at its own speed and puts the items in a buffer from where the consumer(s) picks them at its own speed.

Depending on the buffer type, the problem may have

- *Unbounded buffer:* The producer produces without any bound or limit and puts items onto a buffer of infinite capacity.
- *Bounded buffer:* Buffer size is fixed; the producer stops when the buffer is full. It can only resume when at least one item is consumed from the full buffer.

Recall that in **Sec 3.1.2.2**, we discussed a single producer-single consumer problem and tried to solve it using a bounded-buffer circular message queue in **Fig 3.4**. The producer and consumer can simultaneously access the buffer asynchronously. As long as the buffer contains some items, there will not be any problems. However, the producer must stop when the buffer is full and loops around in a busy-wait state. Similarly, the consumer must be in busy-wait when the buffer is empty. These two extreme cases lead to wasteful busy-wait CPU cycles. However, that can be avoided with the use of semaphores. Also, the bounded buffer is concurrently accessed by both the producer and the consumer. Access to each slot in the buffer should happen in mutual exclusion, otherwise there can be race conditions. Mutual exclusion can be implemented using semaphores. An example solution to the producer-consumer problem is given in **Fig 3.29** using two counting semaphores `empty` and `full` and a binary semaphore `mutex`.

```
/** Common data structures and initialisations **/

constant n  = #slots in the buffer;/*BUFFERSIZE*/

semaphore empty = n;  /*counts empty slots */
semaphore full = 0;   /*counts occupancy */
semaphore mutex = 1;  /*mut-ex access to slots*/
```

```
/****PRODUCER *****/

while (true) {
   ...
/* produce next item */
   ...
   sem_wait (empty);
   sem_wait (mutex);
   ...
/* put next item in buffer */
   ...
   sem_signal (mutex);
   sem_signal (full);
}
```

```
/****CONSUMER *****/

while (true) {
   sem_wait (full);
   sem_wait (mutex);
   ...
/*pick first item from buffer*/
   ...
   sem_signal (mutex);
   sem_signal (empty);
   ...
/*  consume picked-up item */
   ...
}
```

Fig 3.29: Solution to the producer-consumer problem using semaphores

In case of multiple producers, we need to synchronize simultaneous access for putting items onto the buffer (similar to multiple writes) as well as simultaneous consumption from the buffer by the consumer(s). However, the above solution ensures mutual exclusion of accessing the bounded buffer, no matter how many processes are involved. Progress and bounded wait are met for single producer-single consumer cases, but not for multiple producers.

The problem can also be solved using other synchronizing tools like a critical region (see [Hal15]), a monitor ([Sta12]) or an eventcount and a sequencer ([RK79]).

3.8.2 The Readers-Writers Problem

This is another classical synchronization problem. Even though it has resemblance with the producer-consumer problem, here the shared object is treated as a single unit. The unit can be a database record, a file, a memory block or even a set of processor registers. The shared unit can be read simultaneously by several processes (or threads) without any harm but cannot be concurrently read & written. Also, simultaneous writes cannot be allowed. Hence mutual exclusion is needed between read and write as well as between simultaneous write attempts. Also, the problem has two variations based on the priorities between the readers and the writers. If one or more readers wait along with one or more writers: either the readers can be given priority or the writers.

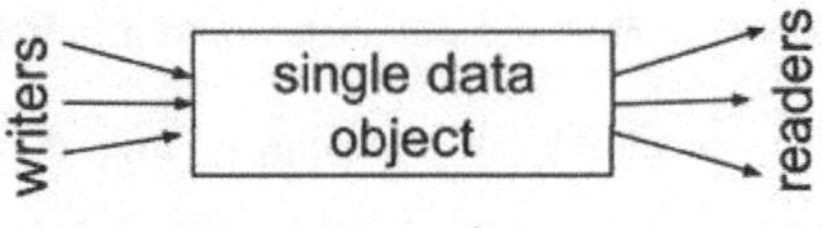


```
/** Common data structures and initialisations **/

semaphore rw_mutex = 1;  /* b/w read & write */
int r_count =0;          /* #simultaneous reads */
semaphore mutex = 1;     /* for update r_count */
```

```
/****WRITER ****/

while (true) {

   sem_wait (rw_mutex);

   ...
  <write operation>
   ...

   sem_signal (rw_mutex);

}
```

```
/****READER *****/
while (true) {
    sem_wait (mutex);
    r_count++;

    if (r_count ==1)
      sem_wait (rw_mutex);
    sem_signal (mutex);
    ...
    <read operation>
    ...
    sem_wait (mutex);
    r_count - -;

    if (r_count ==0)
      sem_signal (rw_mutex);

    sem_signal (mutex);
}
```

Fig 3.30: Solution to the readers-writers problem (readers' priority) using semaphores

We provide a solution here **(Fig 3.30)** considering priority to readers: no reader should wait unless a writer has already accessed the critical section. It allows simultaneous reads and counts the readers using a shared variable `r_count` (initialized to 0). The reader process first increments `r_count` and then checks its value. If it is the first reader, it should stop any writer and thus invokes wait for binary semaphore `rw_mutex` (initialized to 1). Ensuring mutual exclusion with a writer is the responsibility of the first reader only, successive readers need not bother about it. At the end of a read, every reader decrements the `r_count`. Update to `r_count` is also a critical section, which is done in mutual exclusion using another binary semaphore `mutex` (initialized to 1). If the reader is the last reader, it needs to unlock the critical section by signaling `rw_mutex` and allowing a writer.

The writer process is simple. It does write in mutual exclusion to read. If any reader is already within the CS, it waits. As the readers have the priority, the writers may wait indefinitely causing starvation to writers. Hence, mutual exclusion is maintained in the solution, but not progress nor bounded-wait for the writers.

Solution with priority to writers is provided in [Sta12]. [Dow16] contains interesting variations with detailed discussion on the solution using semaphores. [Hal15] provides solutions using critical region and condition variables. [RK79] illustrates the solution using eventcounts and sequencers.

3.8.3 The Dining Philosophers Problem

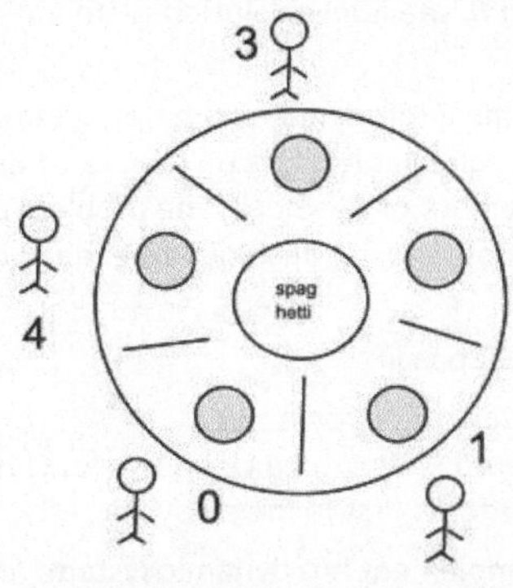

Fig 3.31: Dining Philosophers

This is another classical synchronization problem that was introduced by Edsger W. Dijkstra. Five philosophers (numbered as 0, 1, 2, 3, 4) are sitting around a round-table to dine with spaghetti (an Italian food). They primarily think but attempt to eat when they feel hungry. Each philosopher has a private plate but there are only five forks. Assume, each philosopher needs two forks (both left and right) to eat and thus not all of them can eat at the same time. But when a philosopher finds two forks available beside her, she picks them up, eats some, (washes and) puts down the forks and starts thinking again.

The problem states: *can we devise an algorithm that all the philosophers can complete dining without any issues or difficulties?*

It represents a class of synchronization problems where a subset of the cooperating processes (or threads) can share a limited number of instances of some shared resource(s) to do some job, but not all the processes at the same time. How to serialize their accessing the resource(s) so that all the following properties like

1. mutual exclusion, whenever it is required, is maintained,.
2. there is *no starvation* (every intending process can access the resource) *and*
3. there is *no deadlock* (there is no stalemate).

As the problem states, no two philosophers can use the same fork simultaneously. In other words, forks are to be used in mutual exclusion.

Thus, we can have the first naive attempt to find a solution like the following (**Fig 3.32**).

```
/** PHILOSOPHER 0 **/
int left = 0;
int right = 1;

while (true) {
  wait(fork[left]);
  wait(fork[right]);
   . . .
   /* eats for some time */
   . . .
   signal(fork[left]);
   signal(fork[right]);
    . . .
     /* think again*/
    . . .
}
```

. . .

```
/** PHILOSOPHER i **/
int left = i;
int right = (i+1)%n;

while (true) {
  wait(fork[left]);
  wait(fork[(right]);
   . . .
   /* eats for some time */
   . . .
   signal(fork[left]);
   signal(fork[right]);
    . . .
     /* think again*/
    . . .
}
```

. . .

```
/* PHILOSOPHER (n-1) */
int left = n-1;
int right = 0;

while (true) {
  wait(fork[left]);
  wait(fork[right]);
   . . .
   /* eats for some time */
   . . .
   signal(fork[left]);
   signal(fork[right]);
    . . .
     /* think again*/
    . . .
}
```

Fig 3.32: Naive solution attempt to the dining philosophers problem using semaphores

Let us consider the following shared variables.

n = number of forks (originally n = 5) and an

`semaphore fork [n] = {1, 1, …, 1};` (binary semaphores, all initialized to 1).

The solution tries to see whether both the left and the right forks are available or not for a philosopher. Each philosopher picks up first the left fork and then the right fork, eats for some time and then puts down the fork in the same order (left followed by right). When the philosophers attempt to grab the fork, certainly mutual exclusion will be ensured. If one philosopher can grab both the forks, she can eat as well. In fact, the alternate philosophers from both left and right can eat together [say, (0 and 2) or (0 and 3) or (1 and 3) or (1 and 4)]. However, if we consider only two particular pairs of philosophers eating simultaneously and alternately forever [say (0 & 2) and then (1& 4)] and they keep on taking their turns, one philosopher (Philosopher 3) has to starve indefinitely. Hence, the solution is not starvation-free when *n* is odd (check yourself that for even *n,* the above solution is starvation-free).

Also, in the extreme case, there is a possibility that each philosopher picks up the left fork first and before the right can be picked up, her neighbour picks it up. This leads to a situation where everyone has left fork on their left-hands and their right-hands are empty, nobody can eat and there is a complete stalemate or deadlock. The problem can linger forever unless there is preemption of resources externally. Hence the problem is not deadlock-free (deadlock is discussed in the next unit).

There can be starvation-free and deadlock-free solutions imposing some restrictions like

1. There should be entry for a maximum of *(n-1)* philosophers when there are *n* forks, OR
2. n is *even* and we ensure that even-numbered philosophers (numbered 0, 2, 4, ...) pick up left forks first and then right ones, while odd-numbered philosophers pick up right forks first followed by left, etc.

Obviously, these restrictions are not very general-purpose and are difficult to implement in a dynamic system. Also, remember the fallibility of a programmer while coding the semaphores (the errors are not detectable by compilers and difficult to re-create runtime scenarios always). Let us therefore try a solution with a more powerful tool like a monitor (**Fig 3.33**).

```
monitor DP {
constant n  = #philosophers          /* should be >=2 */
boolean fork[n] = {1,1,....,1}       /*initialised as fork available */
condition cfork[n];                  /* condition for each fork */

void get_forks(int i){

  int left = i;
  int right = (i +1)%n;

  if (!fork[left]) cfork[left].wait();      /*wait for left-fork */
  fork[left] = 0;                           /*left-fork acquired */

  if (!fork[right]) cfork[right].wait();    /*wait for right-fork */
  fork[right] = 0;                          /*right-fork acquired */
}

void put_forks(int i){
  int left = i;
  int right = (i +1)%n;

  fork[left] = 1;                           /*left-fork freed */
  fork[right] = 1;                          /*right-fork freed */

  cfork[left].signal();
  cfork[right].signal();
}
```

```
/* from a philosopher [i], outside monitor */

while (true) {
        ...
        <think>
        ...
        DP. get_forks(i);
        ...
        <eat>
        ...
        DP.put_forks(i);
        ...
        <think>
        ...
}
```

```
/* the main driver program outside monitor */

void main() {

parbegin (philosopher [0], philosopher[1], ....,
          philosopher[n-1]);

/* parbegin indicates parallel or concurrent
execution of its arguments */
}
```

Fig 3.33: Solution to the dining philosophers problem using a monitor & condition variables

Since a monitor ensures mutual exclusion among procedures inside it, `get_forks()` and `put_forks()` execute undisturbed. When the parallel execution starts, the first philosopher that invokes `get_forks()`, gets both the forks and completes eating. Any subsequent philosophers may have to wait, till the first philosopher completes eating and puts down the forks. The solution is deadlock-free, however as it is provided, not starvation-free. If all the philosophers are allowed to go parallel [as shown by **parbegin** in **Fig 3.33**], starvation can happen to one or more philosophers. To avoid starvation, the philosophers need to be called in a sequence (look at the **parbegin** part) – an exercise left for the readers to try.

UNIT SUMMARY

- *This chapter introduced the interprocess communication mechanisms following two models: shared memory and message passing. Different schemes of the message passing model are discussed with examples of implementation.*
- *Interprocess communication in a multiprogramming environment can create race conditions due to concurrent execution of certain sections of code where shared data are being accessed and updated. These sections are called critical sections. Concurrent execution of these sections give rise to a class of problems - known as critical section problems (CSPs).*
- *Critical sections are to be accessed by cooperating processes in mutual exclusion to each other. But the ideal solutions to CSPs need to have the properties of progress and bounded wait also.*
- *Solutions to the CSPs are designed using different synchronization tools. Some of the tools are available at the basic hardware level like atomic memory access and disabling interrupts. Some tools like TSL and CAS offer atomic operations including checking and setting a variable. These primitives help design solutions to CSP involving 2-processes like Peterson's solution as well as that of n-processes (n>2).*
- *Popular synchronizing tools like mutex and semaphores assist developers to design synchronization solutions among various user processes. But using them requires a great amount of care and diligence during coding. Silly mistakes in their uses are neither easily detectable nor reproducible and can cause serious synchronization issues.*
- *Synchronization support in the form of critical region, condition variables and monitors are offered by some higher-level programming languages. A critical region is one or more critical sections which are executed in mutual exclusion. A condition variable forces a process to block until a condition is met. A monitor is an object consisting of local variables, condition variables and methods. Each method here is invoked in mutual exclusion to others. Also, there may be processes blocking on a particular condition variable.*
- *When used intelligently, all these tools offer elegant solutions to the classical synchronization problems like producer-consumer problem, readers-writers problem, dining philosophers' problem etc.*

EXERCISES

Multiple Choice Questions

Q1. A critical region is

A. One which is enclosed by a pair of semaphores and operations on semaphores.

B. A program segment that has not been proved bug free

C. A program segment that often causes unexpected system crash

D. A program segment where shared resources are accessed [GATE(1987)]

Q2. A solution to the Dining Philosophers Problem which avoids deadlock is to

A. ensure that all philosophers pick up the left fork before the right fork

B. ensure that all philosophers pick up the right fork before the left fork

C. ensure that one particular philosopher picks up the left fork before the right fork, and that all other philosophers pick up the right fork before the left fork

D. None of the above [GATE(1996)]

Q3. Let m[0].....m[4] be mutexes (binary semaphores) and p[0]...p[4] be processes. Suppose each process executes the following:

```
wait (m[i]); wait (m(i+1) mod 4]);
...........
release (m[i]); release (m(i+1) mod 4]);
```

This could cause

A. Thrashing B. Deadlock

C. Starvation, but not deadlock D. None of the above [GATE (2000)]

Q4. Consider Peterson's algorithm for mutual exclusion between two concurrent processes i and j. The program executed by process is shown below.

```
repeat
      flag[i] = true;
      turn = j;
      while (P) do no-op;
      Enter critical section, perform actions, then
      exit critical section
      flag[i] = false;
      Perform other non-critical section actions.
until false;
```

For the program to guarantee mutual exclusion, the predicate `P` in the while loop should be

A. flag[j] = true and turn = i B. flag[j] = true and turn = j

C. flag[i] = true and turn = j D. flag[i] = true and turn = i [GATE (2001)]

Q5. The semaphore variables full, empty and mutex are initialized to *0*, *n* and *1* respectively. Process P1 repeatedly adds one item at a time to a buffer of size n, and process P2 repeatedly removes one item at a time from the same buffer using the programs given below. In the programs K, L, M and N are unspecified statements.

P1	**P2**

while(1) {
K;
P(mutex);
Add an item to the buffer;
V(mutex);
L;
}
	while (1) {
	M;
	P(mutex);
	Remove an item from the buffer;
	V(mutex);
	N;
	}

The statements **K, L**, **M**, and **N** and are respectively

A. P(full), V(empty), P(full), V(empty) **B.** P(full), V(empty), P(empty), V(full)

C. P(empty), V(full), P(empty), V(full) **D.** P(empty), V(full), P(full), V(empty) [GATE (2004)]

Q6. Suppose we want to synchronize two concurrent processes P and Q using binary semaphores S and T. The code for the processes P and Q is shown below. Synchronization statements can be inserted only at points W, X, Y and Z

Process P:	Process Q:
while (1) {	while (1) {
W:	Y:
print '0';	print '1';
print '0';	print '1';
X:	Z:
}	}

Which of the following will ensure that the output string *never contains* a substring of the form 01n0 or 10n1 when n is an odd positive integer?
A. P(S) at W, V(S) at X, P(T) at Y, V(T) at Z, S and T initially 1
B. P(S) at W, V(T) at X, P(T) at Y, V(S) at Z, S and T initially 1
C. P(S) at W, V(S) at X, P(S) at Y, V(S) at Z, S initially 1
D. V(S) at W, V(T) at X, P(S) at Y, P(T) at Z, S and T initially 1 [GATE (2003)]

Q7. Consider two processes P1 and P2 accessing the shared variables X and Y protected by two binary semaphores SX and SY respectively, both initialized to 1. P and V denote the usual semaphores

P1:	P2:
While true do {	While true do {
L1 :	L3 : ....
L2 :	L4 : ....
X = X + 1;	Y = Y + 1;
Y = Y - 1;	X = Y - 1;
V(SX);	V(SY);
V(SY);	V(SX);
}	}

operators, where P decrements the semaphore value, and V increments the semaphore value. The pseudo-code of P1 and P2 is as follows:

In order to avoid deadlock, the correct operators at L1, L2, L3 and L4 are respectively.
A. P(SY), P(SX); P(SX), P(SY)
B. P(SX), P(SY); P(SY), P(SX)
C. P(SX), P(SX); P(SY), P(SY)
D. P(SX), P(SY); P(SX), P(SY) [GATE (2004)]

Q8. Given below is a program which when executed spawns two concurrent processes:

```
semaphore X : = 0 ;
/* Process now forks into concurrent processes P1 & P2 */
      P1                    P2
      repeat forever        repeat forever
      V (X) ;               P(X) ;
      Compute ;             Compute ;
```

P(X) ; V(X) ;

Consider the following statements about processes P1 and P2:

1. It is possible for process P1 to starve
2. It is possible for process P2 to starve.

Which of the following holds?

A. Both I and II are true **B.** I is true but II is false
C. II is true but I is false **D.** Both I and II are false [GATE (2005)]

Q9. The *enter_CS()* and *leave_CS()* functions to implement critical section of a process are realized using test-and-set instruction as follows:

```
void enter_CS(X)
{ while test-and-set(X); }

void leave_CS(X)
{X = 0;}
```

In the above solution, X is a memory location associated with the CS and is initialized to 0. Now consider the following statements:

I. The above solution to CS problem is deadlock-free
II. The solution is starvation free.
III. The processes enter CS in FIFO order.
IV More than one process can enter CS at the same time.

Which of the above statements is **TRUE**?

A. I only **B.** I and II **C.** II and III **D.** IV only [GATE (2009)]

Q10. Each process Pi is coded as follows:

repeat
P(mutex)
{Critical section}
V(mutex)
forever

The code for **P10** is identical except it uses **V(mutex)** in place of **P(mutex)**. What is the largest number of processes that can be inside the critical section at any moment?

A.1 **B. 2** **C. 3** **D. None**

Q11. Consider the following threads, T1, T2, and T3 executing on a single processor, synchronized using three binary semaphore variables, S1, S2, and S3, operated upon using standard *wait()* and *signal()*. The threads can be context switched in any order and at any time.

T1	T2	T3

while(true){
 wait(S3);
 print("C");
 signal(S2);
}
	while(true){
	 wait(S1);
	 print("B");
	 signal(S3);
	}
		while(true){
		 wait(S2);
		 print("A");
		 signal(S1);
		}

Which initialization of the semaphores would print the sequence BCABCABCA.... ?
A. S1 = 1; S2 = 1; S3 = 1
B. S1 = 1; S2 = 1; S3 = 0
C. S1 = 1; S2 = 0; S3 = 0
D. S1 = 0; S2 = 1; S3 = 1 [GATE (2022)]

Answers of Multiple Choice Questions

1. D 2. C 3. B 4. B 5. D 6. C 7. D 8. A 9. A 10. D 11. C

Short Answer Type Questions

Q1. What do you mean by interacting processes? When do we say that two processes do not interact?
Q2. What are the models of IPC? Explain how they are similar and different.
Q3. Differentiate between synchronous and asynchronous communication?
Q4. What is parallelism? Mention the similarities and differences between concurrency and parallelism.
Q5. What do you understand by process synchronization?
Q6. What is race condition? What is a critical section and why is it so called?
Q7. What is liveness property? How is it related to starvation?
Q8. Why is strict alternation not a good solution to a 2-process CSP?
Q9. Define a semaphore. Write advantages and disadvantages of a semaphore.
Q10. What is a monitor? How is a condition variable different from a local variable within a monitor?
Q11. What is a producer-consumer problem? How does the problem change when we go from a single producer to multiple producers?
Q12. What is a readers-writers problem? Mention the differences between the cases when readers are given priority over writers and the opposite.

Long Answer Type Questions

Q1. Describe the mutual exclusion problem with a suitable example.
Q2. Define a critical section problem (CSP). Describe the necessary and desirable properties in a solution to a CSP.
Q3. Describe the hardware synchronization tools TSL and CAS. When do they behave the same and how are they different? Which one is more powerful, according to you? Justify.

```
while (1) {
    flag[i] = 1;
        while (flag[j]) {
            if (turn == j) {
                flag[i] = 0;
                while (turn == j)
                    ; /* do nothing */
                flag[i] = 1;
            }
        }
    <critical section>
    turn = j;
    flag[i] = 0;
}
/* remainder section */
```

Fig 3.34: Dekker's Solution (for process Pi)

Q4. The first correct solution to 2-process CSP was proposed by *Dekker* and is known as *Dekker's solution*.

Two processes P0 and P1 share the following variables:

```
boolean flag[2];/*initially 0 */
int turn;
```

Fig 3.34 provides the solution for process Pi (i=0 or 1).

How does the solution differ from Peterson's solution? Check and justify whether the solution satisfy all the necessary criteria.

Q5. Consider the Dijkstra's solution to n-process CSP ($n > 1$) as given in **Fig 3.35**. The processes $p_0, p_1, ..., p_{n-1}$ share the following variables with the given initialisation among them.

```
enum pr_state = {idle, want_cs, in_cs};
int n;                    /* no. of processes >1 */
shared volatile pr_state flag[n] = {idle,..., idle};
shared volatile int turn =0;
```

Check and justify whether the solution meet all necessary criteria or not. If not, how to make necessary changes in the given pseudo-code to fulfill the unmet criteria.

```
while (true){
   flag[i] = want_cs;
   j = turn;

   while ( j != i) {
      if (flag[j] == idle) turn = i;        /* grab it */
      else  j = (j+1)%n;
   }
   flag[i] = in_cs;   /* assume to get into CS */

   j=0;
   while ((j <n) && (j == i) || flag[j] != in_cs))
      j++;
   if ( (j >= n) && (turn == i || flag[turn] == idle))
      break;    /* come out of busy-wait */
}

<critical section>

flag[i] = idle; /* no more interested in CS */

<remainder section>
```

Fig 3.36: Dijkstra solution (for *Pi*) to n-process CSP

```
choosing[i] = true;                  /*interested to be in CS */
token[i] = 1 + max{token[0], token[1], ..., token[n-1]};
choosing[i] = false;

for (int j =0; j<n; j++){ /*busy-wait arbitration */
   while (choosing[j]);  /* wait while someone getting token*/

   while (token[j] !=0 && (token[j], j) < (token[i], i));
         /* wait while someone has preference^ */
}

<critical section>

token[i] = 0; /* no more interested in CS */

<remainder section>

^(token[a],a) < (token[b], b) means
Either token[a] < token[b]
Or if token[a] = token[b], then a < b
```

Fig 3.37: Bakery Algorithm (for *Pi*) to n-process CSP

Q6. Bakery algorithm is one of the first solutions for n-process CSP. **Fig 3.37** shows the pseudocode for process Pi. The algorithm is proposed by Leslie Lamport and named by him as it mimics the service to customers in a bakery (or a bank or a reservation counter, a pizza outlet etc.). n processes arrive at the bakery and each one first takes a token (sequence number of getting the service). Each process gets the chance to enter into CS strictly according to its token number.

The processes share the following variables with their initialization.

```
int n;                          /* no. of processes >1 */
shared volatile boolean choosing[n] = {false,..., false};
shared volatile int token[n] = {0, ..., 0};
```

Each process modifies its own variable but checks the values of others' in the *for* loop and waits. Analyze the algorithm given and answer the following:

i. Justify whether two or more processes can get the same token number or not.
ii. How mutual exclusion of CS is maintained?
iii. Does the solution have all necessary properties of a solution to a CSP? Justify.
iv. Is there a bound on the token number?
v. What can be the issues in the above solution for uniprocessor and multiprocessor systems? How can they be addressed?
vi. Discuss if a bakery algorithm can be designed with the help of eventcounts and sequencers.

Q7. Provide an algorithmic solution to n-process (n>2) CSP using CAS. Does it meet all the necessary properties? Justify.

Q8. Discuss the similarities and differences between a mutex and a binary semaphore.

Q9. Design a solution to the readers-writers problem with priority to writers, i.e., no writer should wait for a reader when no reader is reading?

Q10. Describe the dining - philosophers problem and solution using a monitor for 7 philosophers.

Numerical Problems

Q1. Consider three concurrent processes P1, P2 and P3 as shown below, which access a shared variable D that has been initialized to 100

P1	P2	P3
. . D=D+20	. . D=D-50	. . D=D+10

The processes are executed on a uniprocessor system running a time-shared operating system. If the minimum and maximum possible values of D after the three processes have completed execution are X and Y respectively, then the value of Y - X is______?

[GATE (2019)]

ANS : 80

Q2. Two concurrent processes P1 and P2 use four shared resources and , as shown below.

P1	P2
Compute;	Compute;
Use R1;	Use R1;
Use R2;	Use R2;
Use R3;	Use R3;
Use R4;	Use R4;

Both processes are started at the same time, and each resource can be accessed by only one process at a time. The following scheduling constraints exist between the access of resources by the processes:

P2 must complete use of R1 before P1 gets access to R1

P1 must complete use of R2 before P2 gets access to R2

P2 must complete use of R3 before P1 gets access to R3

P1 must complete use of R4 before P2 gets access to R4

There are no other scheduling constraints between the processes. If only binary semaphores are used to enforce the above scheduling constraints, what is the minimum number of binary semaphores needed?

[GATE (2005)]

ANS : 2

Q3. Processes P1 and P2 use critical_flag in the following routine to achieve mutual exclusion. Assume that critical_flag is initialized to FALSE in the main program.

```
get_exclusive_access ( )
{
        if (critical _flag == FALSE) {
                critical_flag = TRUE ;
                critical_region () ;
                critical_flag = FALSE;
```

```
    }
}
```

Consider the following statements.

i. It is possible for both P1 and P2 to access critical_region concurrently.

ii. This may lead to a deadlock.

How many of the following statements hold?

ANS : (i)=true and **(ii)=false**

Q4. The **enter_CS()** and **leave_CS()** functions to implement critical section of a process are realized using test-and-set instruction as follows:

```
void enter_CS(X)
{
while(test-and-set(X));
}

void leave_CS(X)
{
X = 0;
}
```

In the above solution, **X** is a memory location associated with the **CS** and is initialized to **0**. Now consider the following statements:

I. The above solution to **CS** problem is deadlock-free

II. The solution is starvation free

III. The processes enter **CS** in **FIFO** order

IV. More than one process can enter **CS** at the same time

How many of the above statements are true? [GATE (2009)]

ANS : 1, Only Statement I.

Q5. The following two processes P1 and P2 that share a variable B with an initial value of 2 execute concurrently.

```
P1()
{
  C = B – 1;
  B = 2*C;
}

P2()
{
  D = 2 * B;
  B = D - 1;
}
```

The number of distinct values that B can possibly take after the execution is______? [GATE (2015)]

ANS: 3

Q6. A counting semaphore was initialized to 10. Then 6P (wait) operations and 4V (signal) operations were completed on this semaphore. The resulting value of the semaphore is_____? [GATE (1998)]

ANS : 8

Q7. Consider a non-negative counting semaphore S. The operation P(S) decrements S, and V(S) increments S. During an execution, 20 P(S) operations and 12 V(S) operations are issued in some order. The largest initial value of S for which at least one P(S) operation will remain blocked is_____? [GATE (2016)]

ANS: 7

PRACTICAL

1. Write a program to create two child processes (or two threads) that share a variable. You allow the processes (or threads) to concurrently run. While in one process (thread), increment the variable, in the other, decrement it along with simultaneously printing the values. See whether race conditions appear or not.
2. In the same manner, implement the producer-consumer problem using a bounded buffer by enacting a process (or thread) as a producer and another a consumer respectively. From the producer process (or thread) write onto the buffer and print the item (may be an integer representing the item). Do you observe any situation where nothing is printed for an indefinite amount of time (deadlock)?
3. Create a shared memory. Write a program to write onto the shared memory and print the content written. Write another program to read from it and print the content. Every time you print the process id as well. From a number of different terminals, run several instances of readers and writers and see their concurrent execution. Observe starvation and deadlock, if any.
4. See necessary documentation from the web and references, learn and solve the concurrency using semaphores.
5. Implement the dining philosophers' problem in Java using a monitor.

KNOW MORE

Interprocess communication mechanisms in general are described in [Hal15]. For practical implementation in UNIX, necessary details can be found in [RR03] and [SR05]. However, in a very detailed discussion with theoretical treatment on IPC, semaphores in UNIX systems can be obtained in [Vah12] and [Bac05].

Race conditions, mutual exclusion, critical sections and different synchronization tools are discussed in general in [Hal15], [SGG18] and [Sta12].

Different algorithmic efforts towards CSPs like Dekker solution, Dijkstra solution, Bakery algorithm, Sleeping Barbers problem and several others are discussed briefly in [Hal15] and elaborately in [Dow16] with implementation help.

Classical synchronization problems like producers-consumers problems, readers-writers problem and dining philosophers' problem in general are well explained with elaborate diagrams in [Sta12].

Synchronization primitives as offered in Windows OS are discussed in [YIR17].

REFERENCES AND SUGGESTED READINGS

[Bac05] Maurice J Bach: The Design of the UNIX Operating System, Prentice Hall of India, 2005.

[Dow16] Allen B. Downey: The Little Book of Semaphores, 2e, Green Tea Press, 2016 (available at https://greenteapress.com/semaphores/LittleBookOfSemaphores.pdf as on 9-Oct-2022).

[Hal15] Sibsankar Haldar: Operating Systems, Self Edition 1.1, 2015.

[RR03] Kay A. Robbins, Steven Robbins: Unix™ Systems Programming: Communication, Concurrency, and Threads, Prentice Hall, 2003.

[SR05] Richard W Stevens, Stephen A Rago: Advanced Programming in the UNIX Environment (2nd Edition), Addison-Wesley Professional, 2005.

[SGG18] Abraham Silberschatz, Peter B Galvin, Greg Gagne: Operating Systems Concepts,10th Edition, Wiley, 2018.

[Sta12] William Stallings: Operating Systems Internals and Design Principles, 7th Edition, Prentice Hall, 2012.

[Vah12] Uresh Vahalia: UNIX Internals, The New Frontiers, Pearson, 2012.

[YIR17] Pavel Yosifovich, Alex Ionescu, Mark E. Russinovich, and David A. Solomon: Windows Internals, Seventh Edition (Part 1 and 2), Microsoft, 2017. https://docs.microsoft.com/en-us/sysinternals/resources/windows-internals (as on 8-Jul-2022).

Dynamic QR Code for Further Reading

4 Deadlocks

UNIT SPECIFICS

Through this unit we have discussed the following aspects:

- *Deadlocks: Definition, Necessary and sufficient conditions for Deadlock, Deadlock Prevention*
- *Deadlock Avoidance: Banker's algorithm, Deadlock detection and Recovery.*

This chapter discusses a negative fallout of concurrent execution - deadlocks. A process (or more specifically a thread) needs a number of resources to accomplish a job. While some are hardware resources like processors, registers, main memory, printers, scanners etc.; some are software like files, shared objects, sockets etc. and some are combination of hardware and software objects including synchronizing constructs (e.g., locks, semaphores, mutex, critical regions, monitors etc.). If the resources are non-shareable (i.e., they need to be accessed mutually exclusively) and finite in numbers, simultaneous demands from several threads throws a challenge to the system - while one thread holds a resource, others demanding for the same resource have to wait. If the holding and waiting for a set of resources by several threads are such that everyone waits for release of one or more resources held by some other, none can proceed and fall into a state of indefinite starvation known as a deadlock. The concept of deadlock, its formation criteria, prevention and avoidance principles and mechanisms are discussed. If deadlocks cannot be prevented due to some reasons, how they can be detected and how the system can recover from it are also explained. For every concept, wherever required, necessary definitions, algorithms and adequate examples are provided.

Like previous units, a number of multiple-choice questions as well as questions of short and long answer types following Bloom's taxonomy, assignments through a number of numerical problems, a list of references and suggested readings are provided. It is important to note that for getting more information on various topics of interest, appropriate URLs and QR code have been provided in different sections which can be accessed or scanned for relevant supportive knowledge. "Know More" section is also designed for supplementary information to cater to the inquisitiveness and curiosity of the students.

RATIONALE

This unit on deadlocks starts with an informal introduction to the concept of different stalemate situations. Few real-life examples of deadlocks are provided, clearly pointing out the differences with livelocks before going into the technical terms in the context of operating systems. Necessary definitions are then introduced so that the concept can be discussed with appropriate rigor and preciseness. Different types of computing resources are mentioned, and which type can cause deadlock are clearly pointed out. Also, under what conditions a deadlock will result (the necessary and sufficient conditions) is discussed with reasonable detail. How to prevent occurrence of a deadlock, whether it can be avoided in the runtime, or, if it happens, how to recover from it are explained with necessary algorithms and examples.

This unit builds the fundamental concepts to understand deadlocks - a negative fallout of the concurrent execution environment of an OS. The concepts developed here are central and critical to comprehend and appreciate the interaction of threads (also processes) with computing resources.

PRE-REQUISITES

- *Basics of Computer Organization and Architecture*
- *Fundamentals of Data Structures*
- *Fundamentals of Graph Theory and Graph Algorithms*
- *Fundamentals of Vectors and Matrices*
- *Introductory knowledge of Computer Programming*
- *Introduction to Operating Systems* (**Unit I, II and III** *of the book)*

UNIT OUTCOMES

List of outcomes of this unit is as follows:

U4-O1: Define deadlocks, livelocks, resources, necessary conditions for deadlock formation.

U4-O2: Describe a deadlock situation and its difference with a livelock, different deadlock handling techniques, Banker's algorithm for deadlock avoidance and detection, recovery from a deadlock.

U4-O3: Understand the connection among several conditions leading to a deadlock and thus how to prevent, avoid and recover from a deadlock.

U4-O4: Realize the overhead involved in deadlock prevention, avoidance mechanisms.

U4-O5: Analyze and compare different deadlock handling mechanisms.

U4-O6: Design cost-effective and practical solutions for handling deadlocks in an OS.

Course Outcomes

After completion of the course the students will be able to:

1. Create processes and threads.
2. Develop algorithms for process scheduling for a given specification of CPU.
3. Utilization, Throughput, Turnaround Time, Waiting Time, Response Time.
4. For a given specification of memory organization develop the techniques for optimally allocating memory to processes by increasing memory utilization and for improving the access time.
5. Design and implement file management system.
6. For a given I/O devices and OS (specify) develop the I/O management functions in OS as part of a uniform device abstraction by performing operations for synchronization between CPU and I/O controllers.

Unit-4 Outcomes	*EXPECTED MAPPING WITH COURSE OUTCOMES* (1- Weak Correlation; 2- Medium correlation; 3- Strong Correlation)					
	CO-1	*CO-2*	*CO-3*	*CO-4*	*CO-5*	*CO-6*
U4-O1	1	2	3	2	3	3
U4-O2	1	2	3	2	3	3
U4-O3	1	2	3	2	3	3
U4-O4	1	2	3	2	3	3
U4-O5	1	2	3	2	3	3
U4-O6	1	2	3	2	3	3

4.1 INTRODUCTION

The term deadlock comes from two words *dead* and *lock.* It symbolizes a lock that is closed and whose key is, as if, lost. In real-life, deadlock means a situation where a group of entities (at least two people or objects) are engaged with each other in such a way that none in the group can proceed as another from the group obstructs. As a *dead* lock cannot open on its own and needs to be broken by external forces, a deadlock situation does not resolve on its own.

Fig 4.1[9]: Deadlock on road

Fig 4.2[10]: Not a deadlock

Deadlock or stalemate situations are often found in real life. At a road crossing, uncontrolled traffic often causes deadlock (**Fig 4.1**). No cars can move as there are no spaces in any of the directions. These deadlocks are not resolved unless some external efforts are applied (by traffic police or voluntary efforts from individuals).

However, sometimes a group of entities temporarily face obstructions from each other, but they themselves can try and resolve it. If the entities involved can come out of the stalemate on their own - it is not a deadlock. Even though their attempts may fail repeatedly, eventually they can come out of the stalemate, maybe after several attempts. For example, in **Fig 4.2** the cars are not actually in a deadlock, if there are spaces behind them. The cars can come a little backward. The apparent lock can be easily resolved if a pair of opposite cars come back and wait (say, the north and the south-bound cars) and allow the other pair (say, the east and the west-bound ones) to go forward.

If both pairs of cars simultaneously come back and try to go forward at the same time, there will be a locking situation. Their attempts to go forward may fail, if the attempts are synchronized each time - this kind of lock is called a *livelock,* and not a deadlock. In a livelock, the entities do *not hold the resources* (here free space in front of the cars) *continuously*. Rather, they can attempt to make progress, but the attempts *continuously fail* due to some reason. One can hope that their attempts will succeed, and they can come out of the lock after one or more attempts. How many attempts will be needed, however, is completely unpredictable.

On the contrary, the situation would be a deadlock if there are no spaces behind when other cars also line up in all the four directions as illustrated below (**Fig 4.3**).

Traffic deadlock at a crossroad can be explained with an example. Suppose four fleets of cars are approaching the crossroad from four directions but have not crossed the junction. There are open spaces in front marked as A, B, C, D (**Fig 4.3a**). All the cars want to go straight crossing the junction. For example, cars from west would like to go straight to the east crossing region A & D, cars from south head north crossing B & A and so on. If the junction is signalled and the cars stop at the crossing, there need not be any problem.

However, if there is no signaling system, there is a possibility of a deadlock. The deadlock happens when every car proceeds straight simultaneously such that the east-bound first car occupies space A, the north-bound space B, the west-bound space C and the south-bound space D. No space is left for any of the cars to move ahead, neither to move back as well (*almost*) unlike **Fig 4.2**. The stalemate will continue forever (**Fig 4.3b**). The open spaces (A, B, C, D) are important resources here. Deadlock happened as each car on the front occupied a piece of

---

[9] Picture courtesy: https://www.worldatlas.com/articles/the-biggest-traffic-jams-in-history.html

[10] Picture courtesy: https://twitter.com/cartoonlka/status/1069775359695093761

land and needed another that was occupied by another car and their occupation and requirement of space made a chain or cycle.

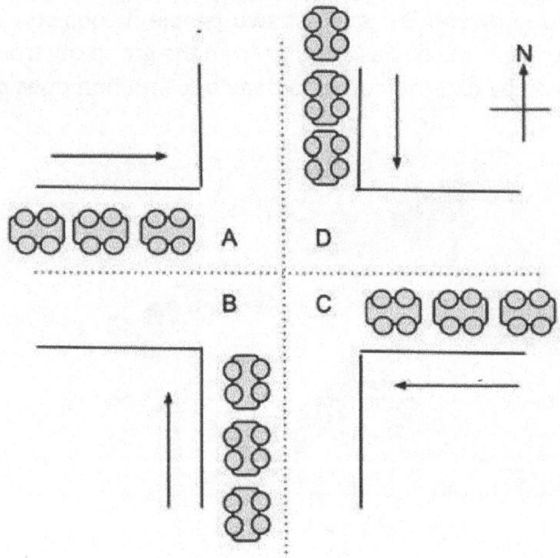

Fig 4.3a: Possibility of deadlock

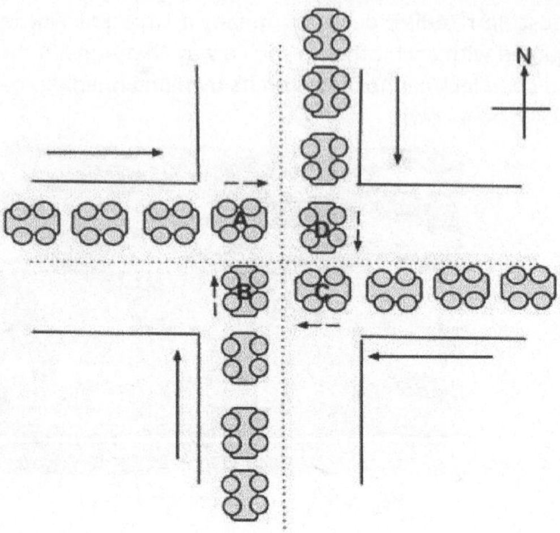

Fig 4.3b: Deadlock

4.2 DEFINITION

In operating systems, deadlock is a serious problem caused by concurrent execution of processes (or threads). It refers to a situation where a set of concurrent processes (or threads) perpetually block or starve for want of some resources held by some other processes (or threads) within the set. The processes (or threads) cannot come out of the situation on their own.

Concurrency offers a set of advantages like increased CPU utilization and throughput but throws serious challenges as well. In the last unit (**Unit 3**), we studied the issue of race conditions due to attempts of concurrent execution of critical sections. Remember that two of the necessary conditions of solutions to CSPs are *progress or liveness* (all processes or threads involved will progress and no process or thread will block forever) and *bounded wait* or *starvation freedom* (no process should wait or starve indefinitely). Critical section problems can cause starvation to *one or more* processes (or threads), specific to execution of critical sections.

But the issue of deadlock is more general and pervasive. The processes (or threads) involved in a deadlock cannot proceed any further (not only execution of critical sections but non-critical sections as well). Deadlock is characterized by the following:

i. it is caused for the want of *computing resources* (of any type).
ii. nature of *starvation* is *perpetual.*
iii. *starvation* occurs to *more than one* processes (or threads) simultaneously.
iv. the set of processes (or threads) have dependencies on each other in such a manner that they cannot come out of the perpetual stalemate on their own.

A deadlock differs from a livelock in the starvation. In a livelock starvation is not permanent and the entities involved in the livelock can resolve on their own without necessarily requiring external efforts.

4.2.1 Examples

Recall the dining philosophers' problem in **Sec 3.8.3.** In the first naive attempt to solve the problem, every philosopher picks up the left fork first and then the right fork. Picking up the forks was considered a critical section and thus was guarded using semaphores. However, in an extreme case, when every philosopher is hungry at the same time, everyone can pick up her left fork and cannot get the chance to pick up the right fork. All the philosophers wait for the right fork, but nobody gets it as nobody puts down the fork as their eating is not complete. This literally creates an *indefinite starvation* or deadlock (*In real-life, this can be a livelock as any of the philosophers can voluntarily release a fork by courtesy and allow her neighboring colleague to proceed to eating! But in a programmed environment, this courtesy cannot be seen unless programmed!!).*

```
/****** main process ***************/
...
pthread_mutex_t mutex1;
pthread_mutex_t mutex2;
...
pthread_mutex_init(&mutex1, NULL);
pthread mutex init(&mutex2, NULL);
...
```

```
/****** thread1 ***********/
void *function1(void *param)
{
  pthread_mutex_lock(&mutex1);
  pthread_mutex_lock(&mutex2);
  ...
  /** * some work****/
  ...
  pthread_mutex_unlock(&mutex2);
  pthread_mutex_unlock(&mutex1);

  pthread_exit(0);
}
```

```
/****** thread2 ***********/
void *function2(void *param)
{
  pthread_mutex_lock(&mutex2);
  pthread_mutex_lock(&mutex1);
  ...
  /** * some work****/
  ...
  pthread_mutex_unlock(&mutex1);
  pthread_mutex_unlock(&mutex2);

  pthread_exit(0);
}
```

Fig 4.4: Possibility of a deadlock in a multi-threaded program

```
/****** thread1 ***********/
void *function1(void *param)
{
  while (1){
    pthread_mutex_lock(&mutex1);
    if (pthread_mutex_trylock(&mutex2)) {
        ...
        /** * some work****/
        ...
        pthread_mutex_unlock(&mutex2);
        pthread_mutex_unlock(&mutex1);
        break;
    }
    else
        pthread_mutex_unlock(&mutex1);
  } /* end of while */
  pthread_exit(0);
}
```

```
/****** thread2 ***********/
void *function2(void *param)
{
  while (1){
    pthread_mutex_lock(&mutex2);
    if (pthread_mutex_trylock(&mutex1)) {
        ...
        /** * some work****/
        ...
        pthread_mutex_unlock(&mutex1);
        pthread_mutex_unlock(&mutex2);
        break;
    }
    else
        pthread_mutex_unlock(&mutex2);
  } /* end of while */
  pthread_exit(0);
}
```

Fig 4.5: Possibility of a livelock in a multi-threaded program

In a multithreaded environment, semaphores or mutex locks can cause deadlocks as illustrated in **Fig 4.4**. The example uses POSIX mutex locks (**Fig 4.4**). Two threads `thread1` and `thread2` acquire two locks `mutex1` and mutex2 for doing some thread-specific critical section. thread1 acquires the locks mutex1 followed by mutex2, whereas thread2 acquires them in the reverse order. In a single processor system, thread1 can acquire lock mutex1 immediately followed by thread2 acquiring mutex2. Or, in a multiprocessor system, both the threads can acquire the first mutex locks simultaneously before either can get the next lock. Then, no thread can successfully acquire two mutex locks. The thread1 holds mutex1 and waits for mutex2 held by thread2 and vice-versa. Thus, neither can proceed. This kind of deadlock, although happens occasionally, is quite commonplace and not easily detectable.

The above problem can be resolved using POSIX pthread_mutex_trylock() **(Fig 4.5)**. Here, each thread attempts to acquire the lock only if it is available, otherwise it immediately releases the already held mutex. However, this may cause a livelock situation if both the threads acquire a mutex lock simultaneously. None gets the other lock as the invocation of pthread_mutex_trylock() fails and simultaneously releases the already-acquired mutex locks (mutex1 by thread1 and mutex2 by thread2). Livelocks continue when threads retry simultaneously. The stalemate can be broken if each thread attempts retry at random times.

With the background, we shall discuss deadlocks in more detail, specifically in the context of operating systems. To that end, we are required to define and discuss a few concepts as given below.

4.2.2 Resources

A computing resource can be any object (hardware or software) that a process (or thread) requires to complete its execution. Hardware resources can be processors, network cards, memory elements, I/O devices; software resources can be files, shared objects (In UNIX, .so files), sockets, messages or synchronization tools like semaphores. mutex locks etc. A computing system can have one or more instances of each resource type, but only a finite number of instances. If the resources are *shareable* among the processes (or threads), i.e., the resources can be accessed simultaneously by more than one threads (like read access to a file by several readers) - there will not be problems of deadlock. But often the resources are *non-shareable,* i.e., they cannot be accessed simultaneously by more than one thread (e.g., using a CPU core or simultaneously both read and write of a file or simultaneous writes to it). This non-shareable use can happen on the following two types of resources.

Reusable resources: The use of the resource does not expire, i.e., the resource can be used by several threads one after another without any loss. Example: processors, memory elements, network devices, I/O devices, files, sockets, locks, semaphores etc.

Consumable resources: The resource is for single-use. Once it is used by a thread, it no longer exists. For example: ephemeral messages.

Typically, each resource category has only a finite number of instances of each resource type. For example, a computer can have only a few processors, a finite number of registers, memory cards, network cards, printers, scanners, sockets, buffers, semaphores, mutex locks etc.

Deadlocks occur because of the non-shareable use of reusable and consumable resources that are finite in numbers. When the total demand of a resource type is more than the available number of its instances (e.g., there are 3 processors in a system, but 5 processes want to simultaneously run) - some of the demanding process(es) (or thread(s)) need to be blocked. If there are one or more processes (or threads) that demand for one or more non-shareable resources held by one or more in the group in such a way that everyone blocks - deadlock happens.

4.2.3 Processes or threads? User context or system context?

Remember that resources are allocated to processes by an operating system. But a process can further allocate resources to threads and resources are used by threads. Threads do request for resources that are finally allocated to processes by the OS kernel, some kernel threads are responsible for resource allocation. Deadlock is a fallout of these demands and allocation of resources. It can happen in the *user context* among several user threads (within a single process or across processes) or in the *system context* (among kernel threads and user threads). Thus, from this point onward, we shall consider threads as stakeholders in a deadlock. *Resources* are considered demanded / requested by threads and used by *threads* (and not processes). Also, the discussion of deadlocks will be done in the *system context* as deadlocks in the user context are supposed to be dealt with by the application developers.

4.2.4 Resource access

Threads need resources for completing their tasks. During execution, a thread needs and uses several resources. However, the uses always obey the following sequence.

i. *Request:* A thread makes a request to the OS kernel for one or more instances of a resource. If an instance of the resource is not available, the kernel cannot grant it to the thread immediately. The thread waits (or blocks) till it acquires an instance of the resource.
ii. *Use:* Once acquired, the thread uses the instance of the resource non-shareably.
iii. *Release:* After the use, the thread returns the resource back to the kernel.

In most cases, both request and release are system calls. Use may be in user or system context. If the resource is a mutex lock or a semaphore, use can be executing a critical section guarded by the mutex lock.

4.2.5 Resource Allocation Graph

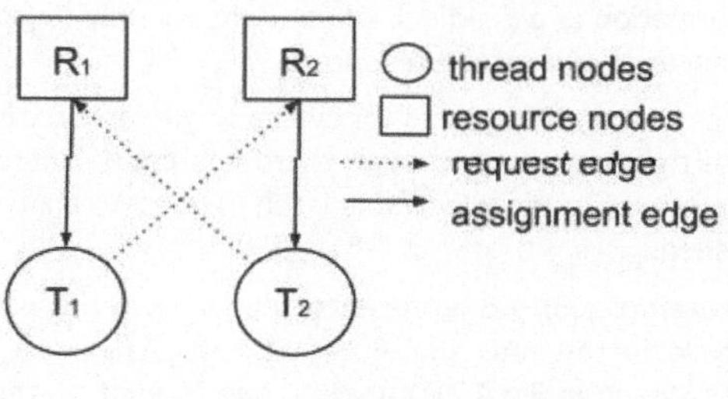

Fig 4.6: A resource allocation graph *G = (V, E)*

Concepts from Graph Theory help understand and define deadlocks precisely. Resource allocation to threads can be modeled as a *heterogeneous directed graph* having two types of nodes (resources and threads) and two types of edges. A thread requests for a resource of a particular resource-type - it is represented by a *claim edge* or a *request edge* from a thread to a resource. When the request is granted, the thread holds the resource - it is represented by *allocation edge* or *assignment edge*. Such a representation is called a resource allocation graph (**Fig 4.6**).

Let us take a simple example involving two threads $\{T_1, T_2\}$

and two resources $\{R_1, R_2\}$. Suppose T_1 requests resource R_1 (request edge $T_1 \rightarrow R_1$). When it is granted, the request edge is converted to an *assignment edge* ($R_1 \rightarrow T_1$). Similarly, resource R_2 is assigned to thread T_2 ($R_2 \rightarrow T_2$).

Now if T_1 requests resource R_2 and T_2 requests R_1, then there will be *request edges* ($T_1 \rightarrow R_2$) and ($T_2 \rightarrow R_1$). If there are only single instance of R_1 and R_2, they cannot be granted anymore and request edges cannot be converted to assignment edges.

The resultant graph is an example of resource allocation graph *G = (V, E)* where *V* = $\{T \cup R\}$, *E* = $\{E_{assign} \cup E_{req}\}$, $T = \{T_1, T_2\}$ and $R = \{R_1, R_2\}$. $E_{assign} = \{R_1 \rightarrow T_1, R_2 \rightarrow T_2\}$ and $E_{req} = \{T_1 \rightarrow R_2, T_2 \rightarrow R_1\}$.

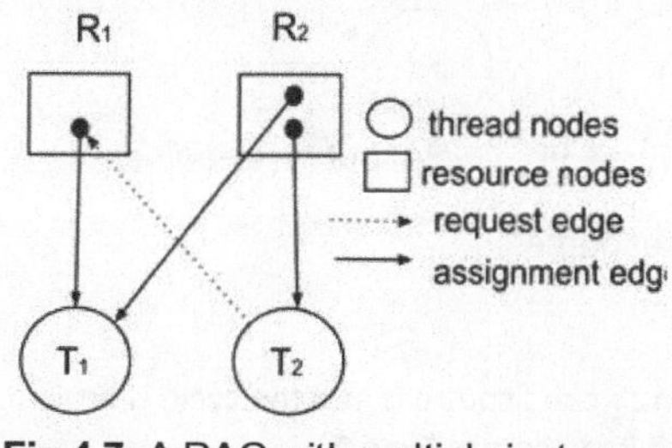

Fig 4.7: A RAG with multiple instances of resources

The above RAG (**Fig 4.6**) represents the case when there are single instances of resources.

Resource allocation graph can also represent multiple instances of resources. If a resource has multiple instances, the same resource node can show multiple instances with dots as shown in **Fig 4.7.** Note that it is the same RAG as in **Fig 4.6** with two instances of R_2. If there are multiple instances of a resource, a resource can be simultaneously held by multiple threads non-sharably, each thread acquiring one instance. A claim / request edge ($T_1 \rightarrow R_2$) in **Fig 4.6** is thus changed to an assignment edge in **Fig 4.7**.

4.3 CONDITIONS of a DEADLOCK

With the technical background given above, we can now define a deadlock more precisely. A deadlock can occur if all the following conditions are satisfied simultaneously.

i. **Mutual Exclusion** *in use of resources*: When resources are used by threads non-sharably, then only there may emerge a possibility of deadlock. There should be at least one resource that is used by threads in a mutually exclusive way - i.e., only one thread can use an instance of the resource at a time. If another thread wants to use the same instance of the resource, the thread needs to wait till the first thread releases the resource.

ii. **Hold and Wait** *for resources*: During execution, threads are allowed to hold one or more resources and, at the same time, request to acquire a few more resources held by other thread(s).

iii. **No Preemption** *of resources*: None of the resources are preempted from the threads that hold them. A thread releases the resources voluntarily when either their need is over, or the thread terminates.

iv. **Unresolvable Circular Wait:** A set of threads $T = \{T_1, T_2, \dots, T_n\}$ hold and wait for resources from a set R = $\{\{R_1, R_2 \dots, R_n\}$ in such a way that $R_1 \rightarrow T_1, T_1 \rightarrow R_2, R_2 \rightarrow T_2, \dots, R_n \rightarrow T_n$ and $T_n \rightarrow R_1$. i.e., threads and resources make a cycle in the resource allocation graph with assignment and request edges.

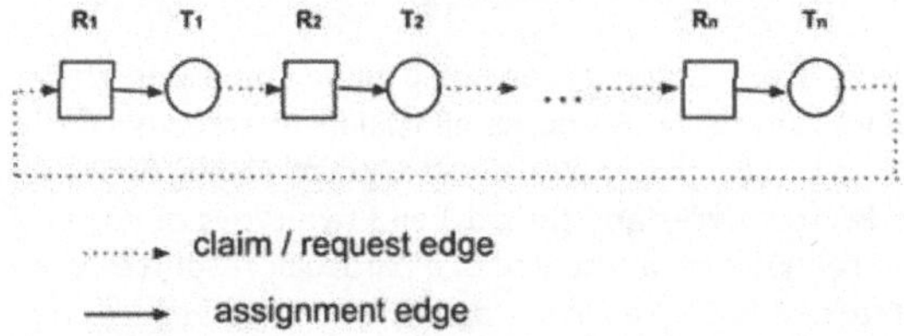

Fig 4.8: Circular wait (RAG contains a cycle)

Formation of the cycle in the RAG (**Fig 4.8**) is a *confirmation of a deadlock when there are only single* instances of each of the resources.

If the number of instances for even a single resource is more than one, even though there is a cycle - there may not be a deadlock if all the requests can be satisfied.

For example, **Fig 4.6** represents a deadlock as there is a cycle in the RAG ($R_1 \rightarrow T_1, T_1 \rightarrow R_2, R_2 \rightarrow T_2, T_2 \rightarrow R_1$). But when a resource has more than one instance (as shown in **Fig 4.7**), a cycle is not formed, as the request is met by the second instance of R_2.

At times, even if the demands cannot be met immediately and a cycle appears to be formed along with other three conditions (**Condition i - iii**), there may not always be a deadlock. For example, in **Fig 4.9a,** R_2 has two instances, both are held by threads T_2 and T_3 respectively. No instances of any of the resources are left free. Hence. request for R_2 by T_1 cannot be met, neither that of R_1 by T_2. Hence, a cycle appears to form: $R_1 \rightarrow T_1 \rightarrow R_2 \rightarrow T_2 \rightarrow R_1$.

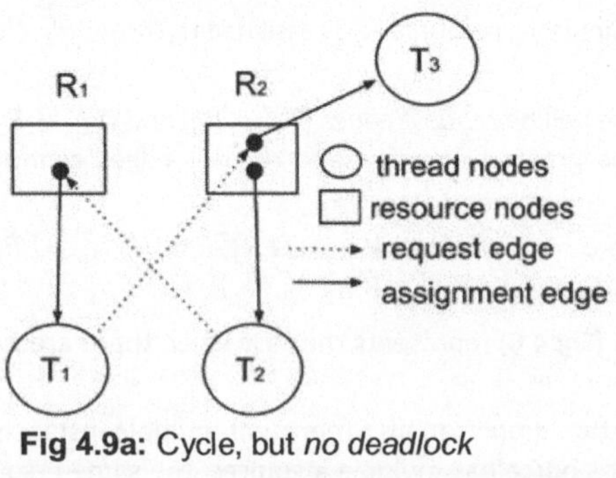

Fig 4.9a: Cycle, but *no deadlock*

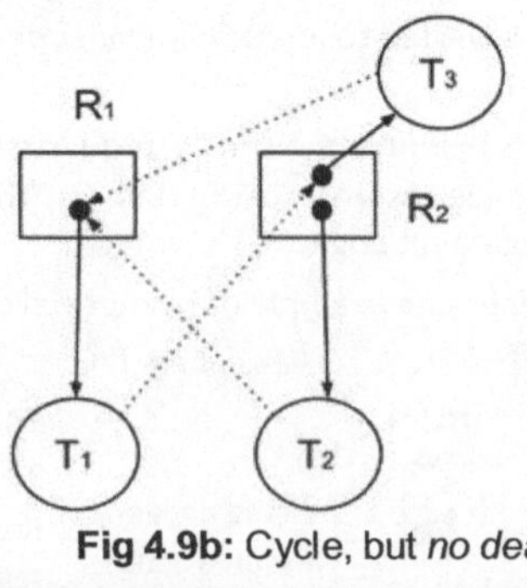

Fig 4.9b: Cycle, but *no deadlock*

Fig 4.9: RAGs with multiple instances of resources

But as soon as T_3 is complete, it can release an instance of R_2, and then T_1 can acquire it and the cycle is broken. A deadlock-like situation (not actual deadlock) is thus resolved (then **Fig 4.9a** becomes **Fig 4.7**).

However, if thread T_3 requests for resource R_1, there will be two cycles as follows (**Fig. 4.9b**):

$R_1 \rightarrow T_1 \rightarrow R_2 \rightarrow T_2 \rightarrow R_1$ and $R_1 \rightarrow T_1 \rightarrow R_2 \rightarrow T_3 \rightarrow R_1$.

Neither can be resolved if the other three conditions (**Condition i - iii**) also hold true. Then, threads T_1, T_2 and T_3 are deadlocked.

All the above four conditions (**i - iv**) are therefore *necessary* and *sufficient* to form a deadlock. They are necessary as not fulfilling even a single condition can stop forming the deadlock. For example, in most of the running systems, the first three conditions (**Condition i - iii**) are often satisfied - meaning that there is a possibility of a deadlock in the system, but the system may not be in a deadlock. If the fourth condition is also satisfied then a deadlock happens, for sure, when all resources have a single instance. When there are multiple instances of resources, a cycle denotes only a possibility of a deadlock. Whether there is a deadlock or not depends on whether the requests can be fulfilled after some time or not.

No more criteria other than the above four (**Condition i - iv**) are needed to form a deadlock - hence these four conditions are sufficient.

4.4 HANDLING DEADLOCKS

Deadlocks are undesired fallout of concurrency. They happen when all the four conditions stated above hold true simultaneously. To stop occurrences of deadlocks, we must make sure that not all the four conditions are true at any point of time. In other words, at least one of the four conditions must be negated.

In most cases, the condition of **mutual exclusion** is non-negotiable, simply because the resources which are non-shareable cannot be shared. We must thus negate one of the other three conditions.

Now requests for resources and their allocations are very dynamic in nature. Keeping track of this dynamism for hundreds of threads and resources and then taking appropriate actions require both space and time. It is thus up to the OS designers to decide what strategy can be adopted to handle deadlocks, based on the constraints in space and time. The strategies are clubbed into the following three categories.

1. *Deadlock Prevention*: Requests to resources are monitored and allowed to be made only if all the four conditions are not satisfied simultaneously.

2. *Deadlock Avoidance*: The threads notify their overall need of resources in advance and the resources are allocated only if the allocation is *safe* (it does not lead to the possibility of a deadlock).

3. *Deadlock Detection & Recovery*: Deadlocks are allowed to happen. But they are detected, and appropriate recovery actions are taken.

Let us discuss each of the strategies below.

4.4.1 Deadlock Prevention

Steps are taken so that, at no time, all the four conditions of a deadlock are met simultaneously. We consider each of the conditions again and discuss how a particular condition can be prevented to occur.

4.4.1.1 Preventing 'Mutual Exclusion'

As we know, shareable resources cannot cause a deadlock. For example, simultaneous reads to a file by several threads is always allowed and cannot cause a deadlock. However, simultaneous attempts to both read and write are not allowed as writing on a file is non-shareable. Similarly, acquiring a semaphore or a mutex lock is non-shareable. Hence, when the resources are non-shareable, mutual exclusion is an absolute necessity and thus cannot be compromised.

4.4.1.2 Preventing 'Hold & Wait'

This is possible if we force all the threads to acquire all the resources they need at a single time and release them all, again at one go. A thread is not allowed to hold one or more resources and simultaneously make incremental requests for others. The threads can request resources, only after releasing the resources held earlier. However, implementing this scheme has the following issues.

- It will require the threads to request for all resources at the very beginning, and release at the very end. The threads must block unless all the resources are acquired. Threads are not allowed to proceed with partially allocated resources that they could have done otherwise.
- Also, resources that might be needed for a short duration, are unduly held up for long. Smaller threads thus must wait if long threads hold resources. In sum, it severely slows down the performance of concurrent execution and leads to drop in resource utilization.

4.4.1.3 Preventing 'No Preemption'

Preventing 'No Preemption' means allowing preemption. If a thread holds some resources but waits for some other resources not available now, the OS is empowered to preempt the resources already held by the thread. In that case, the status of such a victim thread (or *thread-context*) needs to be saved so that it can resume from the same point of execution when all required resources are available. This is often applied to resources where states of resources (such as CPU registers and files in database transactions) can be saved and restored. But it cannot be applied for resources where thread context cannot be saved like mutex locks and semaphores (which are responsible for most of the deadlocks!).

4.4.1.4 Preventing 'Circular Wait'

Preventing circular wait is basically stopping the formation of cycles in the RAG. Instead of circular ordering of the threads and resources (recall **Sec 4.3**), if we can enforce a non-circular (linear or otherwise) ordering, the problem can be solved. For example, we can enumerate the threads and resources in such a way that a thread can always request for resources in increasing order and not the other way i.e., if a thread T_i while holding a resource R_i can request for another resource R_j only if $j > i$ (recall that request from T_n for resource R_1 caused a cycle in RAG). Alternatively, if T_i requires R_j such that $j < i$, it should release R_i first, and then request for R_j.

It can be proved that this does not allow a deadlock to form. If a thread T_i holds a resource R_i and requests R_j, then $j > i$. If another thread T_j holds R_j and, requests R_i, then there is a deadlock. But according to the scheme, again $i > j$. At the same time, both ($j > i$ and $i > j$) cannot be true. Hence, this kind of scheme cannot allow a deadlock to happen.

Out of the four prevention schemes, this is the most feasible one. Still, when there are hundreds of resources like mutex locks, enforcing an order while dynamically allocating them is not a trivial task. Also, like hold & wait, it reduces the amount of concurrency as threads block for want of resources.

4.4.2 Deadlock Avoidance

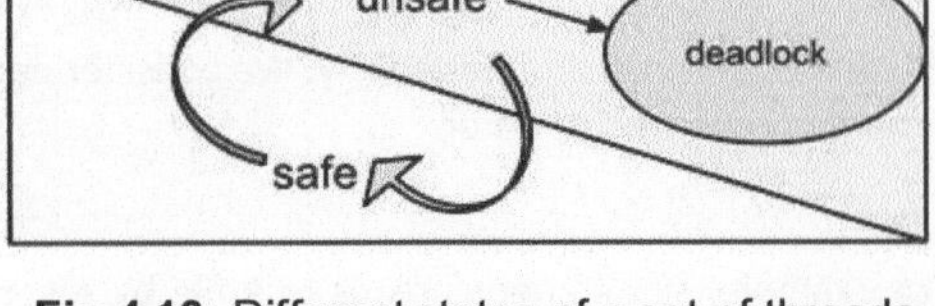

Fig 4.10: Different states of a set of threads

Deadlock avoidance techniques are less restrictive than the preventive ones. They allow the first three conditions (mutual exclusion, hold & wait, and no preemption) to continue, but only check whether the new allocation of resources can cause an unresolvable circular wait or not. Technically speaking, in deadlock avoidance, safety of a system of threads is checked before any new allocation of resources. The system is assumed to have the information of available instances of all the resources, current state of resource allocation to different threads and their outstanding resource-needs to complete execution. We call a system safe if all the threads in the system can complete their execution with the available resources without facing any deadlock. When the outstanding needs of a system of threads (even for a single thread) cannot be met with the available resources, we call the system unsafe. An unsafe system does not necessarily mean a deadlock but indicates the possibility of a deadlock in future (that may or may not come in reality) (**Fig 4.10**). A system can go from a safe state to an unsafe one, and vice versa. However, from an unsafe state, it can go to a deadlocked state from which a system cannot come out on its own.

Deadlock avoidance algorithms check when a system attempts to slip from a safe state to an unsafe one and stops it so that a deadlock can never arise. Given any scenario of resource allocation, the algorithms try to find a safe sequence of threads $(T_1', T_2', \ldots, T_n')$ in which the outstanding needs of resources for each of the threads $\{T_1, T_2, \ldots, T_n\}$ can be met ($n > 1$ and T'_i not necessarily = T_i) without putting any of the threads in an unsafe state. If a sequence can be found, resource allocation and resource reclamation (when a thread completes its execution, all its resources are reclaimed, and they add to the available resources) must be done in the sequence to avoid deadlock. If more than one such sequence is found, randomly anyone can be used. If no such sequence exists, the system is in an unsafe state which can lead to a deadlock. Requests for new resources (incremental demands) are not granted then.

Example: Let us consider a system of three threads $\{T_1, T_2, T_3\}$ using a single resource R that has $(3m + 2)$ instances $(m > 2)$. T_1, T_2 and T_3 require $(2m + 1)$, $(m + 2)$, and $(2m - 1)$ instances to complete their execution respectively.

Initially (at time t_0), if all the threads notify their total requirement and the threads execute only sequentially one after another, each can complete its execution safely in any order.

However, during concurrent execution, at some time, say t_1, thread T_1, T_2 and T_3 hold $(m + 1)$, 2, and $(m - 1)$ instances of R respectively. Hence, number of unallocated or available resources is = $(3m + 2) - \{(m + 1) + 2 + (m - 1)\}$ = m units. The outstanding needs of T_1, T_2 and T_3 are m, m and m units respectively. Here, total outstanding need by all the threads = $(3m)$ units $> m$. Hence, all the outstanding needs of all the threads cannot be met simultaneously. But, if allocation and reclamation of resources happen in any of the following six orders sequentially:

(T_1, T_2, T_3) or (T_1, T_3, T_2) or (T_2, T_1, T_3) or (T_2, T_3, T_1) or (T_3, T_1, T_2) or (T_3, T_2, T_1),

there is no possibility of a deadlock. Hence, these sequences of allocation is safe. Hence, the system is in a safe state.

However, after t_1, at another time t_2, consider each of T_1, T_2, T_3 make an incremental request of one more instance of R . If such requests are met, T_1, T_2 *and* T_3 will hold $(m + 2)$, 3 and m instances respectively with each having outstanding needs at $(m - 1)$ instances. But number of available resources = $(3m + 2)$ - $\{(m + 2) + 3 + m\}$ = $(m - 3)$ units. Hence, the outstanding need of no thread can be satisfied, or no safe sequence can be obtained. This will be a deadlock situation. This kind of allocation at time t_2 throws the system in an unsafe state which then leads to a deadlock.

However, note that allocation to only a single thread (say, T_1) will not put the system in an unsafe state as there will be $(m - 1)$ instances available. Even though other two threads (T_2 *and* T_3) have outstanding need of m units, we can allow the thread T_1 to proceed allocating all the available $(m - 1)$ instances. When it completes, all the resources it holds can be reclaimed ($2m + 1$ for T_1) and allow any one of the other two threads (T_2 or T_3) to proceed till its completion first and then the third in a sequence.

A little thought will reveal that, at time t_2, we can always have at least one safe sequence if allocation is made to a single thread. As soon as we allocate any resource to the second thread (at time t_2, before the first thread completes its execution), we enter an unsafe state (we fail to find a safe sequence).

A deadlock avoidance algorithm checks safety of the system based on total outstanding needs whenever a new request is made (at time t_2) and allows allocation only if the system remains safe after such allocation. If the system becomes unsafe (as in the above case), the allocation is not granted.

4.4.2.1 Banker's Algorithm

One of the most popular deadlock avoidance techniques is known as Banker's algorithm - which always ensures that a system of threads is in a safe state before and after any allocation of resources. The name comes from the fact that a bank needs to allow withdrawal of cash in such a way that it can meet cash requirements of all its customers at any given time.

The algorithm considers n threads $\{T_1, T_2, \ldots, T_n\}$ and m resource-types $\{R_1, R_2, \ldots, R_m\}$ each having one or more instances. Let us define some vectors and matrices necessary for discussing the algorithm.

Resources: Total available resources are represented by a m-dimensional vector,

$RES = [r_1, r_2, \ldots, r_m]$ where each r_j indicates total number of instances for resource-type R_j in the system.

Each thread T_i has allotment or requirement of resources represented as a vector $[r_{i1}, r_{i2}, \ldots, r_{im}]$ where r_{ij} represents the number of instances of resource-type R_j in T_i.

Maximum resource needs: Total requirement of all resource types by different threads is represented by a $(n \times m)$ matrix

$MAX = [[r_{11}, r_{12}, \ldots, r_{1m}]\ [r_{21}, r_{22}, \ldots, r_{2m}]\ \ldots\ [r_{n1}, r_{n2}, \ldots, r_{nm}]]$ where $MAX[i][j]$ indicates maximum need of thread T_i for resource type R_j, given by r_{ij} .

Resource allocation: Similarly, current allocation of resources at a given time, is also represented by another $(n \times m)$ matrix,

$ALLOC = [[r'_{11}, r'_{12}, \ldots, r'_{1m}]\ [r'_{21}, r'_{22}, \ldots, r'_{2m}]\ \ldots\ [r'_{n1}, r'_{n2}, \ldots, r'_{nm}]]$ where r'_{ij} stands for number of instances of type R_j allocated to T_i.

Available resources: As resources are allocated to threads, free and available instances of resources reduce. The current number of available instances of resources is represented by an m-dimensional vector

$AVAIL = [r'_1, r'_2, \ldots, r'_m]$ where each r'_j indicates number of instances available at a given moment for resource-type R_j

Outstanding needs: Once the threads are allocated resources, remaining resource needs of the threads are also represented by an $n \times m$ matrix

NEED = $[[r''_{11}, r''_{12}, \ldots, r''_{1m}]\ [r''_{21}, r''_{22}, \ldots, r''_{2m}]\ \ldots\ [r''_{n1}, r''_{n2}, \ldots, r''_{nm}]]$ where r''_{ij} stands for number of instances of type R_j still needed by T_i to complete its execution.

Resource requests: Another matrix of $(n \times m)$ dimension represents new (incremental) need of all the threads,

REQ = $[[r'''_{11}, r'''_{12}, \ldots, r'''_{1m}]\ [r'''_{21}, r'''_{22}, \ldots, r'''_{2m}]\ \ldots\ [r'''_{n1}, r'''_{n2}, \ldots, r'''_{nm}]]$ where r'''_{ij} stands for number of instances of type R_j newly needed by T_i.

The following relationships and constraints always hold true.

1. $RES\ [j] \geq MAX[i][j]$ for all i, j *(maximum need of any thread for any resource-type cannot be more than the available number of instances in the system)*

2. $RES[j] \geq \sum_i ALLOC[i][j]$ for all i, j *(sum of allocated instances of any resource-type cannot be more than total number of instances at any moment)*

3. $AVAIL\ [j] = RES[j] - \sum_i ALLOC[i][j]$ for all i, j *(available number of resource-instances is whatever remains after allocation to all threads)*

4. $NEED[i]\ [j] = MAX[i][j] - ALLOC[i][j] \geq 0$ for all i, j

5. $REQ[i]\,[j] \;\le MAX[i][j] - ALLOC[i][j]\,for\ all\ i,j$ *(incremental request cannot be greater than the outstanding need of a thread for a given resource-type)*

We also mention that

- $ALLOC[i]$ indicates a m-dimensional vector for thread T_i (a row vector) with its current allocation of m-resource types
- Similarly, $NEED[i]$ is the outstanding need of thread T_i (i-th row from matrix NEED)
- $REQ[i]$ is the immediate need (incremental) of thread T_i (i-th row from matrix REQ)

We shall use the following vector notations.

- X=Y if and only if X[i] = Y[i] for all i.
  For example, [0 1 2] = [0 1 2], but [0 1 2]≠ [0 1 3] as X[3] ≠ Y[3]
- X < Y if and only if X[i] < Y[i] for all i.
  For example, [0 1 2] < [1 2 3], but [0 1 2] < [0 2 3] as X[2] not < Y[2]

... and so on.

The algorithm can be seen as having the following two components (**Fig 4.11**).

```
bool check_safety (AVAIL, ALLOC, NEED) {

  0. INITIALISATION:
     bool finish_possible[n] = {0, 0, ..., 0}; /*flag*/
     bool safe = 1, unsafe = 0;
     int WORK[m];
        /* n = #threads, m=#types of resources */

        WORK = AVAIL;

  1. Find an index i such that
     (NEED[i] < WORK)&&(finish_possible[i] == 0)
     if not found, goto Step 3.

  2. WORK = WORK + ALLOC[i];
     finish_possible[i] = 1;
     goto Step 1.

  3. if (finish_possible[i] == 1 for all i) return (safe);
     else return (unsafe);
}
```

```
bool grant_request (AVAIL, ALLOC, REQ[i], MAX) {

  0. bool grant_possible = 1, grant_not_possible = 0;

  1.  NEED[i] = MAX[i] - ALLOC[i];

  2.  if (REQ[i] > NEED[i])
        return (error); /*request is more than max-need */

  3.  if (REQ[i] > AVAIL[i])
        return (grant_not_possible); /* Ti must wait */

  4. /* as if Ti is allocated the resources */
        AVAIL  = AVAIL – REQ[i];
        ALLOC[i]  = ALLOC[i] + REQ[i];
        NEED[i] = NEED[i] –REQ[i];

  5.  if( check_safety(AVAIL, ALLOC, NEED) == safe))
        return (grant_possible);
      else return (grant_not_possible); /* Ti must wait */
}
```

Fig 4.11: Banker's Algorithm

1. Checking safety of the system, given the available resources (vector $AVAIL$), current state of allocation (matrix $ALLOC$), and the outstanding need (matrix $NEED$), is done by function ***check_safety()***. It tries to first find a single thread whose current requirements can be fulfilled with the available instances of resources (Step 1). If the thread gets the resources, completes its execution and returns all the resources, it is checked for another thread (Step 2) and so on. This way it is checked whether current needs of all the threads can be satisfied or not. Thus, if a complete sequence of all the threads that can complete their execution is found, the function declares safety (Step 3) and the sequence is called a safe sequence.

Step 1 here needs a search of maximum n threads to find the first thread in the sequence, followed by that of maximum $(n-1)$ threads for the second, and so on. For each thread T_i, we need to check $REQ[i]$ vector requiring m comparisons. Hence, the function has a complexity of $O(mn^2)$.

2. Whenever a thread makes an additional request as given by $REQ[i]$ by a thread, say T_i, before granting, the algorithm checks whether the request can be granted safely (shown in function ***grant_request()***). First, if the incremental request is more than its outstanding need, it is outright rejected flagging error message (Step 1 & 2). If the request is within declared maximum need, but less than available resources at present, the thread is not granted resources and must wait till the resources become available (Step 3). Otherwise, it is assumed as if the resources

are granted, we modify the vectors (Step 4) and check for safety (Step 5) before the actual allocation. If the assumed allocation is safe, permission for allocation is granted and actual allocation is done. This function is called for each thread requesting resources and involves comparisons of m resources, thus has the complexity of $O(m)$.

Example: *Consider the following snapshot of a system:*

	Allocation				Max				Available			
	A	B	C	D	A	B	C	D	A	B	C	D
T0	0	0	1	2	0	0	1	2	1	5	2	0
T1	1	0	0	0	1	7	5	0				
T2	1	3	5	4	2	3	5	6				
T3	0	6	3	2	0	6	5	2				
T4	0	0	1	4	0	6	5	6				

Answer the following questions using the banker's algorithm:
a. What is the content of the matrix ***Need****?*
b. Is the system in a safe state?
c. If a request from thread T1 arrives for (0,4,2,0), can the request be granted immediately?

Soln. *a. NEED = MAX - ALLOC*

=

	A	B	C	D
T0	*0-0*	*0-0*	*1-1*	*2-2*
T1	*1-1*	*7-0*	*5-0*	*0-0*
T2	*2-1*	*3-3*	*5-5*	*6-4*
T3	*0-0*	*6-6*	*5-3*	*2-2*
T4	*0-0*	*6-0*	*5-1*	*6-4*

=

	A	B	C	D
T0	*0*	*0*	*0*	*0*
T1	*0*	*7*	*5*	*0*
T2	*1*	*0*	*0*	*2*
T3	*0*	*0*	*2*	*0*
T4	*0*	*6*	*4*	*2*

b. T0 does not need any resources. So, when T0 is complete, AVAIL = AVAIL + ALLOC[0] = [1 5 3 2].

Then, either T2 or T3 can complete, considering T2 first, AVAIL = [2 8 8 6]

After T3 gets over, AVAIL = [2 14 11 8]

Now, either T1 or T4 can complete. Considering T1 gets over first, AVAIL = [3 14 11 8] > NEED [4]. Hence, T4 can also complete. The system is safe, and one of the safe sequences is T0→T2→T3→T1→T4.

c. Here, REQ [1] = [0 4 2 0] < NEED [1], also [0 4 2 0] < AVAIL = [1 5 2 0]

If the request is granted, then AVAIL = AVAIL – REQ[1] = [1 5 2 0] - [0 4 2 0] = [1 1 0 0]
ALLOC [1] = ALLOC[1] + REQ [1] = [1 0 0 0] + [0 4 2 0] = [1 4 2 0]
NEED[1] = NEED[1] –REQ[1] = [0 7 5 0] - [0 4 2 0] = [0 3 3 0]

Hence, modified ALLOC =

	A	B	C	D
T0	0	0	1	2
T1	1	4	2	0
T2	1	3	5	4
T3	0	6	3	2
T4	0	0	1	4

modified NEED =

	A	B	C	D
T0	0	0	0	0
T1	0	3	3	0
T2	1	0	0	2
T3	0	0	2	0
T4	0	6	4	2

T0 can complete as NEED[0] < AVAIL = [1 1 0 0], after which AVAIL = [1 1 1 2]
T2 can complete, after which AVAIL = [2 4 6 6]
T1 or T3 can complete. Considering T1 completes, AVAIL = [3 8 8 6]
T3 completes, then AVAIL = [3 14 11 8]
T4 can be completed as AVAIL > NEED[4]

Hence, the system will be safe (one safe sequence is T0→T2→T1→T3→T4) after grant of the request from T1. It can be immediately granted safely.

Banker's algorithm can be easily implemented at the user level and students should be encouraged to do it as a programming exercise.

Tools: Linux kernel ensures that the resources are acquired in a proper order so that deadlock does not occur. However, Linux also provides a feature-rich tool `lockdep` to check locking order in the kernel[11].

4.4.3 Deadlock Detection & Recovery

This is the most relaxed approach where no restrictions are enforced on resource allocation. Threads request for resources and are granted without thinking about the safety of the system. Rather, the operating system tries to detect if there is any deadlock in the system. If detected, the system tries to recover from the deadlock through external interventions.

4.4.3.1 Detection Algorithm

In this approach, the OS does not care about the first three conditions of the deadlock but the last one of unresolvable circular waits. A deadlock is possible only if there is a cycle in the resource allocation graph. However, deadlock is a certainty with circular wait only when each resource has a single instance. Otherwise, there is only a possibility. Hence, we shall consider the two cases separately.

Each resource has a single instance:

The detection is done using a *wait-for* graph of the active threads in the system. A *wait-for* graph involves only threads (or processes) and is essentially a RAG with its resource nodes short-circuited. The resource nodes and their connecting edges are not shown in the wait-for graph. An edge $T_i \rightarrow T_j$ exists between thread T_i and thread T_j if

[11] https://www.kernel.org/doc/Documentation/locking/lockdep-design.txt (as on 4-Nov-2022)

and only if $T_i \rightarrow R_k$ and $R_k \rightarrow T_j$ in the original RAG. The edge $T_i \rightarrow T_j$ indicates that T_i waits for a resource held by T_j. For example, a wait-for graph for the RAG in **Fig 4.6** can be drawn as in **Fig 4.12. Fig 4.13** shows how a wait-for graph can be drawn from a RAG. A cycle in the wait-for graph denotes a deadlock and all the threads in the cycle are deadlocked. A cycle in a graph can be detected in $O(n^2)$ time, where n is the number of nodes in a graph.

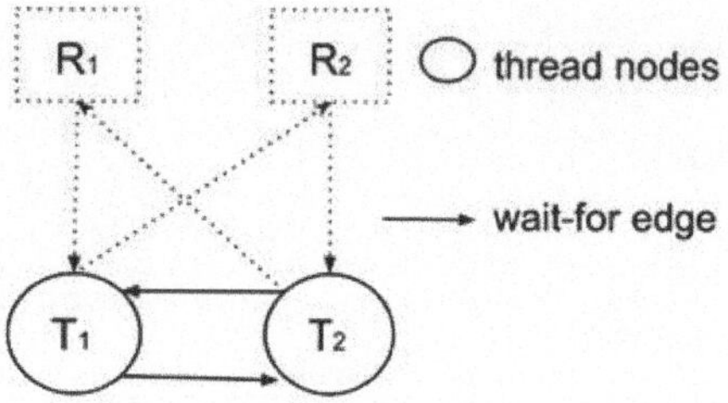

Fig 4.12: A wait-for graph (b/w T1 & T2 only) from **Fig 4.6**

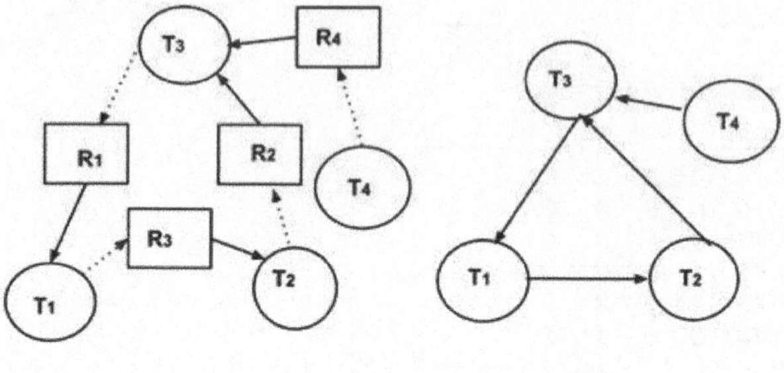

(a) (b)

Fig 4.13: (a) RAG to (b) Wait-for graph

Tools: In Linux, BCC toolkit can detect potential deadlock using `deadlock_detector` that finds cycles in the mutex locks in the user code[12].

Resources with one or more instances:

When resources have multiple instances, we know that mere presence of a cycle is not a confirmation of a deadlock (see **Sec 4.3**). We use a deadlock detection algorithm (***detect_deadlock()***), which is similar to ***check_safety(),*** with little necessary modifications (**Fig 4.14**).

[12] https://github.com/iovisor/bcc (as on 4-Nov-2022)

```
bool detect_deadlock (AVAIL, ALLOC, REQ) {
 0. INITIALISATION:
      bool hold_res[n] ; /*flags for threads*/
      int WORK[m];
            /* n = #threads, m=#types of resources */
      WORK = AVAIL;

  1. For all i, do
      if (ALLOC[i] == [0, 0,...,0]) hold_res[i] = 0;
      else hold_res[i] = 1;

  2. Find an index i such that
       (REQ[i] <= WORK) && (hold_res[i] == 1)
       if not found, goto Step 4.

  3. WORK = WORK + ALLOC[i];
      ALLOC[i] = [0,0,...,0]; hold_res[i] = 0;
      goto Step 2.

  4. if (hold_res[i] == 1 for some i)
       return (system in deadlock & Ti in deadlock);
      else return (no_deadlock);
}
```

Fig 4.14: Deadlock detection algorithm

Step 1: If a thread does not hold any resources, (i.e., $ALLOC[i] = [0,0,\ldots,0]$) it is not part of any deadlock and can bypass Step 2. The step has time complexity $O(n)$.

Step 2: Similar to Banker's algorithm, Step 2 looks for a thread that satisfies both the conditions. It requires a maximum of n searches, each requiring another m comparisons for each resource instance. Hence, a maximum of $O(mn)$ comparisons are needed in Step 2.

Step 3: We assume that the thread T_i completes the execution and returns all resources back to the OS and the flag *hold_res* is reset. We need to search for the next thread that can complete and thus need to go to repeat Step 2.

Hence, Step 2 needs to be executed a maximum of n times (first iteration searches among n threads, second among $(n-1)$ threads, and so on). Thus, the Step 0-3 has a time complexity of $O(mn^2)$.

Step 4: We come here at the end, which is outside the repetitive loop (Step 2-3). Even if a single thread cannot complete, the system is in deadlock and the corresponding thread is starving. All such threads are forming a deadlock. It also has the time complexity $O(n)$.

Hence, overall time complexity of the detection algorithm is $O(mn^2)$ [as $O(n) + O(mn^2) + O(n) = O(mn^2)$].

Example: *For the following matrices, check whether there is any deadlock or not?*

	Allocation					Request					Available				
	A	B	C	D	E	A	B	C	D	E	A	B	C	D	E
T0	1	0	1	1	0	0	1	1	0	1	0	1	0	0	1
T1	1	1	0	0	0	0	0	1	0	1					
T2	0	0	0	1	0	0	1	0	0	1					
T3	0	0	0	0	0	1	0	1	0	1					

Soln. *Here, for T3, present allocation is all zero. Hence, it can not cause any deadlock and thus is left out in the deadlock detection algorithm.*

We can find REQ[2] = [0 1 0 0 1] = AVAIL = WORK. Thus, thread T2 can complete.

Once T2 completes, WORK = WORK + ALLOC[2] = [0 1 0 0 1] + [0 0 0 1 0] = [0 1 0 1 1]
Now, the WORK cannot satisfy any remaining REQ[i], i.e. neither REQ[0] nor REQ[1].

Hence, the detection algorithm stops with T0 and T1 unmarked or, with hold_res[0] = hold_res[1] = 1, i.e. deadlock exists in the system and T0 & T1 are in deadlock.

When to run a deadlock detection algorithm?

Ideally it should be run whenever a deadlock occurs, so that some actions can be taken to recover from it. But a deadlock is ascertained only when the detection algorithm is run.

Thus, the frequency of running the algorithm depends on the following two factors:

i. how often deadlock occurs in the system?

ii. how many threads / processes get affected in a deadlock?

When a deadlock occurs, the resources are held but not used for completion of the threads that hold them. On the contrary, some other threads need them, but cannot use them. Thus, resources are held but under-utilized. Threads occupy memory disallowing other waiting ones to be active but they themselves cannot complete. This leads to reduced throughput. Performance of the system thus deteriorates. Hence, frequency of running the algorithm should match that of its occurrences, in general.

Again, deadlocks happen when resource requests cannot be granted due to lack of available resources. Hence, it can be run whenever a resource requested cannot be granted. But running the algorithm has cost in terms of computational overhead. Running it frequently can burden the system. One practical solution thus is to run in a suitable regular interval (say, once per hour) or when CPU utilization falls below a threshold (say, 40 percent).

4.4.3.2 Recovery from Deadlock

A deadlock can be prevented or avoided. But if it happens, it needs external forces to come out of it. Typically, the condition of the circular *wait* is broken. Recovery, initiated by the OS kernel after detection, thus terminates either the threads / processes or preempts resources from the circular wait.

Thread / Process Termination: Threads can be terminated, and all the resources held by them can be reclaimed by the kernel. But an OS cannot handle threads directly if they are user threads. Processes are terminated and resources are reclaimed in that case. Either *all the involved processes are terminated* at one go or incrementally *one process at a time* is aborted until the cycle is broken.

Aborting processes is costly. A process may have run for considerable time, aborting means re-starting and re-running the process. Hence, aborting all the processes is a brute-force technique. On the other hand, when selecting one process at a time, selection of the victim process needs analysis of the priority-level (how important the process is: high, moderate or low), running history (how long it has run), resource holding status (how many resources it holds) of the process. It also needs re-running the deadlock detection program several times until the deadlock is broken. In either case, it has computational overheads.

Process abortion is thus easy, but costly in general.

Resource Preemption: The other alternative is to forcefully take the resources from the threads that are involved in the cycle and give them to other threads of the cycle that can complete execution. Pertinent questions are as follows:

(i) selection of victims: which resources are to be chosen and from which threads? The deciding factor can be the cost of preemption: number of resources, percentage of completed execution, etc. The preempted resources need to be re-assigned to the thread and the thread re-executed, if not the entire process.

(ii) rollback: The victim process cannot proceed for want of preempted resources. If it is not aborted, then it needs to be rolled back to a safe state from which it can resume its operation when the resources are re-assigned. Appropriate mechanisms should be in place so that process states are stored for possible rollback.

(iii) starvation: If cost is the only deciding factor behind victim selection, then it is possible that the same victims are selected repeatedly. The victim processes then face repeated denial of progress or starvation. To mitigate this, the victim selection algorithm may incorporate the number of rollbacks happening to a thread as one of the deciding factors.

UNIT SUMMARY

- *This chapter discusses deadlocks in concurrent execution of threads (or processes).*
- *Deadlocks happen when requests for non-shareable computing resources cannot be met at all.*
- *Deadlocks emerge when two or more threads hold some resources and simultaneously request for some more which are held by some other threads. All the involved threads make a cycle in the resource allocation graph.*
- *There are four necessary and sufficient conditions needed to form a deadlock: mutual exclusion, hold and wait, no preemption and circular wait.*
- *Mutual exclusion of resources means resources are used in a non-shareable manner (i.e., one resource instance is used by only one thread at a time).*
- *Hold & wait means a thread can hold some resources and wait for getting some more.*
- *No preemption does not allow forceful release of resources from any threads.*
- *Circular wait is the formation of a cycle in the resource allocation graph involving threads and resources.*
- *Deadlocks are handled in three ways: prevention, avoidance and detection & recovery.*
- *Prevention techniques are the most restrictive ones that negate at least one of the four necessary conditions.*
- *Avoidance techniques are comparatively lenient, where safety of the system of threads is checked before each new allocation of resources. Banker's algorithm is a popular deadlock avoidance technique.*
- *In detection & recovery, deadlocks are allowed to happen. At appropriate intervals, detection algorithms are run. When detected, either involved processes are terminated or resources are preempted.*

EXERCISES

Multiple Choice Questions

Q1. Which of the following statements is/are TRUE with respect to deadlocks?

A. Circular wait is a necessary condition for the formation of deadlock.
B. In a system where each resource has more than one instance, a cycle in its wait-for graph indicates the presence of a deadlock.
C. If the current allocation of resources to processes leads the system to unsafe state, then deadlock will necessarily occur.
D. In the resource-allocation graph of a system, if every edge is an assignment edge, then the system is not in a deadlock state. [GATE (2022)]

Q2. A system has 6 identical resources and N processes competing for them. Each process can request at most 2 resources. Which one of the following values of N could lead to a deadlock?

A. 1 **B.** 2 **C.** 3 **D.** 4 [GATE(2015)]

Q3. Which of the following is not true with respect to deadlock prevention and deadlock avoidance schemes ?

A. In deadlock prevention, the request for resources is always granted if resulting state is safe

B. In deadlock avoidance, the request for resources is always granted, if the resulting state is safe

C. Deadlock avoidance requires knowledge of resource requirements a priori

D. Deadlock prevention is more restrictive than deadlock avoidance [ISRO(2017)]

Q4. Consider a system with 3 processes that share 4 instances of the same resource type. Each process can request a maximum of K instances. Resources can be requested and released only one at a time. The largest value of K that will always avoid deadlock is ___. [GATE (2018)]

Q5. In a system, there are three types of resources: E, F and G. Four processes P0, P1, P2 and P3 execute concurrently. At the outset, the processes have declared their maximum resource requirements using a matrix named Max as given below. For example, Max[P2, F] is the maximum number of instances of F that P2 would require. The number of instances of the resources allocated to the various processes at any given state is given by a matrix named Allocation. Consider a state of the system with the Allocation matrix as shown below, and in which 3 instances of E and 3 instances of F are the only resources available.

Allocation

	E	F	G
P0	1	0	1
P1	1	1	2
P2	1	0	3
P3	2	0	0

Max

	E	F	G
P0	4	3	1
P1	2	1	4
P2	1	3	3
P3	5	4	1

From the perspective of deadlock avoidance, which one of the following is true?
A. The system is in *safe* state
B. The system is not in *safe* state, but would be *safe* if one more instance of E were available
C. The system is not in *safe* state, but would be *safe* if one more instance of F were available
D. The system is not in *safe* state, but would be *safe* if one more instance of G were available

[GATE(2018)]

Q6. Consider the following snapshot of a system running **n** concurrent processes. Process **i** is holding **Xi** instances of a resource **R**, **1<=i<=n** . Assume that all instances of **R** are currently in use. Further, for all **i**, process **i** can place a request for at most **Yi** additional instances of **R** while holding the **Xi** instances it already has. Of the **n** processes, there are exactly two processes **p** and **q** such that **Yp=Yq=0** . Which one of the following conditions guarantees that no other process apart from **p** and **q** can complete execution?

A. $Xp + Xq < Min\{Yk \mid 1 \leq k \leq n, k \neq p, k \neq q\}$

B. $Xp + Xq < Max\{Yk \mid 1 \leq k \leq n, k \neq p, k \neq q\}$

C. $Min(Xp, Xq) \geq Min\{Yk \mid 1 \leq k \leq n, k \neq p, k \neq q\}$

D. $Min(Xp, Xq) \leq Max\{Yk \mid 1 \leq k \leq n, k \neq p, k \neq q\}$ [GATE(2019)]

Q7. A system has 3 user processes each requiring 2 units of resource R. The minimum number of units of R such that no deadlock will occur-

A. 3
B. 5
C. 4
D. 6

Answers of Multiple Choice Questions

1. A, D 2. D 3. A 4. 2. 5. A 6. A 7. C

Short Answer Type Questions

Q1. What do you mean by deadlock in the context of an operating system?

Q2. How is a deadlock different from a livelock situation?

Q3. List the conditions that lead to a deadlock.

Q4. Mention the ways of handling deadlocks.

Q5. Can a deadlock happen in a single programming environment? Justify.

Q6. Suppose we have a system with a single resource. Can the resource induce a deadlock in the system?

Q7. How is deadlock prevention different from deadlock avoidance?

Q8. Mention two ways of recovery from deadlock.

Q9. What is a resource allocation graph?

Q10. What is a wait-for graph? How is it different from a RAG?

Long Answer Type Questions

Q1. "Livelock can be opened, but a deadlock needs to be broken." Justify or refute the statement.

Q2. Justify why the necessary conditions of a deadlock are sufficient.

Q3. Construct a resource allocation graph using four process and four resources such that

a. *the graph has a cycle and processes are deadlocked,*

b. the graph has a cycle but the processes are not in a deadlock.

Q4. Discuss different types of deadlock prevention techniques.

Q5. What do you mean by safety of a system? Explain how it is related to deadlock in the system.

Q6. Illustrate with examples when a system is not safe, but a deadlock is not formed in the system.

Q7. Discuss how banker's algorithm is related to avoidance as well as detection of deadlocks.

Q8. Discuss different issues with recovery from a deadlock.

Q9. Why do most commercial OS not implement any OS handling mechanisms? Explain.

Numerical Problems

Q1. A system has 9 user processes each requiring 3 units of resource R. What is the minimum number of units of R such that no deadlock will occur?

[*Hint: a deadlock happens when each process holds resources less than its maximum demand, but outstanding need of none is fulfilled from available resources. Hence, for deadlock, NEED[i] > AVAIL for all i. No deadlock means NEED[i] >= AVAIL for at least one i]* **[Ans. 19]**

Q2. If there are 7 units of resource R in the system and each process in the system requires 2 units of resource R, then how many processes can be present at maximum so that no deadlock will occur? **[Ans. 6]**

Q3. Consider a system having **m** resources of the same type being shared by **n** processes. Resources can be requested and released by processes only one at a time. Derive the condition necessary for the system to be deadlock-free. **[Ans. sum of max need < m+n]**

Q4. Suppose there are 4 tape drives, 2 plotters, 3 scanners and 1 CD drive in a system. They are allocated to 3 processes in the following order: P1: [0 0 1 0] P2: [2 0 0 1] and P3: [0 1 2 0]. If the processes request for additional needs as P1: [2 0 0 1] P2: [1 0 1 0] and P3:[2 1 0 0], check whether the requests can be safely met.

PRACTICAL

Q1. Implement a deadlock detection algorithm while there are single instances of every resource. Input number of resources and that of processes and different edges among resources and processes. Use any language of your choice.

Q2. Implement banker's algorithm in any language of your choice with number of processes, number of resources as inputs. Also take the maximum number of resource instances, allocation matrix and immediate need matrix as inputs to determine safety of a system.

Q3. Explore `lockdep` and `bcc` toolkit to learn their use in Linux kernel.

KNOW MORE

Deadlocks are discussed in general with good detail in [SGG18]. It nicely points out the differences with livelock with examples from POSIX threads.

[Sta12] explains deadlock with timing diagrams to illustrate the difference between the possibility of a deadlock and actual deadlock. It also contains good examples of different types of resources that can cause deadlock. The book also provides a nice summary of three deadlock handling techniques.

[Hal15] sees deadlock as part of process synchronization and provides a brief and summarized version in general.

[Dow16] illustrates a few examples of deadlock involving synchronizing tools: semaphores, barriers, mutex locks.

[Dha09] gives a general introduction followed by brief discussion on deadlocks in UNIX and Windows systems. The book also provides rich references to the seminal and original work on deadlocks.

[Bac05] and [Vah12] discuss deadlocks and their avoidance in the UNIX system, specifically in the locks and file system both in single-processor, multiprocessor and distributed environments.

[YIR17] contains the issue of deadlock in Windows operating systems.

REFERENCES AND SUGGESTED READINGS

[Bac05] Maurice J Bach: The Design of the UNIX Operating System, Prentice Hall of India, 2005.

[Dha09] Dhananjay M. Dhamdhere: Operating Systems, A Concept-Based Approach, McGraw Hill, 2009.

[Dow16] Allen B. Downey: The Little Book of Semaphores, 2e, Green Tea Press, 2016 (available at https://greenteapress.com/semaphores/LittleBookOfSemaphores.pdf as on 9-Oct-2022).

[Hal15] Sibsankar Haldar: Operating Systems, Self Edition 1.1, 2015.

[SGG18] Abraham Silberschatz, Peter B Galvin, Greg Gagne: Operating Systems Concepts,10th Edition, Wiley, 2018.

[Sta12] William Stallings: Operating Systems Internals and Design Principles, 7th Edition, Prentice Hall, 2012.

[Vah12] Uresh Vahalia: UNIX Internals, The New Frontiers, Pearson, 2012.

[YIR17] Pavel Yosifovich, Alex Ionescu, Mark E. Russinovich, and David A. Solomon: Windows Internals, Seventh Edition (Part 1 and 2), Microsoft, 2017. https://docs.microsoft.com/en-us/sysinternals/resources/windows-internals (as on 8-Jul-2022).

Dynamic QR Code for Further Reading

5 Memory Management

UNIT SPECIFICS

Through this unit we have discussed the following aspects:

- *Memory Management: Basic concept, Logical and Physical address map, Memory allocation: Contiguous Memory allocation – Fixed and variable partition– Internal and External fragmentation and Compaction; Paging: Principle of operation – Page allocation – Hardware support for paging, Protection and sharing, Disadvantages of paging.*
- *Virtual Memory: Basics of Virtual Memory – Hardware and control structures – Locality of reference, Page fault, Working Set, Dirty page/Dirty bit – Demand paging, Page Replacement algorithms: Optimal, First in First Out (FIFO), Second Chance (SC), Not recently used (NRU) and Least Recently used (LRU).*

This chapter discusses the role of memory in computers. Memory is the second most important hardware after the processor. A processor constantly interacts with the memory during execution. While all the programs persistently remain in either secondary (HDD) or tertiary memory (removable media), they are temporarily brought in main memory for execution. The processor can fetch (and store) instructions and data from (to) the main memory and not from secondary or tertiary storage. Hence all processes are loaded in the main memory. But main memory is costly in price and thus small. How this space can be judiciously utilized so that we can maximize CPU utilization, throughput and overall performance of a computer is the motivation of this chapter. First, we study how main memory is managed by an operating system and how secondary storage can augment the management to improve performance.

Like previous units, several multiple-choice questions as well as questions of short and long answer types following Bloom's taxonomy, assignments through numerical problems, a list of references and suggested readings are provided. It is important to note that for getting more information on various topics of interest, appropriate URLs and QR code have been provided in different sections which can be accessed or scanned for relevant supportive knowledge. "Know More" section is also designed for supplementary information to cater to the inquisitiveness and curiosity of the students.

RATIONALE

This unit starts with enumerating and introducing different types of memories available in a computer and their interaction with the processor. The largest memory unit that a processor can directly fetch (and store) instructions and data from (to) is the main memory. All programs residing in secondary or tertiary memory are therefore brought into main memory for execution. The main memory is costly and thus small in size. Different parts of a program may be stored in different areas of memory. How they are uniformly referenced and accessed is discussed through logical and physical addressing schemes. It is followed by a discussion on how processes are allocated space in the memory. When the main memory is inadequate and/or a process is so large that it cannot be accommodated in the main memory, how secondary memory can support as a back-up memory is talked about in the virtual memory section. The intricacies and nuances of data transfer between main memory and secondary memory, intervention of the processor and responses of the operating system in the memory management are discussed.

This unit builds the fundamental concepts to understand memory management issues of an OS, introduces necessary terms and terminologies, and details important techniques. The concepts form the core of computation and interaction between the processor and memory under the control of an operating system.

PRE-REQUISITES

- *Basics of Computer Organization and Architecture*
- *Fundamentals of Data Structures*
- *Introductory knowledge of Computer Programming*
- *Introductory knowledge of Compilers*
- *Introduction to Operating Systems (***Unit I, II and III** *of the book)*

UNIT OUTCOMES

List of outcomes of this unit is as follows:

U5-O1: Define different concepts like address binding, logical address, fragmentation, paging, segmentation, virtual memory, demand paging, working set, thrashing, degree of multiprogramming and so on.

U5-O2: Describe the principle and techniques of address binding, memory allocation, implementation of paging and demand paging, different page replacement algorithms.

U5-O3: Understand the issues in memory management of a multiprogramming environment, memory allocation and reclamation procedures, data transfer between main memory and secondary storage.

U5-O4: Realize the role of an operating system in memory space allocation and deallocation, the support from the hardware and software techniques.

U5-O5: Analyze and compare pros and cons of different memory allocation techniques, page replacement techniques, between memory management and virtual memory.

U5-O6: Design memory allocation techniques, page placement and replacement policy and implement them in a given system within its hardware constraints.

Course Outcomes

After completion of the course the students will be able to:

1. Create processes and threads.
2. Develop algorithms for process scheduling for a given specification of CPU.
3. utilization, Throughput, Turnaround Time, Waiting Time, Response Time.
4. For a given specification of memory organization develop the techniques for optimally allocating memory to processes by increasing memory utilization and for improving the access time.
5. Design and implement file management system.
6. For a given I/O devices and OS (specify) develop the I/O management functions in OS as part of a uniform device abstraction by performing operations for synchronization between CPU and I/O controllers.

Unit-5 Outcomes	EXPECTED MAPPING WITH COURSE OUTCOMES (1- Weak Correlation; 2- Medium correlation; 3- Strong Correlation)					
	CO-1	CO-2	CO-3	CO-4	CO-5	CO-6
U5-01	1	2	3	3	2	1
U5-02	1	2	3	3	2	1
U5-03	1	2	3	3	2	1
U5-04	1	2	3	3	2	1
U5-05	1	2	3	3	2	1
U5-06	1	2	3	3	2	1

5.1 INTRODUCTION

Memory is the second most important resource after the processor in a computer. Although there are several memory elements like registers, cache, ROM, RAM, secondary memory (hard disk), tertiary memory (recall Ch.1, **Fig 1.1**) in a computer, RAM or random-access memory is known as the *main memory*.

While registers and cache memory are closer to the processor (**Fig 1.7** - **1.8**) that a processor can directly access, they are very expensive and thus of very small capacity. They cannot accommodate either the operating system or other programs that are executed by the processor. Main memory is the furthest memory unit from a processor that it can directly access which can accommodate the OS as well as user applications during their execution. Processors make all memory references with respect to this memory. Main memory is volatile in nature - it keeps the code and data (both for system and application programs) as long as the computer is on. Hence, both the OS and other programs need to be loaded on the main memory (hereinafter referred to as memory only) from the secondary or tertiary memory after each start-up and/or execution (**Fig 5.1**).

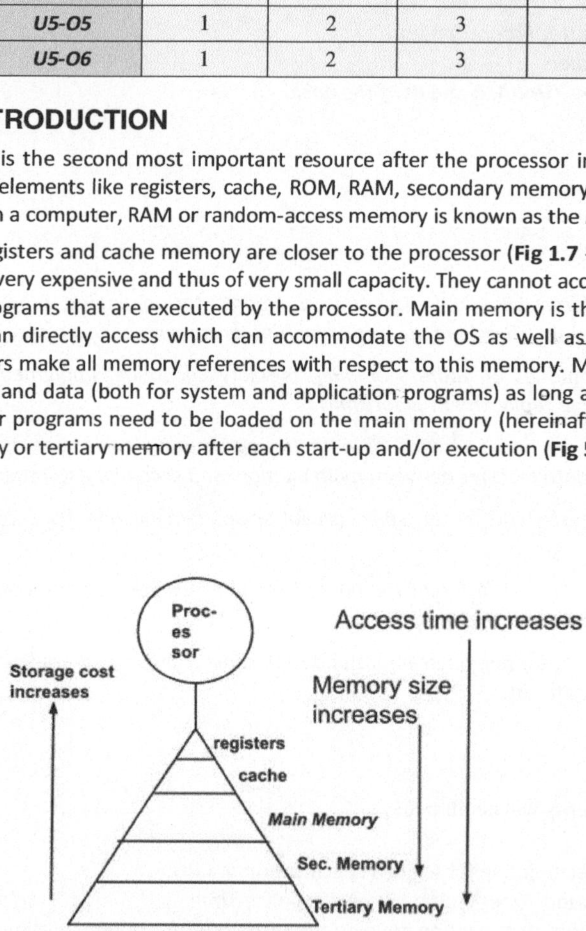

Fig 5.1: Hierarchical Memory organization

The OS kernel remains loaded in the low memory region of the memory as long as the system runs (**Fig 1.9, Fig 2.1**). Once loaded, the OS divides the memory into two parts: *kernel space* for storing the OS; and the *user space* for storing the application processes. In a single-programming system, the OS remains in the kernel space and only one application program can reside in the user space. But in today's multi-programming environment, the OS needs to further divide the user space so that several user programs can coexist in the memory. How many programs can be accommodated in the memory decides the *degree of multiprogramming*. When one process goes for I/O, the CPU remains idle. We can schedule another process only if it is available in main memory. Thus, CPU usage can be maximized if we can accommodate in the memory as many processes as possible. But the main memory is much smaller compared to other permanent storage devices. If a process with a large address space is loaded in the memory, it potentially precludes loading of other processes, reducing the degree of multiprogramming. Can a process be partially loaded? If yes, how much of it is to be loaded now, when and where is the remaining portion to be loaded later? - These are some of the important issues. Main memory space management is thus an important OS task.

Specifically, some of the critical questions related to this space management are as follows.

1. How many processes are to be loaded in the memory?

2. Which processes will be allocated space? In other words, what will be the selection criteria for the processes during memory allocation?
3. How much space will be allocated to a given process and in what way?

We shall investigate these broad questions in this chapter of memory management. The first part will focus on the basic space allocation techniques in the main memory. The later part (*virtual memory*) will discuss how to handle space requirements of large processes that may go beyond the available main memory space with the help of secondary memory.

5.2 BASIC CONCEPTS

Before going into the details of the memory allocation principles and techniques, we need to briefly discuss some concepts from computer hardware organization and compilers.

5.2.1 Basic hardware and software

Main memory (also, secondary memory) is a linear array of memory elements. Each memory element, implemented by a flip-flop or a latch, can store a *bit* (short form of *bi*nary digi*t*). A sequence of eight (8) such bits make a *byte.* Memory can also be thought of as a linear array of millions or billions of bytes (MBs/GBs respectively). A program (system or user) written in a high-level language is finally translated into a sequence of machine-level instructions (code section of a process address space). These instructions, before execution are loaded on the main memory. The instructions are sequentially accessed from memory locations one at a time and executed by the CPU. Typically, a memory location of one word length (4 bytes) stores one machine instruction. Once an instruction is fetched, it is decoded (to understand what operation is to be performed) and then necessary operands are fetched. The operands might be available on the processor registers or memory locations. If the operands are available on registers, the CPU can complete the operation in the quickest possible time. If not, it first searches on the cache (*a short-term memory unit that lies between the processor & the main memory and temporarily stores earlier referenced memory-contents*). If no copy is available there, the operands are fetched from the memory (data section of the process address space). Each process has a valid start address (or base address) of its process address space and the length of the address space to mark the end-boundary of the address space. Two processor registers: **base register** and **limit register** store the base-address and length of an address space respectively. Any memory reference, either to the code or data section of a process, must lie between its base-address (= *val*[**base-reg**]) and end-address (= *val* [**base-reg**] + *val* [**limit-reg**]) and is checked using a hardware (**Fig 5.2**).

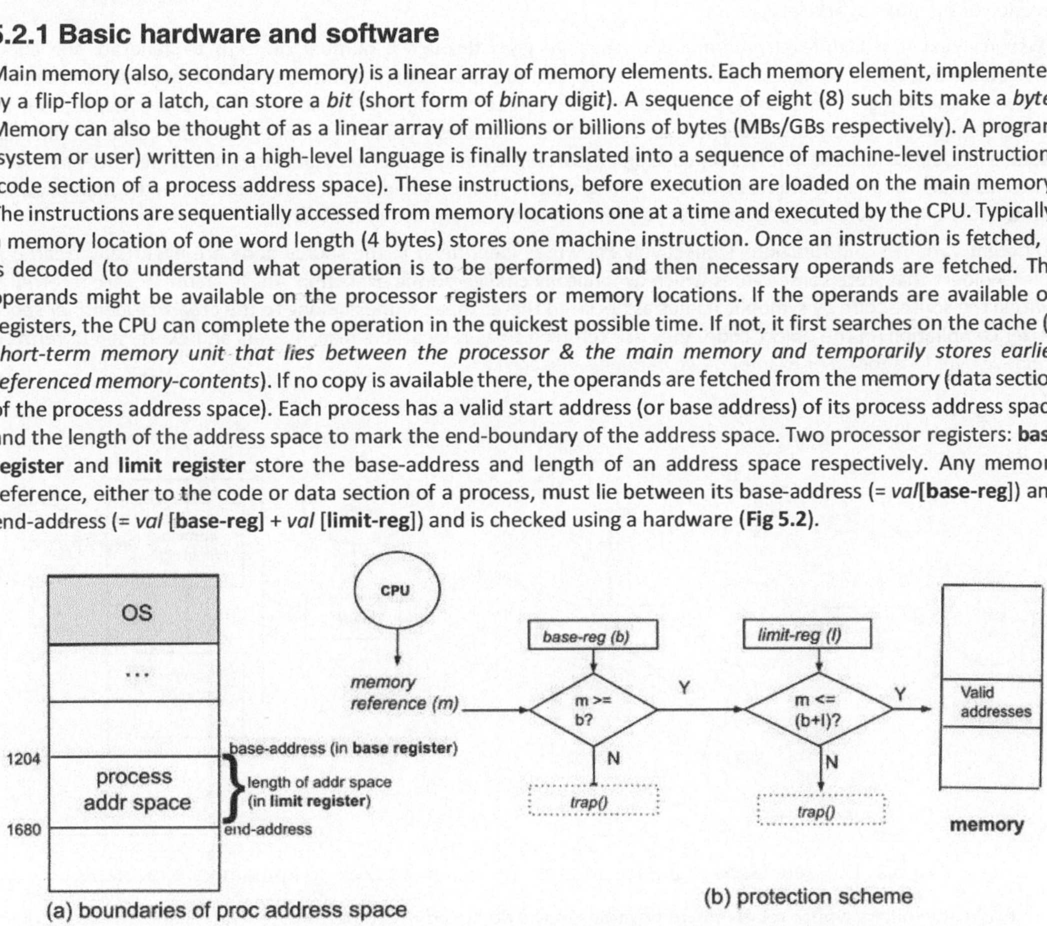

(a) boundaries of proc address space (b) protection scheme

Fig 5.2: Memory access and its protection scheme

For example, suppose a process has an address space with base address 1204 and length 476 bytes. The base register will contain value 1204 and limit register 476. The end-address of the address space is then (1204 + 476) = 1680. If the memory reference (m) generated from the CPU is between these two locations (both inclusive), such an address is valid. But, if the reference address is beyond the two boundaries (less than base address or greater than end-address), the address reference is illegal. A hardware scheme traps the error and invokes a suitable interrupt routine (illegal memory access). Both base register and limit register thus provide protection from illegal memory references.

These registers are handled only by the OS in kernel mode. Appropriate values are populated there whenever a process is scheduled to run in CPU. The OS thus can save its own kernel space from illegal memory access, as well as address spaces of other processes.

5.2.2 Address binding

The memory references shown in **Fig 5.2(b).** should be actual main memory addresses. But it may not be possible for the CPU to always generate the actual addresses. The CPU on its own does not generate the address references but uses whatever is present in the machine instructions in the *in-memory binary executable* (loaded in the code section of the process address space).

A source text in a high-level programming language goes through a number of steps to generate the above executable (**Fig 5.3**). A *compiler* first analyses the source code and generates an object file of low-level instructions. However, the object file may need and refer to other source modules and/or libraries (static or dynamic) that are either separately compiled or available as separate executables. A *linker* (or *link*age *editor*) connects different source modules and static libraries to make an executable. Even such an executable may have references to shared libraries whose addresses are resolved by a *linking loader*. This modified executable is loaded on the memory as an in-memory binary executable, which may still refer to one or more dynamic libraries.

Different variables and functions (collectively known as *identifiers*) in the source code are eventually treated as placeholders that store some values which dynamically change during execution. These identifiers are referred to within the source code by symbolic names as declared there. These names belong to the *program-identifier space.* After compilation, in the object code, they are referred to as relocatable placeholders and expressed in terms of *relative* byte locations. For example, two variables declared as

```
int a, b;
```

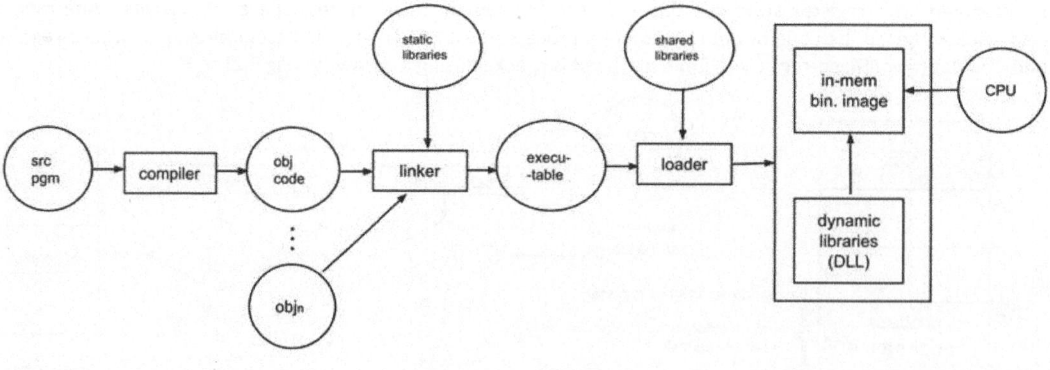

Fig 5.3: Different steps of a user program (from source code to in-memory executable)

are two placeholders whose relative byte positions in the object code can be 14 bytes (for a) and 18 bytes (for b) from a particular reference point (say, the starting location of the program or of the current module). We may not know the actual memory address (known as *absolute* or *real addresses)* of the identifiers until the process is loaded in the main memory. This kind of relative addressing does not refer to the real addresses in the main memory but is helpful in doing address calculations and address references in a logical space. Also, some of the addresses remain unknown in the compiled code if they belong to different source codes and static libraries. These are resolved, only after linking, (however, as relative / relocatable addresses). Similarly, some of the addresses are resolved only after loading (due to shared libraries), while some are only possible during execution of the in-memory executable (dynamically linked libraries or DLLs).

Hence, generating absolute memory addresses involve several resolution-related steps. We call this procedure of resolving addresses to different identifiers as **address binding.** This binding depends on the computer architecture and programming environment. Address binding is divided into three categories based on the time of its occurrence as given below.

1. **Compile-time address binding:** The absolute addresses are generated during the compilation of the source code by the compiler itself. In other words, the object code itself is the final in-memory binary executable. This is only possible if the source has only a single file and does not use any other sources, static libraries, shared files or dynamic libraries (see **Fig 5.3**). Also, the executable must be placed only at a fixed location in the memory every time it is loaded and is limited by the maximum size allowable by the memory manager. Obviously, this is the most restrictive address binding technique and is rarely used nowadays. In MS-DOS, .COM files are examples of compile-time binding.
2. **Load-time address binding:** If all the real addresses are not known during compilation time, the compiler generates *relocatable code* based on relative addresses. The unresolved addresses till compilation are resolved by the linker (static parts like other source files or static libraries) or linker-loader (shared files). All these addresses are in relocatable format. The absolute addresses are generated during loading of the executable based on the relocation-value of the base address (e.g., if the relocation-value is 0, all relocatable addresses themselves become absolute addresses; if the value is 12000, all real addresses are 12000 + relocatable addresses). Once the executable image is loaded, the addresses are fixed in the memory and the image cannot be relocated any further during execution. However, in a separate loading (or re-loading), the image can be relocated based on relocation-value. This binding does not need re-compilation of source text for reloading. But dynamic relocation of the executable in run-time is not possible.
3. **Run-time address binding:** This is the most flexible address binding scheme. Real addresses are computed only before accessing the identifiers. Otherwise, they are referenced in the relative addressing mode, even after loading. The in-memory image does all references in relative or relocatable addressing style. A *memory management unit* (MMU) generates the actual or real addresses during the memory accesses. Since address resolution is done at run-time, the executable image can be dynamically relocated anywhere in the memory anytime - and it does not need any re-compilation of the source code, even across the systems. Most modern operating systems support run-time address binding.

5.3 LOGICAL and PHYSICAL ADDRESSES

In high level languages, variables and functions are known by their symbolic names (e.g., variables like `a`, `count`; function `calculate_interest` etc.) as supported by the languages. This namespace is called *program identifier space*. Again, during compilation, they are represented as numbered identifiers (`id1, id2, id3` etc.) or placeholders in different memory elements (either registers, memory or stack). In the object code, they are referred to in terms of relocatable addresses relative to some reference point (say, start of an object code). All these references are done in the relocatable or relative addressing mode as if the identifiers are available at those addresses. This namespace is called *logical address space*, as the address references and address arithmetic here are computed logically, and not physically. All the addresses generated and referenced in logical address space are called *logical* or *virtual addresses.*

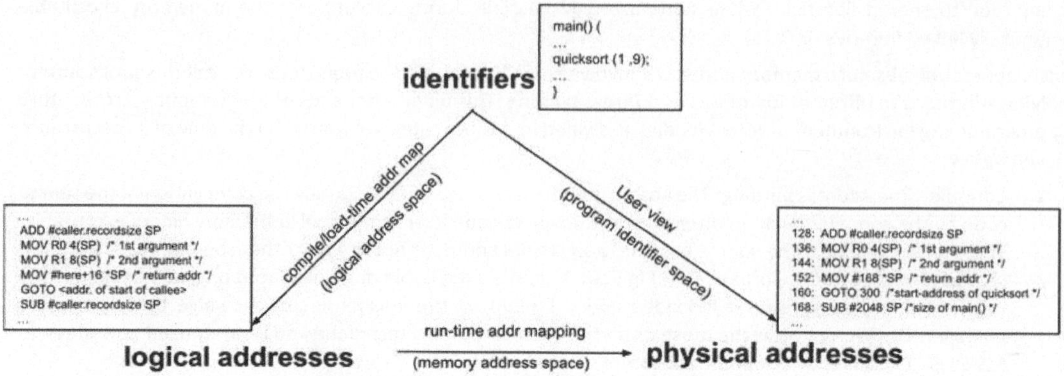

Fig 5.4: Different address spaces and address mapping

However, in the run-time, when the identifiers need to be accessed, their real or absolute addresses in the memory are evaluated. These addresses are called *physical* or *real addresses*.

There is a one-to-one mapping between identifiers, their logical addresses and physical addresses (**Fig 5.4**). The *identifiers from program address space go through logical address space to physical memory address space but* users see the correspondences between identifiers and their physical addresses.

For compile-time and load-time bindings, the in-memory executables already have all the addresses resolved, and thus the CPU here can generate physical addresses.

But, nowadays, for most of the modern systems (run-time bindings), CPU generates logical addresses from an in-memory image of the executable. The MMU calculates the real addresses, based on the memory allocation technique used, and puts the physical addresses on the memory address register (MAR).

Alternatively, it is also said that addresses generated by the CPU are logical addresses, but addresses written on MAR are physical addresses. For compile-time & load-time bindings, logical addresses and physical addresses are the same.

We shall discuss some of the memory allocation techniques in the following sections. However, a simple implementation of MMU can be thought of using a relocation register that stores the value of relocation. When the value is added to a logical address generated by the CPU, we obtain the physical address (**Fig 5.5**). A limit register stores the length of the process and checks whether every logical address remains within the logical limit to prevent illegal memory access.

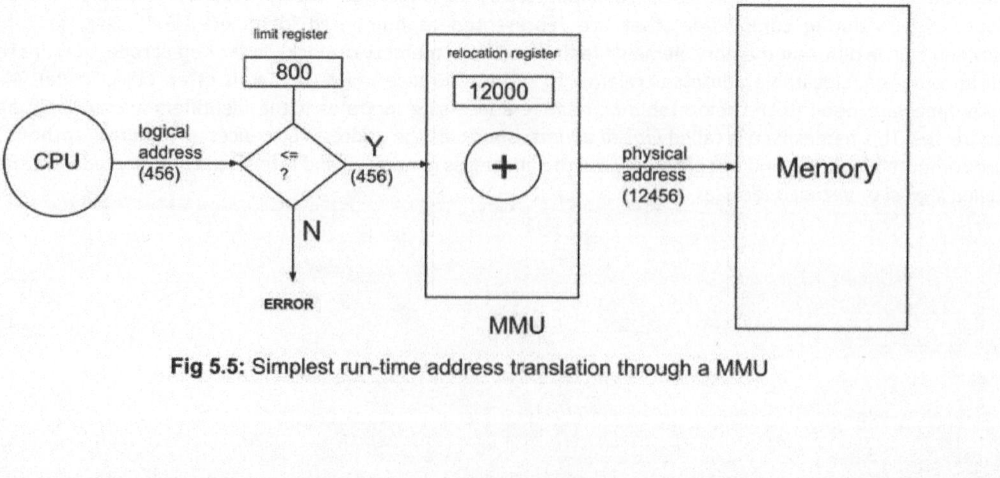

Fig 5.5: Simplest run-time address translation through a MMU

5.4 MEMORY ALLOCATION

Memory allocation is the primary task in memory management. Main memory is the largest memory element that CPUs can directly access. It is smaller and faster than secondary memory but volatile in nature. Hence, programs along with data need to be loaded there each time before their execution.

If a program is large, requiring more than available memory, it cannot be loaded entirely. In the earlier days (single programming environment), the application developer had to decide which part of the program would be loaded at a given time. The program had to be designed into several parts (modules) so that the main module with a currently executed one along with its necessary data fit in the available memory. When another module needed to be loaded, it used to replace the in-memory counterpart from the secondary memory. This technique is called **overlaying**.

Obviously, overlaying was a concern for application developers, as program development was constrained by the hardware. It did not have portability even in a single-programming environment as program design may require changes if available memory space is different. In a multiprogramming environment, it is almost impossible for the program developer to keep track of the available memory space that changes dynamically. Also, the application developer ideally should be kept free from the burden of this kind of micro-management.

Hence, the job of memory allocation is delegated to the OS in most of the modern systems. The OS itself remains in the main memory, and fulfills this responsibility in kernel mode to optimize the overall performance of the system. An OS accomplishes this with the help of secondary memory using different allocation schemes. We shall start with the following three *basic schemes*.

i. ***Contiguous Allocation***: a process in its entirety is allocated contiguous memory space
ii. ***Paging***: a process is divided into a number of equal sized pages; pages are loaded
iii. ***Segmentation***: a process is divided into a number of unequal-sized segments; segments are loaded.

We shall briefly discuss each of the above allocation techniques along with the issues involved therein followed by some of the combinational schemes.

5.4.1 Contiguous Allocation

Here, a process in its entirety is loaded into the memory at one go, if enough space is available, otherwise not at all. The OS occupies a fixed portion of the memory at one of the ends (either the low memory region or the high memory region) and leaves the rest of the memory free for application programs. The OS divides the available space into a number of partitions and allocates at least one partition to each process in a contiguous manner. If no partition is free, but there is a new process ready to be loaded, one of the processes, not ready to run, is swapped out of the partition. Partitioning can be done using fixed boundaries or adjustable boundaries as detailed below.

5.4.1.1 Fixed Partitioning

The OS divides the available space into a few partitions before actual space allocation to processes. The partitions can be of either equal or unequal size (**Fig 5.6**).

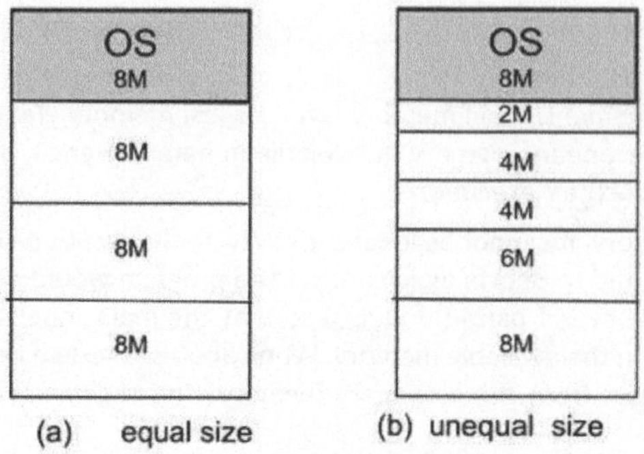

Fig 5.6: Two types of Fixed Partitioning in 32M of memory

Equal partitions: All the partitions are of equal size (**Fig 5.6a**). If a process fits within the size, it is allocated a partition, otherwise it is denied. Either the developer must manage using overlaying or the program is not run at all.

Even if a process is much smaller (say, 1M) than the partition size (8M here), an entire partition is allocated to the process. Since the boundaries are pre-decided and fixed, the remaining space (7M here) is wasted as it cannot be used by any other processes. This phenomenon is called *internal fragmentation* as fragments are created within the partitions. Equal partitions are easy for the OS to manage as any process can be allotted any free partition if there is one. But the scheme suffers from high number of denials and low memory utilization due to high degree of internal fragmentation.

Unequal partitions: Internal fragmentation is less severe in unequal partitions, as each process can be allotted a partition that is just enough to accommodate it, leaving minimum possible waste space (**Fig 5.6b**). However, to implement it effectively, each partition should have a scheduling queue of processes based on the partition size, i.e., smaller processes (say 2M) will be in a queue of 2M partition, larger processes (6M < size < 8M) in a queue for an 8M partition, and so on. This scheme can reduce internal fragmentation with an increased overhead of extra queues. Also, this may cause denial to a process when several partitions of different sizes are free except the one the process is waiting for.

Unequal partitioning is more flexible than equal partitioning but requires comparatively more management effort from the OS. Nevertheless, fixed partitioning is relatively simple, requiring minimal management overhead and processing. However, fixed partitioning in general suffers from the following drawbacks.

- The number of processes that can be allowed memory space is limited by the number of partitions.
- Small processes suffer from fixed partitioning as they cannot leverage the benefits of available space in memory due to internal fragmentation.
- Since partitioning is done much before processes are allocated space, it is only possible if the process sizes of a system are known apriori. This is not very realistic in today's multiprogramming environment.

Hence, fixed partitioning contiguous memory allocation is not seen in modern systems. IBM OS/MFT (Multiprogramming with a Fixed number of Tasks) - an early mainframe OS had implementation of fixed partitioning.

5.4.1.2 Variable (or Dynamic) Partitioning

Here the partitioning is not done apriori but done at the time of space allocation. As the processes arrive, available space is allocated to them from one end of the memory exactly as per their need. When no more space is available, either the new process is denied, or a not-ready process is swapped out. The partitions are thus dynamically created. They are of variable sizes. However, when processes leave the memory or are swapped out, new processes need not be of the same size. When a new process of smaller size replaces an old process, the boundary comes closer, and a 'hole' is created in memory. The partition gets smaller, and the fragmentation is outside the partition. This phenomenon is different from internal fragmentation discussed in fixed partitioning and is called **external fragmentation** (**Fig 5.7**).

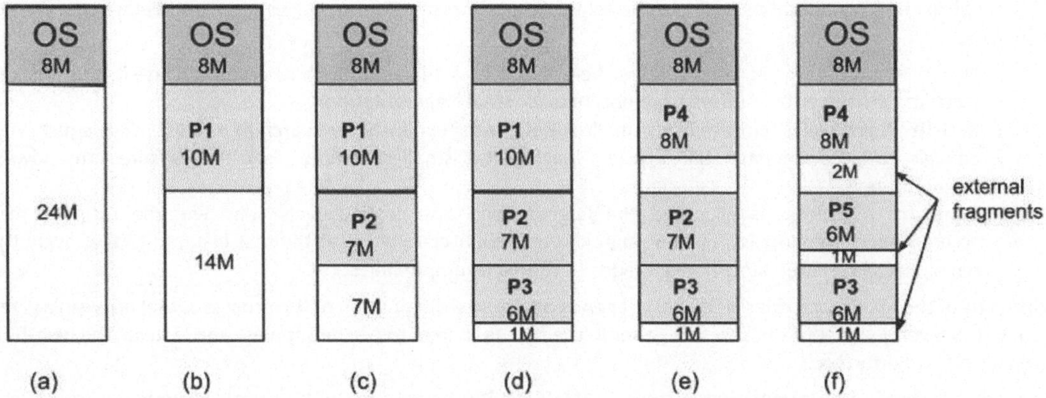

Fig 5.7: Dynamic partitioning and external fragmentation in 32 MB of memory

Dynamic partitioning starts with no external fragmentation at all. But gradually it keeps on adding external fragmentation as processes leave and occupy the memory. Often it comes to a situation where the total available memory is more than the required space of a new process, but it cannot be allocated as the space is not contiguous, but fragmented.

For example, suppose in a memory of 32 MB, the OS occupies 8 MB space leaving 24 M space free (**Fig 5.7a**). A process P1 of size 10M arrives and is allocated space (b). Similarly, P2 and then P3 arrive and occupy (c-d), leaving 1M of space. Now, process P4 of size 8M comes but there is not enough space. P1, the only process that occupies the space large enough is then swapped out (assuming it was not running). P4 takes 8M of space, leaving 2M empty (e). Similarly, P5 leaves another 1M hole (f). Now, suppose a process P6 with say, 3M size arrives. Even though we have 4M space empty, but not contiguous. Hence, P6 cannot be allocated space due to external fragmentation.

How can the issue of external fragmentation be effectively managed, as it keeps on increasing with continuous arrival of newer processes? Two popular solutions applied are: *i. compaction* and *ii. placement algorithms.*

Compaction: Processes are pushed towards one end of the memory and small holes are acquired and added to make a bigger hole. Compaction routine is run by the OS to reclaim the wasted space at regular intervals or when memory utilization falls below a pre-decided threshold. This is like the *defragmentation* utility that Windows systems provide as 'Disk Defragmenter' to make the hard disk drives organized in a compact way and to free some disk space.

Compaction, however, cannot solve the problem of internal fragmentation. Often dynamic partitioning also leaves traces of internal fragmentation. Instead of allocating part of a word (4 bytes), spaces are allocated in multiples of a word to minimize the overhead of management (e.g., if a process needs 2046 bytes of space, 2048 bytes of space is allocated).

Compaction involves movement of many live processes within memory and needs resolving a lot of memory references. This is hugely time consuming and takes substantial processor time.

Placement Algorithms: Another way out to minimize the fragmentation is done while placing new processes into the available holes. The OS maintains a list of available holes with their sizes when processes leave the memory. Before a new process is allocated space, the search is made on the list to find the most appropriate hole. There are different algorithms for allocating holes to the requesting processes. The strategies discussed below are some of them.

i. **First-fit:** A process is allocated the first hole that is found large enough to accommodate it. It is quick to place the processes but suffers from potential external fragmentation.
ii. **Best-fit:** A process is allocated the smallest hole, after exhaustively searching the list, that is just large enough to accommodate the process leaving the smallest empty space. It ensures the lowest fragmentation.
iii. **Worst-fit:** A process is allocated the largest hole, after exhaustively searching the list, that can accommodate the process. Even though it seems counter-intuitive at the first instant, it takes away the remaining space after allocation and adds to the list of empty holes.

Which one of the above strategies is the best depends on the size-distribution of the processes that arrive in a given system. However, in most of the cases, in general, the first-fit is seen to be the simplest and fastest. The best-fit is often the worst performer.

One of the IBM's mainframe operating systems, OS/MVT (Multiprogramming with a Variable Number of Tasks) used dynamic partitioning.

5.4.1.3 Buddy System

Fixed partitioning limits the number of active processes depending on the pre-decided partitions. Dynamic partitioning is a complex scheme to manage and requires time-consuming compaction. A compromise between the two is the buddy system. Memory is dynamically divided in multiples of 2^i words ($L \leq i \leq U$; i, L, U are positive integers) where 2^L = smallest possible block-size that can be allocated; and

2^U = largest possible block-size, close to the entire available memory before allocation.

In the beginning, entire memory of 2^U words are available. When a process of size s comes, where $[(2^{U-1} - 1) < s < 2^U]$, the entire memory is allocated to it. Otherwise, memory is divided into 2 equal buddies of block-size 2^{U-1} words. If $(2^{U-2} < s < 2^{U-1})$ randomly one buddy of size 2^{U-1} words is chosen for allocation and the other is kept available. Otherwise, the process continues until we find an i s.t. $2^{i-1} \leq s \leq 2^i$ and a block of 2^i is allocated. In the extreme case, s occupies a block of 2^L words. The system maintains several lists of holes (unallocated blocks), where list i corresponds to the holes of size 2^i. When 2 blocks of size 2^i are free, they are merged to make an available block of size 2^{i+1}. Two buddies from list i are then removed to make an entry in the list $(i + 1)$. When a process of size s comes, such that $2^{i-1} \leq s \leq 2^i$, necessary algorithm is shown in **Fig 5.8** along with illustrations.

```
void alloc_hole(int i){
   if (i > U) error;
   if (list_i == NULL) {
       alloc_hole(i+1);
       <split hole into two>;
       <put buddies on list_i>;
   }
   <take 1 hole from list_i>;
}
```

(a) Algorithm

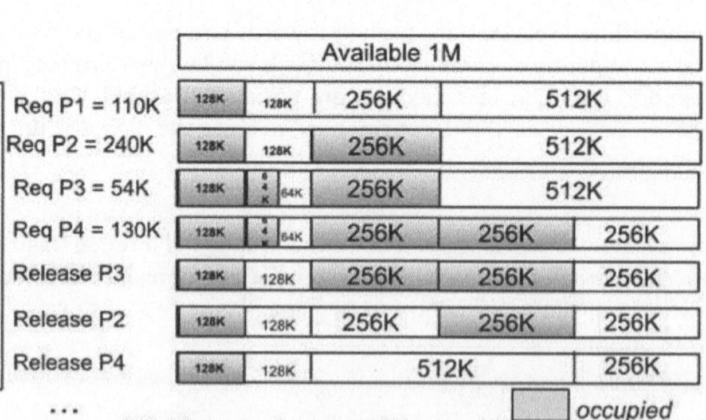

(b) Memory changes with requests and releases

Fig 5.8: Buddy System

Even though the buddy system minimizes external fragmentation to some extent, internal fragmentation is very much there as we have to allocate space in the size of 2^i words, whereas need may be much less (See P4 in **Fig**

5.8b). Also, two empty blocks can only be merged if they are next to each other. Otherwise, compaction is necessary.

As evident from the discussion so far, memory utilization would improve if we can

i. reduce the block size so that internal fragmentation is minimum.
ii. instead of allocating a single big block, more than one small block can be allocated to a process.
iii. compaction will not be necessary if some mechanism is in place to know what blocks are allocated to a process and where they are.

Essentially, these are done in the other two basic memory allocation techniques: paging and segmentation.

5.4.2 Paging

Memory is divided into several small blocks of equal size. For the convenience of address translation and data transfer, block-size is kept in the power of 2, like 1024 bytes (1K), 4K, 1MB or higher. The blocks in the (main) memory are called *frames*. Program code and program data residing in the secondary device are also considered a sequence of blocks of the same size, called *pages*. Processes are loaded in units of pages into the available frames. The frames need not be allocated contiguously in the memory.

5.4.2.1 Principle of operation

A logical address is referred in terms of page number and offset within the page as a tuple `<page#, offset>`. Address translation is done using a per-process kernel data structure, called a *page-table* (PT). A PT maintains a mapping between pages and frames. Given a page (p), the page-table returns the frame-id (f) where it is loaded. Since the pages and frames are of the same size, the offset remains the same within the frame. In Boolean representation of a logical address, page number is given by a prefix part (most significant bits or MSBs) while the offset within a page by LSBs. Since the page-table provides a frame-id for each page referenced, the prefix-part, when replaced by the frame-id gives the real address of any location (**Fig 5.9**).

For example, a logical address of 2056 byte (100000001000) with 1024B (1K) of page-size has `<page#, offset>` representation as <10, 0000001000>. If the page-table shows the corresponding frame as 517 (i.e. mapping 10 → 1000000101) then the real address in the memory is <1000000101, 0000001000> or byte location 529,416 (**Fig 5.9**).

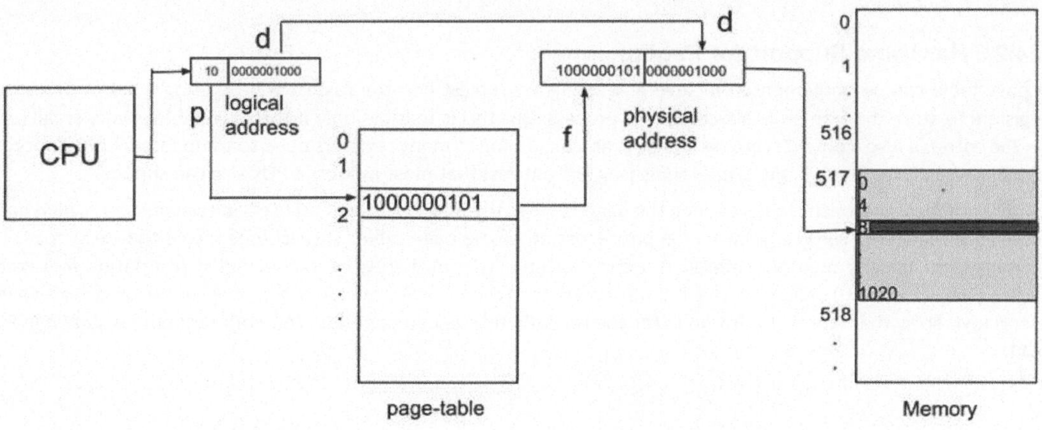

Fig 5.9: Address translation in paging using a page-table

5.4.2.2 Page Allocation

The pages, frames, page-tables are managed by the OS. The kernel allocates a page-table to each process and keeps track of the allocated frames. A process address space is considered as a contiguous sequence of pages, each of the same size as that of a frame. The OS also maintains a global *frame-table (FT)* to keep track of the occupied and available frames. When a frame is allocated to a process, its page table as well as the global frame table are updated. An entry in the FT is made for the corresponding process id. If the page is also used by other processes, it stores those process ids along with reference counts of the page. If the frame is free, it is added to the list of available frames. When a process needs a page to be loaded, the list is searched, and the first available frame is allocated. When a process terminates, or is idle, its frames are reclaimed by the OS so that they can be allocated to a new process. When a process is no more active, its page table is also destroyed. The allocation and release keep on occurring dynamically in a system, and the pages belonging to a process thus are unlikely to get contiguous frames (**Fig 5.10**).

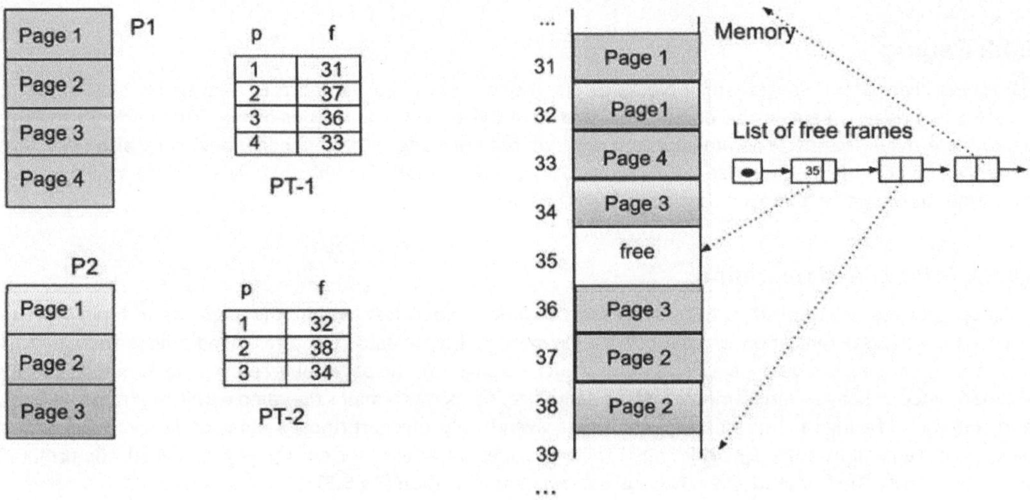

Fig 5.10: An example of different page tables and their page allocation in the memory

5.4.2.3 Hardware Support for Paging

A page-table can be implemented in several ways. The simplest and the fastest will be using a set of processor registers to store the frame-ids allocated to a process. But this is feasible only if the page-table is very small (say, <= 256 entries). Also, context switches will be time-consuming as many registers need to be updated. Contemporary processes can have much larger page-tables (say, 2^{20} entries) that most modern CPUs also can support.

A more practical approach is thus to keep the page-table in the main memory and use a special register, called *page table base register* (PTBR) to point to the base-location of the page-table. This scheme incurs the extra cost of a memory-read for any memory reference. Hence, often a special, hardware cache, called translation *look-aside buffer* (TLB) is used to minimise the memory-read for recently referenced pages. TLB works as a high-speed associative array that stores the frame-id for the recently referenced page-ids. The entire scheme is shown in **Fig. 5.11**.

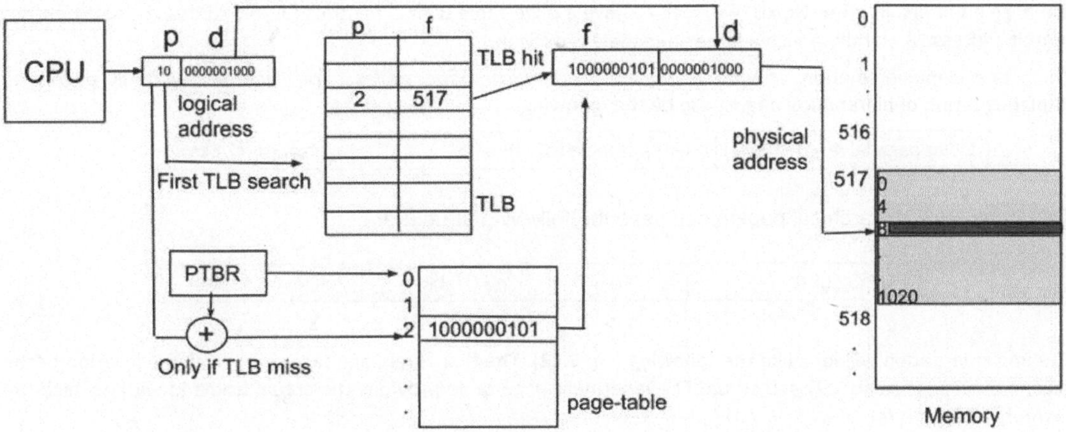

Fig 5.11: Address translation with in-memory page-table and TLB

For any memory references, first its logical address `<page#, offset>` is determined. Page number is first searched in the TLB. If it is found (*TLB hit*), the corresponding frame number is directly used in getting the physical address. If not (*TLB miss*), the page-table needs to be searched. PTBR provides the base address of the in-memory page table. The rest of the address translation mechanism is similar to what is already discussed earlier.

The use of TLB saves a search in the page-table and thus saves one memory access in case of a TLB hit. In case of a TLB-miss, at least 2 memory accesses (1 for finding frame + 1 for actual addr) are required. Out of the total number of memory references, the fraction of TLB hits is called *hit-ratio* ($0 \leq$ *hit-ratio* ≤ 1), and TLB misses are represented by ($1 -$ *hit-ratio*).

Average memory access time MAT_{avg} is given by (assuming negligible TLB cache lookup time)

MAT_{avg} = hit-ratio x mem-access time + (1 - hit-ratio) x 2 x memory-access time.

For example, if memory access time is 20ns, with hit-ratio = 0.7, effective memory access time or MAT_{avg} = *0.7 x 20 + (1 - 0.7) x 2 x 20 = 14+12 = 26ns.*

Hence, placing page tables in the memory slows down effective memory access time (here, from *20ns* to *26ns*). It is better if TLB hits can be increased (say, 90 percent or higher). This, however, requires a large size of TLB in the processor unit which is costly.

Alternatively, some processors use multiple layers of TLB caches in a cascaded fashion (for TLB misses in L1, L2 is searched and so on). For example, Intel Core i7 has 128-entry instruction cache and 64-entry data cache in L1 followed by 512-entry L2 cache. Effective memory access time requires information on hit-ratio and the required number of clock-cycles to search in each layer and time of the memory-access.

Since TLBs are hardware features that come with the processor, the OS must customize paging implementation according to the TLB implementation in the system.

Page Table Structure

In-memory page tables can also be implemented in several ways. Most systems nowadays support large logical space (of several GBs). 1 GB means 2^{30} bytes. For a byte addressable machine, we need to deal with logical addresses with 30 or more bits. The page-size decides the offset or LSBs (a 4K page has 4×2^{10} bytes and uses 12 bits for addressing). The rest of the logical address (for 32-bit addresses, 20 bits; for 64-bit addresses, 52 bits) represents the page numbers. In other words, we need to have a page-table with 2^{20} entries (32-bit addresses) to 2^{52} entries (64-bit addresses). Handling such a large page table is difficult.

Thus, one popular solution scheme is to use *hierarchical page tables*. For example, with 4K pages, an implementation of hierarchical paging can be the following.

Outer page table (*p1*, 10bits)	inner page table (*p2*, 10 bits)	offset (*d*, 12 bits)

Or a three-level hierarchical paging can have the following structure.

p1 (32 bits)	*p2* (10 bits)	*p3* (10 bits)	offset (*d*, 12 bits)

The implementation will look like the following (**Fig 5.12**). The first-level page table (p1) gives the location of the second level page table (p2) and so on. The innermost page table provides the actual frame id within which the memory address is found.

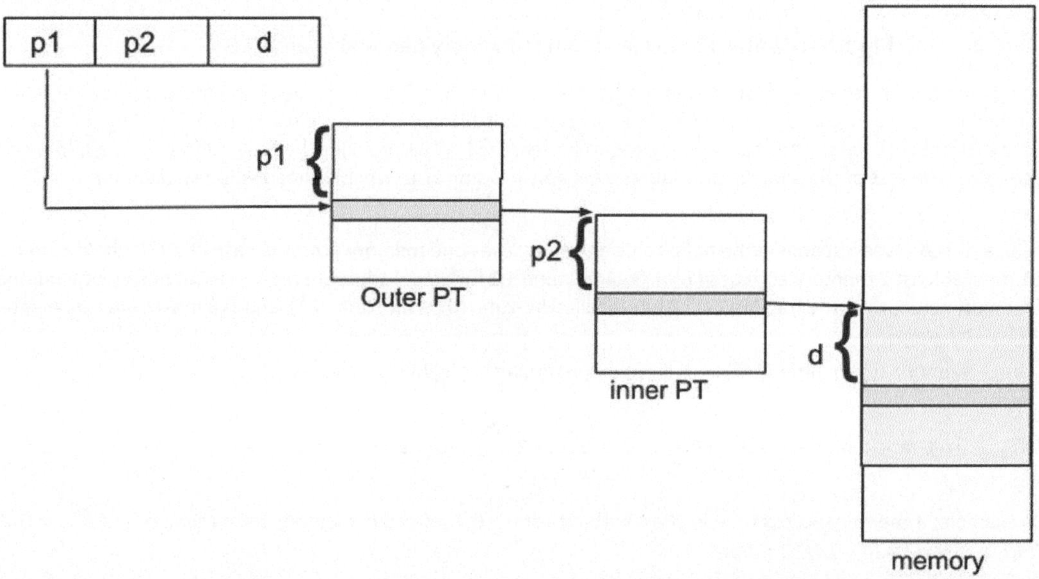

Fig 5.12: Hierarchical page table (32-bit addressing scheme)

Less entries per page table means reduced search time in the page table. But high number of hierarchies involves high overhead of address translation, both in terms of space and time. Depending on the maximum allowable page-size and average process address space, the designer must make a trade-off on the number of hierarchies.

To minimize the space requirement due to high number of page tables in the hierarchical scheme, two other implementations are also popular: *hashed page table* and *inverted page table*.

In *hashed page-table* implementation, the page-id of log -addr are passed to a hash function. The hash function maps all pages to a smaller set of hash-values. Corresponding to each hash-value, page-id and its frame-id are stored. To avoid collisions among several pages with the same hash-value, a linked list is maintained, whenever necessary. Hash table is much smaller than a page table. Search time is also linear in length of the linked list, in case of collision. The scheme is shown in **Fig 5.13**.

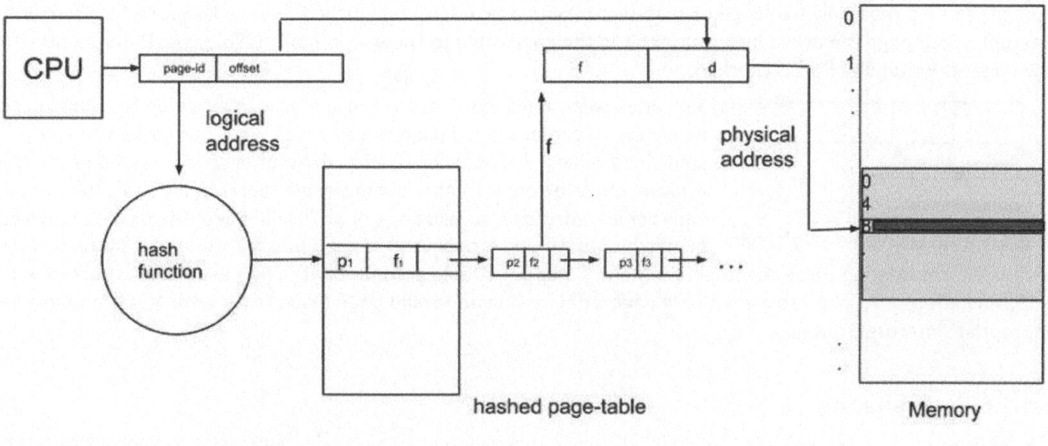

Fig 5.13: Address translation with hashed page-table

In the *inverted page table* implementation, only one global page-table is maintained for all the live processes. The logical address thus needs to include process-id (pid) also and looks like the tuple: `<pid, page-id, offset>`.

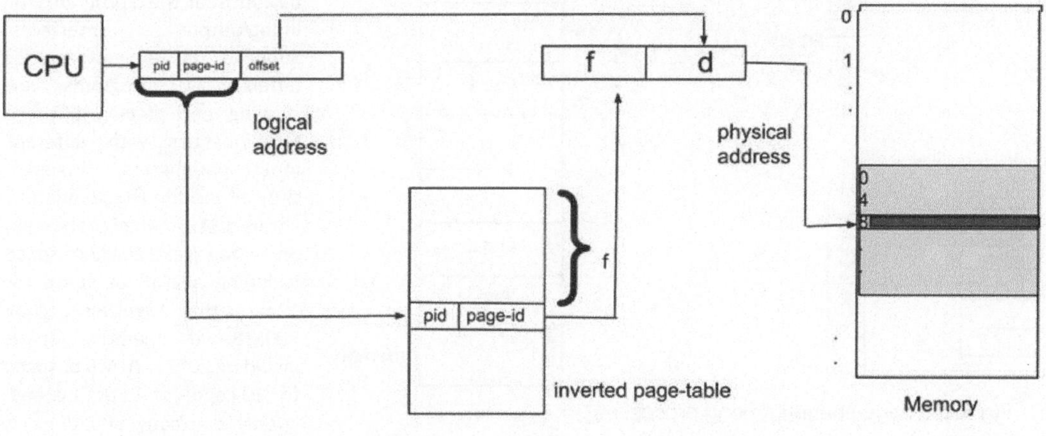

Fig 5.14: Address translation with inverted page-table

Inverted page table is a frame table (also termed as page-frame-table) with entries in the form of `<pid, page-id>` arranged in the increasing order of allocated frame-ids. For each address-reference from a process, the entire page-frame-table is sequentially searched for the query <pid, page-id> and the index of the table itself provides the frame-id. This frame-id is used in forming the physical address as <frame-id, offset>. The scheme is shown in **Fig 5.14.**

The table is sorted in the increasing order of frame-id, but the search is on <pid, page-id>. Thus, searching is exhaustive. To cut-down the search time, a hash table is used where a given <pid, page-id> is hashed into a hash-table that stores the frame-values.

5.4.2.4 Protection in paging

Memory references need to be protected from two aspects: 1. writability 2. legality or validity.

A page can be a read-only (**ro**) page or read-write (**rw**) page. A read-only page needs to be protected from write attempts. Each page is marked by a special bit in the page table to show whether it is **ro** or **rw**. Before writing on any page, its writability field is checked.

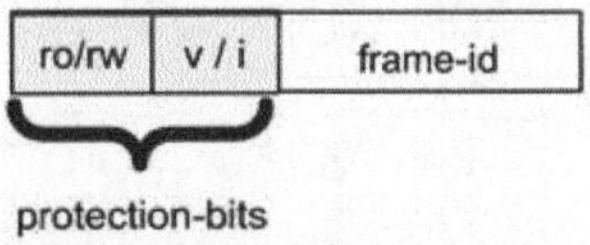

Fig 5.15: An entry in a page table

Similarly, sometimes entries on a page-table may refer to some pages belonging to earlier loaded page-tables which were not flushed properly, or some junk values existed for the frame-id. Another special bit shows whether a given entry belongs to the current page-table or not. In other words, whether an entry is for a valid page or an invalid page. The bit is called **valid-invalid** bit. A frame-id is only used to get a physical address if a valid bit is set (**v**). Hence, considering these together, each entry in a page-table accommodates two extra bits as shown in **Fig 5.15**. Any attempt to write to a read-only page or accessing an invalid page leads to an error (trap) and invokes appropriate interrupt routine.

5.4.2.5 Page sharing

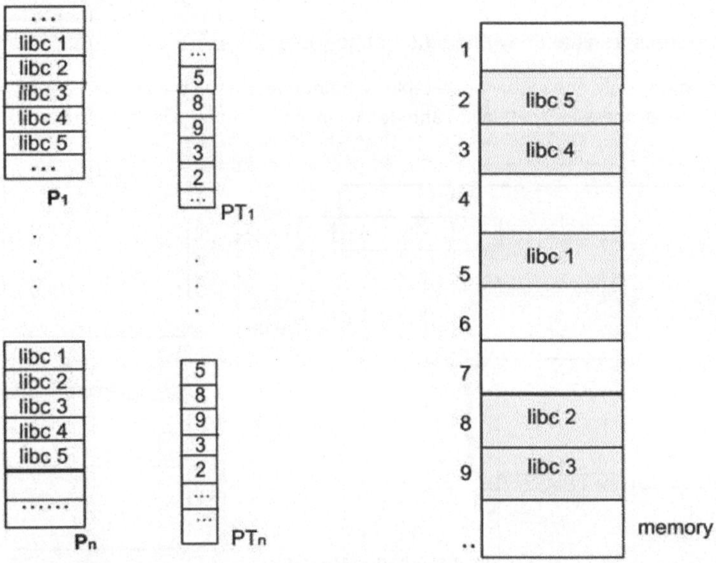

Fig 5.16: Page-sharing among processes

One great advantage of paging is the page sharing among several in-memory processes. *Often a piece of code is used by* several processes, *e.g.,* a standard C library `libc` is used by almost all the C programs for input/output interfaces. Suppose in a system, 20 different C programs are running, each having different functionalities with different input parameters. However, they all include the standard C library `libc`. If all of them on an average take 20MB of space including a 2MB of space for `libc`, they together occupy 400MB of memory space including 20*2 = 40 MB of space for 20 copies of `libc`. Instead, if only one copy of `libc` is shared by all, 38MB of memory space is saved. **Fig 5.16** illustrates this with `libc` occupying 5 pages.

Shared libraries mentioned in **Sec 5.2.2** implement the above idea. This is used in many applications like compilers, window systems, database systems wherever the code is *re-entrant* (a reusable routine that does not change and multiple processes can invoke, interrupt, and re-invoke simultaneously). Also recall Shared Memory Model (**Sec 3.1.1**) that can be implemented using paging and page sharing.

5.4.2.6 Disadvantages of paging scheme

Since a process can be allocated as many frames as it has pages at maximum, there is no external fragmentation in paging. However, if the process size is not exactly multiple of page-size, some spaces in the last page remain unused. E.g., a process of size 5200 bytes in a paging scheme of 1K page-size needs = *ceiling* [5200/1024] = 6 pages with internal fragmentation (here [6 × 1024 – 5200] = 944 bytes remain unusable within a 1K page). Even 1 byte space beyond the multiple of page-size requires a new page allocation. Hence, on an average, half-the page-size per process is wasted due to internal fragmentation. Thus, smaller the page-size, less the fragmentation. On the other hand, programs and data are loaded in terms of pages. Hence, it is convenient, if page-size matches block-size of data transfer, otherwise the number of I/O required will be high.

5.4.3 Segmentation

Segmentation is another non-contiguous memory allocation technique where space is allocated to processes in the units of logical blocks or segments from a user's perspective. Any program can be considered as a collection of logical segments. For example, a C- implementation of quicksort algorithm may have the following logical sections: functions `main()`, `read()`, `quicksort()`, `partition()`, `swap()` etc. and data section. Each of the functions and data sections can be considered as a segment and they can be independently loaded onto the memory (**Fig 5.17a**). Each segment is assigned a number (numbering is not done by the OS, but by either the compiler, linker or loader) and any memory reference in the logical space is done relative to the beginning of a segment. Hence, logical addresses have the form `<seg-id, offset>` where seg-id represents segmentation id and offset is the location of the address from the base-address of the segment. Base-addresses of all the segments are maintained in a *segment table* by the OS.

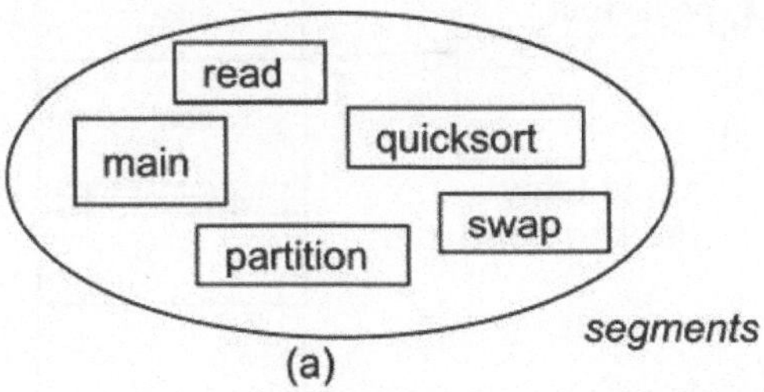

(a)

segment table

name	size	address
main (*seg1*)	642	23576
read (*seg2*)	378	32012
partition (*seg3*)	500	76248
quicksort (*seg4*)	476	54500
swap (*seg5*)	188	23204

(b)

Fig 5.17: Segmentation

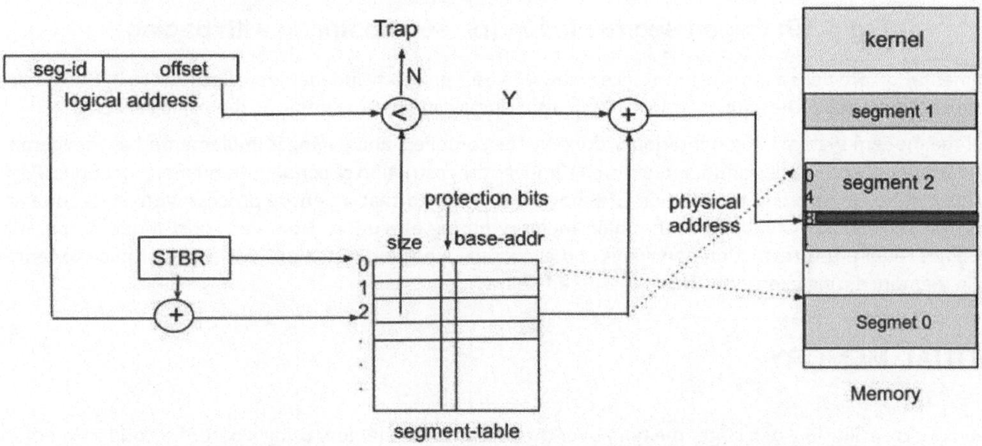

Fig 5.18: Address translation in segmentation (contiguous allocation to segments)

Segmentation can be implemented using contiguous allocation where the segment table stores the base-address and size of each segment (**Fig 5.17b**). For each logical address in the form <seg-id, offset>, the offset is first checked whether it is within the size of the corresponding segment. If yes, the base-address of the segment is added to the offset to get the physical address (**Fig 5.18**).

5.4.4 Paged Segmentation

In paged segmentation, each segment is allocated space independently in the units of pages. Each segment gets a variable number of pages based on its length. The segment table provides a list of base-addresses of the page tables for all the segments. Address resolution is done in two steps. First, from the segment table, the appropriate page-table is identified from the `<seg-id>` field and its based-address is located. Second, the appropriate page-id is obtained from the MSBs of the `<offset>` field. The rest of the offset (LSBs) provide offset within a page (**Fig 5.19**).

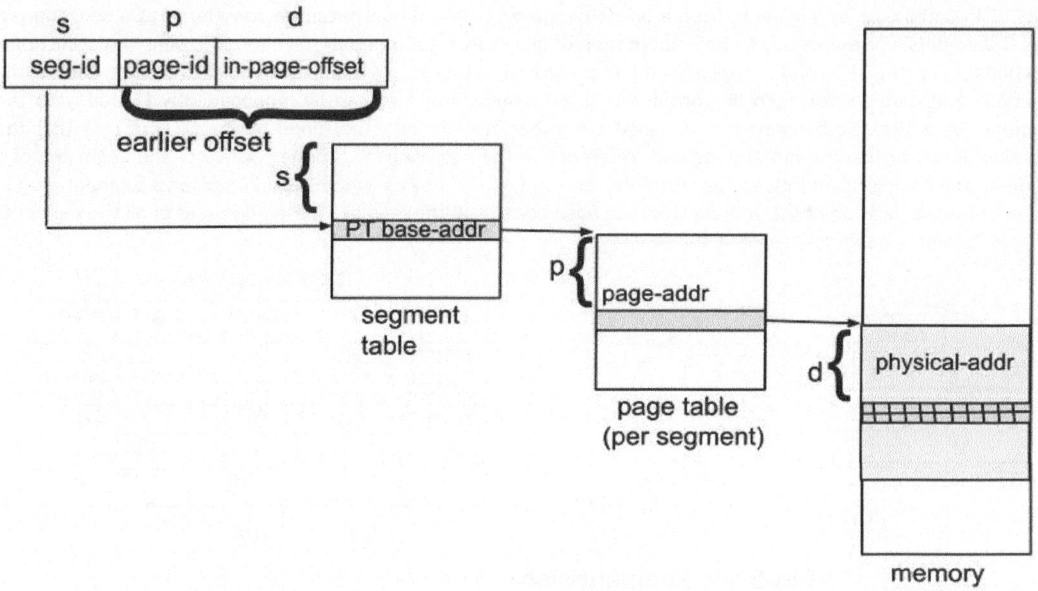

Fig 5.19: Paged segmentation (or, segmentation with paging)

While segmentation provides a more user-oriented view of a user program and memory allocation to it, the unequal sizes of the segments make the address translation a little clumsy and not as simple as the paging scheme.

In most of the modern systems, segmentation is done by the compilers and paging is implemented as the memory allocation technique. Both paging and segmentation removes the restriction of contiguous memory locations. Pages or segments can be anywhere in the memory. Till now, it is assumed that an entire process with all its code and data is loaded and remains stationed in the main memory during execution. However, most modern operating systems do not require this restriction nowadays and allow only a portion of the process address space to remain in the main memory during execution. This is discussed below.

5.5 VIRTUAL MEMORY

Virtual memory is an 'illusion' of a larger memory over the real physical memory using a part of secondary memory. As the name suggests (the word *virtual* is inspired from the field of Physics where *virtual images* are formed in mirrors and some types of lenses), this memory is not real main memory, but an illusion of the same. In a loose analogy, virtual memory is like the inflated *market capitalization* of a business organization while real memory is its *enterprise value* or real worth. However, an organization can also be under-valued in market capitalization, but virtual memory always projects an enlarged main memory hiding the loans from the secondary memory.

Technically, virtual memory (VM) is seen as a memory management scheme to enable execution of processes without requiring them to be fully memory-resident, i.e., only a small part of their code and data can be in the memory, while the remaining majority can reside in a back-up store of the secondary memory.

Virtual memory is a logical extension of the following facts:

1) *non-contiguous memory allocation* techniques: MMU allows loading and accessing of the code and data of a process scattered all over the memory.

2) every program has a *locality of references*: memory references within a time window are usually made to locations that are spatially close to each other (e.g., accessing successive array elements or nodes in a linked list) and often the same instructions are executed several times repeatedly (within a loop)
3) a program may have a lot of non-essential code to tackle error conditions and/or special cases that are rarely encountered.

The above facts facilitate realization of virtual memory in which the frequently used code and data within a locality reside in the memory and infrequently accessed portions are brought to memory only when they are required.

VM also provides the application programmers the freedom from the constraints of physical memory space and its allocation policies. An application program can go beyond the boundary of limited and costly real memory space, and the programmer need not bother about placement of the program and data (or process address space) in the memory during execution.

Even though the scheme is convenient to the programmers, VM is complicated to implement. It needs support from the hardware units and operating system software. The hardware units provide support for *address translation*. The software called the virtual memory manager (VMM) takes care of the issues like when to load a portion of code and/or data (page or segment), and when and how to replace them to the backing store. VMM implements a set of *placement* and *replacement algorithms*. We shall discuss in detail the nuances of virtual memory in the following subsections.

5.5.1 Basics of Virtual Memory

Virtual memory allows partial loading of a process to begin its execution. The OS thus starts by loading only the initial piece of the process (a few pages or a segment) to the memory that includes the initial set of instructions and the data that it refers to. This portion of the process that is in the memory is called the **resident set** of the process. Execution goes smoothly if memory references are within the resident set. However, when the references are beyond it, as flagged by the page table or the segment table, an software interrupt is generated indicating a memory access fault. The OS then suspends the ongoing process and puts it in the waiting state. The OS also issues a disk I/O request to bring the page or the segment corresponding to the logical address that caused the memory access fault. Once the demanded piece (page or segment) is brought to the memory, an I/O completion interrupt through the processor notifies the OS. The OS then places the blocked process to the ready queue to resume its execution. When there is not enough space in the main memory, some piece of the process address space is replaced to the backing store of the secondary memory. A coarse-level broad overview is shown in **Fig 5.20.**

5.5.2 Hardware and Control Structures

In VM, main memory is not increased, but the programmer is provided a perception (or illusion) of a larger main memory with the support from several hardware units. Following units and/or phenomena cover the contribution of different hardware components in implementation of VM.

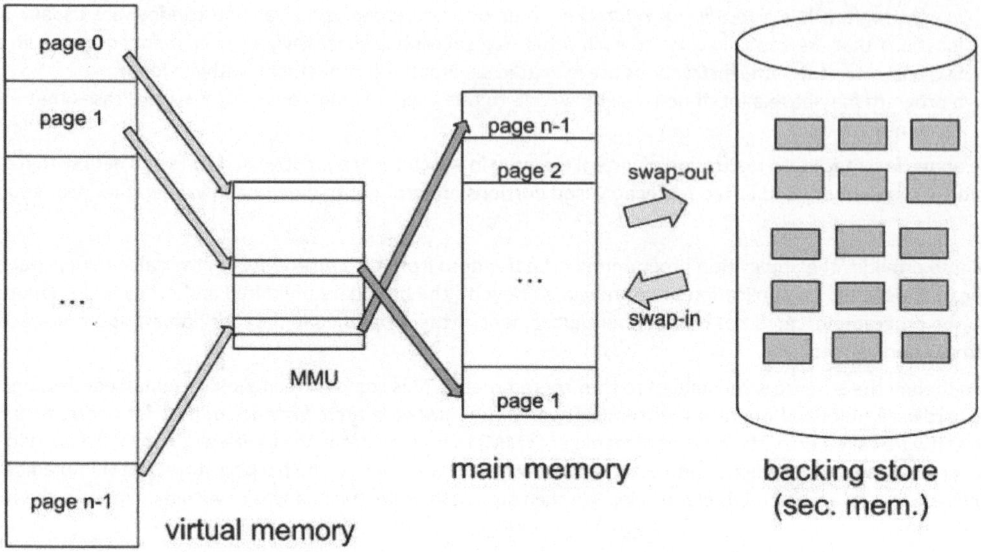

Fig 5.20: A schematic view of virtual memory

5.5.2.1 Backing Store

As shown in **Fig 5.20**, a portion of the secondary memory serves as a backing store of the active processes. While some portions of a process remain in the main memory, other portions are stored in a designated area of the secondary memory. This backing store in the secondary memory is what creates the virtual memory. This is also known as *swap space*. During OS installation, a hard disk is formatted with sufficient space for the swap space (usually kept equal to the size of the main memory space or higher).

5.5.2.2 Page Faults

Most of the OSs implement VM with the help of simple paging or segmentation with paging. A page is almost invariably considered as a preferred unit of placement and replacement. Implementational basics of paging are already provided in the preceding section. However, necessary modifications are incorporated into the above scheme to handle a memory access fault, or more specifically a *page fault*. A page fault is defined as a phenomenon in which a page referenced by a running process is not available in the main memory and needs to be loaded from the backing store or secondary memory. This is typical of virtual memory and not observed in simple paging or segmentation with paging. Page-fault is a serious performance bottleneck as handling a page-fault involves several time-consuming steps, the most time-taking being the disk I/O. The necessary steps are shown in **Fig 5.21.**

In VM, during execution of a process, either the code (instruction) or the data (one or more operands) may not be available in the memory. Corresponding memory reference (Step 1) will result in an illegal memory access, indicated by an invalid bit in the page table. The fault will invoke a trap (Step 2) that needs to be attended by the OS. If the memory reference is legal (within the logical address space of the process), this is a page-fault, i.e., the page must be available in the backing store (Step 3). The OS then must invoke a disk I/O operation and suspend the process or put it in the wait/block state. It can also do context switching (saving the context of the running process and loading the context of another ready process). Disk I/O is a long procedure. The OS is notified by the processor when I/O completes through I/O completion interrupt. The OS puts the page in a free frame of the memory (Step 4) and updates the page table with appropriate frame id and changing status field (invalid to valid) (Step 5). Since the memory reference is resolved, the instruction can be completed now and therefore, is restarted (Step 6).

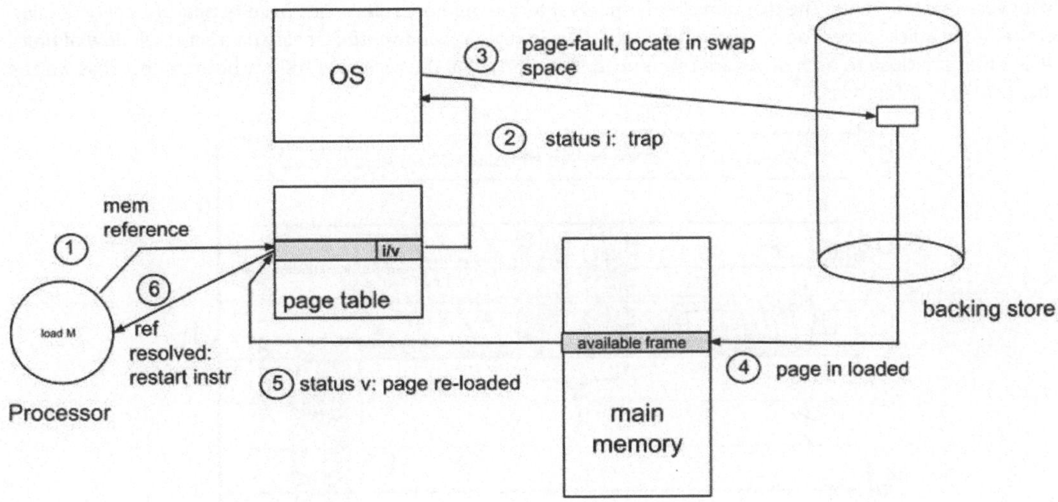

Fig 5.21: Page-fault handling

A page-fault incurs the logistic and temporal cost of several operations:

1. understanding that it is a page-fault (through a trap)
2. understanding that the reference is legal, and the page is available in backing store
3. context switch (suspending the current process and starting another)
4. searching the page in the backing store (incurs disk seek-time + rotational latency)
5. loading the page on I/O bus
6. loading the page on the memory and updating page table
7. putting the blocked process on the ready queue so that the instruction can be restarted.

Understanding page-fault needs at least one memory access. If the page table is long and implemented in a hierarchical fashion (**Sec. 5.4.2.3, Fig. 5.12**), understanding page-fault itself (Step 1) will take more than one memory access. Once the page is re-loaded, when the instruction is restarted, another memory access is required. Hence, handling page-fault needs at least 2 memory accesses (in the order of nanoseconds). However, the major time goes into the I/O as disk access is much slower (in the order of milliseconds). If we assume that a memory access takes 100 nanoseconds, and disk I/O takes 10 milliseconds then, with page fault rate p (p is the fraction of page-faults among all page references, $0 \le p \le 1$),

effective memory access time = $100 * (1-p) + p * 10 * 10^6$ nanoseconds = (100 + 9,999,900* p) nanoseconds.

Even after ignoring several other factors, a page-fault increases memory access time enormously. To keep the effective memory access time within a tolerable limit (say, 10% of usual memory access time), we have, $(100 + 9{,}999{,}900 * p) \le 110$ or, $p \le 0.000001$ i.e., page-fault needs to be very rare, in the order of one in a million page-references.

5.5.2.3 Locality of References

Even though virtual memory seems to be appealing in theory, it is only feasible in practice if the page-fault rate can be kept extremely small. A favourable reality is that an overwhelming majority of programs show a strong locality of references. For any program, only a few pages are accessed within a time window. In **Fig 5.22**, initially only a few pages were referenced as shown by region **a** (Page 18-26), region **b** (Page 31) and region **c** (Page 34). Then region **d** (Page 29, 30) and region **e** (Page 18-24) were active. Similarly, region **f, g** and **h** became active. Page 32 was used only for very few moments. The diagram clearly shows that the memory references have *temporal locality* (a page is referred to in quick succession for some time, as shown in region **t**) and *spatial locality* (in a short window of time, locations that are close to each other are referenced frequently). All the regions **a-h** show both temporal as well as spatial locality of references.

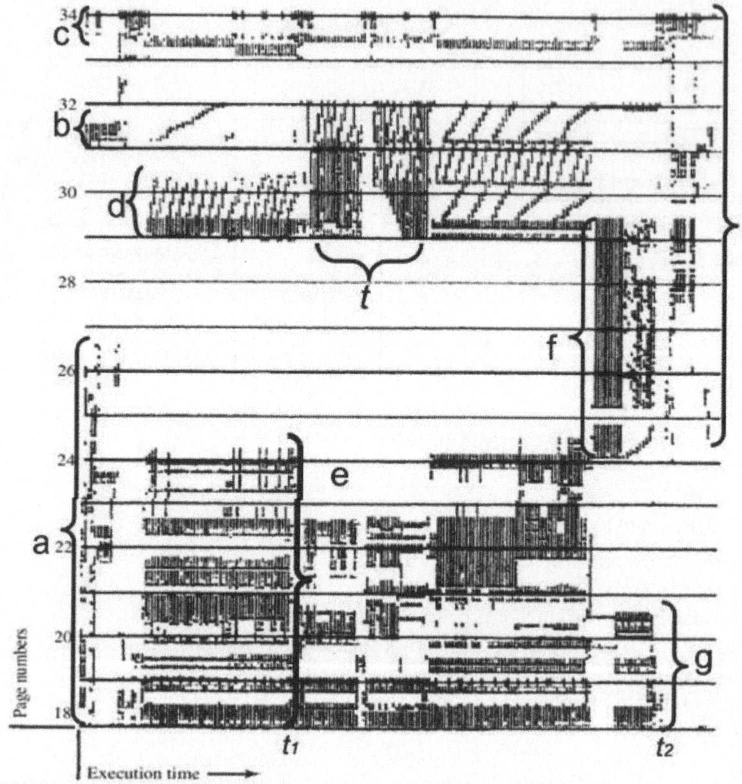

Fig 5.22: Any program execution shows strong locality of references ([Hat72])

Even though the above corresponds to execution of a particular program, all program executions follow this locality model. When a function is invoked, the program control jumps from the locality of the calling function to that of the called function. Local variables are accessed, and computations happen in that locality. Once the function returns to the caller, execution again happens in the spatial locality of the caller. Memory references thus move from one locality to another, with or without overlap among them (see localities at time t_1 and t_2). If we can load into memory only the pages from the active regions instead of all the pages, we can save main memory space. This can accommodate more processes in the memory. It leads to an increase in the degree of multiprogramming. Also, temporal locality helps in reducing the number of page-faults.

5.5.2.4 Working Set

The working set model leverages the benefits of the locality model. Based on a parameter Δ, known as the *working set window*, it analyzes the patterns of the most recent page references. If Δ=5, we see the last 5-page references. The pages belonging to the last Δ forms a working set. If the page references for a program are as follows:

Page id: . . 2 6 1 5 7 7 7 5 1 6 2 3 4 1 2 3 4 4 3 4 3 4 4 4 1 3 2 3 4 4 3 4 4 4 . . .

$\leftarrow \Delta \rightarrow|$ T_1 $\leftarrow \Delta \rightarrow|$ T_2

Working-sets at different time-points with Δ = 5 will be like: $WS(T_1) = \{2,6,1,5,7\}, WS(T_2) = \{3,4\}$.

However, with Δ = 10, working sets will be different at the same time-point, $WS(T_2) = \{1,2,3,4\}$.

The choice of the working set window (Δ) is thus very important. The working set can correctly capture the locality only if Δ is wide enough. If Δ is too small, it cannot provide the correct working set. On the other hand, if Δ is very large, it can span over several localities, even the entire process address space in the extreme case.

For an appropriate size of Δ, cardinality of the working set or working set size (WSS) is helpful in determining the number of frames needed by a process to cause minimum number of page faults. WSS also helps decide the number of processes that can be allocated space in the main memory, or the degree of multiprogramming.

If WSS_i is the maximum working set size for a process i, then $S = \sum_i WSS_i$ gives the number of frames required for a number of processes.

Operating system monitors the working set of different processes and accordingly manages memory usage and allocation. If WSS_i is less than the total number of available frames, more processes can be accommodated in the memory. When a new process is allocated frames, the degree of multiprogramming increases. On the other hand, if S exceeds the total number of available frames, a victim process is selected and forcibly suspended. The frames allocated to the victim process are reclaimed and re-allocated to another process that requires them.

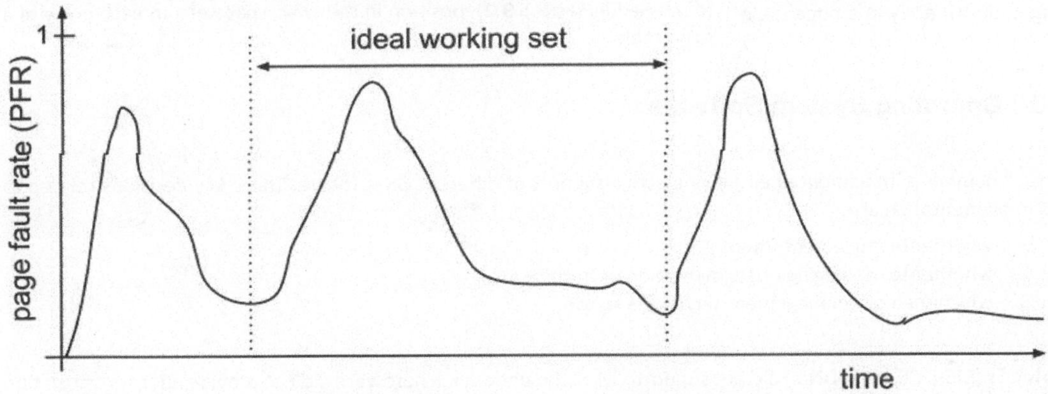

Fig 5.23: Relation between working set and page faults

WSS and page-fault rate (PFR) have a close relationship (**Fig 5.23**). When a process starts execution in a new locality, page faults increase as the pages referenced are not available. However, the same set of pages are soon referred again due to locality. As the pages are available in the memory, page fault rate drops. Hence, it is important to estimate the working set window () and allocate an adequate number of frames to accommodate all working sets for a process. An ideal working set size is the number of pages referenced between two troughs in the above time-diagram. If it is made smaller, more page-faults will result in average.

Working set changes as the program executes. A new page is added to and an old page is removed from the working set as the working set window moves. Keeping track of dynamically changing working sets for all the processes needs considerable hardware support. Each page reference needs to be remembered to decide whether to keep the page in the memory or not. Necessary book-keeping and protection mechanisms are to be in-place for each page in the page table.

5.5.2.5 Page-level Protection and Maintenance

Recall the protection mechanism discussed in **Sec 5.4.2.4** for the simple paging scheme. We added a bit in each entry of the page table to notify whether the page is valid or invalid. An invalid bit indicates the corresponding page is not available in the memory. In the simple paging scheme, it means that the page is not a legitimate page of the process. But in virtual memory, a non-resident page may be a legal page of the process, but not loaded in the memory. In that case, the trap generated is analyzed by the OS and if it is a legitimate page, it is loaded from the secondary memory. Also, another bit per page is used to notify whether the page is read-only (**ro**) or read-write (**rw**). If the page is writable (**rw**), the process can modify it. If the page is modified by the process, the modified copy needs to be backed up in swap space, especially when there is no free frame, and the page needs to be swapped out. But, if the page is **ro,** or it is **rw** but not modified, we do not need to swap out the page as the swap space has a copy of it. Instead, just invalidating the page will serve the purpose. This can save time-consuming I/O. We thus need to check whether a **rw** page in the memory is modified. Another bit is, therefore, assigned for each entry in the page table to mark whether the page is modified or not. This bit is called a **dirty / modify** bit. If the bit is set, the page is understood to have been modified and needs to be backed up when swapped out (see **Sec 5.5.3.2** below) or the process terminates.

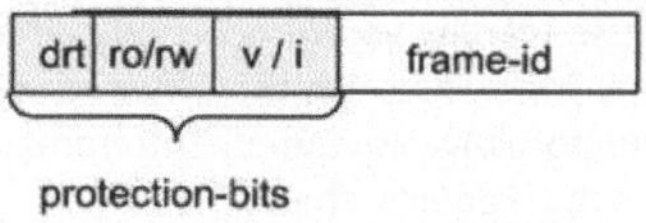

Fig 5.24: An entry in a page table

Hence, virtual memory implementation needs at least 3 bits for each entry in the page table as shown in (**Fig 5.24**). The dirty bit (*drt*) is particularly useful when we decide to swap out a victim page from the main memory.

There can be a few more control information like reference number (discussed in **Sec 5.5.3.2**), position in the swap space etc. in each entry of a page-table.

5.5.3 Operating System Software

Virtual memory is implemented employing active support of different OS software. Three key decisions related to VM implementation are:

1. whether to implement VM or not
2. whether to use paging or segmentation or both
3. which memory management technique to use.

Early OSs (MS-DOS, early UNIX) did not support VM as the underlying hardware did not provide address translation mechanisms and support other necessary functions.

Pure segmentation where each segment is provided contiguous memory space is becoming rare. Most OSs use paging as the basic memory management technique. Hence, even if segmentation is used, segmentation with paging is mostly used.

Although the first two decisions are hardware-driven, performance of the VM implementation depends on a few software issues as follows.

1. *Fetch policy*: when to bring pages (or segments) to the memory
2. *Placement & Replacement policy*: where and how to place the fetched page(s)
3. *Resident Set Management*: how many frames to be allocated per process
4. *Load Control*: how many processes to be accommodated in the memory (degree of multiprogramming).

The issues are discussed as follows.

5.5.3.1 Demand Paging

Demand paging is a technique that implements the fetch policy (*demand segmentation* is not discussed as it is very rarely used). VM allows a process to start execution with only a portion of its process address space in the main memory and to load a page as and when it is required. In other words, pages are fetched on-demand and the pages not referenced are not loaded at all. Thus, it is called demand paging. Demand paging saves time-consuming I/O of loading redundant pages that are not referenced during a particular run of a program, especially the routines that are rarely invoked.

But, how much of the address space needs to be loaded before a process can start? In simple paging (without VM), all the pages need to be loaded. If this is one extreme (a stringent restriction for simple paging!) of the spectrum in the paging scheme, the other extreme can be 'do not load a page until and unless it is required'. That is, each page of a process is fetched only when it is demanded. This is called *pure demand paging*. Pure demand paging, at the first instant, seems beneficial as no unnecessary page is loaded. It saves main memory space that can accommodate more processes. It can thus increase the degree of multiprogramming, CPU utilization and throughput. But pure demand paging also causes 100% page faults, as each page-reference results in a page-fault leading to a serious performance issue. Hence, pure demand paging is not a good idea either. Typically, demand paging is implemented to increase the degree of multiprogramming but keeping the page-fault-rate (PFR) as low as possible.

5.5.3.2 Page Replacement Algorithms

Demand paging is implemented using page placement and replacement. During scheduling a process, the OS allocates a certain number of frames to the process. The process is supposed to execute using only those frames in the memory. If a page referenced is not available within the frames (a page-fault) and there is no free frame, a victim frame is selected, and its content (page) is invalidated. If the frame contains a modified (known by checking the dirty-bit) page, the page is copied back to the backing store (swap space) before invalidation. The frame then accommodates the demanded page fetched from the secondary memory. The frame is simply overwritten with the new page. Selection of a free frame (Step 4) during page-fault handling (**Sec 5.5.2.2** and **Fig 5.21**) thus needs the following modifications:

i. selecting a victim frame
ii. checking the dirty-bit of the victim-frame
iii. if the dirty-bit is set, swap out the page in backing store (extra I/O)
iv. swap-in the demanded page in the selected frame

In case the dirty-bit is set, demand paging must incur the cost of loading back the page to the swap space. This increases the effective memory access time even further.

An OS also has to manage this extra work (i-iv). To be specific, it must *select a victim frame*, *free the frame* and *replace its page*. An OS uses different algorithms to select the victim frame. They are called *page replacement algorithms*. Choice of the algorithm may be based on many factors - but its performance is decided by the number of page faults. For a fixed number of frames, the less the number of page-faults, the better is the algorithm in performance. We shall discuss the following page replacement algorithms here.

1. Optimal (OPT)
2. First in First Out (FIFO)
3. Second Chance (SC)
4. Not recently used (NRU) and
5. Least Recently used (LRU)

For the sake of comparison, we shall consider a single sequence of memory references in a small-time window (assume they are coming from a program execution). For example, this string of references (called a *reference string*) in terms of byte locations are:

1240, 2243, 3450, 4456, 2345, 1645, 5658, 6745, 2234, 1343, 2654, 3674, 7856, 6542, 3654, 2346, 1234, 2543, 3432, 6676

Considering 1 KB (1024 bytes) page-size, corresponding page references are:

1, 2, 3, 4, 2, 1, 5, 6, 2, 1, 2, 3, 7, 6, 3, 2, 1, 2, 3, 6.

We shall primarily assume that four (4) frames are allocated to the process.

1. Optimal (OPT) Page Replacement Algorithm

This is the best possible algorithm that has the minimum page fault rate. The principle used here is: *replace a page that is not going to be used for the longest time.*

The algorithm ensures that a page once brought into the memory is kept if it is to be used in the future. When a new page is required to replace an old one, the victim must be the one not to be used in the future. If such a page is not found, then the victim must be the page to be used in the most distant future. Let us consider the example to understand the algorithm better (**Fig 5.25**).

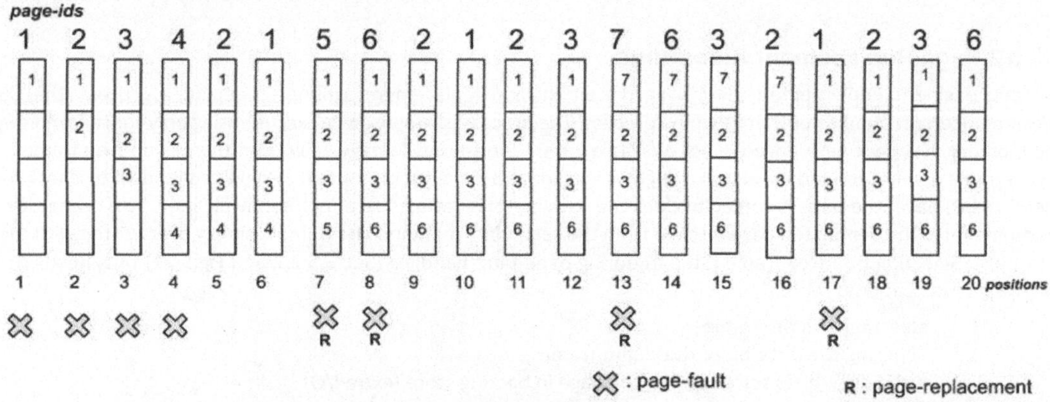

Fig 5.25: Example of Optimal Page Replacement Algorithm

The first four page-references cause mandatory page faults. At position 5, page-id 2 is already there in the memory (frame 2). Similar is the case at position 6 for page-id 1. At position 7, page-id 5 must replace a page. Here, page-id 4 is chosen, as it is not used at all in future. Similarly, at position 8, frame 4 (page 5) is again chosen as the victim. Positions 9-12 do not cause any page-faults. But at position 13, page 7 needs to replace page 1 even though page 1 is used again in future. We did not have a choice as this is the most distant page in the future. At position 17, page 1 again replaces page 7.

Thus, we have a total of 8 page-faults with 4 page-replacements for the given reference string of 20 pages.

You can check that, with a higher number of frames allocated to the process, the number of page-faults can be reduced, but not the other way (try with 3 and 5 frames to get convinced).

This is called the optimal algorithm as we cannot reduce the number of page faults any further using any other algorithms for the given reference string and given number of frames.

But this is impossible to implement as it is based on future page references. During program execution, at a given instant, we do not know, for sure, which page will be used in future. Nevertheless, it is used as the benchmark for evaluating the performance of other algorithms.

2. First in First Out (FIFO) Page Replacement Algorithm

This is the simplest possible algorithm for page replacement. When replacement is required, the page that came in first (to memory), goes out first. In other words, the algorithm replaces the page that has been staying in the memory for the longest time. To understand this, let us illustrate with the same reference string (**Fig 5.26**).

The algorithm results in 14 page-faults with 10 page replacements for the given string with 4 frames. One can try with different numbers of frames and check that: with 1 frame, there will be 20 page-faults; 2 frames → 18 page faults; 3 → 16, 5 → 12, 6 → 10, 7→7, 8 →7. For the given string, 7 is the minimum number of page-faults that is bound to happen as there are 7 different page-ids.

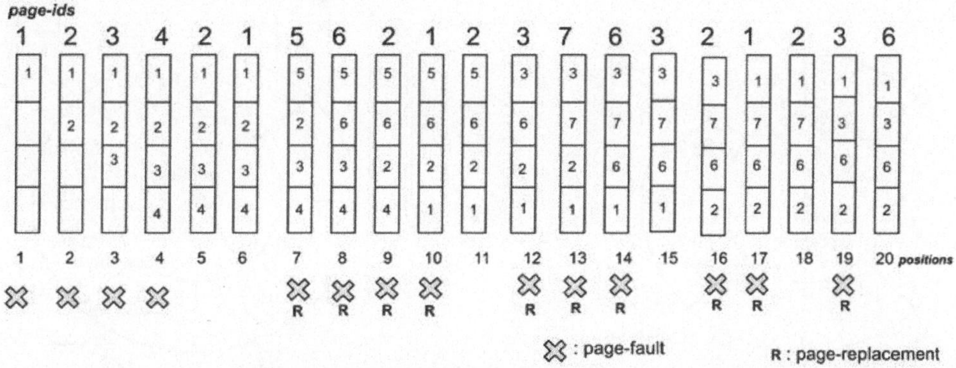

Fig 5.26: Example of FIFO Page Replacement Algorithm

In general, with increase in the number of frames, the number of page-faults decreases (Fig 5.27a). But this is not always true. In some of the page replacement algorithms including FIFO, increasing the number of frames sometimes causes an increase in the number of page faults. For example, for the page-reference string: 0, 1, 2, 3, 0, 1, 6, 0, 1, 2, 3, 6, we see the number of page-faults increase from 3 frames (9 faults) to 4 frames (10 faults) in FIFO (Fig 5.27b). This anomalous phenomenon is called Belady's anomaly (named after László "Les" Bélády).

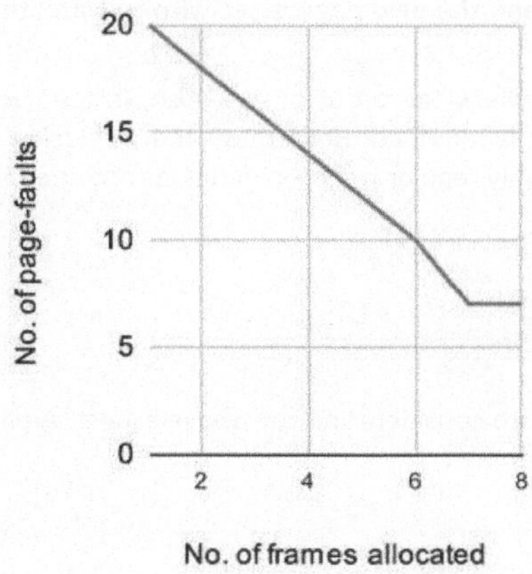

Fig 5.27a: Page-Faults vs no. of frames

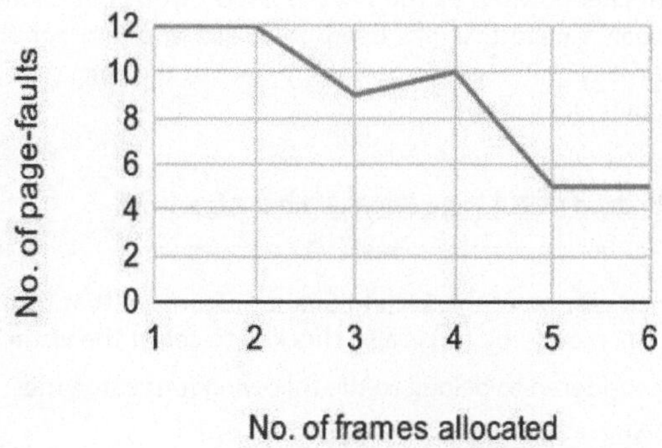

Fig 5.27b: Belady's Anomaly

FIFO algorithm presumes that a page that is brought in the memory first, is the best candidate to go out first. Because of the locality, it is thought less likely to be used again. But reality might be different as illustrated in the example. The most striking drawback of FIFO is that it does not consider the usage history of a page. No matter whether a page is used in the recent past (one or more times), the oldest page is chosen as the victim.

3. **Second Chance (SC) Page Replacement Algorithm**

This is a modified and refined FIFO algorithm with the help of hardware support. Every page is provided with a *reference-bit* or *use-bit*. Whenever a page is referenced or used the *use bit* is set to 1. Initially, when a page-table is allocated to a process, the use-bits are refreshed to 0. As soon as a frame is loaded with a page, its use-bit is set to 1. When a page is to be replaced, in a circular manner a sequential search is carried out (as if the frames make a circular buffer) (**Fig 5.28**). Each time a frame with use-bit 1 is found, it is skipped but its use-bit is reset to 0 (given a second chance). The first frame with its use-bit 0 is chosen as the victim frame. If no such frame is found i.e., all the frames have use-bit 1 in the first round, we come back to the first frame which has its use-bit 0 now and is selected in the second round.

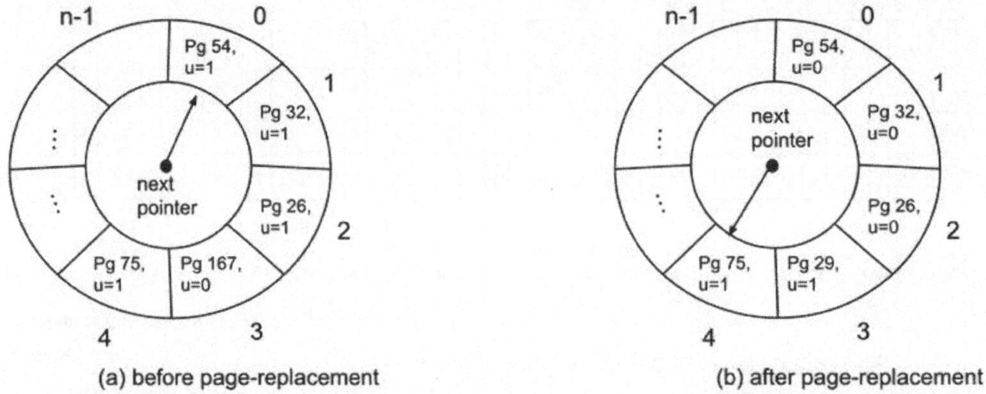

Fig 5.28: Second-Chance (SC) Page Replacement Algorithm

In the example, starting from the frame-id 0, the next pointer moves in the clockwise direction to find the victim frame that has use-bit = 0. Frame-id 3 fulfills such a criterion, the page 167 is replaced (**Fig 5.28a**) with the new page 29 (**Fig 5.28b**). All the pages with u=1 are reset to 0 [frame-id 0, 1, 2] and the new page is set with u=1 and the pointer points to the next frame 4.

The SC algorithm checks whether the page is used or not but cannot check the order of use. Also, it does not distinguish between a page that has been only read and another that is modified. Remember that replacing a modified page is costly as it needs to be backed up. But the page that is only read or not modified does not need to be backed up. It thus can save I/O.

4. **Not Recently Used (NRU) Page Replacement Algorithm**

It is a more refined version of the Second Chance algorithm that takes into consideration the above aspect. Along with the use-bit (u), modify-bit (m) is also checked to select the victim frame.

The frames are considered to belong to the following four categories:

i. not recently used and not modified (u=0, m=0)
ii. not recently used but modified (u=0, m=1)
iii. recently used but not modified (u=1, m=0)
iv. recently used and modified (u=1, m=1).

Step 1: The first frame belonging to the first category (u=0, m=0) is selected as the victim frame as it has the lowest I/O cost involved. Since the page is not modified, it does not need to be backed up. When a frame is bypassed by the moving next pointer, use-bits are not changed (unlike simple SC algorithm).

Step 2. If such a frame is not found in the first sweep of the circular buffer, the first frame from the second category (u=0, m=1) is chosen as the victim frame. Even though the frame is modified, since it is not used in the recent past, it is assumed unlikely to be used in future.

However, when the next pointer moves clockwise, but skips a frame, it changes its use-bit from u=1 to u=0.

Step 3. If Step 2 fails, the moving next pointer comes back to the starting position, but all use-bits are 0 now. We re-run Step 1 or if needed, then Step 2 to find the victim frame.

NRU is also known as enhanced SC algorithm. Although it may need several iterations, and thus need little more time for victim selection, it can minimize the cost of page-faults (due to minimization of I/O cost for back-up).

The SC and NRU are also called *clock algorithms,* as they use the principle of clock.

5. Least Recently Used (LRU) Page Replacement Algorithm

This is another important page replacement algorithm that performance-wise goes quite close to the OPT algorithm. Although it is not possible to exactly predict the future use of a page, its past usage can help us in arriving at a better guess for most of the pages.

We assume that if a page has not been used for long it is less likely to be used again soon. On the contrary, the pages that are recently used are likely to be used soon due to locality of references. Hence the victim should be the frame that holds the page used in the most distant past or is the least recently used page. **Fig 5.29** shows the running example again using LRU.

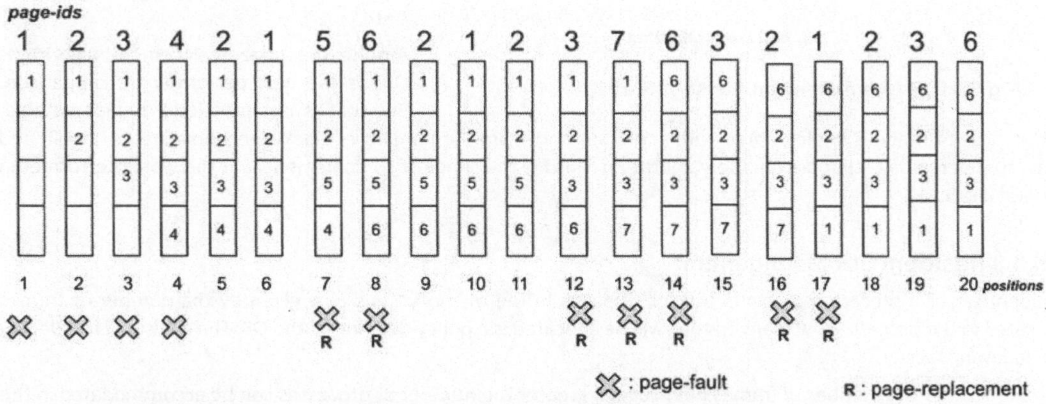

Fig 5.29: Example of LRU Page Replacement Algorithm

The algorithm causes 11 page-faults with 7 page replacements. LRU performs much better than FIFO. It rectifies the problem in FIFO where, no matter whatever be the recent usages of a page, the oldest page is replaced. If LRU is seen in the opposite direction (right to left), it is the reverse of the optimal algorithm.

However, implementing LRU is not trivial without hardware support. The past usage of a page needs to be kept track of before choosing a victim frame. This can be done if every page-use is *time-stamped.* Before the page replacement, the timestamp of last use is checked for each frame and the one with the oldest timestamp is chosen as the victim. Instead of timestamp, *counters* can also be used. For every page reference, a counter associated with a frame is incremented by 1. The frame with the lowest counter-value is selected as the victim.

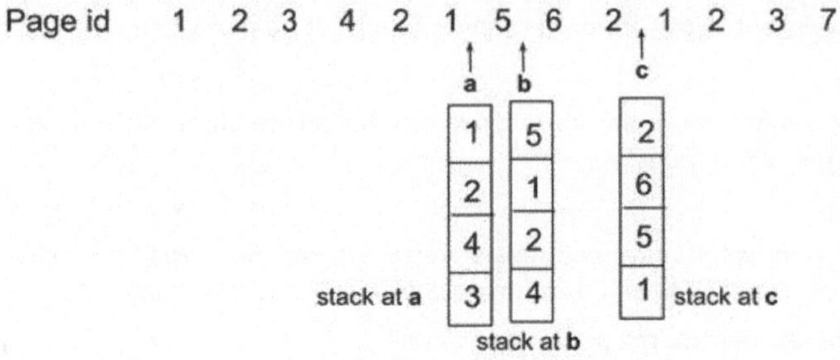

Fig 5.30: Stack-based implementation of LRU

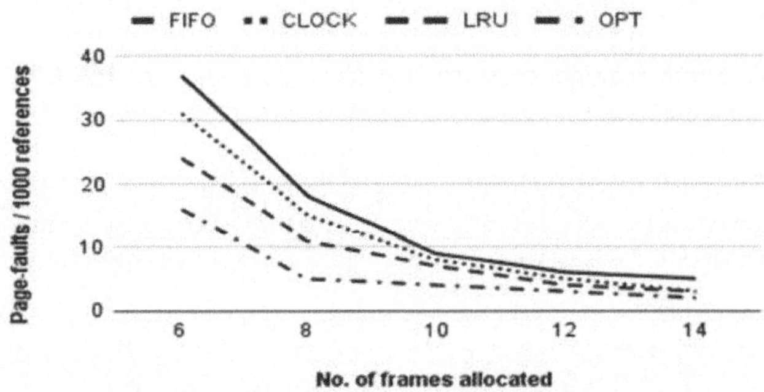

Fig 5.31: Performance comparison [Sta12]

Another alternative is the use of a *stack*. Whenever a page is referenced, it is put on the top. If the page is already available in the memory, it is taken out of the stack (anywhere in the stack, not necessary on the top) and pushed on top again. When a page is to be replaced, the page is available at the bottom of the stack (**Fig 5.30**). Because of this reason, LRU is also called a stack-based algorithm.

However, the above algorithms are not the exhaustive list. There can be other algorithms like:

- **LIFO (Last-In-First-Out) or MRU (Most Recently Used):** The last page will be replaced. Even though it seems counterintuitive, for some cyclical reference strings, it may be the closest approximation to OPT.
- **MFU (Most Frequently Used):** the most frequently occuring page is replaced.

...etc.

Among the page replacement algorithms OPT is the best performer in comparison. But that is not practically implementable. LRU is close to it and is implemented with active support from the hardware. Clock algorithms are next best, and thus, considered as LRU approximation algorithms. FIFO is the simplest to implement, but the worst performer in general (**Fig 5.31**).

5.5.3.3 Resident Set Management

Resident set of a process represents the set of pages in the memory. Its size is given by the number of frames allocated to the process. How many frames will be allocated is a policy decision of the OS. The decision is guided by the following facts.

- Smaller the number of frames per process, greater the number of processes can be accommodated in the memory increasing the degree of multiprogramming and possibly increasing CPU utilization and throughput. But this may also cause increased page-faults.
- Higher the number of allocated frames, the lesser the occurrence of page-faults. But beyond a certain point, there is no noticeable gain.

Keeping these two factors into account, two frame allocation policies are adopted.

- **Fixed Allocation:** Each process gets a fixed number of frames decided during loading of the process or process creation time. The number may depend on the type of process (batch, interactive, or the application-type) and its size. If a page-fault occurs and there is no free frame in the allocated set, page-replacement must be done. Allocated number of frames does not change during the execution of the process.

- **Variable Allocation:** Number of frames allocated to a process change during the execution of the process depending on the paging behavior. If the occurrence of page-faults increases, more frames are allocated. On the contrary, if page fault rate decreases, some of the frames allocated are taken away so that they can be used for other processes.

Variable allocation is more powerful but at the cost of increased software overhead. The OS has to monitor page fault rates (PFRs) of all the processes and the allocation needs support of the hardware including processor.

The use of allocation policy also depends on the page-replacement policy: *local* or *global*.

- **Local Replacement Policy:** When a page-fault occurs and there are no free frame available in the allocated set, a victim frame is chosen from the set only. The referenced page must be loaded in the victim frame replacing (overwriting or swapping out) the old page.

- **Global Replacement Policy:** All the unlocked frames or resident pages are candidates for replacement, regardless of the processes that own the pages. The benefits of variable allocation can be best leveraged in global replacement policy only. A process facing high occurrences of page-faults can take free frames from any of the processes.

When there are no free frames, a process encountering a high PFR will snatch frames from another process. This new process, may, in turn, suffer from increased PFR. It may again snatch frames from other processes. Gradually this may have a spiralling effect leading to very high overall PFR.

Hence, blind use of variable allocation with global replacement is not good. The use can be moderated by adopting the local replacement policy first, monitoring the page-fault-rates of different processes and if needed, adjusting the allocation by taking extra frame(s) from a process with very low page-fault-rate and allocating to another with very high PFR.

Such a dynamic mechanism is difficult to implement. However, the working set strategy (**Sec 5.5.2.4**) is a useful and popular attempt.

5.5.3.4 Load Control

Another important policy decision by OS, related to virtual memory management is the number of processes resident in the memory - or the degree of multiprogramming *aka* multiprogramming level. The decision is also guided by the following observations.

Very few processes residing in the memory may lead to under-utilisation of the processor, especially when all such processes are blocked for I/O. This low processor utilization causes low throughput.

Too many processes mean very few resident pages per process. This may lead to high page-fault rates. Very high PFR causes a peculiar phenomenon called *thrashing*.

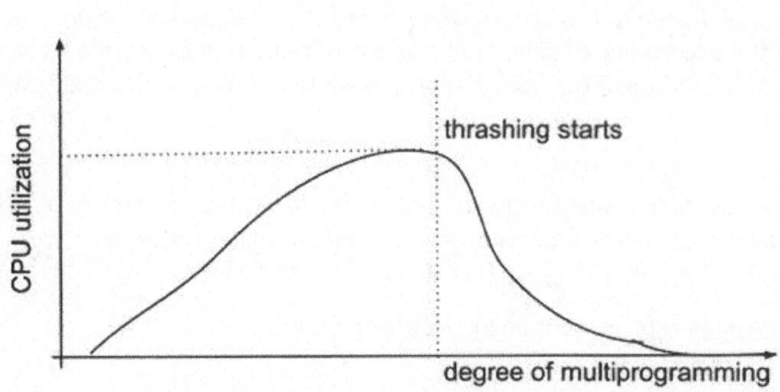

Fig 5.32: Thrashing

Thrashing: If the degree of multiprogramming is very low, CPU remains idle, and its utilization remains low. If the OS monitors utilization, it can increase the multiprogramming level by introducing more processes into the system. This steadily increases the CPU utilization, but up to a certain point. As multiprogramming level increases, there is also an increase in the PFRs as the number of frames availed by each process decreases. As page-faults involve swap-in and/or swap-out, with high PFRs, processes remain more busy with I/O than actual computation in the CPU. CPU utilization thus further dips giving a false notion that more processes can be loaded into the memory or degree of multiprogramming can be further increased. If that is done, CPU utilization further falls, and the situation gradually aggravates in a spiraling manner to such an extent that no process can execute while all remain busy in page faults and I/O. This phenomenon is called thrashing (**Fig 5.32**). Throughput also dives down leading to very poor overall performance. Thrashing is mostly seen in variable allocation with the global replacement scheme.

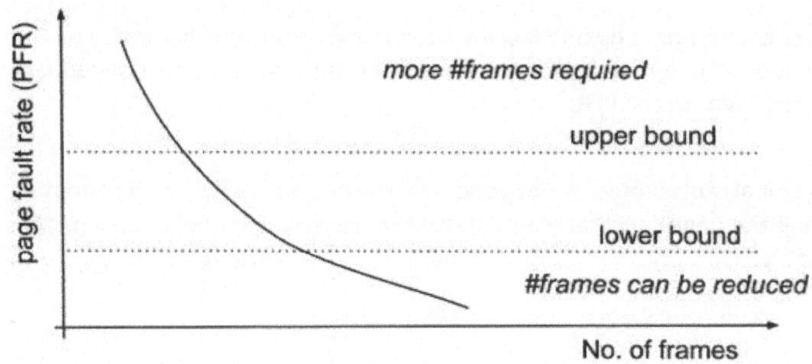

Fig 5.33: Dynamic allocation based on PFR

Thrashing is a highly undesirable phenomenon and should be avoided. Thrashing is invariably associated with high page-fault rates. PFR is monitored by the OS and if it goes above a threshold (upper bound), it indicates that thrashing may start, and the process needs more frames. On the contrary, if PFR goes below the lower bound, it means that the process has more frames than required. It may release frame(s) for other processes.

If thrashing is detected, degree of multiprogramming should be reduced by suspending one or more processes. Which process(es) need to be suspended - depends on lot many factors like

- *process-priority*: low priority processes are easy targets
- *page-fault rates*: processes with high PFRs may be chosen
- *resident set size:* processes with small resident set size can be re-loaded easily later
- *process-size*: largest process will free lot of frames
- *activation-time*: last process activated has the lowest cost of re-starting
- *remaining time*: process(es) with large remaining time will hold and use lot of resources

...etc.

The choice is decided by the OS designer based on one or more of the above factors.

Virtual memory implementation with demand paging is summarized in the following flow-diagram.

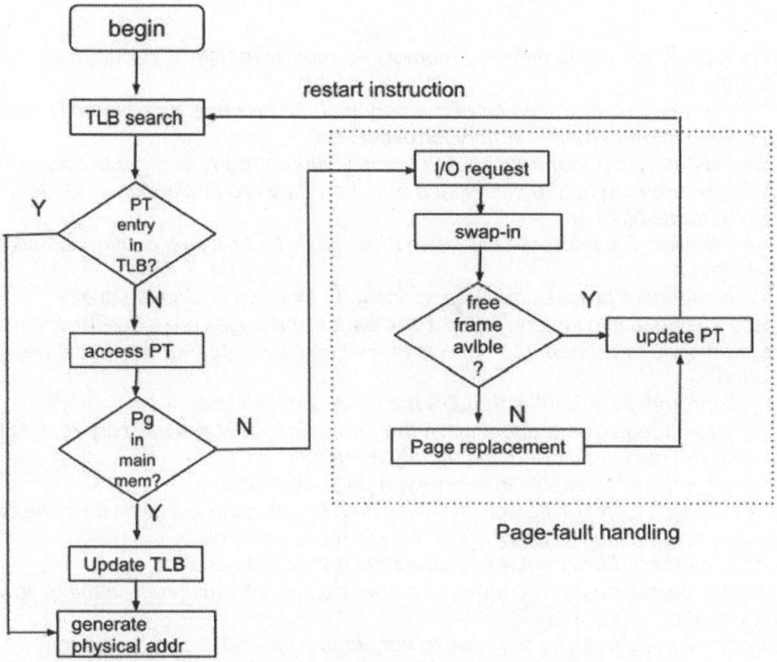

Fig 5.34: Page-fault handling with TLB

Calculation of Effective memory access time

1. Simple memory with a cache (with cache hit-ratio r): $t_{avg} = r \times t_{cache} + (1-r) \times t_{mem}$
(Neglecting cache-search time) [t_{cache} = *cache access time* ; t_{mem} = memory access time]

2. 1-level simple paging with TLB (hit-ratio = p) & in-memory page table:
$t_{avg} = p \times (t_{TLB} + t_{mem}) + (1-p) \times (t_{TLB} + 2 \times t_{mem})$ (Neglecting TLB-search time)

(for TLB misses, one t_{mem} to access PT, the other to access physical address)

3. 2-level simple paging with TLB (hit-ratio = p) & in-memory page tables:
$t_{avg} = p \times (t_{TLB} + t_{mem}) + (1-p) \times (t_{TLB} + 3 \times t_{mem})$
(for TLB misses, 2*t_{mem} to access PTs, the other physical address) ...

4. Demand paging (PFR = f) with TLB (hit-ratio = p), single-layer in-memory page table:

$$t_{avg} = p \times (t_{TLB} + t_{mem}) + (1-p)\{t_{TLB} + t_{mem} + (1-f) \times t_{mem} + f \times (t_{pfh} + t_{TLB} + 2 \times t_{mem})\}$$

(for TLB miss, $(t_{TLB} + t_{mem})$ is compulsory. One more t_{mem} if page is in memory; for a page-fault, page-fault handling (reloading) is followed by restarting page-search $(t_{TLB} + 2 \times t_{mem})$.

UNIT SUMMARY

- *This chapter starts with enumerating different memory elements: registers, cache, main memory, secondary and tertiary memory.*
- *Main memory is the largest and farthest unit of memory that the processor can directly access.*
- *All programs are loaded into the main memory for execution.*
- *A program can have different components spread across different parts of main memory.*
- *The components are referenced in a logical space and then they are finally converted to physical addresses through address binding.*
- *Main memory space is allocated to processes using three basic techniques: contiguous allocation, paging and segmentation.*
- *In contiguous allocation, entire process address space gets memory in a single space.*
- *In paging, a process is divided into several equal-sized pages and pages are loaded in the memory.*
- *In segmentation, a process is divided into several logical components that are of different sizes; segments are loaded.*
- *Pages are managed through page-tables that OS maintains per process.*
- *In virtual memory, not all the pages are loaded at the same time; few are memory resident while the majority remain in the backing store of secondary memory.*
- *When a referenced page is not available in memory, a page-fault occurs.*
- *Page-fault handling is a time-consuming activity: it involves swapping in the page from the backing store and swapping out a modified page when no free frame is available.*
- *Pure demand paging causes 100% page-faults and thus not recommended.*
- *No page-fault means simple paging scheme with low degree of multiprogramming, low CPU utilization and throughput.*
- *Very high degree of multiprogramming may cause very high page-faults and thrashing.*
- *Thrashing is an undesired phenomenon when a process remains busy in handling page-faults without doing any computation.*
- *Page-fault-rate thus should be kept as minimum as possible within an upper and a lower threshold.*
- *If page-fault rate goes beyond the upper threshold, one or more processes need to be suspended and page-frames released should be allocated to processes suffering from high PFR.*

EXERCISES

Multiple Choice / Objective Questions

Q1. Which of the following actions is/are typically not performed by the operating system when switching context from process **A** to process **B**

A. Saving current register values and restoring saved register values for process **B** .

B. Changing address translation tables.

C. Swapping out the memory image of process **A** to the disk.

D. Invalidating the translation look-aside buffer. [GATE (1999)]

Q2. A 1000 Kbyte memory is managed using variable partitions but no compaction. It currently has two partitions of sizes 200 Kbytes and 260 Kbytes respectively. The smallest allocation request in Kbytes that could be denied is for
A. 151
B. 181
C. 231
D. 541 [GATE(1996)]

Q3. Consider six memory partitions of size 200 KB, 400 KB, 600 KB, 500 KB, 300 KB, and 250 KB, where KB refers to kilobyte. These partitions need to be allotted to four processes of sizes 357 KB, 210 KB, 468 KB and 491 KB in that order. If the best fit algorithm is used, which partitions are NOT allotted to any process?

A. 200 KB and 300 KB
B. 200 KB and 250 KB
C. 250 KB and 300 KB
D. 300 KB and 400 KB [GATE(2015)]

Q4. In which one of the following page replacement policies, Belady's anomaly may occur?
A. FIFO **B.** Optimal **C.** LRU **D.** MRU [GATE (2009)]

Q5. The page size is 4 KB (1KB = 210 bytes) and page table entry size at every level is 8 bytes. A process P is currently using 2 GB (1 GB = 230 bytes) virtual memory which OS mapped to 2 GB of physical memory. The minimum amount of memory required for the page table of P across all levels is _________ KB
A. 4108
B. 1027
C. 3081
D. 4698 [GATE(2021)]

Q6. Consider the virtual page reference string: 1, 2, 3, 2, 4, 1, 3, 2, 4, 1
On a demand paged virtual memory system running on a computer system that has a main memory size of 3 pages frames which are initially empty. Let LRU, FIFO and OPTIMAL denote the number of page faults under the corresponding page replacements policy. Then

A. OPTIMAL < LRU < FIFO
B. OPTIMAL < FIFO < LRU
C. OPTIMAL = LRU
D. OPTIMAL = FIFO [GATE(2012)]

Q7. In a system with 32 bit virtual addresses and 1 KB page size, use of one-level page tables for virtual to physical address translation is not practical because of
A. the large amount of internal fragmentation
B. the large amount of external fragmentation
C. the large memory overhead in maintaining page tables
D. the large computation overhead in the translation process [GATE (2003)]

Q8. Consider a virtual memory system with FIFO page replacement policy. For an arbitrary page access pattern, increasing the number of page frames in main memory will
A. always decrease the number of page faults
B. always increase the number of page faults
C. sometimes increase the number of page faults
D. never affect the number of page faults [GATE(2001)]

Q9. Assume that in a certain computer, the virtual addresses are 64 bits long and the physical addresses are 48 bits long. The memory is word addressable. The page size is 8KB and the word size is 4 bytes. The Translation Look-aside Buffer (TLB) in the address translation path has 128 valid entries. At most, how many distinct virtual addresses can be translated without any TLB miss?
A. 16 x 210
B. 8 x 220
C. 4 x 220
D. 256 x 210 [GATE(2019)]

Q10. Consider a process executing on an operating system that uses demand paging. The average time for a memory access in the system is M units if the corresponding memory page is available in memory, and D units if the memory access causes a page fault. It has been experimentally measured that the average time taken for a memory access in the process is X units. Which one of the following is the correct expression for the page fault rate experienced by the process?
A. (D – M) / (X – M)
B. (X – M) / (D – M)

C. (D – X) / (D – M)
D. (X – M) / (D – X) [GATE(2018)]

Q11. A processor uses 2-level page tables for virtual to physical address translation. Page tables for both levels are stored in the main memory. Virtual and physical addresses are both 32 bits wide. The memory is byte addressable. For virtual to physical address translation, the 10 most significant bits of the virtual address are used as index into the first level page table while the next 10 bits are used as index into the second level page table. The 12 least significant bits of the virtual address are used as offset within the page. Assume that the page table entries in both levels of page tables are 4 bytes wide. Further, the processor has a translation look-aside buffer (TLB), with a hit rate of 96%. The TLB caches recently used virtual page numbers and the corresponding physical page numbers. The processor also has a physically addressed cache with a hit rate of 90%. Main memory access time is 10 ns, cache access time is 1 ns, and TLB access time is also 1 ns. Assuming that no page faults occur, the average time taken to access a virtual address is approximately (to the nearest 0.5 ns)
A. 1.5 ns
B. 2 ns
C. 3 ns
D. 4 ns [GATE(2003)]

Q12. A multilevel page table is preferred in comparison to a single level page table for translating virtual address to physical address because
A. It reduces the memory access time to read or write a memory location.
B. It helps to reduce the size of the page table needed to implement the virtual address space of a process.
C. It is required by the translation lookaside buffer.
D. It helps to reduce the number of page faults in page replacement algorithms. [GATE(2009)]

Answers of Multiple Choice Questions

1. C *2.* B *3.* A *4.* A *5.* A *6.* B *7.* C *8.* C *9.* D *10.* B *11.* D *12.* B

Short Answer Type Questions

Q1. What do you mean by logical addresses? How are they different from physical addresses?
Q2. What is address binding? How many types of address binding are possible?
Q3. Why does a computer keep several processes in main memory?
Q4. What is fragmentation? What are its different types? How can it be dealt with?
Q5. What is paging? How is it different from contiguous allocation?
Q6. What is virtual memory? How is it different from real memory?
Q7. What are the advantages of a page table? Where can a page table be stored?
Q8. What is demand paging? How is it different from paging?
Q9. Why do we need page replacement algorithms?
Q10. What is Belady's anomaly?
Q11. What is thrashing? How can it be dealt with?

Long Answer Type Questions

Q1. Describe with necessary diagrams different stages of compilation.
Q2. Explain the differences between different types of address binding with advantages and disadvantages.
Q3. Briefly discuss different types of memory allocation techniques and point out the pros and cons in them.
Q4. Why is virtual memory used? Justify why it is used despite substantial increase in memory access time.
Q5. Describe page-fault handling technique.
Q6. How can you measure the performance of demand paging? Derive a formula of average memory access time in virtual memory implementation with a cache, TLB and an in-memory page table.
Q7. What are the steps to modify the page-fault service routine to include page replacement?
Q8. Why can no page replacement algorithm beat the optimal one? Try to illustrate an algorithm where FIFO can be better than LRU.
Q9. Write differences between the following:

a. fragmentation vs segmentation

b. segmentation vs paging
c. best-fit vs worst-fit
d. buddy system vs equal partitioning
e. paging vs demand paging
f. LRU vs NRU

Q10. Write short notes on:

a) compaction
b) working set
c) thrashing
d) page-fault-rate (PFR)
e) degree of multiprogramming
f) resident set management
g) relationship between PFR and working set

Numerical Problems

Q1. Consider a main memory system that consists of 8 memory modules attached to the system bus, which is one word wide. When a write request is made, the bus is occupied for 100 nanoseconds (ns) by the data, *address, and control signals. During the same 100 ns, and for 500 ns thereafter, the addressed memory module* executes one cycle accepting and storing the data. The (internal) operation of different memory modules may overlap in time, but only one request can be on the bus at any time. The maximum number of stores (of one word each) that can be initiated in 1 millisecond is________? *(ANS : 10000)* [GATE(2014)]

Q2. A process has been allocated 3 page frames. Assume that none of the pages of the process are available in the memory initially. The process makes the following sequence of page references (reference string): 1, 2, 1, 3, 7, 4, 5, 6, 3, 1. If optimal page replacement policy is used, how many page faults occur for the above reference string ______? *(ANS :7)* [GATE (2007)]

Q3. A demand paging system takes 100 time units to service a page fault and 300 time units to replace a dirty page. Memory access time is 1 time unit. The probability of a page fault is p. In case of a page fault, the probability of page being dirty is also p. It is observed that the average access time is 3 time units. Then the value of p is_______? *(ANS : 0.019[approx])* [GATE (2007)]

Q4. A system uses FIFO policy for page replacement. It has 4 page frames with no pages loaded to begin with. The system first accesses 100 distinct pages in some order and then accesses the same 100 pages but now in the reverse order. How many page faults will occur? *(ANS: 196)* [GATE (2010)]

Q5. A system uses 3 page frames for storing process pages in main memory. It uses the Least Recently Used (LRU) page replacement policy. Assume that all the page frames are initially empty. What is the total number of page faults that will occur while processing the page reference string given below? 4, 7, 6, 1, 7, 6, 1, 2, 7, 2 *(ANS: 6)* [GATE(2014)]

Q6. Consider a computer system with ten physical page frames. The system is provided with an access sequence (a1, a2, ...a20, a1, a2, ...a20), where each ai is a distinct virtual page number. The difference in the number of page faults between the last-in-first-out page replacement policy and the optimal page replacement policy is_________ number. *(ANS: 1)* [GATE (2016)]

PRACTICAL

Q1. Write a program to implement the contiguous memory allocation and visually display the output when dynamically a set of processes comes and memory is allocated.

Q2. Write a program that will take a page-reference string as input and determine the number of page-faults for (i) OPT (ii) FIFO (ii) LRU and (iv) SC algorithms.

Q3. In a UNIX or Linux system, explore the following commands (learn using `man <command>`) to see page table, page-faults and other page-related activities for a process or several processes:

(i) `ps` command

(ii) `top` command

(iii) `time` command

(iv) `sar` command.

KNOW MORE

Memory Management and Virtual Memory are discussed in general with good detail as two separate chapters in [SGG18], [Sta12], [Hal15] and [Dha09].

[SGG18] covers address binding and explains implementation of paging hardware specially in different architectures and commercial systems. It also discusses newer technologies like memory compression.

[Sta12] also covers securities issues including attacks and protection to memory. This also provides a very organized and holistic view of virtual memory with emphasis on implementation of TLB.

[Hal15] clarifies different types of address spaces and illustrates their interaction. It provides segmentation well in memory management and virtual memory.

[Dha09] sees memory management as two separate entities like heap space management and that for kernel stack. It provides a good account of kernel space allocation and a mathematical framework for finding memory access time.

[Bac05] and [Vah12] discuss memory management in the UNIX system. While [Bac05] discusses swapping and demand paging there, [Vah12] is more comprehensive. [Vah12] discusses UNIX virtual memory implementation in several architectures and systems like SVR4, SVR 4.2, Mach, Solaris 2.4, 4.3 & 4.4 BSD.

[YIR17] contains implementational details of memory management and virtual memory in Windows operating systems across different architectures.

REFERENCES AND SUGGESTED READINGS

[Bac05] Maurice J Bach: The Design of the UNIX Operating System, Prentice Hall of India, 2005.

[Dha09] Dhananjay M. Dhamdhere: Operating Systems, A Concept-Based Approach, McGraw Hill, 2009.

[Hal15] Sibsankar Haldar: Operating Systems, Self Edition 1.1, 2015.

[SGG18] Abraham Silberschatz, Peter B Galvin, Greg Gagne: Operating Systems Concepts,10th Edition, Wiley, 2018.

[Sta12] William Stallings: Operating Systems Internals and Design Principles, 7th Edition, Prentice Hall, 2012.

[Vah12] Uresh Vahalia: UNIX Internals, The New Frontiers, Pearson, 2012.

[YIR17] Pavel Yosifovich, Alex Ionescu, Mark E. Russinovich, and David A. Solomon: Windows Internals, Seventh Edition (Part 1 and 2), Microsoft, 2017. https://docs.microsoft.com/en-us/sysinternals/resources/windows-internals (as on 8-Jul-2022).

Dynamic QR Code for Further Reading

6 I/O Management

UNIT SPECIFICS

Through this unit we have discussed the following aspects:

- *I/O Hardware: I/O devices, Device controllers, Direct memory access, Principles of I/O Software: Goals of Interrupt handlers, Device drivers, Device independent I/O software, Secondary-Storage Structure: Disk structure, Disk scheduling algorithms*
- *Disk Management: Disk structure, Disk scheduling - FCFS, SSTF, SCAN, C-SCAN, Disk reliability, Disk formatting, Boot-block, Bad blocks*
- *File Management: Concept of File, Access methods, File types, File operation, Directory structure, File System structure, Allocation methods (contiguous, linked, indexed), Free-space management (bit vector, linked list, grouping), directory implementation (linear list, hash table), efficiency and performance.*

This chapter discusses the role of input and output devices in a computer. I/O devices are the gateways to interact with a computing system. Users and application programs provide inputs through input devices and receive outputs through output devices. Each such device has some hardware components like device controllers, DMA, I/O ports, and I/O bus, that are connected to other hardware components like CPU and memory through system bus. However, there are also few software components like I/O subsystem and device drivers provided by the operating system that coordinate with different hardware components and the device. We start with an introduction to different hardware devices and components and then the software needed in I/O operations. We also discuss disk, an important I/O device to persistently store code and data for a computer. Its physical structure, functionalities and management is discussed in detail. We then delve into files, the software abstraction of data. With reasonable depth and rigor, we cover the structure and management of files.

Like previous units, a number of multiple-choice questions as well as questions of short and long answer types following Bloom's taxonomy, assignments through a number of numerical problems, a list of references and suggested readings are provided. It is important to note that for getting more information on various topics of interest, appropriate URLs and QR code have been provided in different sections which can be accessed or scanned for relevant supportive knowledge. "Know More" section is also designed for supplementary information to cater to the inquisitiveness and curiosity of the students.

RATIONALE

A computer interacts with users or applications through I/O devices: it takes inputs through one or more input devices and provides output through one or more output devices. How this interaction happens, specifically how the operating system manages this interaction is the content of this chapter. The chapter begins with the definition of I/O devices and their interaction with other necessary hardware components like I/O controllers, DMA, I/O ports, I/O bus, processor, memory and system bus. It is followed by discussion on necessary software components like I/O subsystem and device drivers. We then focus on the most important I/O device that persistently stores code and data across - a disk. Necessary details of disk management are discussed. Data is stored in the storage device as well as used in applications in the abstraction of files. Files are software entities that are used across the multitude of physical storage media. Files and their management is thus an important concept. How an operating system creates and manages files are discussed in reasonable detail in the last part.

This unit builds the fundamental concepts to understand I/O devices and their management in a computer. It introduces necessary terms and terminologies related to different I/O devices and I/O operations.

PRE-REQUISITES

- *Basics of Computer Organization and Architecture*
- *Fundamentals of Data Structures*
- *Introductory knowledge of Computer Programming*
- *Introduction to Operating Systems (**Unit I-V** of the book)*

UNIT OUTCOMES

List of outcomes of this unit is as follows:

U6-O1: Define different hardware components like device controllers, DMA, I/O ports, I/O buffers, I/O bus, files, directories and so on

U6-O2: Describe the data transfer mechanism between memory and an I/O device, operation of a DMA, disk formatting, disk scheduling algorithms, disk space allocation, implementation of file system and directory structure

U6-O3: Understand the issues in I/O management, variety and diversity in I/O devices, their interfaces, intricacies in disk management, disk space allocation and access

U6-O4: Realize the need of files, the concept of device-independent abstraction of storage units and their management from OS perspective

U6-O5: Analyze and compare pros and cons of different disk scheduling algorithms, disk allocation techniques, directory structure implementations

U6-O6: Design an I/O management system choosing the most appropriate techniques available or prescribing one for a given use-case scenario to minimize overall I/O time

Course Outcomes

After completion of the course the students will be able to:

1. Create processes and threads.
2. Develop algorithms for process scheduling for a given specification of CPU.
3. utilization, Throughput, Turnaround Time, Waiting Time, Response Time.
4. For a given specification of memory organization develop the techniques for optimally allocating memory to processes by increasing memory utilization and for improving the access time.
5. Design and implement file management system.
6. For a given I/O devices and OS (specify) develop the I/O management functions in OS as part of a uniform device abstraction by performing operations for synchronization between CPU and I/O controllers.

Unit-6 Outcomes	EXPECTED MAPPING WITH COURSE OUTCOMES (1- Weak Correlation; 2- Medium correlation; 3- Strong Correlation)					
	CO-1	CO-2	CO-3	CO-4	CO-5	CO-6
U6-O1	1	1	2	2	3	3
U6-O2	1	1	2	2	3	3
U6-O3	1	1	2	2	3	3
U6-O4	1	1	2	2	3	3
U6-O5	1	1	2	2	3	3
U6-O6	1	1	2	2	3	3

6.1 INTRODUCTION

A computer interacts with the user through a variety of hardware devices. While some of them are used to accept inputs (keyboard, mouse, joystick, scanner, screen-reader etc.), some to show the outputs (display unit, printer) or to run other systems (computer-driven robotic devices), or to communicate with other computing units (network devices). These devices are in general called input/output devices or I/O devices. These hardware devices do not form the core of computational components (processor, bus and memory) and remain in the periphery of a computer (they are, hence, also called peripheral devices) (see **Fig 1.1**). I/O devices vary widely in shape, size, functionality, input and output format. Handling I/O devices involves complexities and is thus the most difficult part of a computer system.

Despite differences at different levels, one thing is common at a very high level. All I/O devices either store or carry data that are used by the processor.

Recall from Unit 1 that an operating system provides an "easy-to-use" interface for the users to use the barebone hardware. The OS not only takes care of the computing components of the hardware, but also of these I/O devices which deal with data for storage or communication. An OS provides "easy-to-use" interfaces to different application programs and kernel modules for a huge variety of devices. I/O management is thus a very important job of an OS.

First, we shall discuss the I/O hardware units followed by the software involved in the interaction with them in general. We shall then focus on a particular device type: the disk device (in *disk management*). Finally, we shall discuss storage, organization and management of data in the hardware devices in the abstraction of files (in *file management*).

6.2 I/O HARDWARE

Wide variety of hardware is used in computers. Except the essential few like processor, memory and communication bus, the most belong to the peripheral devices. They are mostly used by a computer to interact with the outer world and thus are known as I/O devices (however, not all peripheral devices are I/O devices, e.g., a timer is a peripheral device but not an I/O). The interaction needs both hardware and software. In the following we first discuss different hardware units.

6.2.1 I/O devices

I/O devices can be used for various purposes. However, they can be clubbed into two broad categories according to their purpose of uses, as follows.

1. *communication*: data is taken in or sent out through communication devices

2. *storage*: data is persistently stored in storage devices.

Communication Devices: These devices transmit data from or to processors and do not store data persistently. They can be used for *user interaction*. In this category, there are strictly *input devices* like keyboard, mouse, scanner, joystick etc; strictly *output devices* like monitor, printer etc.; or both *input-output devices* like touchscreen.

Again, there are purely communication devices or network devices like NIC or Ethernet cards.

Storage Devices: Data is stored in these devices for persistent use and can stay even after shutdown of the computer. Programs and data are loaded from these devices and written onto. They include secondary memory like HDD, CD-ROM, and tertiary memory like tape, flash media etc.

The devices can be classified differently based on different characteristics. Following are a few examples.

- *character* or *block*: a device can transfer one character or a single byte of data (e.g., a keyboard), while another can transfer a multi-byte block at a time (e.g., a disk). The block size is fixed for a device but can vary across devices.
- *read-only / write-only / read-write*: A device can only take input (e.g., a keyboard) or produce only output (e.g., a printer) or does both read and write (e.g., a disk or a touch-screen).
- *slow* or *fast*: A device can be very slow transferring a few bytes a second (e.g., a keyboard), while another can be very fast, transferring several MBs per second (e.g., NICs).
- *transient* or *persistent*: Some devices store data for very short duration (e.g., NICs), while some can store for long periods (e.g., disks).
- *serial* or *parallel*: A device can transmit one bit at a time (bit-stream device), while another can transmit several bits simultaneously in parallel.
- *sequential* or *random access*: A device can support access of data only sequentially (e.g., a tape drive) or can support random access from any region of the storage (e.g., a magnetic disk).
- *sharable* or *exclusive*: A device can be concurrently accessed by several processes (e.g., a disk) or can be used by only a single process at a time (a graphics plotter).

Each of these devices get connected to the host computer through a hardware component called device controller or I/O controller. An I/O device is controlled by the controller and transmits data through an I/O bus (**Fig. 6.1**).

6.2.2 Device Controller

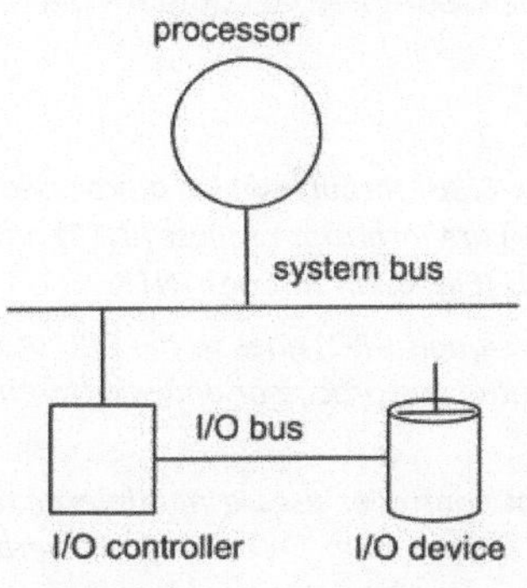

Fig. 6.1: I/O device, bus, controller

All I/O devices are connected to the computer through a device controller or I/O controller. A controller is an electronic unit with different levels of circuits. For example, a serial-port controller can contain a small chip that controls signals on a few wires. Again, a disk-controller can contain a small processor with microcode to control several disk-data related checking. Whatever be the complications in its circuitry, a controller essentially controls the operation of the I/O device and communicates with the CPU. At one side, the controller is connected to the system bus (address bus + data bus + control bus, where each bus is a set of parallel wires to carry address, data and control signals from/to CPU respectively) and on the other side, with the I/O bus (**Fig. 6.1**). A controller acts as an intermediary between the CPU and the device. Controllers can be housed in the host computer, or the device may have an in-built controller. A single controller can control operations of several I/O devices of the same type.

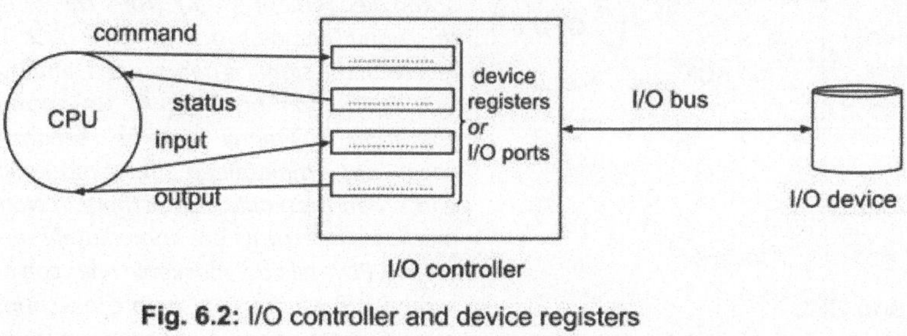

Fig. 6.2: I/O controller and device registers

Each controller implements a few registers, known as *control registers* or *operating registers* or *I/O ports*. There are four categories of I/O ports (**Fig. 6.2**):

i. Command
ii. Status
iii. Input
iv. Output.

The CPU sends the instruction by populating the Command port. It also provides the input data to the device by writing on the Input ports. When the I/O is complete or stops due to error(s), it is notified to the CPU by an appropriate status message written on the Status port. The output of the device, if any, is written by the device on the Output register, which is read by the CPU. There may be other registers as well, like configuration registers used for configuring the controller during initialization. Again, sometimes, more than one category of ports are merged. These ports exchange data with CPU registers. A popular example of an I/O controller is SCSI (acronym for Small Computer System Interface)-HBA (Host Bus Adapter).

6.2.3 Processor (*an additional subsection)

A processor is the most important hardware unit in any computer. The principal processor of a computer is not an I/O device. But often a small processor is housed inside an I/O controller for assisting I/O related processing. Certainly, it is not an essential part of the I/O device or the device controller, but this processor is dedicated to a specific task to assist the device controller. Here we are not referring to these I/O specific processors, but a general-purpose processor. This section is added to illustrate the differences between a processor and its different components, specifically to highlight that between a CPU and an interrupt controller.

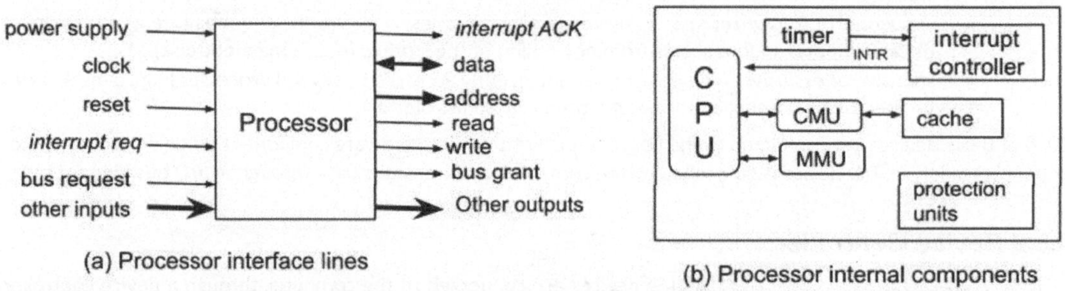

Fig. 6.3: Processor interconnections and components

*There are different interface lines connected to a general-purpose processor (**Fig. 6.3a**) through which a processor gets various signals and inputs as well as sends and provides output. Two of them are interrupt request (INTR) and interrupt acknowledgement (ACK) lines. I/O devices draw the attention of the CPU (**Fig. 6.3b**) through INTR.*

*Even though there can be several I/O devices, only one of the interrupt activation signals (IRQ) goes to the CPU at a time - which one will go is decided by the interrupt controller (another component of the processor and is different from an I/O controller) (**Fig. 6.3b**).*

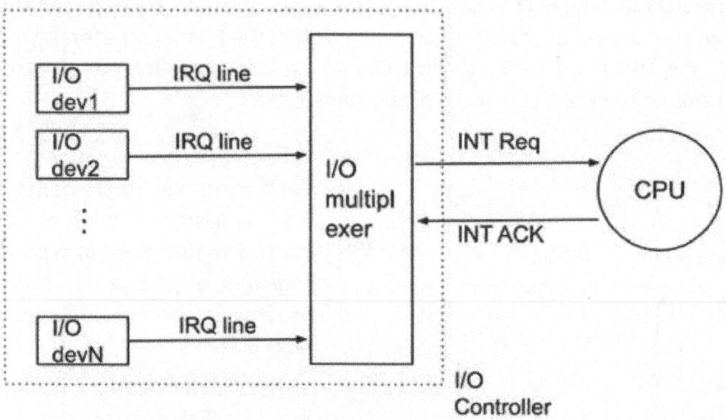

Fig 6.4: I/O Controller and CPU

*Interrupt controller uses a multiplexer to select only one, out of several simultaneous IRQ lines, based on priority of the device or some other criteria (**Fig 6.4**). Until the I/O controller receives an acknowledgement (ACK) from the CPU, the signal remains active. Once ACK is received, the signal is deactivated, and the I/O device can go back to its normal operation. In many systems, separate lines are maintained for maskable and non-maskable interrupts. Non-maskable interrupts are immediately sent to the CPU while the maskable ones can be turned off by the CPU before executing critical instructions. In programmable interrupt controller (PIC), separate mask registers are provided to control masking of IRQ lines by the CPU.*

CPU - I/O Controller Interaction: An I/O controller works on behalf of a CPU to get some I/O operation done by an I/O device. However, the I/O devices widely vary in user interfaces and the controller insulates the CPU from low-level differences. Processor architecture supports a few special I/O instructions, and the processor executes those instructions (like IN, OUT) to operate the controller. The CPU writes the command on the designated I/O port and input data on the input port, if any, and waits for the completion of the I/O operation intended.

This wait can happen in two ways. The I/O operations are also divided based on the wait-type.

- One, the processor can continuously or intermittently check the Status register of the controller. If the I/O is complete then, it also reads the Output register. The processor remains busy with the I/O operation during the entire interval since issuing an I/O command till its completion (successful or error). This type of busy-wait handshaking is called *programmed I/O*.
- Two, the processor populates the command register along and the Input register(s) and goes back to do other activities. When the device completes the intended operation, the controller raises an interrupt request (INTR) to draw attention of the processor. The processor, on receiving the INTR, invokes appropriate interrupt service routine (ISR). The ISR checks the Status register and Output register of the controller and does other necessary work as per the ISR. This option is called *interrupt-driven I/O*.

Programmed I/O does not need a context switch. It can save time and logistic overhead of context switching. However, it can be used only if the I/O device is quite fast, and the controller responds quickly.

But, in general, most of the I/O devices are much slower than the processor and hence, most contemporary systems implement interrupt-driven I/O. When the I/O device takes time to do the I/O operation, the processor can execute other instructions for other processes. The processor and I/O controllers can execute in parallel.

The processor only needs to check the presence of the INTR signal intermittently. Generally, the processor does it after every clock cycle and addresses the interrupt first, if any, suspending the current process and invoking an interrupt service routine (ISR). When execution of the ISR is complete, then either the suspended process is resumed, or execution of another program is started as decided by the ISR.

The I/O ports of all the controllers in a system make a composite *I/O address space*. I/O activity involving these I/O ports of I/O controllers is called *port-mapped I/O*.

In some systems, instead of I/O ports in the controller, a certain portion of main memory is used for I/O control. The CPU can do I/O operations very much like memory accesses (read/write). This kind of I/O activities are called *memory-mapped I/O*.

6.2.4 Direct Memory Access (DMA)

In the above scheme, data transfer between the main memory and an I/O device happens through the I/O controller and the CPU. Even for a single byte of data transfer, we need active involvement of the CPU. It sends an I/O read or I/O write instruction to the controller. The controller sends the instruction to the device. The device does the exchange and comes back to the controller with the status and output. Finally, the status and output reach the CPU through the system bus. During this time, the CPU either busy-waits or gets interrupted and then runs an ISR. For a large amount of data transfer (say few MBs), this kind of byte-by-byte (or word-by-word) exchange is extremely time-consuming and inefficient as it consumes substantial CPU time. Can we do any better? Direct Memory Access (DMA) exactly does this. DMA is a dedicated processor for large-scale data transfer between two devices without actively involving the CPU. Most modern I/O controllers are fitted with DMA (**Fig. 6.5**). A host computer can have multiple DMAs for different devices.

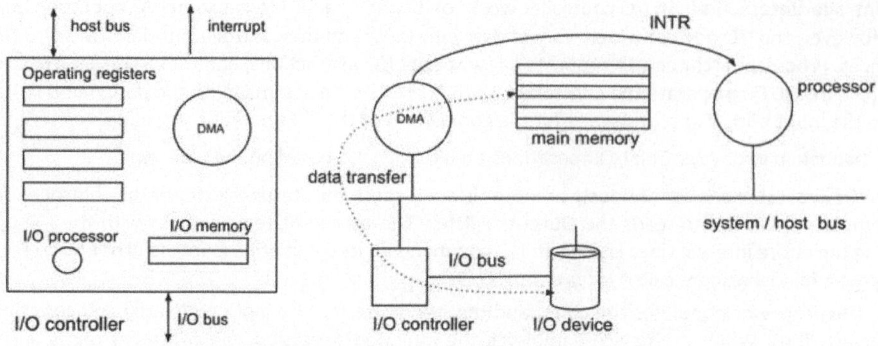

Fig. 6.5: Large-scale data transfer using DMA

For data transfer between main memory and an I/O device, the CPU is involved in the initial setup. The CPU first arranges a memory buffer for data transfer. It conveys the I/O controller address of the buffer, number of bytes to be transferred and direction of transfer (from or to the memory). DMA transfers the data. Only at the end of transfer, DMA (or the I/O controller) interrupts the CPU. In between, the CPU remains free and can do other execution. Instead of byte-by-byte (or word-by-word) involvement, the CPU is involved only at the beginning and end.

However, the DMA transfers the data byte-by-byte or word-by-word or block-by-block. It uses the system bus for the transfer.

When DMA transfers data of one byte or one word at a time, it uses the host bus in an interleaved fashion along with other activities of the CPU. This intermittent use of the host bus is also called *cycle stealing* of DMA transfer.

DMA can also use *burst mode* or *block transfer mode* where DMA uses the host bus uninterrupted. Other devices are not allowed to use the system bus at that time. Obviously, the bus needs to support the burst mode.

DMA can also transfer data in a single clock cycle at high-speed bypassing the DMA registers. DMA needs to activate necessary control signals at both the source and the destination. For example, for a secondary memory to main memory transfer, DMA simultaneously enables read signal at the secondary memory and write request to the main memory. This mode of data transfer is called *fly-by mode* or *single-access mode.*

6.3 I/O SOFTWARE

Interrupts are signals that I/O devices raise to draw the attention of a CPU (**Sec 3.1.2.1**). Modern computing systems are mostly interrupt-driven. Computers achieve multiprogramming because of interrupts. An interrupt disrupts the normal activity of a CPU. Normally a CPU sequentially executes instructions of a program. An interrupt forces it to stop and execute another set of instructions from another program. At the end of each instruction, the CPU checks the interrupt request line (INTR) and needs to handle the interrupt, if there is any.

Interrupt handling is an extremely important task and involves both hardware and software. While handling of a few interrupts can be deferred during critical processing (by masking low priority interrupts), some interrupts need immediate attention of the operating system. Interrupt handling thus requires hardware mechanisms (like identifying an interrupt type, its priority-level, assigning a number to it, putting an entry in the interrupt vector table and pointing to the memory address corresponding to its interrupt service routine or ISR through a pointer etc.) and necessary software like the ISR to handle the interrupt.

6.3.1 Interrupt Handlers

ISRs or interrupt handlers are part of an operating system that are specific to interrupt types. During the boot time, an OS probes the devices attached to the computer system and registers the handlers corresponding to the devices. The registered interrupt handlers have a mapping with the devices. When an interrupt comes from a registered device, the handler is invoked by the hardware mechanism.

Often the handler is split into two parts: *first-level interrupt-handler* (FLIH) and *second-level interrupt-handler* (SLIH). A FLIH is a fast and hardware-dependent handler that immediately does state save (of the currently executing process), context switch, mode switch (to supervisor mode and scheduling of the corresponding SLIH.

SLIH is a slow and more hardware-independent handler. It takes the desired action based on the interrupt signal (e.g., providing input for the I/O operation, or after successful completion or encountering error of the I/O) that can take a longer time. At the end of the SLIH, it can resume the suspended process or can start another process.

Interrupts are caused by hardware devices. But several untoward situations like dividing by zero, memory access errors, illegal memory access etc are captured by exceptions or traps that are also handled by an OS like the interrupts.

The goals of the interrupt handlers are the following.

- A CPU should not be held back and kept idle while an I/O operation is in progress. Both can be concurrently done, and an interrupt should serve as a mode of communication between the two.
- An I/O device should notify the CPU when it needs to, by raising an interrupt.
- Not all I/O devices are of equal priorities. When a critical processing is going on, the CPU can disable or defer (by masking) the interrupt from a low-priority device.
- An operating system must distinguish between high- and low-priority interrupts so that it can respond with an appropriate degree of urgency in case of multiple concurrent interrupts.

Interrupt-driven I/O involves context switching - which is a time-consuming process. On the other hand, programmed I/O needs busy-wait handshaking that wastes CPU cycles. A system can implement any one or both the techniques. Where both are available, programmed I/O is used when I/O responses are quite fast, otherwise interrupt-driven I/O.

6.3.2 Device Drivers

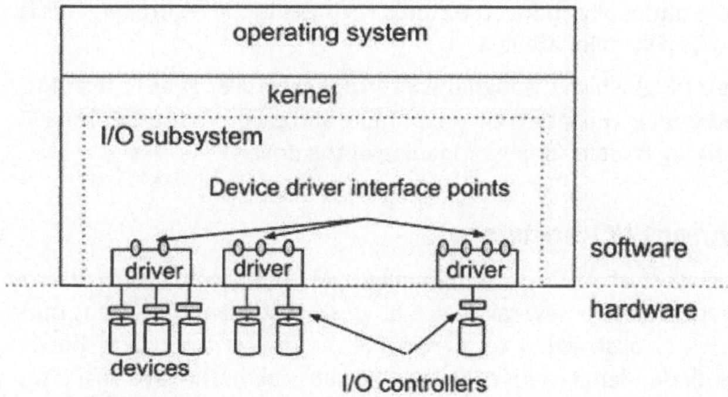

Fig. 6.6: Devices and device drivers

I/O devices widely vary in their functionalities and low-level instructions for control and management. Hence, ISRs also vary widely at the low-level. An operating system thus implements I/O management through layers of abstraction. Each layer hides the complexities and variations of lower level from the upper level and provides convenience to upper level. Device drivers are the lowest level of abstraction from an operating system to control devices. A device driver is an OS kernel module that interacts with the controller of a device. However, a device driver can control several hardware devices of the same type (**Fig 6.6**), including some software device that emulates some hardware (like a pseudo-terminal or a virtual keyboard).

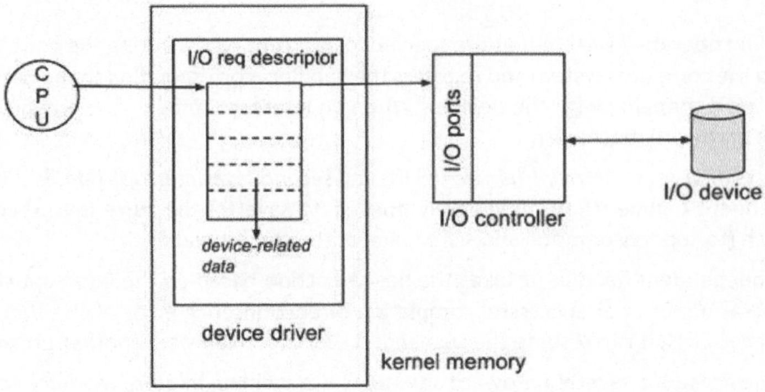

Fig 6.7: Hardware-software interaction for I/O operation

A device driver includes all device-specific codes and ISRs and provides the rest of the OS a set of device-independent interfaces. The OS and application programs can easily interact with the device using the interfaces without requiring the knowledge of its low-level intricacies. The device drivers thus provide modularity and portability to the OS.

Device drivers can be of different types. However, two basic types are: block device drivers (deals with block devices supporting file systems) and character device drivers (standard or stream character devices like keyboard and network devices respectively).

Irrespective of the types, device drivers are implemented following the kernel-device interface model (KDIM). The KDIM defines a set of specifications for the interface between an OS and all device drivers. A device driver maintains some private data, a set of device-specific routines including ISRs and a set of device-independent interfaces as per KDIM. The OS and application programs control / access devices through device drivers by executing the routines.

Device drivers are loadable kernel modules. Device drivers need to be registered to the OS before they can be used. During the bootstrapping of an OS, or when the driver is loaded it is registered and initialized through the KDIM interface functions. The OS invokes these functions to get some services from the devices through the driver. In turn, the driver also seeks some kernel services like getting kernel memory through the interface.

The CPU-controller interaction discussed earlier actually happens through the driver of the device - that resides in the kernel space of the memory. Each I/O request is represented by a request descriptor stored in the kernel memory. An I/O controller gets the address of the descriptor on its I/O ports and then collects the instruction and data to operate the device through DMA. Once I/O operation is done, the driver gets notified by the controller either through polling or an interrupt signal (**Fig. 6.7**).

Polling is done in programmed I/O where the driver continually checks the status registers in the controller. This is time-consuming, but bearable if the I/O device and its controller are fast.

Otherwise, the controller raises an interrupt request (IRQ) which through the interrupt controller goes to the CPU. The CPU finds the appropriate ISR using the INTR address in the interrupt vector table and executes the ISR. The ISR is part of the driver that is registered with the OS during bootstrapping or loading of the driver.

6.3.3 I/O Subsystem (Device-independent I/O software)

As shown in **Fig 6.6**, an operating system maintains layers of abstraction to manage the I/O devices. Device drivers are device-specific low-level abstractions. An OS must manage several device drivers of different types. It is thus convenient for the kernel to maintain a higher level of abstraction to manage all the drivers through a simple, uniform and single interface. This common device-independent layer is called the *I/O subsystem.* This layer insulates the rest of the OS and application programs from the diversity of the device drivers and provides a common gateway to the I/O devices.

The I/O subsystem keeps track of all the device drivers. It maintains a generic driver that drives all the individual device driver propers. The I/O subsystem is responsible for allocation and deallocation of I/O devices to different processes. It also maintains a number of data caches (also known as I/O buffers) in the kernel space to facilitate data transfer between memory and I/O devices.

The I/O subsystem clubs the wide variety of devices into a few categories for the sake of management. In UNIX systems, the devices are managed through three such categories:

1. Network devices 2. Character devices and 3. Block devices.

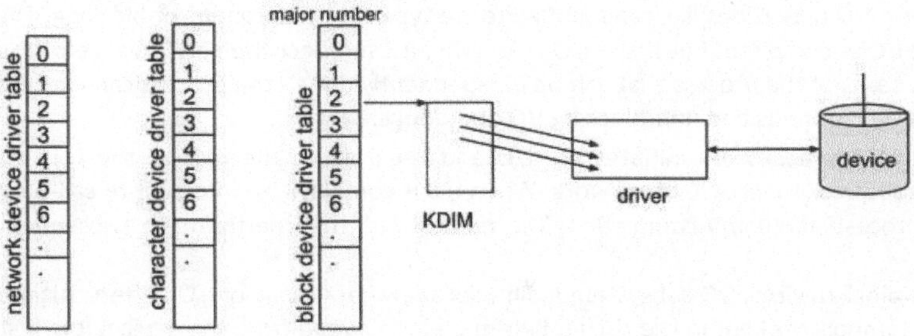

Fig. 6.8: Device driver tables are maintained in the I/O subsystem

Each category of devices is kept track of through three different tables. Each category implements a different set of KDIM interfaces. For example, character devices implement `get` (read a character) or `put` (write a character) while block devices have read, write and repositioning etc. Each such table contains a number of entries corresponding to different device types within the broad category. These device types are represented by integer numbers, called *major numbers* (**Fig. 6.8**).

Each major number may have a few instances of the device type represented by minor numbers (e.g., there can be several instances of the similar printers). Each device is thus uniquely specified by a tuple consisting of device category, major number, and minor number.

Device category along with a pair of integers (major, minor numbers) acts as the symbolic link between the OS and the I/O subsystem. The appropriate driver information is obtained by dereferencing the driver table followed by the major number. When a device driver is registered with the OS, a pointer to the driver KDIM structure is entered into the appropriate entry of its driver table. To use a device, a client program must provide the I/O subsystem the device category and major number which enable the I/O *subsystem to access appropriate interface routines*. The minor number is passed on to and used by the device driver to use a particular device.

Functionalities of I/O Subsystem

An I/O subsystem is responsible for I/O device management. It does the following functions.

- *I/O device allocation:* This is the primary task of an I/O subsystem. If a device is non-sharable, it is exclusively allocated to a process during which other requesting processes must wait. A device can only be allocated if it is available. An I/O subsystem thus has to manage a device status table where their current allocation information is maintained (**Fig. 6.9**). For every device, there is an allocator that is managed by the I/O subsystem.

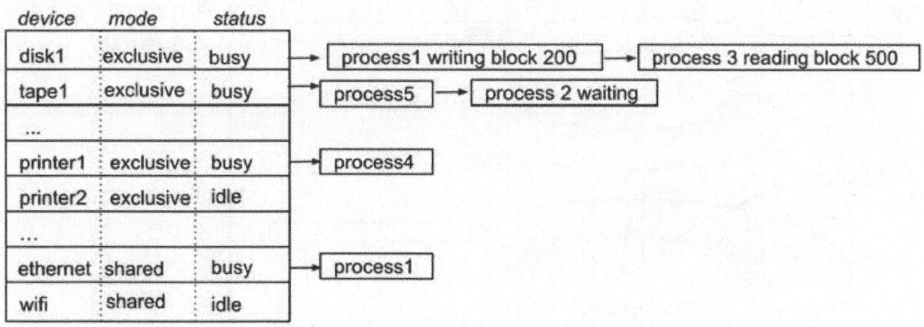

Fig. 6.9: Device status table maintained by the I/O subsystem

- *I/O request scheduling:* For sharable devices, there is no requirement of scheduling. But for non-sharable devices, if there are concurrent requests from several processes, there needs to be a scheduling algorithm (like CPU scheduling discussed in **Unit 2**) (**Fig. 6.9**). While FCFS can work for most of the cases, sometimes process priority or other constraints can play a role. For every device, I/O subsystem determines the best order among the pending requests. While one is allocated a non-sharable I/O device (with a single instance), the others need to wait for it in a queue.

- *Coordinating I/O operations:* I/O operations like read and write are typically synchronous or blocking. The process must wait till the I/O is complete. But if the I/O is lengthy, it can affect the performance of the process. If there are other tasks of the process that can be independently done - the process can execute using an alternative way: asynchronous and non-blocking I/O operations.
- In asynchronous I/O operations, a process initiates the I/O and then leaves the task to the OS (I/O subsystem). The process goes back to its own other work. When I/O is complete, an interrupt or call-back mechanism notifies the process about I/O completion. The process can then perform the subsequent actions.
- *Managing data cache:* For block devices, I/O subsystem maintains a few data cache or I/O buffers. After a block of data is read, it is temporarily kept in the cache. Before a block is read from the device, it is first checked in the cache. If found (i.e., a cache-hit), time for reading from the device (which is a way more costly than from the kernel memory), is saved.

6.4 SECONDARY STORAGE STRUCTURE

Mass-storage medium in any computer system that is closest to the processor where code and data can reside persistently is the secondary storage. Two primary categories in the secondary storage devices are hard-disk drives (HDDs) and solid-state disks (SSDs).

We shall study them in greater detail below.

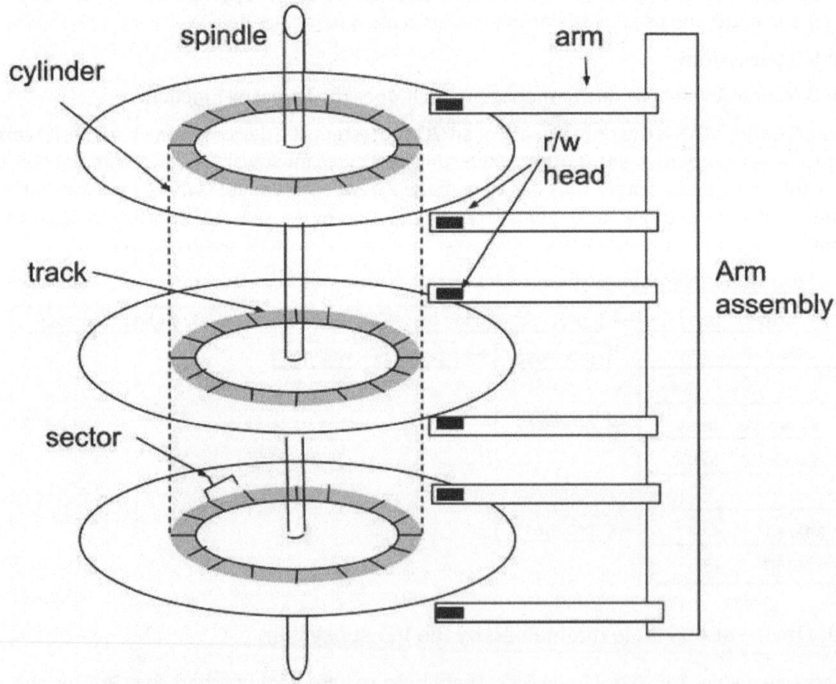

Fig. 6.10: Magnetic Disk Structure

6.4.1 Disk structure

A HDD is simply a collection of magnetic disks, stacked up in a mechanical arrangement. A HDD consists of a number of concentric flat circular platters (typically 1-12 in numbers), each of diameter 1.8 to 3.5 inches, stacked on a single spindle. Platters are very thin (10 - 20 nm) that have coatings of magnetic material (iron oxides) on both sides that store the data (**Fig. 6.10**).

For each platter, there are two read-write heads to access its either side. The heads do not touch the disk surface, although the separation is extremely narrow (about one-millionth of an inch). The heads are mounted on arms that enable horizontal movement over the platters. The arms are fixed on the arm-assembly and can only have linear motion along the radius of the platter.

Data is stored on either side of the platter. Entire space of all the platters together makes the total disk space. Each platter is divided into hundreds of circular rings. Each such ring or circular stripe is called a *track.* A track is divided into a number of *sectors.* However, all the similar tracks with a particular radius across platters together make a *cylinder* or *volume.* A typical sector stores 512 or 1024 bytes of data. All cylinders, tracks and sectors are numbered. Each sector is uniquely referred to by a tuple `<cylinder-no, track-no, sector-no>`.

Cylinder number starts from the periphery (0) and increases towards the center. The one closest to the spindle has the highest cylinder id.

A disk is rotated at a high speed (3600 rpm to 15000 rpm) by a disk-drive motor. To access a particular sector, appropriate volume (or track) needs to be identified and the r/w head to be brought over it through radial movement of the arm. The platter then needs to be rotated so that the beginning of the sector comes under the r/w head. Hence, data-access from a disk involves the time for arm-movement (called *seek-time)* and time of rotation (called *rotational latency*).

Disk-access time = seek-time + rotational latency.

Once the sector is perfectly located, data transfer can take place. Including data transfer, effective disk access time = seek-time + rotational latency + data transfer time.

Seek time is on an average $5 - 25\ ms$ and one complete rotation of the platter takes $8 - 16\ ms$ in modern disks. Data transfer time depends on a few factors like the amount of data, the position of the sectors involved (contiguous or spread over the disk) and speed of rotation of the disk.

6.4.2 Disk Scheduling

In recent times, there have been tremendous advancements in processor and main memory technologies, leading to massive drop in both execution time and memory access time. However, disk technologies, particularly for magnetic disks, have not advanced with that pace, resulting in few orders of differences between disk access time and main memory access time. Overall execution time of a process is thus affected by disk access time. Among the three components in disk access time, seek time is the major one. An operating system, responsible for overall performance of a system, tries to therefore reduce the seek time through proper scheduling of the disk accesses.

For a multiprogramming system, requests for disk access come continuously from different processes. When one request is attended, the others wait in the disk queue. The disk device driver tries to schedule a sequence of such access requests in such a way that total seek time or average seek time is minimized.

The sequence of cylinder numbers that represents intended disk accesses is called a *reference string.* We shall discuss few disk scheduling algorithms and find out average (or total) seek time for a given reference string:

97, 182, 36, 121, 13, 123, 64, 66 (the cylinder is assumed to be located initially at cylinder 52 from an earlier access). We assume that the disk has 200 cylinders (0 - 199).

6.4.2.1 First come First Serve (FCFS) Scheduling

This is the simplest possible algorithm as all the requests are met in the same order as they appear in the wait queue for the disk. The read-write head moves to Cylinder 97 from its start position (Cylinder 52), then to Cylinder 182, followed by 36 and so on. Finally, the r/w head stops at Cylinder 66 (**Fig. 6.11**).

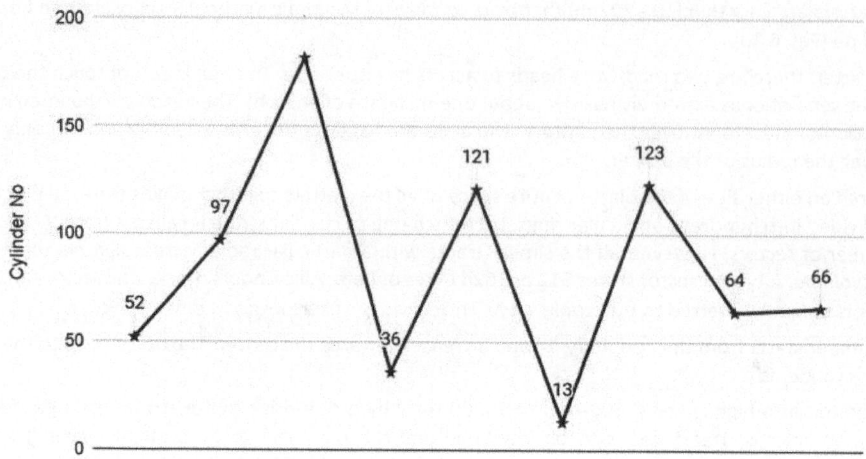

Fig 6.11: FCFS Scheduling

The total number of *to and fro* movement of the r/w head is = (97- 52) + (182 - 97) + (182 - 36) + (121 - 36) + (121 - 13) + (123 - 13) + (123 - 64) + (66 - 64) = 45 + 85 + 146 + 85 + 108 + 110 + 59 + 2 = 640 cylinders.

The algorithm is easy to understand and implement, but not good at all from the performance point of view. The r/w arm has to move back and forth several times that results in very high overall seek-time.

6.4.2.2 Shortest Seek Time First (SSTF) Scheduling

R/W head movement is costly, it increases seek time. It can be reduced if the head moves to the nearest cylinder among the pending requests from its current position. This is the idea behind the SSTF algorithm. Before moving the head each time, the closest cylinder number is searched from the remaining requests and the head goes to that cylinder. For our example reference string, the movement of the head is shown in **Fig. 6.12.**

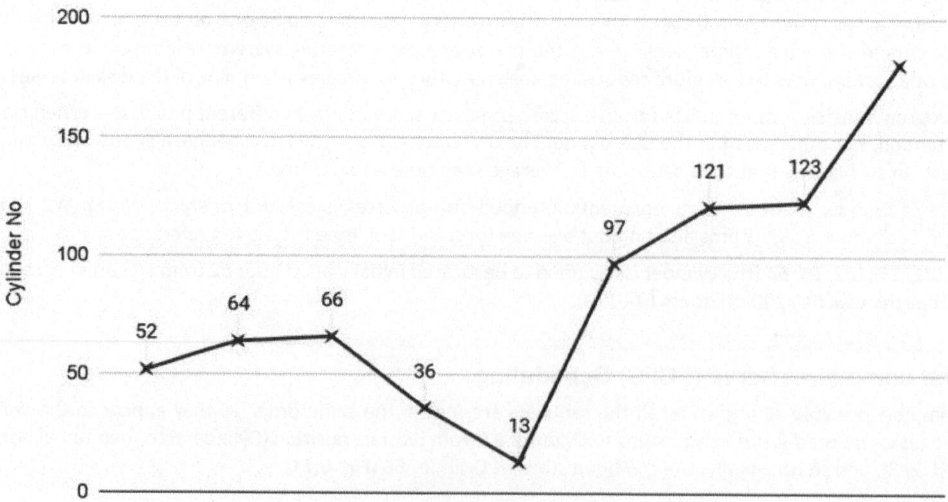

Fig 6.12: SSTF Scheduling

The total number of to and from movement is = (64 - 52) + (66 - 64) + (66 - 36) + (36 - 13) + (97 - 13) + (121 - 97) + (123 - 121) + (187 - 121) = 243 cylinders.

The performance is much improved over FCFS, even though it may not be the best for the given reference string.

The algorithm can be implemented using a min-heap built over the remaining disk cylinder requests and using the min-value as the destination of head movement each time.

The algorithm is elegant and easily implementable. However, it suffers from a few problems. The algorithm always looks for the local minimum (the closest cylinder from the current position) without considering the global minimum. Hence, it can involve few back-and-forth movements of the head (though much less than FCFS). More serious is the starvation problem. When some requests keep on coming that are near the current head, they will be served before an old request that is far off from the current position.

6.4.2.3 SCAN Scheduling

In the SCAN algorithm, the r/w arm moves in one direction at a time till it reaches the end: either it goes in the direction of increasing cylinder number (from periphery to the center) or the opposite (from center to periphery). While going in a particular direction, it serves all the requests until it reaches the end. After that it changes the *direction and serves the remaining requests in the opposite direction. For the given reference string, we assume* that the head is initially in the direction towards the center serving increasing cylinders first (**Fig. 6.13**).

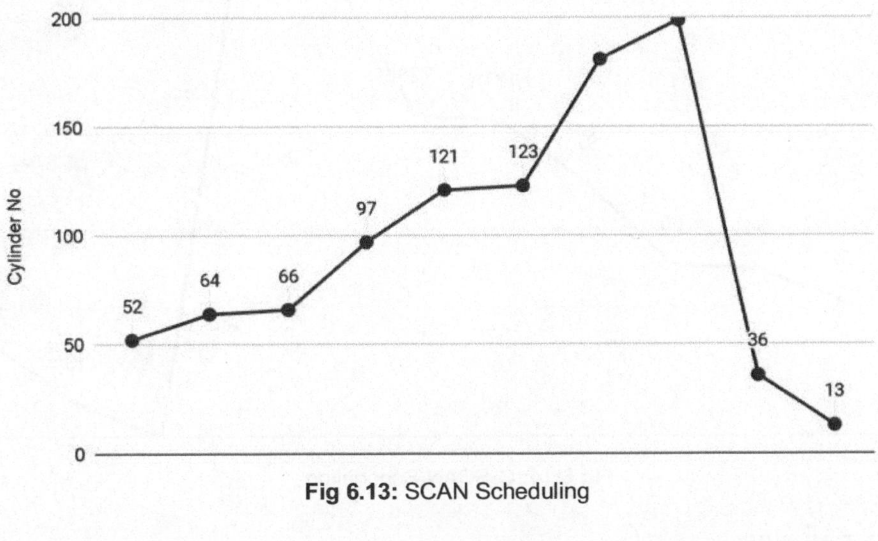

Fig 6.13: SCAN Scheduling

Total head movement for the reference string is = (64-52) + (66 - 64) + (97- 66) + (121 - 97) + (123 - 121) + (187 - 123) + (199 - 187) + (199 - 36) + (36 - 13) = (199 - 52) + (199 - 13) = 147 + 186 = 333 cylinders.

The performance is not that great, although much better than FCFS. When the head moves in a particular direction, if the requests also come in the same direction, the requests will be served immediately. However, the requests coming in the opposite direction will have to wait. The wait is the longest for the requests at the opposite end to the current direction of the head. For example, in the above reference string, requests for Cylinder 36 and Cylinder 13 arrive at position 3 and 5 but are served at position 7 and 8 respectively.

Assuming uniform distribution for arrival of requests, when the r/w head reaches near to one end, very few unattended requests remain on the front. Most of the unattended requests remain on the back of the head that we cover in the reverse direction. However, the most affected (waiting for long) are the ones that lie near the opposite end of the platter. According to uniform distribution, most of them have come earlier than those in the middle of the spectrum. This non-uniform delay in service is a problem in the SCAN algorithm.

6.4.2.4 Circular SCAN (C-SCAN) scheduling

Circular SCAN algorithm attempts to address the non-uniform delay problem of SCAN algorithm. It provides uniform wait time to all the pending requests by servicing in only one direction (either periphery to center or the other way) and not servicing any requests in the return path. Assuming the direction of the periphery towards the center, head movement is shown in **Fig. 6.14.**

Total amount of head movement is = (64 - 52) + (64 - 64) + (97 - 66) + (121 - 97) + (123 - 121) + (181 - 123) + (199 - 181) + (199 - 0) + (13 - 0) + (36 - 13) = (199 - 52) + 199 + 36 = 414 cylinders.

Even though during the return journey the arm has to cover the entire radius of the platter, it does not serve any requests during that time. Thus, this time is very small compared to the case when the r/w head services requests. Hence, it is often ignored. Ignoring the time for return, it is merely 215 cylinders (optimum among the four algorithms discussed).

If we assume the other direction for service also, there will not be much change in the overall seek time, but the order of service will change. C-SCAN considers the list of requests as a circular one and hence the name.

There are many scheduling algorithms in the literature, but SCAN and C-SCAN are quite popular across the operating systems.

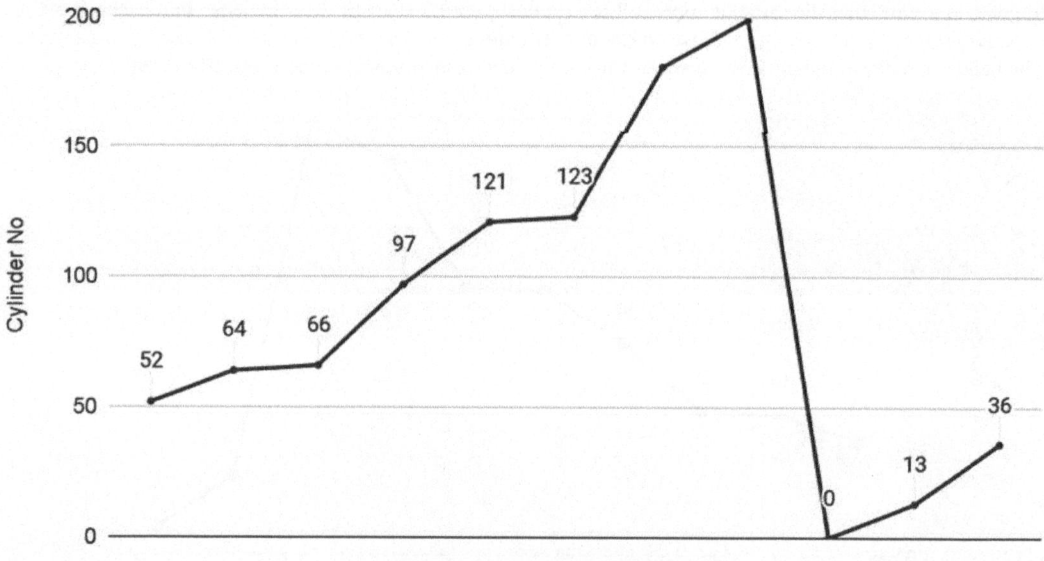

Fig 6.14: C-SCAN Scheduling

6.4.3 Disk Reliability

Reliability of a system represents its consistency of operation or performance. Disk reliability means how long a disk will operate successfully (without fail) by retaining the data and supporting read and write on it. Since disks are used for persistent storage, disk reliability is very important. If the *mean time between failures* (MTBF) is quite large for a disk, we can consider the disk to be highly reliable. But even a highly reliable disk can fail any time, and if it does, the data it stores gets lost. Whatever be the probability of failure for a single disk, if we can instead use multiple disks for storing the same data, the probability of losing data diminishes. This increases the reliability of the storage system. For example, if a disk has MTBF 100,000 hours and *mean time to repair* 10 hours, with another disk used to keep a back-up copy of the same data, *mean time to data loss* becomes = $(100{,}000)^2/(2 * 10)$ = $0.5\ x\ 10^9$ hours or 57,000 years. (Probability of failure for a single disk within 1st hour = 1/100000, prob. for failing 2 disks simultaneously within 1st hour is = $1/100000^2$).

The probability of data loss thus exponentially decreases when we use multiple disks to store the same data with some redundancy. This resulted in a *redundant array of independent disks* (RAID) [the term 'inexpensive' used earlier is now replaced by 'independent'].

RAID technology uses several identical disks to store data. The array of disks is seen as a single 'logical' storage unit managed by a single 'logical' disk controller. The low-level multiplicity of disks is hidden from the user. RAID has different types, depending upon how the data is organized. Data is either divided (or *stripped*) and/or replicated (or *mirrored*) among the disks in a RAID. *Stripping* means dividing data into multiple units and storing each unit in different disks. Stripping can be done at bit level (each bit of a byte is saved in different disks), or byte, word or sector or block levels. Often a parity information is also added in stripping. Initially six levels of RAID were proposed (**Fig. 6.15** and **Fig. 6.16**) as given below.

RAID Level 0: Only stripping is used, without any redundancy. Data can be accessed from the disks in parallel. Data transfer rate is thus very fast.

RAID Level 1: Stripping is used, with mirroring. Total number of disks required is double the size of data that can be stored. Data read can be done very fast in parallel, but data write is slower due to mirroring.

RAID Level 2: Stripping is used. Instead of mirroring, error-detection and correction techniques (for example, Hamming code) are used. Parity bits are stored separately for each stripe in some disks. Depending on the error detection & correction level, the number of extra disks vary.

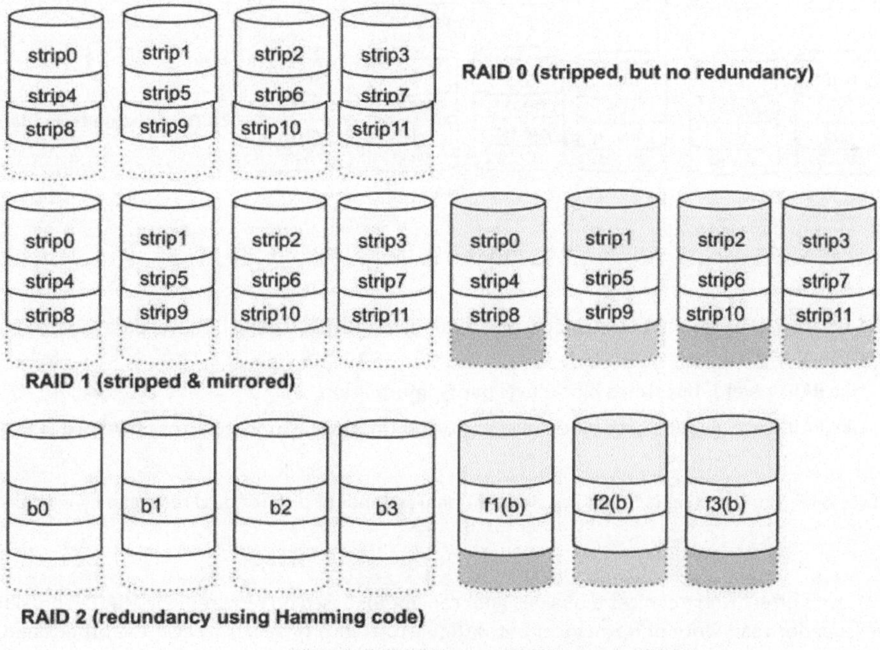

Fig. 6.15: Different RAID Levels (0-2)

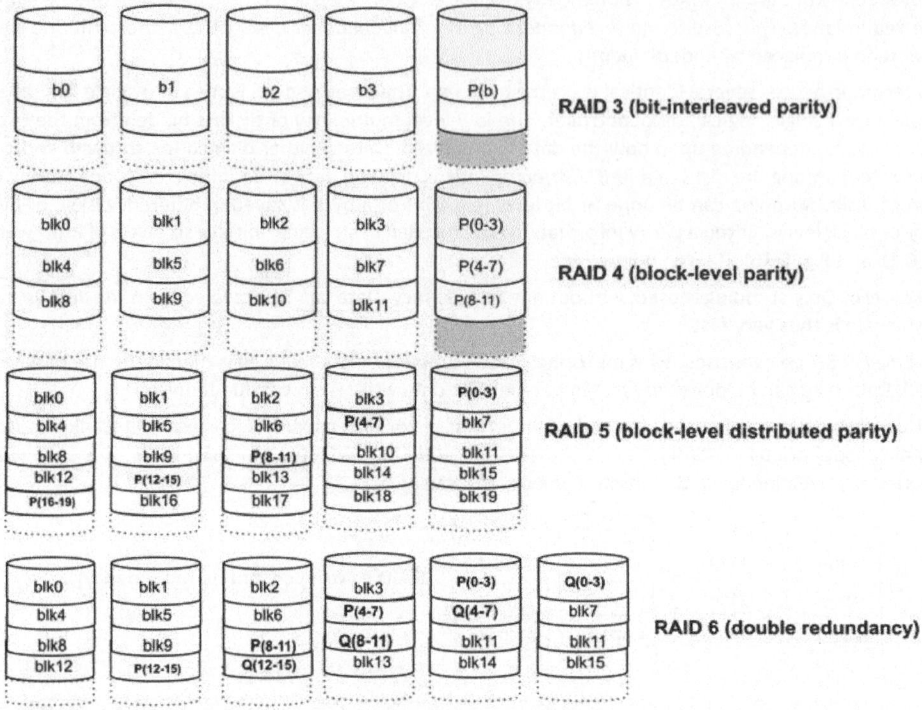

Fig. 6.16: RAID Levels (3-6)

RAID Level 3: Similar to RAID Level 2 but uses only one redundant disk for storing bit-level parity information (also called bit-interleaved parity).

RAID Level 4: Like RAID Level 3, but stores block-level parity information.

RAID Level 5: Like RAID Level 4, but stores block-level parity information distributed across several disks.

A newer RAID Level 6, similar to Level 5, but has an additional redundant disk for dual redundancy with distributed parity.

Different RAID levels offer diverse choices that a designer can opt for based on requirements. RAID 0 provides faster data transfer (superior read-write performance) but no fault-tolerance or reliability. On the other hand, RAID 1 provides good performance in terms of read / write and fault tolerance, but disk usage is halved.

RAID was initially conceptualized to induce reliability against disk failures for cost-effective disks. However, the technology evolved gradually, and RAID is now used in workstations and large-scale data centres involving expensive disks as well.

6.4.4 Disk Formatting

Disks just after being manufactured are not directly usable. The magnetic elements therein initially remain in a random form. They need to be formatted so that they become usable. The formatting is done in three stages as given below.

6.4.4.1 Physical Formatting

This low-level formatting is first done to align the surface particles along the tracks through magnetization. Each platter within a disk is divided into several tracks and each track into a number of sectors. Each sector is again divided into three parts (**Fig. 6.17**). The *header* and *trailer* contain sector related meta-information. A header must contain a sector number, followed by some optional fields like file-type, data type, length of data etc. *Payload* is the actual content stored in the sector. Trailer stores error detection and correction codes (also called *checksum*).

Fig. 6.17: Different components of a sector

Payload area normally stores 512 or 1024 bytes of data. It is populated by a file management system, while the header and the trailer by the disk controller. During reading of the sector, checksum is calculated and compared to see whether the sector content is valid or corrupt.

Once a disk is divided into cylinders, tracks and sectors, the sectors are numbered. Sector number assignment is an important task. Sector numbers can be assigned *linearly* as shown in **Fig. 6.18**.

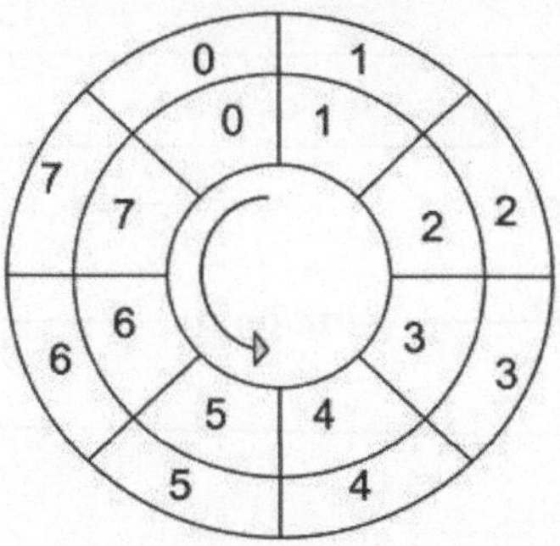

Fig. 6.18: Linear assignment of sector numbers

This scheme, even though simple to implement, has some problems. The sectors are accessed by the r/w head through rotation of the disk and linear movement of the r/w arm. These two mechanical actions have physical limitations with respect to precision. Hence, sufficient gaps need to be maintained between two sectors from the same track as well as between two consecutive tracks.

Even though a small physical gap is maintained between two adjoining sectors, it is not enough, especially when two consecutive numbered sectors are accessed in the same rotation.

This intersectoral gap is increased by clever assignment of the numbering. There are several techniques like *sector interleaving, sector skewing* etc.

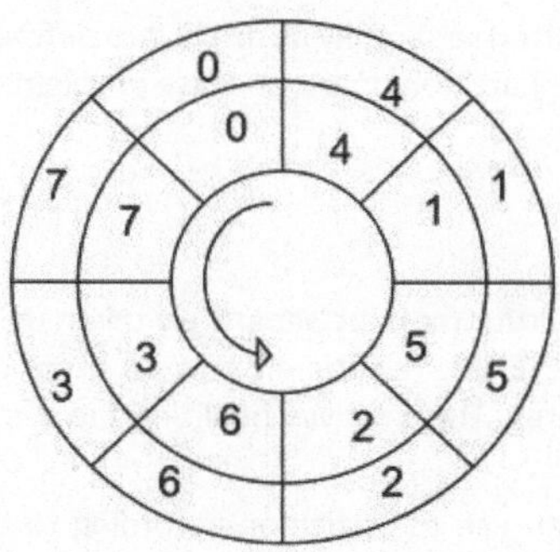

Fig. 6.19: Numbering with one sector interleaving

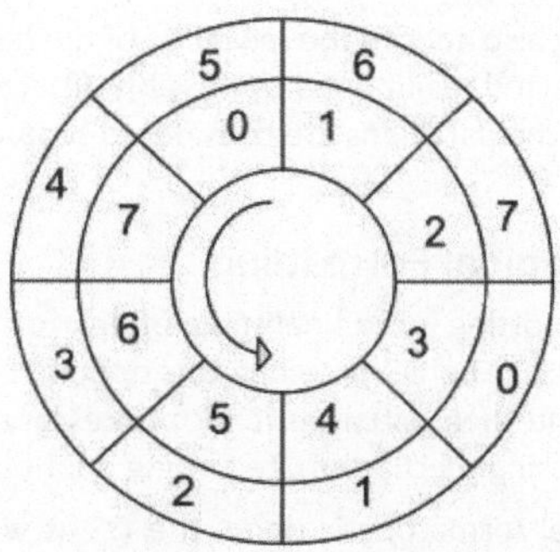

Fig. 6.20: Skew sectoring with skew of 3

In *sector interleaving,* consecutive numbers are assigned keeping the physical distance or gap of one or more sectors. For example, in **Fig. 6.19,** a gap of one sector is interleaved. There can be interleaving of zero or more sectors. Zero sector interleaving is the same as linear numbering.

Two sectors interleaving will create a circular sequence like: 0, 3, 6, 1, 4, 7, 2, 5.

Three sectors interleaving will create a circular sequence like: 0, 2, 4, 6, 1, 3, 5, 7; and so on.

Sector Skewing is aimed at minimizing the delay due to arm movement. Suppose while the arm moves by one track, at the same time the disk rotates by three sectors. To keep continuity of data access from one track to another, the sector numbers are assigned by making an appropriate gap between the seek time (arm movement) and rotational latency. For example, in **Fig. 6.20,** from an inner track, when the arm moves to the outer track, at the same time, the platter can move by 3 sectors. From sector 7 of the inner track, the r/w head can start accessing sector 0 of the outer track.

This is particularly useful when consecutive tracks are accessed across the tracks.

6.4.4.2 Partitioning

Once the physical formatting is done at the production site, logical formatting follows using an OS. However, in-between, a physical disk is optionally divided into a number of partitions using some partitioning tool (e.g. `GParted` in Linux) that comes bundled with the OS software. Each partition is considered as a logical disk and treated as if a hardware disk device (or a mini-disk). A number of consecutive cylinders make a partition. Each partition can hold a file system including a swap system.

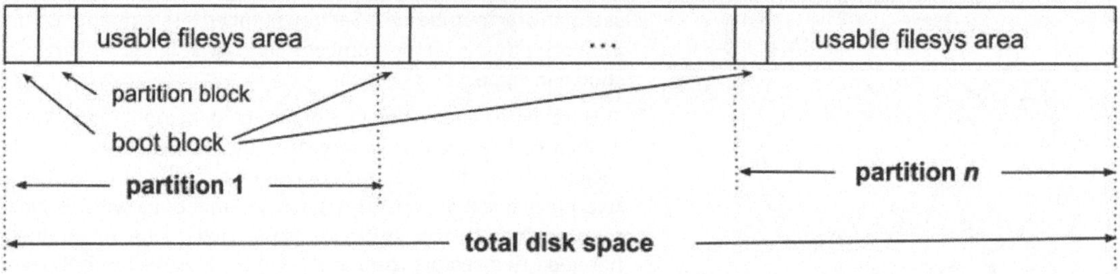

Fig. 6.21: Disk partitions

Each partition mandatorily contains a *boot block* (the 0th block) followed by a usable area. This area is formatted according to the filesystem in the later stage.

In the first partition, the boot block is followed by a *partition block* that stores information about all the partitions in the disk. This partition block can be optionally replicated in all the partitions (**Fig. 6.21**).

Partitioning also adds to the reliability of the disk. Each partition can be formatted separately by an OS into different file systems and maintained by possibly different OSs. Data corruption in one partition does not cause problems in another as the partitions are considered separate.

6.4.4.3 Logical Formatting

Logical formatting is the final stage of disk formatting done by an OS. Each partition can be separately taken up by different OSs. The OS provides the options of the filesystem (FAT32, EXT2, EXT3, reiserfs etc.) to be used in a partition and then initializes it with necessary information and data structures. This involves finalizing the sector size, addressing mechanism, recording boot block, directory structure etc.

Once logical formatting is done, the OS as well as application programs can use the partition according to the protocols of the file-system.

6.4.5 Boot Block

Boot block is a component of a block device (secondary storage device like a hard disk, NVM, flash drive or CD) that stores the initial code to load the operating system into RAM.

When a computer is powered on or rebooted, the processor does the following sequence of tasks.

1. *Power-On-Self-Test (POST):* to check whether all internal units of a processor are in working condition or not.

2. *Basic-Input-Output-System (BIOS):* the CPU points to a fixed location of ROM. This is called BIOS code. It continues the power-on self-test and initializes other hardware components of the computer system including storage devices.
3. *boot loader:* BIOS searches for a kernel image from storage devices like floppy, CD, HDD sequentially. If found, the BIOS loads the tiny code into the RAM. This code is called bootloader. This bootloader is kept in the first block of the device so that the BIOS can easily find it. This bootloader is a simple code that stores the location (e.g., partition information of a disk) of the entire OS where it is saved persistently and from where it can be loaded. This block is called the *boot block* that stores the boot loader.
4. *Loading OS proper:* The entire operating system is stored in a partition the pointer to which is stored in the bootloader of the boot block. When the boot-loader loaded into RAM and is executed, the bootloader in turn refers to the OS proper and loads the kernel and other different subsystems as per requirement.

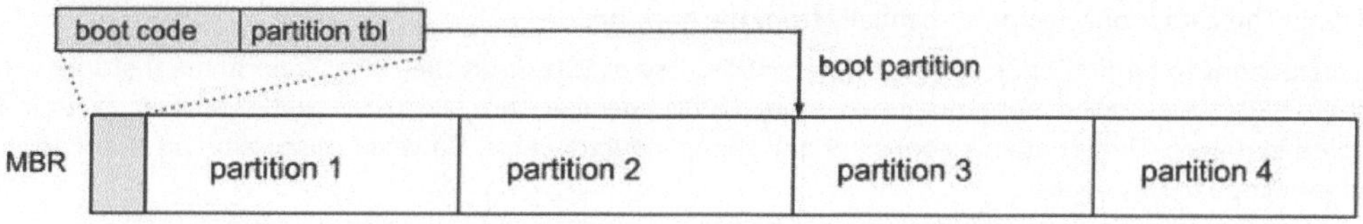

Fig. 6.22: Boot Block in a Windows system and booting from disk

is

This can be explained with a specific example. In Windows systems, a disk drive can be divided into several partitions. A partition can store the OS and device drivers. This partition is called *boot partition*. But the bootloader is placed in the very first block of the hard disk - this boot block is called Master Boot Record (MBR).

The MBR contains the boot code and a partition table. Booting the Windows system starts using the POST and BIOS steps as indicated above. Then the BIOS accesses and executes the boot code of MBR. The boot code enables the storage device controller and the storage device to locate the boot partition through the partition table. The first sector of the boot partition (called the *boot sector*) points to the kernel. The rest of the booting is taken up by the kernel that loads different OS subsystems and services (**Fig. 6.22**).

6.4.6 Bad Block

Hard disks contain mechanical moving parts that can malfunction any time and the disk can fail. Sometimes it can be a complete failure, meaning the entire disk is unusable. It needs to be replaced. But often, few blocks or sectors become unusable. They are known as *bad blocks*. A disk can have bad blocks from the time of manufacture, developed during manufacturing in the factory or later during use. Whatever be the timing, bad blocks need to be handled, if they are very few in numbers, rather than discarding the entire disk.

On old disks having IDE controllers, bad blocks are managed manually. During the formatting of the disk, the disk is scanned, and bad blocks are identified. The bad blocks are then isolated and not allocated to any partition. If blocks get corrupted during normal operation, a special program (e.g., Linux command `badblocks`) is run to search for the bad blocks. Data in bad blocks of such old disks is usually lost, cannot be recovered.

Disk errors mainly come from bad blocks. Some of the errors are recoverable (called *soft errors*) and some are not (*hard errors*).

Modern disks have some bad-block recovery mechanism, for soft errors. The disk controller maintains a list of bad blocks that is initialized during the low-level formatting of the disk at the factory and then updated during its use. Bad blocks found during the low-level formatting are not visible to the operating system also. The controller also maintains a list of spare sectors that are used to replace bad blocks.

Handling at this hardware level is done using a scheme known as *sector sparing* or *sector forwarding*. When the OS tries to read a logical block (say block number 18), the disk controller calculates the error correcting code (ECC) and may find it to be a bad block. The controller reports it to the OS as an I/O error. The controller also replaces the block with a spare block so that the next request to block 18 is transferred to the replacement block by the controller.

This strategy bypasses the involvement of the OS and the OS remains unaware of the replacement. But at the physical level, this can cause unplanned redirections of read/write head and rotations. It also affects optimisation of disk scheduling algorithms. Most disks are thus provided with few spare sectors in each cylinder and a spare cylinder during the time of formatting. The controller tries to replace a bad block from the same cylinder, whenever possible.

An alternative to sector sparing is *sector slipping.* Here, if the bad block is logical block no. 18 and the next spare sector is, say, logical block no. 196, then logical block 195 is mapped to 196, 194 to 195, and so on till logical block 18 maps to logical block 19. Shifting this way leaves the bad block.

Soft errors are thus recovered using sector sparing or sector slipping. Hard errors are not recoverable and result in loss of data. The data is only restored manually from the back-up.

All the discussions so far in Section **6.4** considered HDDs. Use of SSDs is on the rise as a permanent storage device nowadays. SSDs, also called non-volatile memory (NVM) devices, are electrical and electronic, rather than mechanical in nature. They contain a controller and semiconductor chips. However, discussion on these devices is beyond the scope of this book.

6.5 FILE MANAGEMENT SYSTEM

Computers deal with code and data. They are stored in different storage devices (HDD, SDD, CD, DVD, optical drives, flash drives, magnetic tapes and so on) as a stream of bytes. Persistent storage of such byte streams and access mechanisms depends on the physical medium of the device (magnetic tape, HDD, optical disc, flash etc.). Not to bother the users and application programs of the diverse multitude of access techniques, the OS provides a set of uniform device-independent I/O interfaces through the I/O subsystem.

Similarly, to keep the users and applications unconcerned about physical storage of the data, the OS implements an abstract concept of files. The OS implements a software layer on top of the I/O subsystem (including device drivers) that deals with creation, access, manipulation and destruction of files in a device-independent manner. This software layer is called File Management System (FMS) (**Fig. 6.23**). An FMS interacts with the I/O subsystem to implement a filesystem in a storage device.

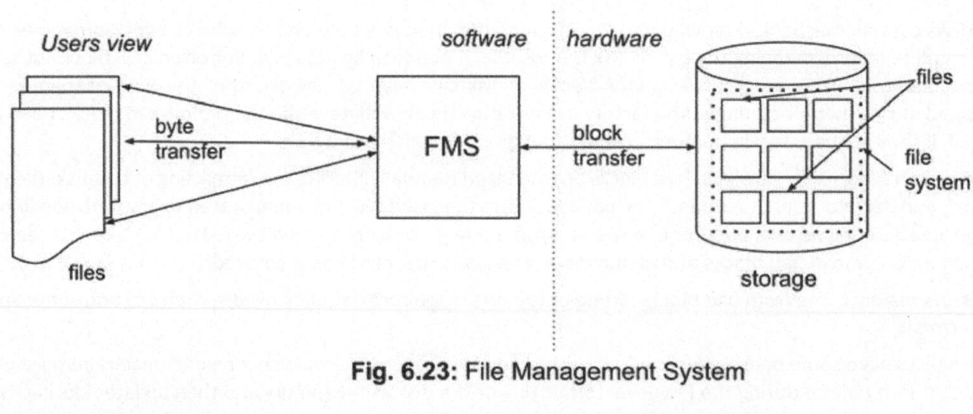

Fig. 6.23: File Management System

6.5.1 Concept of File

Files are logical units of data storage and are handled in a uniform manner, independent of physical storage media. All the code and data that we deal with in a computer are stored persistently in the conceptual units of files. Other than real-time applications, most applications use files as inputs (to read data from) and outputs (to store results). A file outlives the lifetime of a program that uses or creates it and can be shared among several programs simultaneously or at different times. A file can move from one medium (say, flash drive) to another (say HDD or magnetic tape) without any compromises on the content (data) or other logical attributes of the content (data types or permissible operations on the data). However, the data at the physical level can be stored differently in different media. Even though a file may be divided into separate blocks and stored at different physical locations within a device, the user remains unaware of these physical variations and sees the file as a continuous stream of bytes (**Fig. 6.24**).

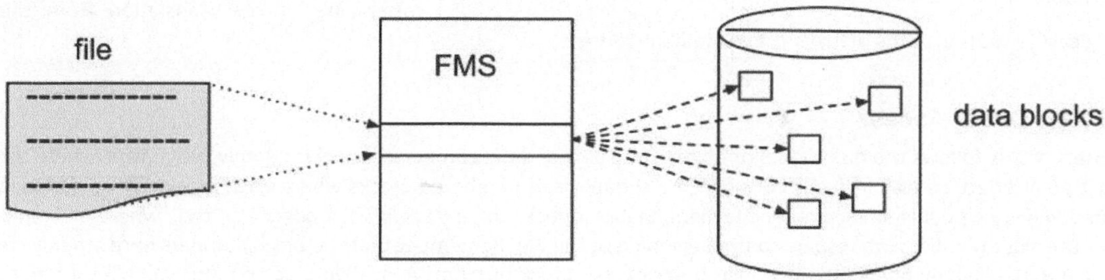

Fig. 6.24: Mapping from a logical file to physical disk blocks

A file may consist of one or more sub-units. The smallest logical unit within a file is called a **field**. A field can be a single value like firstname of a person, employee-number, a date, or a hash-value of a password etc. A field is characterized by length (a single byte or several bytes), and data type (e.g., binary, ASCII string, decimal value etc.).

A **record** is a collection of related fields within a file that can be considered as a logical unit by a program. For example, an employee name with employee number, date-of-birth, address is a record.

A file may contain a single field or several records. The records may be of similar nature, of similar length or of variable nature and/or length.

A **database** contains several files logically related to each other. Database management systems is another layer of software working on top of a file management system and is beyond the scope of the book. We focus on files, file systems and file management systems here.

A file is created, accessed, manipulated, and deleted by a user or an application program and is referenced by a name. Every file belongs to a class of files depending on a set of properties. Such classes are called filesystems. An operating system supports one or more filesystems. An OS also manages files belonging to different file systems through file management systems. A file can belong to only one filesystem at a time in a given system.

6.5.2 Access methods

Files, stored in storage media, are accessed by users or applications. However, they can be used only when brought to the main memory by the operating system. There are different access methods. Most OSs support one access method, but few (e.g., mainframe OS) can support more than one. Let us discuss below a few access methods.

6.5.2.1 Sequential Access

Sequential access follows the tape model where the file is treated like a tape. Data in a file can only be accessed sequentially starting from the beginning to the end. It must start from the very first field of the first record, then second field, and so on till the last field of the last record. This is called sequential access of a file. Most of the applications including editors and compilers access files this way.

Two most common operations on files are: reads and writes. File management systems provide abstract methods `read_next()` and `write_next()` respectively for them and track the current position of the read/write operation through a pointer (called *file pointer*). `read_next()` reads the next record from the current position of the pointer and then advances the pointer. Similarly, `write_next()` starts writing from the current position and, at the end of writing, places the pointer after the end of the unit written.

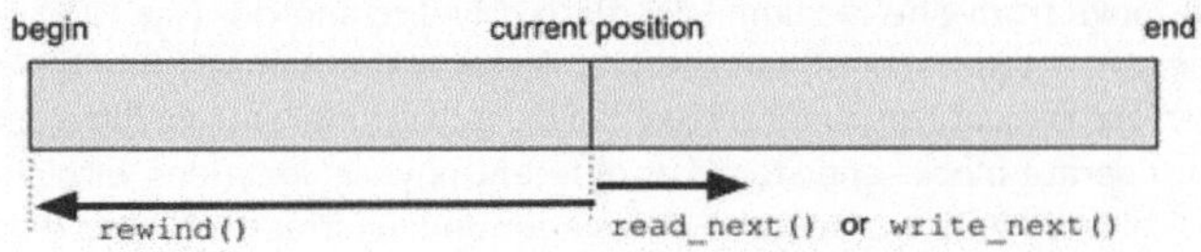

Fig. 6.25: Sequential access of a file

Some systems also provide abstract method `rewind()` to get to the beginning of the file from any position (**Fig. 6.25**). Even though the records seem to be consecutive, in the real disk, they can be sparsely located. File management system takes care of the translation from this logical file address to the actual storage medium address.

6.5.2.2 Direct Access

Direct access follows the disk model of access. Any part of a file can be accessed randomly, no matter where the last point of access was. A file is considered a sequence of numbered blocks where each block can be accessed randomly. Two popular and common file manipulation operations are `read(n)` and `write(n)` where `n` stands for the block number with respect to the beginning of the file. Remember that the block numbers here are not the actual disk block numbers, rather a logical or **relative block number**. A relative block number acts like an index relative to the beginning of the file. An example of direct access can be referring to the relative block numbers 12, then 3, followed by 54 and so on. In a real disk these references can be physical block numbers 540, 234, 650 and so on. The file management system translates the relative block number to actual disk block number without bothering the user or the application program about the low-level implementation of the translation.

Operating systems intrinsically support either of the access methods. But the sequential access method can be considered as a special case of direct access method as given in **Fig. 6.26** (the current position of the file-pointer is given by `fp`).

Sequential Access	Direct Access
rewind()	fp = 0;
read_next()	read(fp); fp = fp +1;
write_next()	write(fp); fp = fp +1;

Fig. 6.26: Sequential access is a special case of direct access file

6.5.2.3 Other Access methods

There are some sophisticated methods built on the base of direct access. These methods create an index file for each of the files. The index is a sorted metadata that facilitates random search on the data. For example, the index found at the end of a book is an alphabetically sorted list of terms that helps us find the page where a term appears. The index this way helps find a record by checking the index value. An index file stores only the search terms and the address of the record corresponding to the search term. The detailed records are stored in another file (called **relative file) (Fig. 6.27)**.

Index files are generally small and can be comfortably loaded into the main memory. However, for a very big file, the index file itself can be quite big and may not fit in the available memory. In that case, there can be two level indexing where the 1st level index file maps to the second level index file which maps to the actual relative file. This scheme has close resemblance to hierarchical paging scheme in main memory management (cf. **Unit 5**).

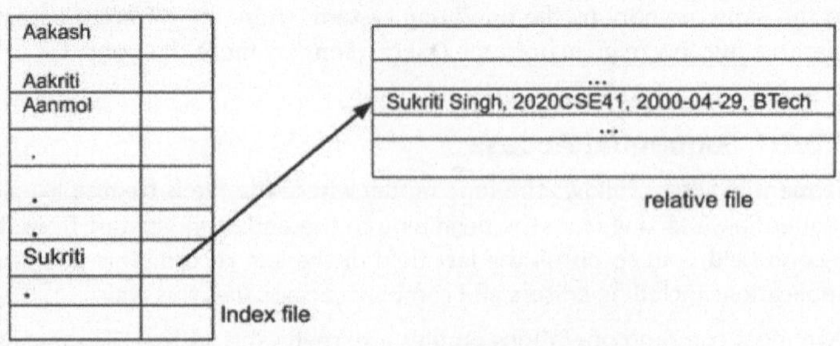

Fig. 6.27: Index file and relative file

6.5.3 File Types

A FMS categorizes the files into a certain number of classes, known as *file types*. Every file belongs to a file type that holds a certain set of attributes or characteristics. Some OSs recognize the file types and process them in a certain way, some may not treat them in any special way. File type is generally denoted as part of filename. Every file is recognized by a name, where a period (.) is allowed. File type is denoted by one or more characters after the dot or period. The set of characters after the dot is called file-extension. For example, *abc.txt* is a text file, *pqr.exe* is an executable file, *quicksort.c* is a C source file etc. **Table 6.1** shows some examples of file types.

Table 6.1: File types

File type	Meaning	Examples of extension
source code	from different programming languages like C, C++, Java, Perl, assembly languages	.c, .java, .pl, .asm
object code	compiled code before linking	.obj, .o
executable	ready to run, loadable program	.exe, .com, .bin
batch/script	command line interpreted code	.bat, .sh
library	libraries or shared objects used in source code	.lib, .a. .so, .dll
markup	textual data with formatting info	.html, .xml, .tex
archive / compress	for compression of files, storage and archives	.zip, .rar, .bzip, .bz2, .tar
word processor	word processor formats	.doc, .docx, .abi, .rtf
image	file for viewing / printing images	.jpeg, .jpg, .gif
multimedia	audio-visual content	.avi, .mov, .mpeg, .mp3, .mp4

MacOS supports file type. Along with the file-type, it also keeps track of the application that created the file as file-creator. For example, if a file is created by a word processor, the application is invoked by the OS while opening the file.

UNIX supports six different file types: 1. regular 2. directory 3. symbolic link 4. device (character or block device) file 5. FIFO (named pipe) and 6. socket.

A regular file is unformatted data. Most of the file-types in **Table 6.1** belong to this type. The FMS is not supposed to interpret the data. Users are supposed to maintain the internal structure of the data, and the application is supposed to interpret the structure. Other file-types, not mentioned in the table above, however, are interpreted by the FMS. For example, a directory contains a list of filenames and a reference to its metadata. This way UNIX associates names to file objects, but the file objects themselves are treated as nameless entities.

6.5.4 File Operations

Files can be considered as abstract data types. There are a few operations allowed on them as follows that are supported by an FMS.

6.5.4.1 Create

Users are allowed to create new files and/or directories within a file system, unless the concerned file system is read-only. Every file is associated with a set of attributes.

Create operation requires the name of the file / directory to be created, its container directory and the values for the attributes. On successful completion, the FMS creates an empty file / directory, allocates space for it, makes an entry in the container directory, and initializes the attributes with supplied values or default ones. FMS populates some fields like creation time, owner of the file / directory, and permission attributes. If the space is allocated, its address is also recorded in the metadata of the file.

Creating a directory involves a few extra steps like initializing directory content, search structures etc.

6.5.4.2 Delete

Users are also allowed to delete a file or a directory with all the files under it, unless the concerned file system is read-only. A delete operation only requires the name of the file / directory to be deleted. On success, the FMS frees the space held by the file / directory along with its metadata. It also removes the entry from its container directory. The removal of the entry from its container directory is done first. In a multiprogramming environment, a file may be used by other processes also. Hence, the file content is deleted and the space allocated is freed only if no other process is using the same file / directory.

6.5.4.3 Open

Every file needs to be opened before any application can access it for any purpose. The FMS *needs the name of the* file to be opened along with a few additional values like opening mode (read / write / append etc). An open operation checks whether the user has required access permission or not. If not, the operation replies with a negative response. If yes, two objects called *file descriptors (fd)* are created for the file and the application pair. One *fd* (called *external fd*) is returned to the application and another (called *internal fd*) is for the operating system. They are used to operate on the same file. The external fd works as the symbolic link to the internal one that operates on the file.

In some operating systems, open operation also creates a *file pointer (fp)* to keep track of the read / write operations. File pointer points to the byte offset position with respect to the start of the file (start position considered as byte 0) (**Fig. 6.28**).

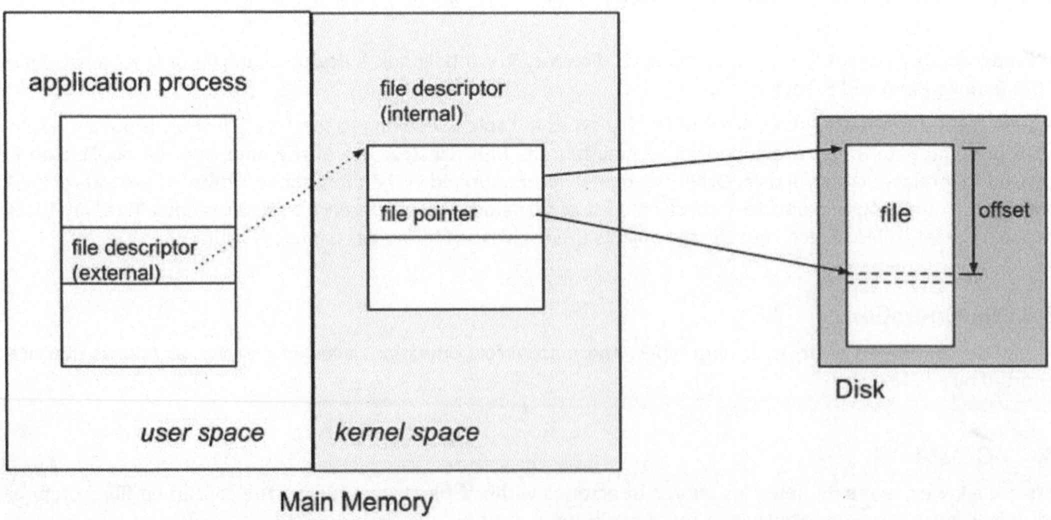

Fig. 6.28: A typical file session related to open and other operations

6.5.4.4 Close

Any opened file, at the end of use, needs to be closed. A close operation requires the file descriptor as an argument. It releases the internal file descriptor, file pointer and other resources allocated during open operation. The time between opening and closing the file is called a file session (**Fig. 6.28**).

6.5.4.5 Reposition

Reposition operation is related to positioning the file pointer. It takes the file descriptor and offset as the inputs and positions the file pointer at the desired location of the file (**Fig. 6.28**). This operation is only allowed in random access files.

6.5.4.6 Read

Reading a file means copying the contents of a file to an I/O buffer. Read operation takes as inputs a file descriptor (of the opened file), a positive integer (the number of bytes to be read), and a buffer address. On success, the required number of bytes starting from the current file pointer is copied into the buffer. At the end of read, the file pointer is repositioned to the end of the last byte read.

6.5.4.7 Write

A write operation writes a string onto a file starting at the position of the current file pointer. It takes as arguments a file descriptor, the string to be written and the length of the string. It can overwrite the earlier content of the file or can append after the current file pointer. If space is needed to complete the write, the space is also allocated for the same if available. At the end of the write, it repositions the file-pointer to the end of the last byte written.

6.5.4.8 Truncate

Truncate operation cuts the file length. It takes a file descriptor and a positive integer as inputs and reduces the file size to the specified number of bytes. The extra space is freed.

The above operations are considered as basic operations on files. There can be a few more operations depending on the operating system and the file management system involved therein like memory mapping, locking a file from access etc.

6.5.5 Directory Structure

A directory is a special file that contains control information or metadata about a group of subdirectories and/or files. Each entry in a directory refers to a subdirectory or a file, its type, organization, location, access mode etc. Directory structure helps the system map file names to its actual objects and track them when in use.

file name	type & size	location info	protection info	open count	lock	flags	misc info

file name: name of the file / subdirectory. Name beyond the allowed length will be truncated
type & size: file type is denoted by the extension like .c, .exe etc, size expressed in bytes
location info: information about the file's location in the disk, expressed in the form of table or linked list of disk blocks
protection info: information about the users having access permission to the file and manner of access
open count: number of processes that opened the file
lock: whether a process is having exclusive access
flags: information about whether the file is a directory, a link, a mounted filesystem or regular file
misc. Info: miscellaneous information like owner of the file, creation time, last modification time etc.

Fig. 6.29: Different fields in an entry of a directory

Fig. 6.29 provides an example of different fields that a directory entry may contain. How this information will be stored varies across the file systems. Some of this metadata may be stored as a part of the header record of a file, and the rest as part of the directory. This splitting reduces the directory size, making it easier to be loaded into the main memory. But on the contrary, a file needs to be accessed to ascertain whether a user can access the file or not.

The simplest form of directory structure can be a list of entries, each for a file within the directory. A directory thus can be implemented as a sequential file. But this will take a good amount of time to search for a particular file, when the directory contains a lot of entries. Before creating a file, it is to be ensured that the same filename is not present, and this involves searching the entire list. Even though it is possible for a single user, it is problematic for multiple users of the directory as concurrent accesses will involve synchronization issues.

One advancement over it can be a two-level structure: one directory implementing a sequential file for each user and a master directory containing all the users only. Even if this serves the purpose for a small size multi-user system, it is not scalable to a large system. Both these schemes do not allow subdirectories - which we often need to logically organize the files in some particular order.

A more flexible and popular approach employs a hierarchical arrangement, or a tree-structure as shown in **Fig. 6.30**. At the root, there is a system-wide master directory. All the files within the system are divided into a set of subdirectories. Each subdirectory can get further divided into another set of subdirectories and so on. All the files remain as leaves whereas subdirectories as intermediate nodes (**Fig. 6.30a**). A file and/or subdirectory, other than the master directory, can be added, deleted or modified at any level if the user has necessary permissions.

UNIX system implements the scheme where root (/) is the master directory that contains a set subdirectories like *dev* (for managing devices), *bin* (executables), *usr* (users) and so on. Each of the first level subdirectories can have few files or subdirectories. Each file or subdirectory is uniquely referenced by a branch starting from root. For example, */bin/ls* or */dev/disk1* etc. Each user is supposed to have a home directory (*/usr/home*) where user contents can be saved. Nevertheless, a user can create any subdirectory, and store any file at any level below the root directory, if she has necessary permissions (**Fig. 6.30b**).

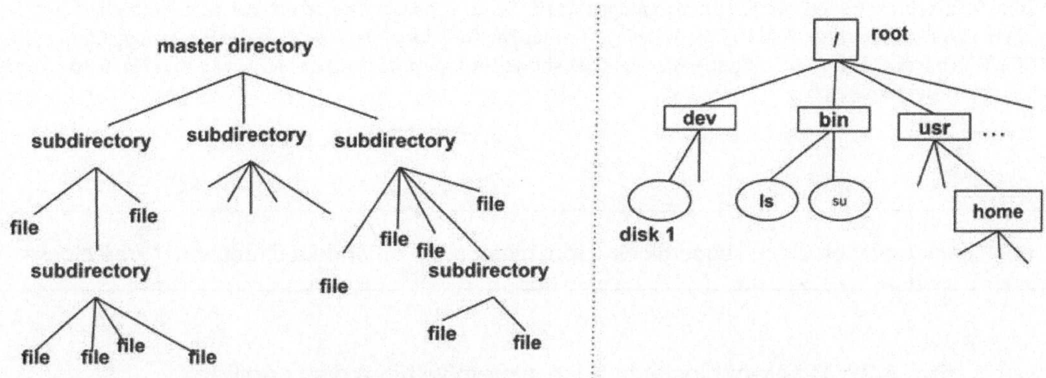

(a) Hierarchical Directory Structure (b) UNIX file organization

Fig 6.30: A popular, flexible, powerful directory structure

6.5.6 File System Structure

A file system is considered as a collection of files and directories following a certain set of design principles. There are different types of file systems used and supported by different operating systems. For example, UNIX supports UNIX File System (UFS) based on Berkeley Fast File System (FFS); Windows supports FAT, FAT32, NTFS; Linux supports more than 130 file systems along with its own extended file systems (ext2, ext3, ext4).

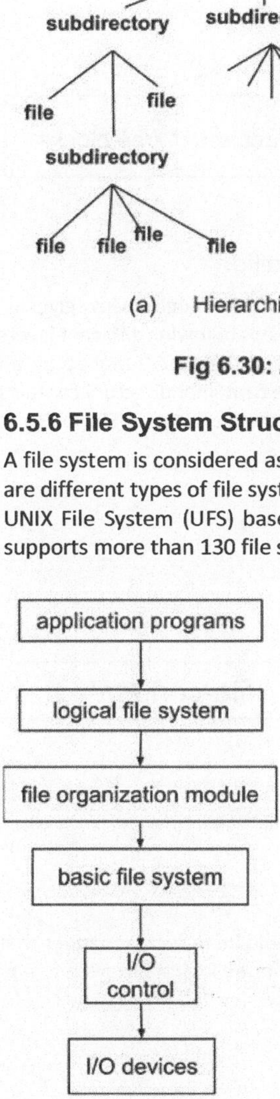

Fig. 6.31: File system layers

A file system provides convenient access to the storage medium in terms of easy and efficient mechanism to store, locate and retrieve data. A file system involves multiple layers as shown in **Fig. 6.31.**

Each layer at the lower level is more basic compared to the upper one. For example, I/O control level consists of device drivers and interrupt handlers to enable data transfer between the storage media and main memory through I/O controllers.

Basic file system (also known as block I/O subsystem in Linux systems) issues generic commands to the appropriate device drivers for reading and writing data blocks on the storage devices. This layer also manages I/O scheduling, memory buffers and caches during data transfer.

File organization module knows about files and their logical blocks. It has a free space manager that manages block allocation.

Logical file system manages metadata of the files. This metadata includes every control information of the files and the filesystem except the content of the files. It provides directory information to the file organization module for a symbolic file name obtained from the user or application program. File structure metadata is maintained through file-control blocks (FCBs). A FCB (called an **inode** in UNIX) stores information related to ownership, permissions and location of the file content.

Remember that a storage medium is divided into partitions (**Sec. 6.4.4.2**). Each partition can be formatted according to a file system (**Fig. 6.15**). Each partition has a *boot block* as the first block, then a *partition block* followed by a *superblock.* The superblock is the most important block of the file system as it stores all management-specific information like file-system name, partition space size, block-size, address of the root directory, and pointers to other blocks of the file system. Superblock thus acts as the anchor for the file system (**Fig. 6.32**).

A file system may be confined to a particular partition of a disk, a complete disk or even a volume comprising several disks. Along with the control and metadata, a file system also contains all the records or the content. Hence, a file system is a self-contained system that manages itself. Some separate the structural part from the functional aspects. Structural part is called the file system, whereas the functional part is called the file management system (FMS), which is part of an OS. To be specific, **Fig. 6.31** shows the logical structure of FMS, whereas **Fig. 6.30** provides structure of the same.

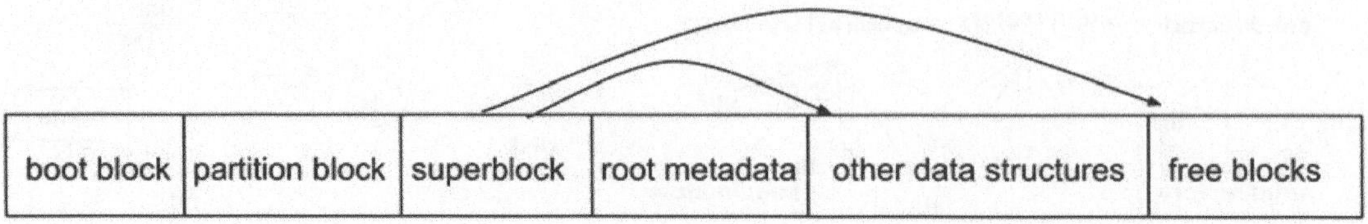

Fig. 6.32: Different blocks of a file system within a disk partition

The applications and the users see a file as a contiguous sequence of records or bytes. This logical view gives us logical blocks (*l-blocks*). FMS translates these l-blocks into physical block (*p-blocks*) in steps following different layers (shown in **Fig. 6.31**) using different metadata in **Fig. 6.32**. For example, for a given filename supplied by an application, the root directory is searched to get the container directory of the file. The container directory contains a pointer to the metadata of the file, which contains a pointer to the start address of the file content (**Fig. 6.33**).

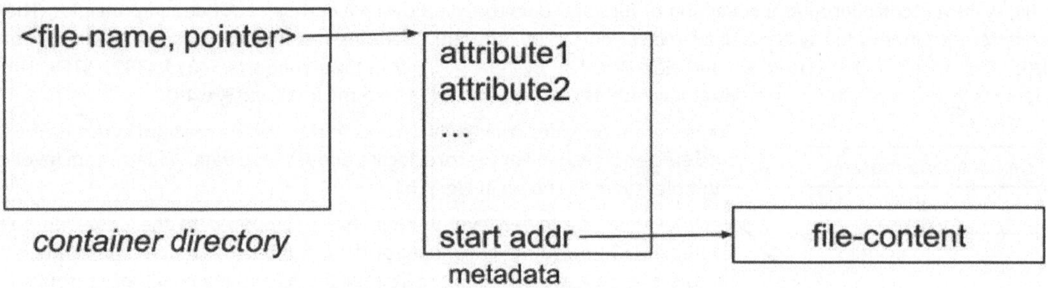

Fig. 6.33: Address resolution across layers in a file system

6.5.7 File Allocation Methods

Files are allocated space in the storage media in units of blocks. Space allocation should be in such a manner that storage space is effectively utilized and files can be easily accessed. For each l-block in the logical file system, a p-block is assigned on the storage medium. Three major techniques are discussed below.

6.5.7.1 Contiguous Allocation

A file is allocated space contiguously. Both the l-blocks and p-blocks follow the same sequence linearly. If there are n l-blocks necessary for a file that is allocated space starting at p-block s, then the file will be allocated space till p-block id $(s + n - 1)$ with l-block id 0 getting p-block s, l-block id 1 getting p-block id $s + 1$, ..., l-block id $(n - 1)$ getting p-block id $(s + n - 1)$ (**Fig. 6.34**).

The scheme is easy to implement and understand. Random file access is also simple, since there is a linear mechanism to get to the p-block for any given l-block.

But the scheme suffers from a few serious issues. As a file dynamically grows, finding contiguous blocks becomes difficult. A file needs to be relocated if the space requirement cannot be fulfilled at the present location. Relocation involves the overhead of book-keeping.

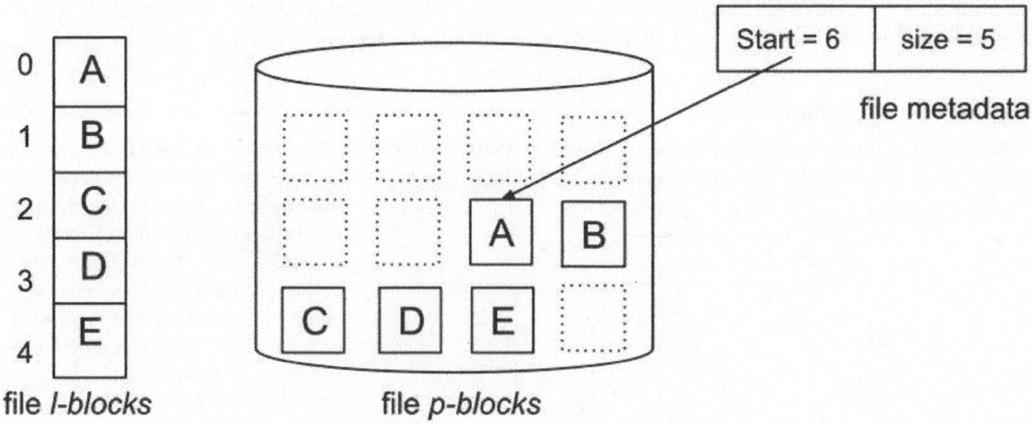

Fig. 6.34: Contiguous Allocation of a file in a storage device

Another problem is that of external fragmentation. As the files are deleted or relocated, p-blocks are freed. But such free spaces are not contiguous. Remember our discussion on contiguous main memory space allocation (**Sec 5.4.1**). The issues and solutions are relevant here as well.

6.5.7.2 Linked Allocation

In the linked allocation, p-blocks are not contiguous but linked in a chain. Here, a l-block can be placed at any available p-block in the storage medium, not necessarily contiguous. The file metadata in the directory stores, like before, pointer to only the first p-block. Each p-block, however, in turn, points to the next p-block of the file. The last p-block points to NULL. Every p-block, therefore, is structured to contain a block header, followed by content and then a pointer (**Fig. 6.35**).

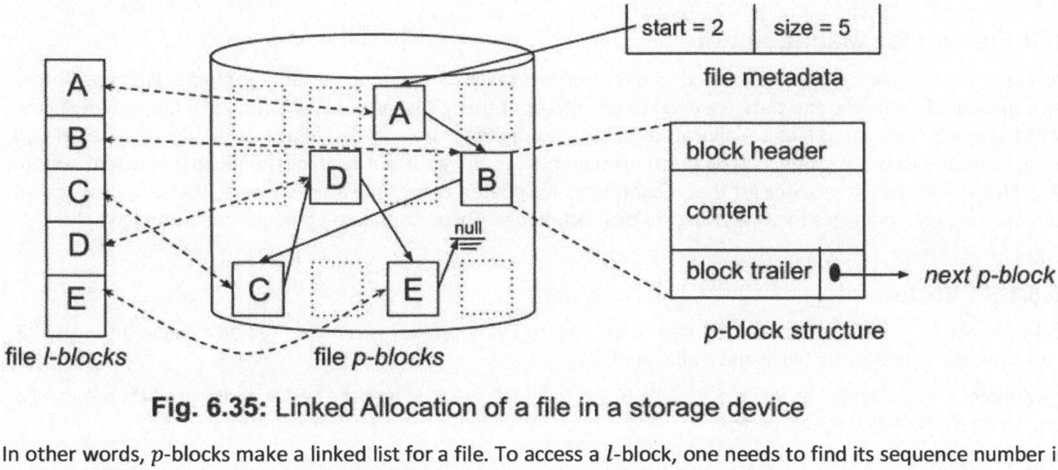

Fig. 6.35: Linked Allocation of a file in a storage device

In other words, p-blocks make a linked list for a file. To access a l-block, one needs to find its sequence number in the logical file space, and then sequentially traverse required number of p-blocks.

Linked allocation solves the issue of external fragmentation. There is also no problem when a file grows. No relocation of p-blocks is necessary due to growth of file size. Only file-metadata needs to be modified.

However, a major drawback is the mandatory sequential access of file blocks. No random access is possible. An l-block search time is linear in length. For a large file, this is costly. Also, each p-block must hold a block header, trailer and a pointer. This increases the overall space overhead of the scheme.

Another problem is the issue of reliability. Since a number of links are involved to track the p-blocks of a file, where damage in a single link may break the entire chain and the file may get partially or fully inaccessible.

6.5.7.3 Indexed Allocation

The problems of the above two schemes are addressed in indexed allocation. The benefit of linked allocation is retained, as any l-block can be placed in any available p-block anywhere. However, two types of p-blocks are maintained: data blocks (or d-blocks) and index blocks (i-blocks). d-blocks only contain data (file content proper) and no pointers; while i-blocks only contain pointers and no data. These pointers can either be pointing to d-blocks or to another i-block (**Fig. 6.36**). In an i-block, all but the last pointer point to a d-block, while the last pointer points to the next i-block. The last i-block will have the last pointer pointing to NULL.

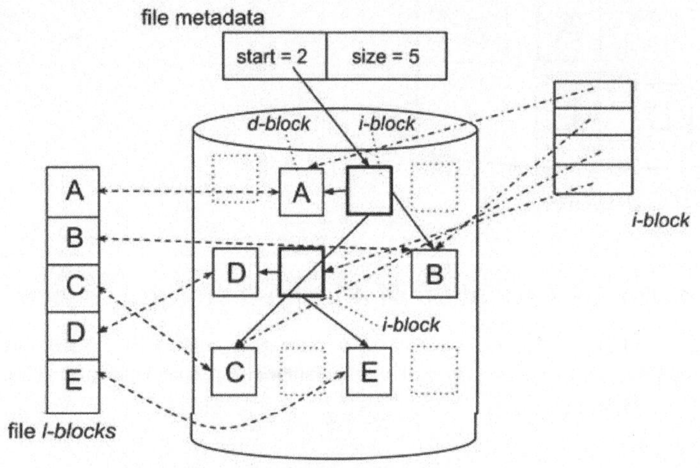

Fig. 6.36: Indexed Allocation of a file in a storage device

A small file can be accommodated with one i-block and a few d-blocks. A large file needs to have several i-blocks. Searching for a particular l-block can force to search several i-blocks. To reduce search time, i-blocks can be arranged in a multi-level index.

Indexed allocation has the advantage of random access, but no external fragmentation.

6.5.8 Free-space Management

p-blocks in the storage space are allocated to different files from only free or available p-blocks. We can allocate only if there are free blocks and thus, we need to keep track of them. Just after initialisation of a file system, all the p -blocks remain free. But as files are allocated space, the number of free blocks reduces. Also, files can be deleted leaving some p -blocks free. Hence, free space management is an important task for the file management system (FMS). FMS maintains a *free-space list* that is continuously updated every time after space is allocated, deallocated and reclaimed. FMS manages the task using various techniques. Three popular techniques are discussed below.

6.5.8.1 Bit Vector

The free-space list is maintained as a bitmap or bit vector. Every **p**-block is represented as a single bit in the bit vector, where 1 denotes free block and 0 allocated.

For example, if in a storage device, blocks 3, 5, 6, 7, 10, 14, 22 are free and the rest are allocated then it can be represented by the following bit vector:

0001011100100010000000100000 ...

The scheme is simple to understand and implement. We can easily find out the first free block scanning the bitmap, and a set of contiguous free blocks on the device. When a request for allocating a p -block comes up, the FMS searches for bit 1 in the bitmap, allocates it and changes its bit value to 0.

For a small disk or storage device, we can easily load the entire bitmap in the main memory and keep it there throughout. However, for a large storage device, (e.g., 1TB disk-space with block size of 1KB, there will be $2^{40}/2^{10}$

$= 2^{30}$ bits = 128 MB of bitmap), this may not be possible. With continuously increasing disk space, keeping the entire bitmap in the main memory, however, can be space-consuming.

6.5.8.2 Linked List

Another method is to make a linked list of free p-blocks. The first free block is pointed to by the head of the free space list. This p -block then points to the next free p-block and so on, in the increasing order of the block-id.

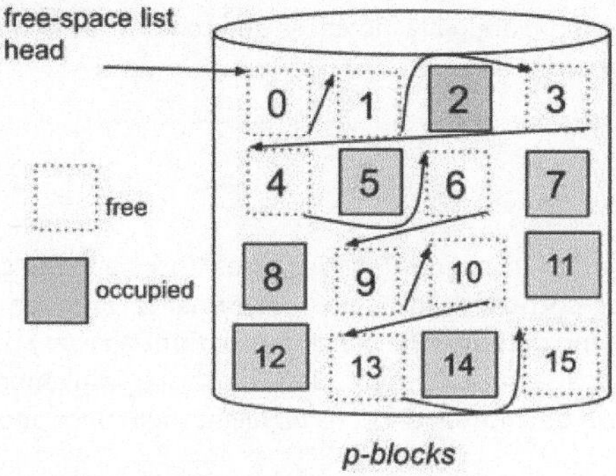

Fig. 6.37: Free space linked list

For example, in **Fig. 6.37**, p-blocks 0, 1, 3, 4, 6, 9, 10, 13, 15, .. are free. This scheme involves traversing through the blocks in the linked list. It is thus time-consuming, especially when the storage medium is huge. Also, the scheme is not usable for contiguous allocation. However, from a practical viewpoint, often, only a single block is required at a time, and that can be provided by the head of the free list. Hence, we do not need to traverse the entire list most of the time.

6.5.8.3 Grouping

Grouping is the modification of the linked free list approach. Here, instead of making a single list containing all the free blocks, a group of n blocks are made. The first free p-block stores the addresses of first n free blocks. While the next $(n-1)$ blocks are free, the n-th free block contains the addresses of the next n free blocks and so on. Hence, a contiguous list of $(n-1)$ blocks can be quickly found, unlike the standard linked list approach above.

6.5.9 Directory Implementation

Directory allocation and directory management play a crucial role in the performance of a file system. Hence the implementation of the directory structure is important. Two popular implementations are described below.

6.5.9.1 Linear List

As already introduced in **Sec. 6.5.5**, simple implementation of a directory can be a linear list of file names, with each file name having a link to data blocks. Creating a file first needs linear search over the list and adding the new file name at the end of the directory. Deleting a file also involves a similar search followed by releasing the space allocated to it. For reusing the space of a directory entry, there can be several strategies. The entry can be marked as unused, or it can be attached to the list of unused entries. Or the last entry can be freed, with other entries shifted to the previous location until the freed entry is filled up.

However, the major issue comes from frequent accessing of file records. Each access needs getting the filename followed by resolution of finding the p-block for a l-block of the file. Since searching filenames is linear in length of directory, this is time-consuming. Hence linear list implementation needs use of caching of the most recent directory entries. Also maintaining a sorted list of file names helps in employing binary search and cuts down search time. But a good amount of management efforts involving movement of several directory information is needed for this. Maintaining a tree structure as explained in **Sec 6.5.5** can therefore be effective.

6.5.9.2 Hash Table

Another popular implementation is using a hash table. From the file name, a hash value is calculated, and the file-related information is obtained from a particular position of a list corresponding to the hash-value. This hashing scheme drastically reduces the directory search time (from linear to constant time). Insertion and deletion of files are straightforward and managed in constant time.

One problem with the hashing scheme is the fixed size of the function. For example, suppose a directory has the hash table of 64 entries and the file names are hashed to values 0 to 63. Even for an increase of one new file (65 entries), one needs to increase the hash table to accommodate 128 entries and a new hash function. All the directory entries need to be changed to reflect the new hash-function values.

Otherwise, we must use an overflow hash table where each hash-value can have multiple entries due to collision. Whenever a collision happens, a linked list is added. Search time marginally increases due to linear search in case of collisions, but still a hash table is much faster than linear search.

6.5.10 Efficiency and Performance

A filesystem is implemented in a storage device, which is a disk in majority of the cases. Disks are the slowest components in any computing system and cause the major bottleneck in overall performance of a computing system. Hence, efforts must be made to minimize disk access and optimize the performance through every possible means. Through efficient file allocation methods, free space management and directory implementation techniques, performance of the filesystem and disk system can be improved. Let us highlight them once again.

6.5.10.1 Use of Directory Structures

Directories are so organized that they facilitate fast search for files. Hash tables and B+ trees are two popular and efficient techniques for searching files and they are used in organizing files within a directory.

6.5.10.2 Disk Space Allocation

Disk space allocation should be such that seek-time and rotational latency is minimized during accessing a file. Contiguous allocation can be preferred for small files. For large files, linked or indexed allocation may be adopted. But care must be taken to choose appropriate pointer size. For example, 32-bit pointers can address a maximum of 2^{32} bytes or 4GB of files. 64-bit pointers allow larger files, but require more space to store and maintain pointers, too.

6.5.10.3 Caching

Caching is an important technique to minimize disk access and to speed up I/O activities. Part of main memory is dedicated for caching to exploit temporal and spatial locality of data blocks. Some operating systems use *page caching* to cache both file data as well process data. Effective cache management techniques can optimize cache-hits and minimize the cache-misses. For majority of cases, the *least recently used (LRU) page replacement technique* proves effective. But, for sequential file accesses, where a seen page is not going to be used again LRU does not work. In such cases, *free-behind* (free a page as soon as a new page requested) and *read-ahead* (reading a requested page along with pre-fetching a few next pages) techniques are employed.

6.5.10.4 Buffering

Sometimes storage device controllers have on-board caches that can temporarily store a track or a few blocks of data.

Some operating systems also maintain a special section in the main memory, called buffer caches, to speed up I/O operations. Buffer cache, along with page cache, sometimes offer *double caching*. Double caching is wastage of memory, CPU cycles and I/O cycles. Also, it leads to potential inconsistencies in the filesystem. Hence, some systems provide *unified buffer cache*.

6.5.10.5 Disk Scheduling

Disk scheduling algorithms attempt to minimize the disk head movement for a reference string and reduce the overall seek time.

All these techniques and algorithms together improve the performance of a file system as well that of a disk. There is no single technique that can be said to be the most effective, nor can it optimize all the performance issues. Based on a given situation, the operating system must dynamically decide the best technique and deploy.

UNIT SUMMARY

- *This chapter discusses the role of input and output devices in a computer.*
- *I/O devices are the gateways to interact with a computer.*
- *Users and application programs provide inputs through input devices and receive outputs through output devices.*
- *An I/O device is connected through an I/O bus to a device controller that has a few I/O ports, and an optional DMA.*
- *Normally, data to/from an I/O device goes to main memory through the processor.*
- *A DMA can bypass the continuous interference of a processor in the data transfer during I/O operation.*
- *I/O operations are managed by an OS through different software components like I/O subsystem and device drivers.*
- *A device driver is a low-level OS module that interacts with I/O controllers and manages I/O activities. A device driver can handle more than one device of similar type.*
- *Disk is an important I/O device that persistently stores code and data for a computer.*
- *Hard disk drives (HDD) are cheap and popular mass storage devices. It is a collection of several very thin magnetic platters that store data. Data is accessed through radial movement of a r/w head and rotation of the disk structure.*
- *A disk is divided into a number of volumes or cylinders, where each volume is a set of concentric circles across the platters. Each circle within a platter is called a track. Each track is further divided into a number of sectors. Each sector is either 512 bytes or 1024 bytes.*
- *When a sector comes under the r/w head, data transfer takes place.*
- *Disk access time is much higher than processor computation time or main memory time. Hence, disk management is a very important activity of an OS.*
- *Different disk scheduling algorithms are proposed to reduce seek time (time of r/w head movement).*
- *Files are device-independent software abstractions to store and use persistent data.*
- *A file is a sequence of data blocks. Users and applications access persistent data in the units of files.*
- *Files are organized in a hierarchy of directories. Efficient file system management needs effective directory implementation.*
- *System performance largely depends on good I/O management that consists of disk management and file management.*

EXERCISES

Multiple Choice / Objective Questions

Q1. Which of the following is an example of a spooled device?
A. a line printer used to print the output of a number of jobs
B. a terminal used to enter input data to a running program
C. a secondary storage device in a virtual memory system
D. a graphic display device [GATE (1996)]
(spooling is a buffering technique to compensate for speed difference between two devices)

Q2. What is the bit rate of a video terminal unit with 80 characters/line, 8 bits/character and horizontal sweep time of 100 μs (including 20 μs of retrace time)?

A. 8 Mbps
B. 6.4 Mbps
C. 0.8 Mbps
D. 0.64 Mbps [GATE(2004)]

(sweep time is the time for a signal to reach its maximum value, retrace time is the time to fall from the maximum to original value)

Q3. Which one of the following is true for a CPU having a single interrupt request line and a single interrupt grant line?

A. Neither vectored interrupt nor multiple interrupting devices are possible.
B. Vectored interrupts are not possible but multiple interrupting devices are possible.
C. Vectored interrupts and multiple interrupting devices are both possible.
D. Vectored interrupt is possible but multiple interrupting devices are not possible. [GATE (2005)]

Q4. Normally user programs are prevented from handling I/O directly by I/O instructions in them. For CPUs having explicit I/O instructions, such I/O protection is ensured by having the I/O instructions privileged. In a CPU with memory mapped I/O, there is no explicit I/O instruction. Which one of the following is true for a CPU with memory mapped I/O?

A. I/O protection is ensured by operating system routine (s)
B. I/O protection is ensured by a hardware trap
C. I/O protection is ensured during system configuration
D. I/O protection is not possible [GATE (2005)]

Q5. Which of the following DMA transfer modes and interrupt handling mechanisms will enable the highest I/O band-width?

A. Transparent DMA and Polling interrupts
B. Cycle-stealing and Vectored interrupts
C. Block transfer and Vectored interrupts
D. Block transfer and Polling interrupts [GATE (2006)]

Q6. Consider a computer system with DMA support. The DMA module is transferring one 8-bit character in one CPU cycle from a device to memory through cycle stealing at regular intervals. Consider a 2 MHz processor. If 0.5% processor cycles are used for DMA, the data transfer rate of the device is __________ bits per second.

A. 80000
B. 10000
C. 8000
D. 1000 [GATE(2021)]

Q7. Which one of the following facilitates the transfer of bulk data from hard disk to main memory with the highest throughput?

A. DMA based I/O transfer
B. Interrupt driven I/O transfer
C. Polling based I/O transfer
D. Programmed I/O transfer [GATE (2022)]

Q8. Suppose the following disk request sequence (track numbers) for a disk with 100 tracks is given: 45, 20, 90, 10, 50, 60, 80, 25, 70. Assume that the initial position of the R/W head is on track 50. The additional distance that will be traversed by the R/W head when the Shortest Seek Time First (SSTF) algorithm is used compared to the SCAN (Elevator) algorithm (assuming that SCAN algorithm moves towards 100 when it starts execution) is __________ tracks

A. 8
B. 9
C. 10
D. 11

Answers of Multiple Choice Questions

1. A 2. B 3. C 4. A 5. C 6. A 7. A 8. C

Short Answer Type Questions

Q1. Define an I/O device. Why is it needed?
Q2. Justify whether a timer device should be called an I/O device or not.
Q3. What is a device controller? How is it different from device drivers?
Q4. What do you mean by I/O address space?
Q5. What is a DMA? Why are they used?
Q6. Why is a disk formatted before use? How many types of formatting are there?
Q7. What is a file? How are files managed?
Q8. What is a file descriptor? Why is it needed?
Q9. What is a directory? How is it different from a file control block?
Q10. What is a bit-map? Why is it used?
Q11. What is a boot block? How is it different from a partition block?
Q12. Why might a system use interrupt-driven I/O to manage a single serial port and polling I/O to manage a front-end processor?

Long Answer Type Questions

Q1. Explain the interaction among a device, a device controller and the CPU.
Q2. Discuss different transfer modes in a DMA.
Q3. Differentiate between port-mapped I/O and memory mapped I/O.
Q4. Explain the scenarios when polling I/O and interrupt-driven I/O are beneficial.
Q5. Describe the organization of a magnetic disk.
Q6. Explain different stages of disk formatting.
Q7. With necessary diagrams, explain different types of blocks like superblock, boot block, partition block.
Q8. Both main memory and disk are storage units. Explain the similarities and differences in the space allocation and free space management.

Numerical Problems

Q1. A disk drive has 8 usable surfaces with 110 tracks per surface. If each track has 96 sectors and each sector is 512 bytes, what is the size of the disk?

Q2. If we want to store 300,000 logical records of 120-bytes long in the above disk (as in **Q1.**), how many surfaces, tracks and sectors will be necessary?

Q3. In **Q2.**, assume that the disk rotates at 360 rpm. The processor reads from the disk using interrupt-driven I/O with one interrupt per byte. If it takes 2.5 microseconds to process each interrupt, calculate the percentage of time spent in I/O handling (neglect seek time).

Q4. Suppose you have a 4-drive RAID array with 200GB per drive. Calculate available data storage capacity for different RAID levels: 0, 1, 2, 3, 4, 5, 6.

Q5. A disk having 500 cylinders (0 to 499) needs to serve a reference string: 144, 10, 123, 75, 304, 281, 480. If the r/w head is at 250, calculate the total head movement (in cylinders) if the disk scheduling algorithm is: (i) SSTF (ii) SCAN (iii) C-SCAN and ((iv) FCFS>

Q6. Suppose a disk has a label "160GB SATA HDD 7200rpm 3MB/s transfer rate" and 200 sectors per track with sector size 512 bytes. What is the average rotational latency? What is the average transfer time to read one sector of data?

PRACTICAL

Q1. In a UNIX or Linux system, Learn and try different shell commands like: `df, ls, fdisk, fsck, mkdir, mkfs, sfdisk, parted` etc.

Q2. Check the filesystem hierarchy in a UNIX or Linux system using command '`ls /`'. make a tree structure to reach to your home directory.

Q3. In a UNIX or Linux system, try '`ls -l`' from your present working directory and see the entire record for each file entry. Learn what each of the letters means in the first string like '`drwxr-xr-w`'. How to change them?

Q4. In a Windows system, open the command prompt and write `dir`. See the output and understand what it shows.

Q5. In a Windows system, on the command prompt, type `tree` / `TREE` to see the filesystem hierarchy.

Q6. In a Windows system, on the command prompt, type `help` to learn about other Windows commands and try some commands related to disk and file management.

Q7. Write a program to design and implement a file management system.

Q8. Write a program to perform operations for synchronization between CPU and I/O controllers.

KNOW MORE

I/O Management is a vast area and is discussed in general with good detail as two separate parts as storage management and file systems each with at least one or more chapters in [SGG18] , [Sta12], [Hal15] and [Dha09].

[SGG18] covers SSD devices and flash drives with reasonable details under NVM storage devices. It also discusses file system mounting and recovery mechanisms.

[Sta12] also covers the DMA and RAID structures vividly. This also provides a brief account of different file systems found in UNIX, Linux and Windows systems.

[Hal15] discusses disk formatting techniques very nicely. It also covers file system journaling and virtual file systems with a focus on UNIX systems.

[Dha09] especially covers error recovery and buffering part quite well.

[Bac05] has a complete chapter each on buffer cache and I/O subsystem, while two chapters on file systems of UNIX OS. [Vah12] dedicates four chapters to UNIX file systems.

[YIR17] contains implementational details of I/O system management in Windows operating systems across different architectures.

REFERENCES AND SUGGESTED READINGS

[Bac05] Maurice J Bach: The Design of the UNIX Operating System, Prentice Hall of India, 2006.

[Dha09] Dhananjay M. Dhamdhere: Operating Systems, A Concept-Based Approach, 18]McGraw Hill, 2009.

[Hal15] Sibsankar Haldar: Operating Systems, Self Edition 1.1, 2016.

[SGG18] Abraham Silberschatz, Peter B Galvin, Greg Gagne: Operating Systems Concepts,10th Edition, Wiley, 2018.

[Sta12] William Stallings: Operating Systems Internals and Design Principles, 7th Edition, Prentice Hall, 2012.

[Vah12] Uresh Vahalia: UNIX Internals, The New Frontiers, Pearson, 2012.

[YIR17] Pavel Yosifovich, Alex Ionescu, Mark E. Russinovich, and David A. Solomon: Windows Internals, Seventh Edition (Part 1 and 2), Microsoft, 2017. https://docs.microsoft.com/en-us/sysinternals/resources/windows-internals (as on 17-Marl-2023).

Dynamic QR Code for Further Reading

REFERENCES FOR FURTHER LEARNING

[Bac05] Maurice J Bach: The Design of the UNIX Operating System, Prentice Hall of India, 2005.

[CKM16] Russ Cox, Frans Kaashoek, Robert Morris: xv6, a simple, Unix-like teaching operating system, available at https://www.cse.iitd.ac.in/~sbansal/os/book-rev9.pdf

[Dha09] Dhananjay M. Dhamdhere: Operating Systems, A Concept-Based Approach, McGraw Hill, 2009.

[Dow16] Allen B. Downey: The Little Book of Semaphores, 2e, Green Tea Press, 2016 (available at https://greenteapress.com/semaphores/LittleBookOfSemaphores.pdf as on 9-Oct-2022).

[HA09] Sibsankar Haldar and Alex A Aravind: Operating Systems, Pearson Education, 2009.

[Hal15] Sibsankar Haldar: Operating Systems, Self-Edition 1.1, 2015.

[Han00] Per Brinch Hansen: The Evolution of Operating Systems, (2000) (available at http://brinch-hansen.net/papers/2001b.pdf) ((as on 8-Jul-2022).

[Mil11] Milan Milenkovic: Operating Systems - Concepts and Design, 2nd edition, Tata McGraw Hill, 2011

[Nar14] Naresh Chauhan: Principles of Operating Systems, Oxford University Press, 2014.

[RR03] Kay A. Robbins, Steven Robbins: Unix™ Systems Programming: Communication, Concurrency, and Threads, PrenticeHall, 2003.

[SGG18] Abraham Silberschatz, Peter B Galvin, Greg Gagne: Operating Systems Concepts,10th Edition, Wiley, 2018.

[SR05] Richard W Stevens, Stephen A Rago: Advanced Programming in the UNIX Environment (2nd Edition), *Addison-Wesley Professional, 2005.*

[Sta12] William Stallings: Operating Systems Internals and Design Principles, 7th Edition, Prentice Hall, 2012.

[Vah12] Uresh Vahalia: UNIX Internals, The New Frontiers, Pearson, 2012.

[YIR17] Pavel Yosifovich, Alex Ionescu, Mark E. Russinovich, and David A. Solomon: Windows Internals, Seventh Edition (Part 1 and 2), Microsoft, 2017. https://docs.microsoft.com/en-us/sysinternals/resources/windows-internals (as on 8-Jul-2022).

CO AND PO ATTAINMENT TABLE

Course outcomes (COs) for this course can be mapped with the programme outcomes (POs) after the completion of the course and a correlation can be made for the attainment of POs to analyze the gap. After proper analysis of the gap in the attainment of POs necessary measures can be taken to overcome the gaps.

Table for CO and PO attainment

Course Outcomes	Attainment of Programme Outcomes (1- Weak Correlation; 2- Medium correlation; 3- Strong Correlation)											
	PO-1	PO-2	PO-3	PO-4	PO-5	PO-6	PO-7	PO-8	PO-9	PO-10	PO-11	PO-12
CO-1												
CO-2												
CO-3												
CO-4												
CO-5												
CO-6												

The data filled in the above table can be used for gap analysis.

INDEX